THE ALMS BAZAAR

THE ALMS BAZAAR

*Altruism under fire —
non-profit organizations and
international development*

IAN SMILLIE

IT Publications 1995

Published by Intermediate Technology Publications Ltd,
103–105 Southampton Row, London WC1B 4HH, UK

© Intermediate Technology Publications 1995

Reprinted 2000

ISBN 1 85339 301 0

Typeset by Dorwyn Ltd, Rowlands Castle. Hants
Printed in UK by SRP, Exeter

Contents

Now the trumpet summons us again, not as a call to bear arms . . . but as a call to bear the burden of a long twilight struggle, year in and year out; rejoicing in hope, patient in tribulation; a struggle against the common enemies of man: tyranny, poverty, disease, and war itself . . .

John F. Kennedy, Inaugural Address, 1961

ACRONYMS AND ABBREVIATIONS

ACFOA   Australian Council for Overseas Aid
ADAB   Association of Development Agencies of Bangladesh
ADRA   Adventist Relief and Development Agency
ADF   African Development Foundation (USA)
AIDAB   Australian International Development Assistance Bureau
AKF   Aga Khan Foundation
AKRSP   Aga Khan Rural Support Programme
AMREF   African Medical and Research Foundation
BRAC   Bangladesh Rural Advancement Committee
CAFOD   Catholic Fund for Overseas Development (UK)
CAPART   Council for the Advancement of People's Action and Rural
           Technology (India)
CARE   Cooperative for American Relief Everywhere (US); else-
           where not usually an acronym
CCIC   Canadian Council for International Cooperation
CEBEMO   Central Agency for the Co-Financing of Development Pro-
           grammes (Netherlands)
CEDEP   Centre for the Development of People (Ghana)
CFC   Chlorofluorocarbons
CIDA   Canadian International Development Agency
CIDSE   Coopération Internationale pour le Développement et la
           Solidarité
CRS   Catholic Relief Services
CUSO   Canadian University Service Overseas (now no longer an
           acronym)
DEC   Disasters Emergency Committee (UK)
DAWN   Development Alternatives with Women for a New Era
EC   European Commission
FAO   Food and Agriculture Organization
FASE   Federation of Organizations for Social and Educational
           Assistance (Brazil)
FINNIDA   Finnish International Development Agency
GAD   Gender and Development
GDP   Gross Domestic Product
GNP   Gross National Product

GONGO	Government-Organized NGO
ICCO	Inter Church Coordination Committee for Development Projects (Netherlands)
ICRC	International Committee of the Red Cross
IDRC	International Development Research Centre
IFAD	International Fund for Agricultural Development
IIED	International Institute for Environment and Development
INGO	International NGO
ISCA	International Save the Children Alliance
ISODEC	Integrated Social Development Centre (Ghana)
ITDG	Intermediate Technology Development Group (UK)
ITN	Independent Television News
IUCN	International Union for the Conservation of Nature
IUEF	International University Exchange Fund
MSF	Médecins sans Frontières
NORAD	Norwegian Agency for Development Cooperation
NOVIB	Netherlands Organization for International Development Cooperation
OAU	Organization of African Unity
ODA	Official Development Assistance
ODA	Overseas Development Authority (UK)
OECD	Organization for Economic Co-operation and Development
OPP	Orangi Pilot Project (Pakistan)
ORAP	Organization of Rural Associations for Progress (Zimbabwe)
PSC	Public Service Contractor
SAP	Structural Adjustment Programme
SCF	Save the Children Fund (UK)
SCF	Save the Children Federation (US)
SEWA	Self-Employed Women's Association
SIDA	Swedish International Development Authority
SSA	Sub-Saharan Africa
TNC	Trans National Corporation
UNHCR	United Nations High Commission for Refugees
UNCED	United Nations Conference on the Environment and Development
UNDP	United Nations Development Program
UNEP	United Nations Environmental Program
UNESCO	United Nations Education and Scientific Council
UNICEF	United Nations Children's Fund
UNIFEM	United Nations Fund for Women
USAID	United States Agency for International Development
VO	Voluntary Organization
VSO	Voluntary Service Overseas
WAD	Women and Development

WDF	Women's Development Federation
WHO	World Health Organization
WID	Women in Development
WWF	Working Women's Forum (India)
WWF	World Wide Fund for Nature
WWF	World Wildlife Fund (US and Canada)

AN IRREVERENT GLOSSARY

(Not in alphabetical order)

Donation	The act of giving; from Latin, *donum*, gift.
Donor	One who makes a donation or gift. In international development work, it can mean someone who gives £5 to ActionAid or $5 to the American Friends Service Committee; it can mean a bilateral agency (see below) or a multilateral agency (also below). Sometimes it can refer to a voluntary organization — like the Red Cross. Where it refers to bilateral and multilateral agencies, it is often used incorrectly, as some of these provide loans or assistance tied to the purchase of goods and services in their own countries. This blends 'giving' with an element of banking, and with subsidies for the private sector.
ODA	'Official Development Assistance' is concessional assistance from governments. It may include tied aid and loans but it must include a grant element of at least 25 per cent. Not to be confused with the British Overseas Development Administration, which is a bilateral agency administering the Official Development Assistance of the British Government.
Bilateral	Something undertaken by two parties. In the development business it means government-to-government aid, but it is also used as a noun, referring to governmental aid agencies such as the British Overseas Development Administration or the US Agency for International Development.
Multilateral	As a noun, it refers to multilateral institutions such as the United Nations, the World Bank and the International Monetary Fund.
Umbrella agency	An odd expression when you think about it. In the development business it usually refers to organizations that act as clearing houses or that provide co-ordinating, information and advocacy services on behalf of member agencies. Most Australian NGOs, for example, belong to the Australian Council for Overseas Aid; in Bangladesh

they belong to the Association of Development Agencies of Bangladesh. Some, like these, are national; others are regional (e.g. Eurostep), and some have functional or religious underpinnings.

Nouns to verbs If adjectives like 'bilateral' and 'multilateral' can be transformed into nouns, nouns can become verbs. Although this practice is not unique to the development business, it has some regulars: 'to network', 'to access', 'to partner' (e.g. 'This project was partnered with the Canadian Hunger Foundation').

Documents Usually just a fancy way of saying 'papers' (as in 'project documents').

Surplusage Mark Twain's Twelfth Rule of Literary Style — 'Avoid surplusage' — is generally ignored. In the development business, people favour long words: 'document' often becomes 'documentation'; 'preventive' turns into 'preventative'. And one does not impose 'conditions'; most documentation refers more politely to 'conditionalities'.

Sector This word is as elastic as 'downtown'. As a subdivision of society, 'the private sector' is well known. This book deals primarily with the 'voluntary sector', sometimes called the 'non-profit sector' or 'third sector'. In development work, there are a lot of other sectors: the 'health sector', the 'education sector', the 'formal sector' (business and industry), the 'informal sector' (unregulated and unregistered business and industry).

Enabling To make possible or easy, to facilitate. Almost always used in connection with the word 'environment', although it has nothing to do with ecology. First used in a development context by H.H. The Aga Khan in a 1982 speech in Nairobi: 'Social institutions in national development; the enabling environment'.

Linkage Any form of communication.

Partnership Any form of linkage (see Chapter X).

Technical assistance This refers to the sending of 'experts', usually from the North to the South, to assist, teach or manage projects. 'Volunteers' like the Peace Corps and VSO are seldom referred to as 'technical assistance', however, even though they may be well qualified. 'Technical assistance' is usually coincident with the expression 'highly paid'. Technical assistance to Africa in 1989 absorbed $3.3 billion. In an article on the subject, UNDP said that

xi

'technical assistance, unlike turnips, has no independent measure of its value to the recipient. Instead, output is measured by input, such as salaries or man-months, conveying a deceptive impression of achievement when nothing may have been achieved.' (UNDP 1994, p.80)

Expert	Technical assistance.
Resources	Many meanings. 'Human resources' means 'people'. 'Human resource development' can mean training, but it usually refers more broadly to building the capacity of people to deal with challenges and opportunities. When the word 'resources' refers to a project (as in 'the project consumed a lot of resources'), it usually just means 'money'.
Inputs	Inputs to a project are usually activities or 'resources': sometimes 'human resources' (i.e. people); sometimes 'technical assistance' (i.e. highly paid people); sometimes equipment or commodities; and usually money.
Outputs	An output is 'what happens'. An output is usually a bit different from a 'result'. For example if you run a training programme, an 'output' will be trained people. There may, however, be no result. Or the result may be something other than what was expected (e.g. the trainees all emigrate to America).
Dev. Ed.	A common abbreviation in both writing and speech ('deved') for 'development education'. Not limited to schools, it refers to the work of Northern NGOs and others to convey messages about development to the general public or to specific target audiences.
Paradigm	Meaning unknown. Seldom used without the word 'shift' attached to it.
Lessons learned	An expression appearing in evaluations. Often it means only 'lessons'.

Other terms, such as 'empowerment', 'participation', 'sustainable' and 'professionalism' will be explained as far as is possible in the text. For a fuller discussion of terms such as 'development', 'progress' and 'standard of living', see *The Development Dictionary*, edited by Wolfgang Sachs (1992 Zed Books, London).

ACKNOWLEDGEMENTS

I began my international career in 1967, in the small West African country of Sierra Leone, working as a teacher in the diamond mining town of Koidu, the third largest settlement in the country. Throughout Sierra Leone, there was a feeling of optimism: of growth, energy and a promising future. Roads and bridges were being built, schools and hospitals were being opened, new businesses and industries were being established. With only two and a half million people, Sierra Leone was a largely unknown country. It was not likely to become a significant player on the world scene, but it was a nation on the move, one unlikely to require the services of people like me for long.

I still have my mark book from those years: Sahr Barbah got 80 per cent in Form III French; Aiah James, the Head Boy, received 58 per cent in History. Had they lived, Sahr Barbah and Aiah James would be in their early forties. Sadly, they did not. Nor did the school. Physically, it may still be there, but in 1993, a ragtag gang of uniformed killers, loosely associated with other killers across the border in Liberia, overran the town, looting and murdering anyone who got in their way. By 1995, the eastern third of the country had reverted to the law of the jungle. A camp for refugees and displaced people had become the third largest settlement in the country. Long before the advent of civil strife, however, the country was on the way down. In 1992, Sierra Leone — which boasted the first university in sub-Saharan Africa — had the fourth lowest GNP per capita in the world. Of 173 countries on UNDP's 1994 Human Development Index, it ranked 170th, an improvement over 1991, when it was *last*.

This book is not about Sierra Leone, nor is it an aid memoir. I begin with Sierra Leone and my own experience of it only because by accident more than design I grew very attached to a country that epitomizes all the frailties and failures of what has become known as 'development'. I was a 'volunteer', working for a Canadian non-governmental organization (NGO), contributing to what most of us thought was the business of 'putting ourselves out of business'. The opposite happened. Those of us who worked for NGOs in those days were on the ground floor of what has proven to be a high-rise growth industry, one that has in recent years become the focus of increasing attention — and sometimes of vilification — for academics, aid agencies, governments and politicians. In one capacity or another, I have worked with NGOs since those long-ago days in Sierra Leone, as a founder of one, director of another, as critic, evaluator, field worker, trustee and consultant. It has taken me this long, however, to get my thoughts around the subject as a whole. *The Alms Bazaar* is not a whitewash, nor is it an attack. It is a practitioner's attempt to cut through some of the syrup and the bile that alternately afflict the development industry in general and the NGO sector in particular.

I have tried to be fair, but I may not always have succeeded. I have tried to make the book readable. As a result, it contains quite a lot of 'anecdotal evidence' to support the points I make. I worried about this as I was writing, until I came across something by American journalist Russell Baker. He believes that 'only anecdotal evidence' is a phrase coined by economists 'to shrug off tales of individual human misery that threaten to spoil their statistical pictures of general and abundant happiness'. This kind of reassurance was helpful in trying to make sense out of the unhappiness and poverty that seem so endemic in today's world. Toni Morrison said it better in her 1993 Nobel Prize address:

> Official language smitheryed to sanction ignorance and preserve privilege is a suit of armour, polished to a shocking glitter, a husk from which the knight departed long ago. Yet there it is: dumb, predatory, sentimental. Exciting reverence in schoolchildren, providing shelter for despots, summoning false memories of stability, harmony among the public.

A few minor editorial comments: the development business has more acronyms than there are people in Peru. I have tried to give the name in full for the first usage, and again later sometimes, to keep the flow going. A key is provided on pages vii–ix. Where a source is used only once, the reference will be noted by chapter at the end of the book. If it is used more than once, a brief description will be given by chapter, and the full reference will be found in the bibliography. Unless otherwise stated, all dollar figures are US dollars.

For reasons that will become apparent in the text, the term 'Third World' has pretty much gone out of fashion. I have tried to use 'North' and 'South' as much as possible, but sometimes other expressions — 'developed', 'developing' — and even 'Third World' — creep in for reasons of style, semantics or flow. I have tried to keep other development jargon — such as the vastly overworked expression 'sustainable development' — to a minimum, or to explain what I think an expression like that means when it becomes unavoidable. A glossary on pages x–xii deals with especially difficult words and expressions.

Accurate statistics are problematic in a world of five or six billion people, two hundred-odd countries and an army of number-crunching aid agencies and economists with points to make and axes to grind. Much of the statistical picture on development is guess-work, but numbers are important in the illustration of volumes and trends. I have provided the source and date wherever statistics are used, but a grain of salt may sometimes be advisable.

By way of acknowledgement, I would like to thank the International Development Research Centre in Ottawa, which gave me a fellowship, and therefore the time, to compose my thoughts and the book. I gratefully acknowledge permission from the OECD Development Centre to update and reprint an earlier essay: what now appears as sections of Chapter VII, 'Mixed messages: NGOs and the Northern public'.

I am very grateful to all the people in many countries, from Ireland to New Zealand, Kenya, Jamaica, Pakistan and elsewhere who helped with important information, advice and editorial comment. If a book can have a keystone among those who helped make it possible, Chris Smart served that function. Shah Abdulla, Gavin Andersson, Stéphane Cardinal, Philip Dunn, Ruth Groberman, Henny Helmich, Richard Holloway, Cynthia King, Bernard Muchiri, Colm Regan, Geoffrey Salkeld, Hameed Shaikh, Heather Shapter, Rob Stevens and Bob Thomson all provided missing pieces to various puzzles. Bob O'Brien and Loren Finnell filled in a variety of American and other gaps; and Robin Munro followed up a chance meeting on a flight from Bangkok to Chiang Mai with helpful information from Human Rights Watch.

Many individuals struggled with early drafts of various chapters and helped to make them more comprehensible for those who would follow. For this, I am tremendously grateful to Barbara Brown, Michael Bryans, Marilyn Carr, Mike Edwards, John Foster, Nazeer Ladhani, Ross Lambertson, Kamal Malhotra, Wendy Quarry (who also ferried copies of a draft to Pakistan), Dorienne Rowan-Campbell, Rieky Stuart and John Watson. Returning to war-torn Bosnia, Brenda Cupper left her chapters on a plane. Unfazed by this excuse, I managed to get duplicates to her and she faxed helpful comments from Zagreb.

Several people struggled with an entire draft, and I am especially grateful for the many hours they took, even if it did mean more reading, phoning, faxing and re-writing for me. Sharon Capeling-Alakija blue-pencilled her way through drafts in Candelaria, New York and Ottawa. Tim Brodhead, Dulan de Silva, Tim Draimin, Aban Marker Kabraji, Andrès Perèz, Brian Rowe and Father William Ryan all provided excellent advice and the occasional warning. I have tried to incorporate as much of the former into the book as possible.

Last, but far from least, I want to thank Neal Burton, Managing Editor at IT Publications, who nursed this book from the idea stage —

over pizza and Chianti in London — to the last dot on the last *i*. His moral support, solid advice, and the steady transatlantic stream of helpful faxes, clippings, ideas and concerns meant that I was seldom alone in my work.

In the end, of course, I alone am responsible for the tone and content of the book, and for any errors or omissions it may contain.

IAN SMILLIE,
Ottawa, 1995

Introduction

BY THE MIDDLE of the last decade of the twentieth century, there were almost a million American philanthropic non-profit bodies, and there were a further four hundred thousand non-profit, but not philanthropic organizations. The combined income of these organizations was more than $400 billion.[1] Together, they accounted for 6 per cent of the gross domestic product and 18 per cent of the national services economy.[2] In the 1990s, American business donated about $6 billion each year to non-profit organizations, and non-profits returned many times that amount to the economy through the purchase of goods and services, creating in the process 1.4 million jobs in business and manufacturing. These organizations employed over eight million people, more than the federal and all state governments combined. Assisting them were volunteers: almost half of all adult Americans do voluntary work of some sort every week.

The 170 000 registered charities in England and Wales had a total 1990 income of approximately £16 billion, representing more than 3 per cent of Britain's gross domestic product.[3] An estimated 700 000 associations make up the French non-profit sector, providing full-time employment to 4 per cent of the national labour force. Sweden, a country of 8.3 million people, has an estimated 200 000 organizations with 31 million members. In Canada, an estimated US$62 billion passed through registered charities in 1993: nearly 13 per cent of the country's entire gross domestic product. Almost half of this was paid out in the form of salaries and benefits to 1.3 million people. At 9 per cent of the labour force, this represented more jobs than the entire construction industry.[4]

In the developing countries of the South — the 'Third World' — there has also been a remarkable explosion of voluntary self-help organizations. Tens of thousands of organizations have sprung up in Asia, Africa, the Caribbean and Latin America, a high proportion of them in the 1980s and 1990s. Most are small, and like some of their counterparts in the North, some are amateurish. However, many are becoming world leaders in innovative health care, education and job creation. Some have become very large; and some have become so effective that they are giving advice and assistance to other countries. Bangladesh's successful Grameen Bank, for example, has provided

1

advice and personnel to anti-poverty projects in Malaysia, Malawi and the United States.

People have always formed organizations. Before there was government, groups of people created associations for self-help and self-preservation, for religious, cultural and political purposes. In Europe and North America, the rise of commerce and government led to newer kinds of organization: guilds, trade unions, pressure groups, reform movements. The emergence of the welfare state obviated the need for much of what some associations had once done, but their numbers continued to expand in order to deal with newer and different needs. By coincidence, the welfare state reached its zenith at the moment in history when the great colonial empires began to unravel: the British, French, Portuguese, Dutch and Belgian empires, and finally the great Soviet imperium. As the metropolitan powers retreated from empire, they left behind an idea of the state as provider, of government as a nation's primary, and sometimes its exclusive, social arbiter and economic actor. It was an idea that was about to fall from grace in the places where it had originated.

In the South, the mantle of the welfare state was inherited by new governments that were ill-equipped both politically and economically to fashion anything even remotely resembling what had emerged over the previous century in Europe. But they tried. Struggling to manage a transition of incredible complexity, and assuming too many roles, they faltered. Over time, some failed badly, descending heavily into debt and falling under the hypnotic sway of international financial institutions and donor agencies. As the state retreated, gaps widened between human needs and the capacity of the state to meet them, and non-profit voluntary organizations sprang-up to deal with some of the worst problems. Initially seen as a short-term, temporary phenomenon — as 'gap-fillers' — these organizations now seem set to remain, and perhaps to play an even more significant role in the years ahead.

This book is about the three or four thousand Northern voluntary organizations that work in the South,[5] and their partners: the small village groups, the national organizations, the movements and coalitions that deal with health, education, jobs, the environment and human rights. Part of the book deals with the origins of these organizations and their work. Some of it deals with the messages they convey. And a large part has to do with the role of organizations and associations in helping to build and maintain responsible and democratic government. But the book is primarily about the challenges they face in a time of unprecedented global change, and during what appears to be a pivotal moment in their evolution.

There are very real and sometimes volatile tensions between governments and the voluntary sectors of the North and the South. On the one

2

hand, more service delivery is expected of voluntary organizations as governmental expansion in health, education and job creation halts or retreats. Faced with static levels of private income, voluntary organizations are easily enticed by the financial blandishments of large benefactors. Governments, however, which are providing them with more and more support, do so on conditional terms. There is increasing pressure to 'professionalize', with management prescriptions lifted indiscriminately from the private sector and government. What is emerging as a 'contracting era' has the potential to change the very nature of the voluntary sector, placing its independence in jeopardy. Advocacy and reform, long an integral part of the voluntary *raison d'être*, are unwanted or even feared by governments, and means are actively sought, through legislation, contracting and spurious theorizing about 'voluntarism', to minimize, subvert or suppress it.

This theme — the independence of the voluntary sector — provides the central framework for the book. From this will flow its other central preoccupations: efficiency, effectiveness, accountability, the role of civil society in governance and democracy, North-South relations. The book will also explore public opinion and the images created by the voluntary sector in the minds of people in industrialized countries, through fundraising and what is known as 'development education'.

The book is about organizations, movements and people that are well known, and about others that are relatively unknown. Oxfam is here, along with CARE, World Vision and Save the Children. The Greens, the women's movement and the appropriate technologists are here as well, as are Sarvodaya in Sri Lanka, the Self-Employed Women's Association in India, flying doctors in Africa, and Chico Mendes and his rubber tappers in Brazil. The book is about development (or lack thereof), and about how voluntary organizations relate to the so-called new world order, to governments, revolution, war, the people who donate money and to the people who eventually get it.

There are some deliberate omissions. International labour organizations and the co-operative movement, being more membership driven than service-oriented, have been largely excluded. Religious organizations are here, but their histories and their scope are so broad that they do not receive the attention that a larger book, or one dedicated solely to them would provide.

Ultimately, the book is an attempt to demystify and explain the aura, the confusion, the inordinate acclaim, the unfair criticism and the very great expectations that are caused by, and heaped in ever-increasing measure onto the many non-profit development organizations that labour in the villages of Africa, the tiny rural bank branches of Bangladesh, the fundraising, research and advocacy departments

3

of organizations from Melbourne to London, Delhi, Nairobi and Washington. It is a story of heroism and folly, of success and failure. It is about one of the greatest endeavours of our time: efforts by ordinary as well as rather extraordinary people to help put an end to the poverty that has plagued the twentieth century; a level of poverty that poses the greatest threat to the health, happiness and well-being of virtually everyone who will live on the planet during the century to come.

The book is also an attempt to deal with the weakness of the words we use to describe needs: the need for fraternity, social solidarity, for civic belonging. 'Needs,' says writer Michael Ignatieff, 'can only live when the language which expresses them is adequate to the times. Words like fraternity, belonging and community are so soaked with nostalgia and utopianism that they are nearly useless as guides to the real possibilities of solidarity in modern society.' What distinguishes the language of needs, he says, 'is its claim that human beings actually feel a common and shared identity in the basic fraternity of hunger, thirst, cold, exhaustion, loneliness or sexual passion.'[6] The basis for hope and the possibilities of peace and stability rest not so much in science, commerce and information, but on this idea of natural human identity.

PART ONE

The flight of the phoenix

CHAPTER I

Doomsters and cornucopians

From the folds of [the spirit's] robe, it brought two children; wretched, abject, frightful, hideous, miserable.

'Spirit! Are they yours?' Scrooge could say no more.

'They are Man's,' said the spirit, looking down upon them. 'This boy is ignorance. This girl is want. Beware them both.'

Charles Dickens,
A Christmas Carol, 1843.

IN THE MIDDLE of December, 1994, the United Nations admitted its 185th member nation. Palau, lying 800 kilometres south-east of the Philippines, is an archipelago of 200 islands and 16 000 people. The last of eleven United Nations Trust Territories, it perhaps has more experience of colonialism than any other member of the United Nations. Colonized first by Spain, then Germany, it was administered by Japan after 1914, and by the United States after 1944. Palau joined a world of nation states that was very different from the world that its 120-odd decolonized siblings had entered over the previous four decades. These were decades of war: cold war and hot war; guerilla war; civil war; clan war; religious war; border war; wars of liberation, invasion and independence. They were also decades of hope; 'Development Decades', so-named by the United Nations, which had optimistically labelled the 1960s a Decade for Development. When ten years proved insufficient, a second Decade was declared in the 1970s. The 1980s, sometimes called 'the lost decade', seemed to mark a slowing of resolve, a waning of enthusiasm as the optimism of the first two Development Decades gave way to the harsh and growing realities of debt, war, environmental degradation, famine and poverty.

Poverty is the key word: the state of being that has contributed more to debt, war, environmental degradation and famine than any other single factor. The effort that has gone into defining, measuring and discussing poverty in recent years is enormous. One reason for this is that governments and those working in development want to know if the situation is getting better or worse. They want to know if their efforts to alleviate poverty are working in the way they had hoped.* Thus, academics and development agencies have given us 'absolute poverty', 'relative poverty', the poor, the 'ultra-poor' and a dozen ways to measure their misery: per capita income levels, household consumption, per capita food consumption, calorie intake, food ratios, 'under-five mortality rates', a 'physical quality-of-life index' and UNDP's 'human development index' which combines a variety of social and economic factors.

In 1988, the International Fund for Agricultural Development (IFAD) put the total number living in absolute poverty at more than a billion people, and in 1991, UNDP estimated the number to be 1.2 billion. The 1995 UN Social Summit in Copenhagen seemed to agree on 1.3 billion. Projections of what might happen by the turn of the century vary: UNDP has suggested a figure of 1.3 billion, IFAD thinks it might reach 1.5 billion, while the World Bank believed in 1990 that with wise investments and a healthy global economy, the number could be reduced to 825 million.[1] This prediction, a repeat of hopeful (and largely unfulfilled) 1980 Bank forecasts,[2] had a fairly shaky basis in reality, as 'wise investments' were repeatedly delayed and a healthy global economy was postponed indefinitely. Accurate prediction, of course, is a rare gift. Lights on a ship's stern reveal turbulent water, and the wreckage of anything that may have passed under the keel. On the bow, however, they illuminate very little.

As for today, at least one person in every five on the planet lives in absolute poverty. The total number — say a billion, plus or minus a few hundred million — looks like this: 1 000 000 000. This is about four times more than the total population of the United States, seventeen times more than the population of Britain and 67 times the population of the Netherlands.

Absolute poverty is a term which suggests an awful permanence. Roughly defined, it describes individuals who spend approximately 75 per cent of their income on food, and who consume about 75 per cent of the calories they would need in order to lead a healthy life. They live in urban slums or in rural areas that are often remote and where land, if they have any, is poor. They have few assets; they are mostly illiterate; they have little access to government services; they are vulnerable to disease, to weather, and to greater poverty. They have no power, no influence, and nothing to invest except their physical labour. There are more women than men in this state, and they are generally less well paid (when they are paid at all), for longer hours of work. More poorly educated than men, they are often denied access to services that might help: education, health, credit and markets.

---

*Poverty alleviation: an expression commonly used among development agencies. What most of them probably mean is 'poverty reduction'. In its principal meaning, 'alleviation' means only 'to make easier to bear'.

8

For children it is worse. Because of their greater need, poverty places them at greater risk than adults. Ultimately, they are beholden to and the victims of adults. With children, numbers start to lose their meaning; of the billion people living in absolute poverty, about three or four hundred million are children and young people under the age of sixteen. Hundreds of millions of children live in appalling conditions, and fifteen million die terrible and mostly unnoticed deaths every year: about twice as many individuals as live in Denmark. It is as though all the people in Finland, Israel and Norway were to die in a year, with hardly anyone except UNICEF and a handful of voluntary organizations saying anything about it.

Apocalypse soon?

Is the situation getting better? Yes. And no. A 1992 IFAD study of 41 developing countries showed that the percentage of the rural population living below the poverty line had declined from 35 per cent of the total to 33 per cent between 1965 and 1988. In 20 countries, including India, there was a decline, and in 18, including China, there was an increase. In some cases, the improvement was dramatic: in 1965, 91 per cent of Lesotho's rural population was poor; by 1988 the number had fallen to 55 per cent. A more recent report shows positive trends in countries such as Ghana, Malawi, Colombia, Costa Rica, Uruguay and Paraguay.[3] In most developing countries, life expectancy has increased over the past ten years, and child mortality has decreased.[4] These positive statistics represent prodigious efforts by governments, multilateral institutions and voluntary agencies to mobilize resources, vaccinate children, train teachers and organize adults.

That is the good news. The bad news is that the statistics are misleading. First, the entire rural population — not just the number of poor — is actually declining in some countries because the poor are flooding into urban areas to look for work. In the 1980s, Argentina showed an absolute decline in rural poverty of 10 per cent, but this was not due to any developmental breakthrough. It was because between 1965 and 1988 a million people left the countryside. During this period, extreme poverty in Buenos Aires increased eightfold.[5] Meanwhile, the percentage of rural people living in poverty actually increased.* In Brazil, the situation was worse: extreme poverty grew

*Argentina, once the economic *wunderkind* of Latin America, is somewhat anomalous. In the early 1990s, hyper-inflation was checked, the economy grew and the peso stabilized. This was expected to help reverse the 14 per cent decline in real wages, and the halving in value of the minimum wage that occurred between 1980 and 1992. At the beginning of 1995, however, urban unemployment stood at 11 per cent, and in the northern provinces it was 25 per cent or higher.

during the 1980s from 12 to 19 per cent of the population. More Brazilians live in absolute poverty than the combined populations of Australia, New Zealand and Switzerland.

In India, where rural poverty decreased from 53 per cent in 1965 to 42 per cent in 1988, population growth meant that there had actually been an 18 per cent increase in the number of rural poor. Other bad news: some of the figures are simply spurious, the brave figments of governmental imagination. Ethiopia, for example, claimed to have decreased rural poverty from 65 per cent to a figure — calculated in the midst of massive on-going starvation, war and general wretched-ness — of 43 per cent. Sub-Saharan Africa as a whole, with almost half its population living in absolute poverty, had a combined 1992 gross domestic product that was only slightly higher than that of Denmark.[6]

Another word on predictions: the World Bank has got many of these wrong over the past few decades, so it will be no surprise that others did as well. *The limits to growth*, an alarming book produced by the Club of Rome in 1972, is often used as a stick to beat would-be seers. It confidently predicted that without dramatic changes in con-sumption patterns, the world's mercury would be depleted by 1983. Tin would be gone by 1985, zinc by 1988 and copper and lead by 1991.[7] It didn't happen. Exploration, prices, commercial opportuni-ties, national priorities and consumption patterns have all affected these estimates dramatically. As of 1992, known world reserves of mercury (which should have run out a decade earlier) still had a life expectancy of 43 years. For tin, the figure was 45 years. Zinc reserves showed a 20-year supply, copper had 33 years remaining and there were 18 years worth of lead left.[8] Known reserves of natural gas were four times higher in 1990 than they were in 1970, and proven recover-able reserves of crude oil were 9 per cent higher in 1990 than they had been only three years earlier in 1987.[9]

Apocalyptic predictions about population, food and the environ-ment have also proven to be exaggerated. The 1969 *Commission on international development*, known as 'the Pearson Commission', said that world population would increase from 3.5 billion in 1968 to a low estimate of 6 billion by the turn of the century, and a possible high of 7 billion. In fact 1995 estimates support the lower figure, about 6.1 billion. More importantly, some of the dire predictions about the im-plications of population growth did not come to pass. Bangladesh, a net importer of food when it had a population of 77 million in 1973, had become virtually self-sufficient in food twenty years later with a population of 115 million, a prodigious achievement for a country unkindly dismissed by many as a basket case. In 1968, Paul Ehrlich, author of *The population bomb*, supported the idea that India 'couldn't possibly feed two hundred million more people by 1980'

10

and in 1970 he predicted a worldwide famine, to occur between 1980 and 1989, in which as many as four billion people would die. In 1974, Lester Brown calculated that the world was nearing the end of its ability to produce more food. Land, energy, water, fertilizer and new technology were available in ever-decreasing supplies, and disaster was on the way. The world fish catch, he said, at 70 million tons a year, was 'at or near the maximum sustainable level'. What actually happened? The 1993 catch was, in fact, 98 million tons, a 40 per cent increase.[10]

As a result of their inaccuracies, people like Ehrlich, Brown and others who have popularized these issues have been written off in some quarters as cranks. In his book, *Eco scam: the false prophets of ecological apocalypse*, Ronald Bailey calls them neo-Luddites, radical egalitarians, arch-environmentalists and eco-doomsters, pointing out the contradictions in their work and listing their failed predictions. He likens them to others in history who predicted plague, pestilence, over-population and the end of the world. Bailey is an optimist. He says, for example, that acid rain is 'at most an environmental nuisance . . . [a] non-problem'. (In 1994 the Canadian Government estimated that 14 000 lakes were devoid of fish because of acid rain.) Bailey says that 'humanity can easily adapt to the projected changes in climate in the next century', and for every 'bio-doomster' he cites a bio-optimist like Winston Brill, who works for an American company called Agracetus: 'Biotechnology will save lives, preserve the environment, feed the hungry and revolutionize industries such as the chemical industry, agriculture and mining. The products and practices will be environmentally more compatible than those that will be replaced.'[11]

Things fall apart

Winston Brill may be right. It is not clear, however, if he is distinguishing between an optimistic future in the US for the products of his company, and the reality that faces a country like Nigeria. Nigeria's population grew by 55 million people between 1950 and 1990, and it will increase from about 110 million in 1995 to 217 million in 2025. Here is the equipment Nigeria has to deal with this projected increase:

○ inflation: between 60 and 100 per cent in 1994;
○ a decade-long negative growth rate in manufacturing (that means it was going backwards economically);
○ a food deficit: in the early 1990s Nigeria was importing three-quarters of a million tons of cereals;
○ debt: in 1994 it paid over $2 billion in interest and principal on $29 billion worth of external debt, and had arrears of about $7 billion.

11

Its interest payments were 25 per cent of its exports: not as bad as some, but worse than most;
o declining social services: fewer Nigerians in rural areas had access to safe drinking water in 1990 than was the case in 1980, government health expenditure dropped by 41 per cent in the 1980s, and education budgets fell by 66 per cent;
o deteriorating terms of trade: the country's major exports had all plummeted in value. In constant dollars, petroleum was earning almost 33 per cent less in 1992 than it did in 1975. The price of groundnut oil stood at one third of its 1975 world price and palm kernels were less than half;
o corruption: in the worst example, a government enquiry found that $12 billion had gone missing from offshore government accounts between 1988 and 1994;
o religious and ethnic conflict: between Muslims and Christians; between the Ogoni and the Adoni; between the Tiv and the Jukun; between the Hausa and the Kataf;
o arbitrary arrest and detention, an emasculated judiciary, and a serious curtailing of press freedoms.[12]

Nigeria's three decades of alternating and mainly botched experiments with military and civilian government rendered the country increasingly unstable, with dire predictions emanating from all sorts of 'doomsters' such as, for example, the US State Department's Bureau of Intelligence and Research: 'The country is becoming increasingly ungovernable . . . ethnic and regional splits are deepening . . . religious cleavages are more serious; Muslim fundamentalism and evangelical Christian militancy are on the rise; and northern Muslim anxiety over southern [Christian] control of the economy is intense . . . the will to keep Nigeria together now is very weak.'[13] Bacteriologist Winston Brill, and perhaps Ronald Bailey too, may have overestimated the ability of silver bullets like biotechnology to deal with debt, plummeting terms of trade, religious fundamentalism, ethnic mistrust and military coups.

Biotechnology has not helped much with the global fish harvest either. True, the global catch did increase by 40 per cent between 1973 and 1993. But by 1993 the situation had changed. In 1990, landings of commercial fish in New England were at their lowest ebb in a generation, causing a loss of $350 million to the fishing industry and the end of 14 000 jobs.[14] Two years later, salmon fishing off Washington state was banned because of shortages and in the Strait of Georgia, the 1995 Chinook salmon fishery had fallen to one-fifth of its 1980 size. In Namibia, the catch declined from nearly two million tons in 1980 to less than 100 000 tons in 1990.[15] According to the FAO, by

1993 nine of the world's seventeen major fishing regions were in decline. 'Decline' is a gentle word. The year before, in an effort to regenerate devastated cod stocks, Canada suspended the entire New-foundland cod fishery indefinitely, putting more than 30 000 people out of work. These are not numbers dreamed up by eco-doomsters.

In Bangladesh, the numbers and their implications are greater. The country had become largely self-sufficient in food by 1995, but how long could this be expected to last? Bangladesh's population will double from 120 million in 1995 to 235 million in 2025. Arable crop-land, currently shared out at less than one-tenth of a hectare per person, will fall, therefore, to half that ratio. This compares badly with one hectare per capita in Bolivia, two in Brazil, almost three in Guyana and Uruguay, and more than seven hectares per capita in Argentina. Water resources in Bangladesh are already overstretched, and while new technologies could increase rice yields somewhat, the infrastructure and pricing mechanisms to support new technologies are weak or non-existent. Deprived of real opportunities, people vote with their feet. Dhaka, a city of less than a million people in 1972, had more than 6 million in 1995. Others head for India, where the popu-lation density across the border is one third of what it is in Bangla-desh. It is estimated that between 12 and 17 million Bangladeshis have migrated in the past two decades, boosting the population of one state, Assam, from 7 million to 22 million in a generation. Ethnic conflict and violence have become endemic in the region.[16]

Thomas Homer-Dixon, Director of Peace and Conflict Studies at the University of Toronto, has demonstrated how resource shortages, crowding and environmental degradation can serve to undermine the legitimacy of the state and its capacity to govern. He traces peasant insurgencies in the Philippines and Peru directly to the heavy migra-tion of poor people to, and the subsequent degradation of, fragile eco-systems. Deepening poverty follows, along with vulnerability to the blandishments of insurgents like Peru's Sendero Luminoso and the Philippines' New People's Army. In China, 300 million people in the interior have less arable land than is the case in Bangladesh. The scope for more irrigation and higher yields is limited. Combined with a growing population, the net effect will be a decrease of 25 per cent in arable land per capita by 2010. Already there is an internal migra-tion, with 150 million redundant workers and tens of millions of people leaving the interior where water and fuel are scarce. They are moving towards the coast and to cities where there is a hope of jobs. 'Environmental scarcity causes violent conflict,' Homer-Dixon says. 'Of immediate concern are scarcity of cropland, water, forests and fish . . . . two others [are] population growth and unequal resource distribu-tion. Scarcity often has its harshest impact when these factors interact.

13

As environmental scarcity becomes more severe, some societies will have a progressively lower capacity to adapt. Of particular concern is the decreasing capacity of the state to create markets and other institutions that promote adaptation.' In addition to China, Bangladesh and India, which have about 40 per cent of the world's people, other candidates for this sort of turbulence are Nigeria, Indonesia and Brazil, which together have another 10 per cent.

In Egypt, the turbulence has already arrived. Corruption, poverty and terror have become the order of the day. In 1995, 12 per cent of the population was destitute and more than half lived below the poverty line, a 30 per cent increase in only a decade. In Algeria, more than 6000 civilians died in 1994 from political and religious terrorism, and in Karachi, where the same sort of chaos prevailed, the murder rate rose to almost a thousand. A ten-year war against Kurdish separatism in eastern Turkey took an estimated 14 000 lives between 1985 and 1995.

The impact of poverty and the concomitant disorder may seem to exact a low and indirect price from industrialized countries. Perhaps cheap labour and cheap commodities will always be available in the South. Perhaps the industrial exports which support current Northern lifestyles will always be in demand elsewhere. It may seem possible to draw a line in the sand between the North and the South, across which AIDS, pollution, nuclear material and technology, terrorism, boat people, fundamentalism, anger, misery and refugees cannot pass. But the impact of poverty can be swift and direct. Mexico's poverty and its second Chiapas uprising at the end of 1994 contributed directly to the sudden collapse of the peso, destabilizing currencies and stock markets throughout the western hemisphere, and wiping out $15 billion worth of US investment in the space of about two weeks.

Mere anarchy: the Kaplan article

American journalist Robert Kaplan drew on Homer-Dixon's work for a landmark article about 'the coming anarchy', published in *The Atlantic Monthly* in February 1994. He chose West Africa as the locus for his illustrations.

West Africa is becoming the symbol of worldwide demographic, environmental, and societal stress, in which criminal anarchy emerges as the real 'strategic' danger. Disease, overpopulation, unprovoked crime, scarcity of resources, refugee migrations, the increasing erosion of nation-states and international borders, and the empowerment of private armies, security firms, and international drug cartels are now most tellingly demonstrated through a West African prism.[17]

14

The chaos and troubles of Nigeria and Liberia do make the occasional Northern headline. Not so well known is the deterioration elsewhere: Togo in turmoil; the Ivory Coast, once a model of economic rectitude, dropped in recent years from the World Bank's list of African 'success stories'. The Ivory Coast now has a growing food deficit, a debt burden that tripled in the twelve years after 1980, a debt service load that represents 32 per cent of its export earnings, and a big cathedral in the jungle. In 1993, Gambia, hitherto a paragon of democratic virtue, fell to a military coup. In 1995, Sierra Leone, a small country rarely in the news up to then, had 400 000 internally displaced people, 400 000 refugees from Liberia, and another 100 000 of its own people living in distress in Liberia and Guinea. Armed gangs roamed the rural areas and the government's writ covered less than two-thirds of the country. This — in a country of 4.4 million, with a young army captain as head of state — did not augur well for the future. Similar situations, some more severe, some less, prevailed during the early 1990s in Somalia, Rwanda, Zaire, Algeria, the Balkans, the Caucasus, Turkey, parts of Sri Lanka and Cambodia, in the hills of Negros and Peru, in Kashmir, Chiapas and in the Chittagong Hill Tracts.

In his influential book, *The transformation of war*, Martin Van Creveld says that this is the shape of things to come. The days of war between nation states are ending, just as the nation state itself goes into decline. In its place is a brave 'new world order', the globalization of capital, manufacturing, knowledge, culture, terrorism and crime, a world of mega-trading blocks, of unrestricted information superhighways, and an end to sovereignty. This end, or at least this decline in sovereignty, manifests itself in the power of transnational institutions like the World Bank and the International Monetary Fund to enjoin structural adjustment upon poor countries, hiking their debt loads higher so they can repay the loans they incurred for failed projects urged on them in other Development Decades.

Structural adjustment and the IMF aside, there are few effective transnational instruments of law, order, peace, security or human rights. What we have instead is a growing horror, described well by Kaplan: 'an epoch of themeless juxtapositions, in which the classificatory grid of nation-states is going to be replaced by a jagged-glass pattern of city-states, shanty states, nebulous and anarchic regionalisms.' Little Palau is an example. The thirtieth new country to enter the United Nations in only five years, its entire population represents about one-quarter of the attendance at a major US football game. Even before its hard-won independence from the US, it had a taste of anarchy, with the murder of its first elected president in 1985 and the apparent suicide of its second president three years later during a corruption scandal.[18]

15

An upsurge of 'tribalism', sometimes politely called 'nationalism', has occurred on almost every continent because globalization has weakened governments and made them less able to deal with people's real needs. Increasingly, people need to define themselves in their own terms, in terms they can understand and influence. This manifests itself in the return to linguistic, religious or cultural communities, and sometimes in attempts to rearrange the geographical polity. This seems reasonable, even agreeable when a polite arrangement can be concluded, as between the Czechs and the Slovaks. But the average nation state dies hard. Countless futile deaths in the Caucasus, the Balkans, Sri Lanka, Somalia and Ethiopia are testimony to this. Unfortunately, what emerges in the process is not always a coherent or shared concept of community. Too often the product is bandits and crooks taking ruthless advantage of fear, poverty and the collapse of government. Van Creveld says that 'once the legal monopoly of armed force, long claimed by the state, is wrested out of its hands, existing distinctions between war and crime will break down much as is already the case today in places such as Lebanon, Sri Lanka, El Salvador, Peru or Colombia. Often, crime will be disguised as war, whereas in other cases war itself will be treated as if waging it were a crime.'[19]

The horn of plenty

For his effort, Robert Kaplan was widely castigated in the South for cultural insensitivity, a lack of historical awareness and for simplistic scare tactics. *The Economist*, somewhat schizophrenic about the environment, development assistance and dire predictions, decided that Kaplan and Thomas Homer-Dixon were 'extreme eco-pessimists', putting them into the same camp as flakes like Joachim of Fiore, a monk who incorrectly predicted that the end of the world would occur in 1260.* 'The neo-Malthusians' pessimism is challenged by others,' *The Economist* observed (others who are presumably not flakes). These others are 'often economists, who believe in the ingenuity of man to adjust to new circumstances and scarcer resources. Scientific inventiveness, for example, will help raise agricultural

---

*Joachim of Fiore may not have had the influence of Kaplan and Homer-Dixon. The US State Department sent Kaplan's article to every US embassy worldwide, and in 1994, Homer-Dixon twice briefed US Vice President Al Gore and his staff, as well as the directors of the CIA and USAID.

productivity and provide ways of feeding the extra billions. Changes in behaviour — especially the education and liberation of women — will bring down birth rates. Population policies . . . have a high likelihood of success.'[20]

More 'others' were quick to join the furious debate that followed the Kaplan article. They pointed out that world child mortality is down, adult literacy and life expectancy are up, and that food production has always outstripped population growth. Economic growth rates in the South have outpaced those in the North, fertility rates have declined, and as for global warming, well, forget about it. There is a growing belief, especially among economists, that the financial cost of cutting emissions of carbon dioxide, methane and chlorofluorocarbons far outweighs what we know about their environmental cost. War? We have had negotiated settlements in Cambodia, El Salvador, Ireland, Mozambique, Angola, Namibia, South Africa and Palestine. Maybe all will hold. And while generally things don't look so good in Africa, South Africa somehow 'promises to be a powerful motor of economic growth for the whole region'.[21]

Such views are held by what Matthew Connelly and Paul Kennedy call 'cornucopians'. Like doomsters, they extrapolate selected past trends uncritically into the future, as though the global fish catch can and will grow to 140 million tons. They ignore the slowing growth in food production and the fact that world population will still reach 6.1 billion by the end of the century and 8.1 billion in the 25 years after that. But let us assume for a moment that there is room for at least cautious optimism about 'the coming global boom'. For Connelly and Kennedy,

> a closer look at this cornucopian literature reveals that its focus is overwhelmingly upon the world's winners: the well-educated lawyers, management consultants, software engineers . . . who sell their expertise at handsome prices to clients in other rich societies. To the extent they consider the situation in the Third World, the cornucopian writers typically point to the model minority of global politics, the East Asians. The techno-liberals pay hardly any attention to the mounting human distress in Calcutta or Nicaragua or Liberia, and no wonder: were they to consider the desperate plight of the poorest two billion beings on our planet, their upbeat messages would sound less plausible.[22]

For this, Kennedy — author of *The rise and fall of the Great Powers* and *Preparing for the Twenty-first Century*, and Director of International Security Studies at Yale — will probably be labelled 'doomster' as well.

He and a legion of others paint increasingly gloomy pictures of faltering international institutions, of Southern governments beset with ever-greater problems, equipped with dwindling amounts of the human, financial and moral capital needed to stave off further decline. These are not campus-bound debates. For anyone with eyes and a television, the evidence of the new world *disorder* is there in the riot-torn slums of Karachi, in the wasted cities and war-torn countryside of Algeria, in the breakdown of Sierra Leone and Somalia, in the killing fields of Cambodia and Rwanda, the battlefields of tomorrow's Angola and next year's Nicaragua. It is evident in an industrial world of governments 'downsizing' and 'outsourcing', relying increasingly on concepts of vaguely regulated transnational 'growth' for their salvation, on the private sector for service delivery and on voluntary organizations for welfare. It is evident too, in the relative values placed on work, entertainment and money. Nike, the giant American running shoe company, posted sales of $3.9 billion in 1994. Most of its shoes are made in China, Indonesia and Thailand, where wages for women workers are about a dollar a day. In 1992, Nike reportedly paid basketball star Michael Jordan $20 million for promoting their shoes, more than the entire annual payroll of the Indonesian factories that make them.[23]

There is other evidence of the new world disorder:

○ In 1973, there were 2.4 million refugees worldwide. By 1993, the number had risen to 23 million, plus an additional 26 million 'internally displaced people';*

○ Although global military spending declined from $995 billion in 1987 to $767 billion in 1994, peacekeeping expenditure remained tiny by comparison — $1.9 billion in 1992. This was about a quarter of one per cent of total military expenditure and about half what the world spends each year on Nike running shoes;

○ Of the 17 million people infected with the HIV virus in 1995, two million lived in India and eleven million lived in Africa. But less than 15 per cent of the world's AIDS prevention budget was being spent in Asia and Africa. AIDS is expected to cost Africa as much as 22 per cent of its gross domestic product over the next two decades;

○ Commitment to the financial agreements reached at the UNCED Summit in 1992 was dead before the last jet took off from Rio. Of the $510 million pledged to promote CFC-free technologies during 1994–6, only $31 million — about six per cent — had been delivered by early 1995;

---

*World population during this period has not quite doubled, while the refugee population has increased tenfold. If displaced people — most of whom feel, act and look like refugees — are included, the number has actually increased by a factor of almost twenty.

- Less money was devoted by industrialized countries to official development assistance in 1993 than in any previous year since 1973. Further cuts took place in 1994 and 1995.

Maybe this last point does not really matter if, as UNDP says, only 15 per cent of aid goes to health and education, and less than half of this is earmarked for human priority concerns.[24] If the 1995 UN Social Summit in Copenhagen provides any indicator, the UNDP figure is probably accurate. At the summit, UNDP and others argued for a '20–20 compact' under which at least 20 per cent of foreign aid would go to meeting basic needs, and 20 per cent of the budgets of recipient governments would be spent in the same way. The arguing that followed over semantics, definitions and calculations is as good an indicator as any of the reluctance to change. Much official development assistance winds up in large infrastructure projects, a substantial proportion is political in nature, and a lot is simply military expenditure. When not 'giving' weapons to countries in the South, industrialized countries sell them: about a billion dollars worldwide in 1992 from France and Britain, two billion each from Germany and Russia, and $8.4 billion from the US. The five permanent members of the ill-named United Nations 'Security' Council are also coincidentally the five biggest arms exporting countries in the world.

Where arms sales are concerned, of course, there must be buyers. In 1992, India ordered 20 MiG-29 fighter aircraft for a sum that could have provided basic education for all the country's 15 million girls not then in school. Nigeria bought 80 British battle tanks for an amount which could have been used to immunize all of the country's two million unimmunized children, and to provide family planning services for 17 of the 20 million couples who lack them. Pakistan bought 40 Mirage 2000E fighters from France, Iran bought two submarines from Russia . . . the beat goes on.[25]

The new disorder has caught us off guard. The end of the Cold War, which should have brought 'peace dividends', seems to have coincided with, or possibly contributed to, greater instability and uncertainty. In the face of this growing disorder, the world seems unwilling or unable to cope. Paul Kennedy says that 'Human beings are usually unwilling to make short-term sacrifices to achieve distant (and uncertain) improvement in the general good — and most politicians' perspectives are shorter still.' He concludes that the doomsters and the cornucopians are probably both correct. Globalization, transnationalism and growth, along with breakthroughs in biotechnology and the availability of yet unimagined silver bullets will give the more stable, industrialized countries greater breathing space, more time. The rest will have to fend for themselves, with predictable results. But if both pessimists and optimists are correct, 'the gap between rich and poor will steadily widen as we enter the twenty-first century, leading not only to social unrest within developed countries but also to growing North-South tensions, mass migration, and environmental damage from which even the 'winners' might not emerge unscathed.'[26]

The light at the end of the tunnel

Development is a product of many things: good education, effective health and welfare services, good and open government, environmental sustainability, high rates of saving and investment, a dynamic private sector, a vibrant civil society and a healthy trading regime. Bringing these things about is not, fundamentally, a question of foreign aid. But aid can help, and in this there is a role for nongovernmental organizations.

Throughout the soothsaying and the worrying about the future, the voluntary sector arises again and again. The American management guru, Peter Drucker, writes extensively about it, saying that as social needs expand, the demand for more and better independent social institutions will grow. Voluntary organizations are important in the charitable sense: to help the helpless in an age of government decline and 'outsourcing'. But they can also provide an integrating function, another way of organizing, of building community and citizenship. 'Historically, community was fate,' he says. 'In the post-capitalist society and polity, community has to be commitment.'[27]

There is something a little too glib, however, about the way many conceive of this 'social sector': what its constituent parts are, where they fit, what they can do. Often, as a writer nears the end of a diatribe against environmental myopia, neo-liberal economics or the official aid establishment, he or she starts looking for alternatives. Nongovernmental organizations invariably emerge as part of the solution. In a massive critique of the World Bank, *Mortgaging the earth*, Bruce Rich says that 'the public should pressure the Bank's member governments to encourage and support a diversity of alternative institutions and channels for foreign assistance. He names four: the Inter-American and African Development Foundations, Appropriate Technology International and Oxfam. These are nominated to help save the world only sixteen pages before the end of the book.[28]

Thomas Homer-Dixon suggests that development assistance policy should focus more on Southern non-governmental organizations.[29] Towards the end of their detailed study of the global economy and transnational corporations, *Global dreams*, Richard Barnet and John Cavanagh talk about the 'crying need for political vision' in a global system characterized increasingly by war, militant fundamentalism,

20

and a growing 'surplus of gifted, skilled, undervalued and unwanted human beings'. In the second to last paragraph of the book, they suggest that change might emerge from 'local citizen's movements and [the] alternative institutions . . . springing up all over the world'. None of these, however, are discussed seriously in the previous 429 pages.[30]

With John Cobb, former World Bank economist Herman Daly has written an opus about economics, community and the environment, *For the common good.* Cobb and Daly do the same as the others. Discussing the importance of community development, they observe that 'the most impressive effort in this direction today is the Sarvodaya Movement in Sri Lanka, led by A.T. Ariyaratne.' Saying that India's continuing poverty is a result of the failure to follow Gandhian principles, they conclude (in only two paragraphs) that 'Sri Lanka has chosen not to follow Ariyaratne. The results will be similar'.[31] It does not stop there. Journalists and pollsters who bemoan the poverty of good international reporting, and the consequent ignorance of people and governments in industrialized countries, also put their hopes for change in the voluntary sector. Journalism expert Daniel Hallin says that the media is pathologically unable to reform itself or to halt the downward rush into trash television, sensationalism and commercially successful pap. He believes, however, that there is room for 'cautious optimism that citizens' organizations can make themselves heard despite the centralization of control over the channels of political communication'[32] — this in the last eight lines of a chapter in a book that does not mention 'citizens' organizations' again.

Is there room for cautious optimism? Or are these melancholy writers casting about for a perfunctory light at the end of the tunnel, the obligatory upbeat book ending, a sign that in the projected worst of times, there may yet be some best of times? Here the question is asked in the first chapter. The next twelve chapters will attempt to find some answers.

CHAPTER II

Naming the rose: what is an NGO?

What's in a name? That which we call a rose
By any other name would smell as sweet.

Shakespeare, *Romeo and Juliet.*

GREAT EFFORT HAS gone into dissecting, disaggregating and defining
non-governmental organizations, to nobody's great satisfaction.
Loosely grouped under an assortment of headings such as 'voluntary',
'non-profit', and 'non-governmental', it is possible that more energy has
gone into unrequited efforts to name and rename them than has been
invested in understanding them. As far as the term 'non-governmental
organization' goes, it is a commonly held view that defining something
in negative terminology is both inappropriate and unimaginative. On
the latter score, enterprising minds have created an innovative assortment of terms that remain unrecognized by most dictionaries.*

Before grappling with non-profit theory and nomenclature, it
would perhaps be useful to look at the historical record. Humanistic
service and the philosophy behind it is neither new, nor does it

---

*Among the exciting alternatives are the following: 'non-governmental develop-
ment organization' (NGDO), 'private development organization' (PDO), 'popular
development agency' (PDA), 'not-for-profit organization', (NFPO), 'voluntary organization', 'non-profit organization' (NPO), and 'voluntary agency' (sometimes
shortened to 'volag'). 'Private voluntary organization' (PVO) is common in the
United States, while 'charities', a word with negative connotations in some countries, is commonly used in Britain. Without success, Alan Fowler tried 'membership organizations' (MO), 'private service organizations', (PSO) and 'donor local
organizations' (DLO) in the 1980s. The term 'civil society organization' (CSO) is
showing up more and more frequently in USAID papers, while the United Nations
began pushing 'non-state actor' (NSA) in the mid-1990s. In Bangladesh there is a
move to adopt 'private voluntary development organization' (PVDO). Sometimes
an acronym can do double duty: for some, VDOs are 'voluntary development
organizations'; for others they are 'value-driven organizations'. David Korten has
created a subset which will be examined later in the chapter: 'people's organization', 'public service contractor', and 'governmental NGO' or GONGO. Other
expressions, related mainly to small village organizations in the South, include
'grass-roots organization' (GRO), 'grass-roots development organization' (GDO)
and 'community-based organization' (CBO). Tom Carroll writes about 'grass-roots
support organizations' (GSO).

emerge from a particular place or time. At its most basic, even in primitive ancient societies, it grew from the elemental obligation of the family, tribe or clan to ensure that its members were fed, housed and clothed. Four thousand years ago the Code of Hammurabi ordered Babylonians to see that justice was done to widows, orphans and the poor. A kind of humanism, focusing on family and society rather than the individual, predominated in ancient Chinese philosophy. The Confucian code of ethics, based on goodness, benevolence and love for all, was developed in the sixth century B.C., and the subsequent evolution of Buddhism imbued it with spiritual underpinnings that have survived 2500 years. The reduction of greed is a core value of Buddhism, and the giving of alms to the poor and to monks is a ritual that can be traced to the dawn of the religion.

Hinduism stresses the transitory nature of life on earth. Doing good works is necessary in order to gain release from the cycle of rebirth and, therefore, to achieve salvation: 'If a man does justice and kindness without sin, his reward is stretched into other lives which, if his virtue persists, will be reborn into a loftier place.'

Jewish law, originating 3300 years ago, stresses the importance of tithing one-tenth of a person's income to charity. Greek philosophy and ethics have influenced western thinking for over 2500 years; it was in the Golden Age of Greece that the common sharing of political authority — democracy — was developed, based on a financial system of contributions (rather than taxes) for education, health, culture and the welfare of the aged. Christ prescribed charity as a means of salvation: 'If thou wilt be perfect, go and sell what thou hast, and give to the poor, and thou shalt have treasure in heaven.' In his first Epistle to the Corinthians, Paul said, 'And now abideth faith, hope, charity, these three; but the greatest of these is charity.' Seven hundred years later, charity — *Al Zakat* — became one of the five pillars of Islam — along with prayer, fasting, pilgrimage and belief in one God. 'Of their good take alms, so that you may thereby purify and sanctify them,' says the Koran in encouragement of giving.[1]

Through the Dark and Middle Ages in Europe, the Christian church became the dispenser of benevolence and charity, establishing hospitals, schools and universities. By the twelfth century in England, it controlled half the country's entire public wealth. With the advent of protestantism across much of Northern Europe, a 'work ethic' developed which equated poverty with sin, and established its alleviation among the helpless as the responsibility of the state (or of parishes and villages). Amongst the able-bodied, poverty was regarded as a punishable evil, a concept resulting in work houses, debtors' prisons and widespread misery. The Elizabethan Poor Law of 1601 codified this approach and influenced charitable thinking and deeds in North America for two centuries, and in Britain for three.

Much medieval charity was a form of self-protection, created by land-holding peasants as a defence against the vagrant poor who wandered from village to village seeking work, but who were equally capable of robbery and violence, of burning barns and plundering harvests. Town walls, constructed as much out of fear of the poor as fear of foreign armies, gradually gave way to a collectivizing process, a process of ritual giving in support of the poor, organized by the church, by municipalities and by charitable entrepreneurs. Put more simply, it was less costly to help the poor than to shun them. It was the gradual spread of education and the evolution of the nation state, and the bureaucracies that accompanied it, that eventually created the conditions which would allow the transfer of social responsibility from the traditional village charitable base to national governments.

In nineteenth-century Europe, however, it was still reformers and reform movements more than governments that brought about changes in working conditions, public health and child labour. Pressure from these reformers, the proliferation of charitable societies, and the political threat of a potentially revolutionary underclass gradually forced governments to take greater responsibility for welfare. Germany's pioneering social welfare programmes of 1880 were followed by France's 1893 National Law for Free Medical Assistance for the poor, and by Britain's old age pension scheme of 1908 and the National Health Insurance and Unemployment Insurance Acts of 1911.

Much analysis of today's voluntary organizations, in both the North and the South, assumes that the phenomenon springs from the same ground. Despite national similarities, however, there are distinct differences. The evolution of the voluntary sector can be categorized under three broad headings. The first is based on the failure of both markets and government to meet the demand for the kinds of services voluntary agencies provide. The second, focusing on disciplines or countries where philanthropy and voluntarism are weak, has to do with a concept of 'voluntary failure'. A weak voluntary ethic allows the state to usurp or bypass what might otherwise be a more vibrant non-profit community.

A third area of study focuses on the organizational culture in which voluntary action develops. In Sweden and Norway, for example, domestic voluntary organizations are a common feature of everyday life, and most people belong to several. These voluntary associations commonly act as interlocutors between their members and government, participating actively in government decision-making and policy formation. In fact official Swedish development assistance was initiated not by government, but by non-governmental organizations. A group

24

of 44 organizations, working with the Ministry of Foreign Affairs in 1952, started the country's first projects in Ethiopia and Pakistan. At the outset, most of the effort was non-governmental, with the Ministry providing only secretarial and co-ordinating services.[2] This Scandinavian corporatism contrasts with what political scientists call 'pluralism' or 'democratic pluralism', in which voluntary associations help to ensure that no single interest or interest group will prevail over others on a given issue. In the Scandinavian model, voluntary organizations work together with government to develop a consensual approach to policy, governance and service delivery. The contrasting pluralist approach is rooted in a clear separation of powers between government, political parties and interest groups.

A common ordering of Northern 'corporatist' countries places Austria, Sweden, Norway, Finland and the Netherlands at the head of the list. Denmark, Ireland, Switzerland, Belgium and Germany are in the middle, while Britain, France and Italy fall into the category of 'weak and unsuccessful' corporatisms. The United States and Canada are at the 'pluralist' bottom of the list.[3]

The corporatist–pluralist distinction provides little guidance in the South, and it is too facile to say that non-profit organizations have sprung up because of state and market failure. The tens of thousands of small community-based organizations that are often missed in the surveys of Asia, Latin America and Africa were there long before the state and market existed in forms that could succeed or fail. And modern Southern non-profits evince very different growth patterns from one country to another. When Bangladesh was a province of Pakistan, a modern NGO movement barely existed. Within five years it had taken off, a phenomenon that did not occur in what had been West Pakistan for the better part of another generation. Need, state and market failure, and *laissez-faire* government attitudes all assuredly played a role in the different growth patterns. The sudden multitude of Northern donor organizations in Bangladesh also made a difference, as did cultural homogeneity. But perhaps most important, the trauma of the war of independence sparked a new kind of civic spirit. Zimbabwe's war of liberation had a similar effect there, as did the shock of complete economic collapse in Ghana in the mid-1980s. The same sudden growth of NGOs can be seen following the Central American wars and in post-apartheid South Africa.

The spending and job creation power of today's non-profit sector is enormous. But it is in their organizing role that non-profits have the greatest impact on society. Although the French historian and political writer, Alexis de Tocqueville, has become something of a cliché in discussions about associational life, he remains an important observer of the American scene. In his 1831 opus, *Democracy in America*, de

Tocqueville commented again and again on the unique American propensity to create and join voluntary organizations:

> Americans of all ages, all stations in life, and all types of disposition are forever forming associations. They are not only commercial and industrial associations in which all take part, but others of a thousand different types — religious, moral, serious, futile, very general and very limited, immensely large and very minute. Americans combine to give fêtes, found seminaries, build churches, distribute books, and send missionaries to the antipodes. Hospitals, prisons and schools take shape in that way. Finally, if they want to proclaim a truth or propagate some feeling by the encouragement of a great example, they form an association. In every case, at the head of any new undertaking, where in France you would find the government or in England some territorial magnate, in the United States you are sure to find an association.

De Tocqueville was pointing out what others have observed about the 'New World' of the seventeenth, eighteenth and nineteenth centuries. Settlers arrived in groups and established their communities in groups. The passengers on the Mayflower and other ships established the Massachusetts Bay Colony, the Ohio Company, the Green and Jersey County Company and others. They travelled west in groups, often establishing new communities when they arrived: the Mormons of Salt Lake City, the gold rush settlements of California, the logging camps that became the towns and cities of Washington state.[4]

It was de Tocqueville's observation — less than fifty years after the effective independence of the United States — that the establishment of groups and associations had formed the basis of America's development, and the roots of her democracy:

> In democratic countries knowledge of how to combine is the mother of all other forms of knowledge; on its progress depends that of all the others. Among laws controlling human societies there is one more precise and clearer, it seems to me, than all the others. If men are to remain civilized, or to become civilized, the art of association must develop and improve among them at the same speed as equality of condition spreads . . . The more government takes the place of associations, the more will individuals lose the idea of forming associations and need the government to come to their help. This is a vicious circle of cause and effect . . .

From the time of the American Revolution, private action, often rooted in religious movements, was seen as the primary route to societal development and political influence. In the post-Civil War era, the concept of private responsibility for public good shifted from religious grounds to new ideas about the role of the élite, and about enhanced private sector responsibilities. Fear of socialism and a fundamental mistrust of governmental action, especially in the social field, encouraged wealthy industrialists in the first three decades of the twentieth century to build on this idea, and to establish philanthropic foundations as an alternative to government. The Carnegie, Sage and Rockefeller Foundations emerged at this time, and helped form a concept of 'welfare capitalism', which maintained a high degree of legitimacy and influence until the 1930s.

Although the idea of welfare capitalism did not survive the Depression, the growth of the welfare state in the 1930s actually stimulated the American non-profit scene. This occurred in part because the 1936 Tax Act allowed corporations, for the first time, to deduct charitable donations from their income tax. It also occurred because the government made a conscious decision to work with, and to provide financial support to non-profit organizations, rather than to set up full-scale alternatives itself. Unlike Scandinavian voluntarism, which sought to build consensual societies in under-populated nations of small, scattered communities, American voluntarism was based on a rejection of government control and a resistance to consensus.

The humanitarian urge

The religious, social and historical background to humanitarianism is underscored by a complex web of motivations. Obviously, one of the first and foremost motives for the formation of a voluntary organization is simple altruism, a motivation with historical roots in religious faith. Compassion for and relief of the sick, the poor, the elderly and the handicapped have always been at the root of the charitable ethic, and remain the primary reason that individuals support organizations like Oxfam and CARE in the North, and organizations like the Edhi Welfare Trust in Pakistan today. The deepest and most profound roots of charitable work are grounded in the capacity of humans to feel a need for others. Guilt, however, is almost as powerful a motivator. Guilt is disparaged by most progressive charities, but it is used — often blatantly — in some of the most effective fundraising campaigns. It motivates the giver, but it also motivates the asker. 'I felt impelled to do it out of a sense of rage and shame,' Bob Geldof said of his fundraising efforts for Ethiopia in the mid-1980s. 'Shame was the over-riding thing. I felt ashamed that we allowed these things to happen to others.'[5]

Fear, sometimes described as self-interest, can also be a powerful motivating force in the creation of, and public support for, voluntary organizations. The medieval fear of marauding bands of paupers has given way to modern fears of disease, international pollution,

27

unchecked immigration and political and economic destabilization. Self-interest and self-preservation have been the motivating forces behind the co-operative movement, farmers' organizations and much of the environmental movement.

Corporatist or populist, consensual or competitive, there is a tendency in the North, borne of an enlightenment tradition, materialism, and an increasingly dogmatic secularism, to analyse society and its institutions entirely from a political and economic perspective, and to disregard the role of religion and religious motivation in both statecraft and associational life. This is certainly a mistake as far as the South goes, but it is probably a mistake in the North as well. Spirituality, values and religious beliefs continue to play a large and highly under-estimated role in both politics and in the motivation of voluntary organizations.[6]

And there is another motivation for voluntary organizations, often forgotten in today's competition for charitable donations. It is the one observed and articulated so well by de Tocqueville: voluntary associations, whether charitable in nature, self-helping or otherwise, form an important part of the way in which societies organize themselves, both politically and economically. Peter Drucker believes that this is more true today than it ever was. Social sector institutions create citizenship. 'Modern society,' he says, 'and modern polity have become so big and complex that citizenship — that is, responsible participation — is no longer possible . . . As a volunteer in a social sector institution, the individual can again make a difference.'[7]

Both altruism and guilt can overshadow the other motivations: fear, self-interest and the socializing or political nature of voluntary organizations. The first two emphasize charity, but the rest have much more to do with reform. Reform, in fact, has for at least two or three centuries been a primary reason for the creation of voluntary associations. Humanitarian reform was very much a part of the early American Quaker tradition in dealing with the poor, as well as with Indians and blacks. Social reformers and their organizations were behind the development of the poor houses and the work houses of the nineteenth century, and social reform underscored the creation of children's aid societies, juvenile reformatories and countless other institutions. Social and political reformers fought slavery in the eighteenth and nineteenth centuries: the Society of Friends (Quakers), the Anti-Slavery Society, founded in London in 1787, and others. Reform movements clamoured for universal suffrage and the right of labour to organize. Moral reform too has been a strong organizational motivator: moral reform of the 'unchurched poor' and of wayward youth; the creation of asylums for reformed prostitutes; an entire — and for some, a completely incomprehensible — movement to abolish the consumption of alcohol.

28

Both the charity ethic and the reform ethic have powerful detractors. 'Do-gooders' and 'bleeding-hearts' are mistrusted and are often regarded as naive or hypocritical, or both. Charity, stigmatized by its association with paternalism, helplessness and pity, seems to come under the heaviest fire during times of greatest stress for the poor, when economies are at their most precarious, or when social revolution seems only a step away. Thomas Malthus, writing at the end of the eighteenth century, said that public relief of the poor should be stopped, that private charity was little more than a palliative. If all relief were withheld, he wrote, the poor would quickly learn 'to defend themselves, [and] we might rest secure, that they would be fruitful enough in resources, and that the evils which were absolutely irremediable, they would bear with the fortitude of men and the resignation of Christians.'[8]

This survival-of-the-fittest assault on charity differs from more radical appraisals, which attack altruism as an inadequate substitute for governmental action. In the early 1950s, John Steinbeck wrote:

> The most overrated virtue . . . is that of giving. Giving builds up the ego of the giver, makes him superior and higher and larger than the receiver. Nearly always, giving is a selfish pleasure, and in many cases it is a downright destructive and evil thing. One has only to remember some of our wolfish financiers who spend two-thirds of their lives clawing fortunes out of the guts of society, and the latter third pushing it back . . .'[9]

Some of the most important advances in governmental provision of social welfare have taken place at times of political peril for liberal democracy: the British reform acts of 1908 and 1911 were instituted in the teeth of massive labour unrest and the incipient revolutions brewing across Europe. The New Deal of Franklin D. Roosevelt was an effort to check the social and economic chaos of the Great Depression, to deal with the ills that preoccupied Steinbeck. The reverse is also true. Continuing the Reagan withdrawal of government support for social services, George Bush spoke in his 1988 inaugural address of the 'brilliant diversity' of private charitable organizations, 'spread like stars, like a thousand points of light in a broad and peaceful sky'. Some saw this as a vindication and recognition of the third sector. David Korten, an American non-profit specialist, cites this passage as an indication that 'the forces of voluntary action were gaining new respect'.[10] Robert Reich, however, who became President Clinton's Secretary of Labor in 1992, saw it as little more than hypocritical escapism. 'No nation congratulates itself more enthusiastically on its charitable acts than America,' he wrote. 'None engages in a greater number of charity balls, bake sales, benefit

29

auctions and border-to-border hand-holdings for good causes. Most of this is sincerely motivated; much of it is admirable. But close examination reveals that these and other forms of benevolence rarely in fact help the poor.'[11] To ignore the fact that a large proportion of the American population cannot afford adequate social services without danger of impoverishment is to encourage what Reich calls 'the politics of secession'.

Reformers too — never particularly pleasing to any government — have their detractors. Reformers are, in fact, critics, demanding change. Unlike health, education and welfare organizations, which often work with government, advocacy groups thrive on making government, and sometimes business, uncomfortable. Advocacy-related organizations are the most independent part of the voluntary sector, and in many ways these organizations are among the most vital to the functioning of a vibrant democracy — in de Tocqueville's 1835 view of America, and perhaps more so today. Communist regimes have recognized this, typically treating any organization outside party control as 'bourgeois' and potentially dangerous.* Mostly they are banned or closely regulated. And rightly so, from a control point of view: in some eastern European countries it was the relaxation of such regulations in the 1970s that allowed newly emerging non-profit and church organizations to become substitutes or covers for political action. Cultural and literary societies, peace movements and environmental organizations all did double duty for many years in Czechoslovakia, the German Democratic Republic and Poland. One of Hungary's most important charities, the Fund for Poverty Relief, sheltered and nurtured the nascent Liberal Party, which subsequently emerged as one of the largest political bodies in the country.[12] The same phenomenon occurred in Rhodesia during the 1970s, and in apartheid South Africa.

Advocacy groups have historically played an important role in providing checks and balances against governmental excess and apathy. Some of the most important social and moral advances have come from such organizations: the anti-slavery movement, child welfare societies and the temperance movement of the nineteenth century; the suffragist movement, the civil rights movement, the independence movement, and the environmental and peace movements of the twentieth century.

All non-profit organizations engage in some form of lobbying and public education, but those focusing primarily on advocacy reflect

---

*A Soviet definition of charity: 'Aid, hypocritically rendered by representatives of the ruling class in an exploiter society, to the poor population in order to deceive the workers and divert them from the class struggle.' (McCarthy *et al.*, (1992), p.373)

and test a country's most fundamental attitude towards non-governmental organizations: freedom of assembly, freedom of belief, freedom of speech. There can be a cost to free speech, and the prices exacted in the United States, Britain and Canada are similar. Charitable organizations (as opposed to organizations that are only non-profit) are often, and sometimes irrationally restricted from activities which seek to influence legislation. The dividing line between public education and political lobbying, although often a grey area, can therefore become one of enormous financial importance if one type of organization can issue receipts for tax purposes and is eligible, say, for government grants, and another is not.

The next generation

Variations in the NGO tradition will be a recurring theme throughout this book, and a reminder that Northern international development NGOs, working with a complex mosaic of Southern partners, may not behave, and may never be able to behave, in quite the way observers, especially government observers, hope or expect they will. Shakespeare, who frequently used the imagery of flowers, said that 'Roses have thorns and silver fountains mud . . . All men make faults'.

David Korten, who created one of the more durable NGO typologies, has done much to disaggregate a rather complex set of organizations, basing his analysis on the type of work an organization does, on its form and governance, and on its sources of income. Korten describes an evolutionary pattern in NGO thinking, programming and growth. 'First generation' NGO strategies, he says, focus primarily on relief and the provision of welfare services. Most of the older Northern international NGOs started with this sort of approach: Save the Children, Oxfam, Foster Parents Plan. Many Southern NGOs have done the same. 'Second generation' strategies focus on self-reliant local development, often small-scale community improvement projects. 'Third generation' strategies involve 'sustainable systems development': strategies that seek to influence the broader policy framework which may well impinge on the success of projects at the micro-level. A third generation strategy might combine, for example, village agricultural projects with a programme aimed at altering a government's policy on the encouragement of local ownership of irrigation systems.

Korten's fourth generation is less a 'strategy' than an approach to the concept of organization: the fourth generation is comprised of social, or 'people's development movements'. These 'are driven not by budgets or organizational structures, but rather by ideas, by a vision of a better world. They move on social energy more than on money. The vision mobilizes independent action by countless

31

individuals and organizations across national boundaries, all supporting a shared ideal . . . in continuously shifting networks and coalitions.'[13]

Subscribing to the generally accepted concept of voluntary organizations as a 'third sector' after government and business, Korten also slices the cake in a different direction, dividing NGOs into four categories:

o *voluntary organizations* that pursue a social mission driven by a commitment to shared values;
o *public service contractors* that function as market-oriented non-profit businesses serving public purposes;
o *people's organizations* that represent their members' interests, have member-accountable leadership and are substantially self-reliant;
o *governmental NGOs* (GONGOs) that are creations of government and serve as instruments of public policy.[14]

Voluntarism is at the heart of Korten's definitions, and at the heart of the American concept of the voluntary organization. 'They depend primarily on appeals to shared values as the basis for mobilizing human and financial resources. Citizens contribute their time, money and other resources to a VO because they believe in what it is contributing to society . . . This value commitment is the distinctive strength of the VO, making it relatively immune to the political agendas of government or to the economic forces of the market place.'[15] This immunity from government, of course, is a clear reflection of the American pluralist ideal, and is quite different from, say, the ideal of Swedish corporatism.

Korten's definitions exclude a wide range of what have come to be called 'NGOs'. NOVIB in Holland, Radda Barnen in Sweden and Médecins sans Frontières in France certainly do not depend on volunteers for the large part of what they do. Some of their income, in varying degrees, may be raised by public subscription, but this is usually done through very sophisticated fundraising techniques where the 'shared value' of donors, as often as not, is a response to emotive appeals for relief or welfare: a first generation response to a first generation plea. This weakness in voluntarism applies, to a greater or lesser extent, to most Northern NGOs, and even to most Southern NGOs of any size or sophistication. The staff may have a high degree of commitment to their work, but this is not the same as voluntarism. The biggest and best known Southern NGOs — Sarvodaya in Sri Lanka; BRAC (the Bangladesh Rural Advancement Committee), Proshika and Grameen Bank in Bangladesh; the Aga Khan Rural Support Programmes (AKRSP) in India and Pakistan — none are membership organizations in the Korten sense; none have more than traces of what could be described as democratic management; and few would survive in recognizable form if they were forced to become financially self-reliant in a short space of time.

Even the easily dismissed GONGO, the government-organized NGO, presents definitional difficulties. Take for example, the Janashakthi Bangku Sangam (Janashakthi Bank) in Southern Sri Lanka. A project of the Women's Development Federation (WDF), it is modelled closely on Grameen Bank, and in its first four years of operation organized 368 women's societies with a membership of 22 000 individuals. Combined shares and savings totalled approximately $309 000 in mid-1994, and outstanding loans, on which the repayment rate averaged 96 per cent, totalled $623 000.[16] The Women's Development Federation is a registered NGO operating on a lean budget, depending heavily on contributions of time from over 2000 volunteer workers. Supported by Canadian and Swiss NGOs, it might well be described by the casual visitor as a people's organization. In many ways more voluntary than CARE or Oxfam, the WDF is in fact a GONGO of the purest sort. The local District Secretary, a dynamic (male) civil servant with his heart firmly rooted in community development, inspired a number of women to take advantage of financial support offered by the Janasaviya Trust Fund. The Janasaviya Trust Fund is a support mechanism for NGOs designed and paid for by the Government of Sri Lanka and the World Bank. None of this makes much difference to the women who now run their own Federation, nor does it matter to the savers and borrowers who look very much like savers and borrowers in any NGO project. Nor does it make much difference to the volunteers who provide the community backbone of the Janashakthi Bank.

The Korten typology describes elements of what anyone familiar with the Northern and Southern NGO scene knows. Its weakness, however, is that by default, because most NGOs are not significantly volunteer-based, it more or less throws all of them into the rather unattractive 'public service contractor' category. As an attempt to nudge NGOs into more thoughtful behaviour, this is perhaps useful. As a way of explaining or describing a complex set of institutions doing a wide variety of very different things, it lacks both rigour and organizing power. Among other things, rigour and organizing power are what a John Hopkins University Non-profit Sector Project has sought.[17]

Using background studies of Germany, France, Britain, Brazil, India, Thailand and others as tests for its thesis, the study concludes that it is the structure and operation of an organization that provide the most rational basis for definition. Thus, occasionally reverting to the term 'third sector',[18] it defines voluntary organizations as those which make 'a reasonable showing' in each of the following categories:

- *formal* — the organization is institutionalized to at least some extent: probably incorporated, but at least formalized in the sense of having regular meetings, office bearers and some degree of organizational permanence;
- *private* — it is institutionally separate from government, although it perhaps receives government support;
- *non profit-distributing* — the organization may generate a financial surplus, but this does not accrue to the owners or directors;
- *self-governing* — able and equipped to control and manage its own activities;
- *voluntary* — there is some meaningful degree of voluntary participation in the conduct or management of the organization. 'This does not mean that all or most of the income of an organization must come from voluntary contributions or that most of its staff must be volunteers'.

A typology of voluntary service

If this definition is accepted, the matter of evolutionary stages remains. It is obvious that the evolution of voluntary humanistic service will vary from country to country, over time, and according to the pace of development and the predominating ideology. The following is a different way of looking at it.

Stage One is *community-based voluntarism*. This stage is characterized by a high degree of direct personal involvement and responsibility for the delivery of humanistic service. Small, community-based self-help efforts, the community-based welfare activities of a village church, and personal voluntary service fall into this category, which was most common, in most countries, until the early years of the twentieth century.

Stage Two could be called *institutionalization*. The institutionalization of humanistic service grows out of necessity because of greater needs, and greater concentrations of people. Responsibility remains with individuals, but through the formation of associations which may complement services being provided by government. A volunteer ethic remains, but it may no longer predominate; the expression 'voluntary' now takes on meanings that extend beyond 'volunteer': elective, non-compulsory, willing, optional.

Stage Three could be called a *professionalization stage*. It evolves more from convenience than conviction: the demand for services, the proliferation of associations and the intensification of fundraising lead to the federation and professionalization of associations, and, often reluctantly, to government funding or to replacement by government agencies and departments.

34

Stage Four might once have been called *the welfare state*. This is the ultimate in humanistic delivery systems, one in which a society decrees that all members will be provided with an appropriate level of health care, education, cultural enjoyment and social well-being. In theory, charities and voluntary organizations become redundant and cease to exist. The extension of government social security programmes throughout Europe and North America after the Second World War represented a growth in the belief that 'collective action' as reflected in the state, rather than the individual, was the most appropriate way to deal with strangers in need.[19]

While Stage One organizations conform more or less with Korten's first generation NGOs, the comparison does not hold through subsequent stages. For example a mature, professional Stage Three NGO, such as the Red Cross, might be involved in relief and welfare, or development projects, or systems analysis. Or it may well be involved in all three. There is no relative value judgement to be placed on development or systems analysis, or welfare. An organization need not 'graduate' from one to the other. Rather it grows in the maturity and professionalism that it applies to the mandate it has chosen for itself.

The stages are not immutable, nor is one necessarily superior to another. Time, societal values and money will make that distinction. In fact much of Europe in the Middle Ages, under heavy church rather than governmental influence, had reached a crude form of Stage Four, only to move backwards to Stages One, Two and Three through the nineteenth century, re-emerging at Stage Four again after the Second World War. State contraction and conservative political ideologies in western Europe, along with the collapse of eastern European communist regimes which espoused Stage Four services (but provided considerably less), suggest a return towards greater reliance on a Stage Three approach.

Because of their motivation and donor base, Northern international NGOs tend to be more reflective of Stage Two than of Stage Three. They are, nevertheless, highly individualistic and territorial, and often have strong Stage One characteristics. Proliferating at a staggering pace in the past twenty years, some of the most successful fundraisers among them make their appeal to the donor's sense of personal responsibility and to the idea of direct delivery of services to those in need.

Some of the great struggles facing international voluntary organizations are glimpsed in the attempt to describe and name it. But there is another dimension. In 1977, Jørgen Lissner observed that altruistic intentions must be translated into concrete action. 'In a world of conflicting interests, that means making choices which are political, accepting compromises which are debateable, and influencing public opinion in one direction, rather than another. In other words, helping people is a political art, just as politics is a way of helping people.'[20] The following chapters will deal with how NGOs turn intentions into action, how they cope with conflicting interests, how they make choices and compromises, and how they influence public opinion.

Finally, it may not have gone unnoticed that the lamentable and much deprecated term 'NGO', assiduously avoided in the early paragraphs of this chapter, has become more common towards the end. Even if a rose is not always a rose, there is a reason for sticking with this ungainly and unloved expression. First, defining something in negatives is not as unusual as development neologists make out. *Non-aggression, non-aligned, non-combatant, noncommittal, nonconformity, nondescript, nonentity, non-fiction and non-starter* all have good Oxfordian and Websterian pedigrees. The NGO term, enshrined in the 1945 UN Charter, is commonly used throughout most international development organizations. It is widely understood in the South, and it seems more or less intent on not going away. There is a better reason for this than habit. One writer has observed, quite rightly, that NGOs see themselves as being what governments are not: 'not bureaucratic, not rigid, not directive, and not stultifying of local initiative. This image plays an important functional role in freeing NGOs from established political hierarchies.'[21] Even if it ignores the close links most NGOs have with governments, the term is probably here to stay, at least through to the end of this book.

CHAPTER III

Northern NGOs: the age of innocence

A voyage is now proposed to visit a distant people on the other side of the globe; not to cheat them, not to rob them, . . . but merely to do them good, and make them, as far as in our power lies, to live as comfortably as ourselves.

Benjamin Franklin, 1771.

NORTHERN NGOs, even the newest of them, have extensive root systems and complex historical origins. This chapter will touch briefly on the beginnings of modern humanitarian and development assistance, and will then examine three strands that have helped form the work and thinking of today's NGO community: volunteer-sending organizations, appropriate technology, and the environmental movement. These are not exclusively Northern in origin and they are by no means predominantly Northern today. But all stories require a starting point and a chapter heading, and so it is with these. Other important strands such as the women's movement and emergency assistance will be the subject of full chapters in Part Two.

Many secular Northern organizations can trace their ancestry to missionary organizations, and these have a long history. Many were designed centuries ago to minister to new-found colonial empires, particularly to colonies in North America, where educational and welfare requirements in the days of the early settlements were great. One of the earliest recorded examples was a shipment of food sent from Ireland to New England in 1647: 'to the poor, distressed by the late war with the Indians'.[1] One of the oldest overseas assistance organizations still extant was itself founded in the colony of New France, in 1653. *Les Soeurs de la Congrégation de Nôtre Dame*, based in Quebec, is still active in literacy and educational work in Latin America. The United Society for the Propagation of the Gospel, a missionary society of the Church of England, was founded in 1701. The Church Missionary Society, the Africa Inland Mission and the Methodist Missionary Society were others. The Royal Society, founded in London in 1660 and the National Adult School Union, founded in 1798 were early educational institutions which had an overseas outreach. French counterparts, established a century later, include the *Ligue Française de l'Enseignement* (1866) and the *Alliance Française* (1883).

37

The history of American assistance abroad pre-dates any organized voluntary efforts. In a foreshadowing of events that would occur two centuries later on the same island, Americans provided impromptu shelter and assistance in 1793 to thousands of people fleeing revolution in Santo Domingo. The American Government sent assistance to the victims of an earthquake in Venezuela in 1812, to Greek war victims in 1820, and to starving families in Ireland during the Great Famine of 1847.

The Red Cross, originally known as the International Committee to the Wounded, was founded in Geneva in 1862 by a young Swiss, Henry Dunant, who had witnessed the carnage of the Battle of Solferino three years earlier. In the following decade, national Red Cross committees were established throughout Europe, spreading to North America and eventually to almost every country of the World. Organized labour also had its outreach programmes: The British Trades Union Congress was established in 1868, the Co-operative Union in 1868, and the American Federation of Labor in 1881. Temperance societies founded in the late nineteenth century formed branches abroad, and organizations formed to promote universal suffrage and the emancipation of women provided scholarships and other educational services to their counterparts overseas. Among these were the *Frederika Bremer Förbundet*, established in Sweden in 1884, the Paris-based International Council of Women and the US National Council of Women, both founded in 1888.

The shape of the modern NGO scene began to form in the years between the First and Second World Wars, for here were people not only ministering to the poor and suffering, but attempting to deal with some of the causes. In 1919 Eglantyne Jebb founded Save the Children in Britain to help young victims of World War I. The 1924 Declaration of Geneva, a precursor of today's UN Rights of the Child, was written and promoted by Jebb in an effort to build awareness and to prevent child victimization. World University Service was founded in Geneva in 1920, and various international work camps were established in efforts to create better cross-cultural understanding. Jewish organizations, many of them founded in the previous century, became increasingly active in support of immigrants and refugees moving to Palestine, while pacifist and church groups throughout Europe and North America raised money for China after the Japanese invasion of Manchuria.

Foster Parents Plan (now Plan International), founded by two Englishmen in 1937, was established to aid child victims of the Spanish Civil War. In its early days, the American Branch was closely affiliated with the pro-Loyalist North American Committee to Aid Spain, while others, such as the American Friends Service Committee,

38

the Committee for Impartial Civilian Relief in Spain, and the Red Cross attempted to provide food and medical assistance to both sides.

During the Second World War and immediately afterwards, a number of today's best-known organizations were formed. Oxfam, initiated to provide famine relief to victims of the Greek Civil War in 1942, is today one of the world's largest NGOs. A close runner-up is CARE, which began by sending food packages from the United States to Europe in 1946. World Vision, one of today's largest and fastest growing Northern NGOs, was the brainchild of an American missionary in Asia during the Korean War. These organizations or spinoffs found support throughout Europe, North America, Australasia, and in some cases, Japan. Redd Barna in Norway and Radda Barnen in Sweden are part of the Save the Children family. Oxfam spread to Belgium, Canada and the United States. CARE established branches in Canada, Australia and throughout Europe. Church organizations were created specifically for relief and development work: the Mennonite Central Committee; *Evangelische Zentralstelle für Entwicklunshilfe* (EZE) in Germany; ICCO and CEBEMO in the Netherlands; *Comité Catholique Contre la Faim* (CCFD) in France; Christian Aid and the Catholic Fund for Overseas Development in Britain.

Many of these organizations began with and retained a strong emphasis on emergency assistance. But most also realized soon after they began that it was more cost-effective to prevent disasters through developmental programmes than to minister to the victims later. Setting up projects themselves, or working through local governments and missionary organizations, they started learning about community development, tropical agriculture, rural health and education. Some helped build schools, clinics and irrigation channels, some shipped books, some shipped teachers.

Smiling faces going places

Paul Theroux, author of a dozen best-selling novels and an accomplished travel writer, produced his first two books in Malawi when he was a Peace Corps Volunteer. Entitled *Foundation secondary English* (Book One and Book Two), they were co-authored with an official of the Ministry of Education, and twenty years after they were published, Theroux was still earning royalties. As a volunteer from 1963 to 1965, he saw his first hyena, smoked his first hashish, witnessed his first murder (so he said) and caught his first dose of gonorrhoea.* And a month before his two-year assignment was to end, he was 'terminated' after being accused of involvement in an assassination plot

---

*The total number is not a matter of public record.

against President-for-Life, Hastings Banda. He ended up back home with $200 and a grudge against the Peace Corps that would be slow to fade. 'When I think about those years,' Theroux wrote in 1986, 'I don't think much about the Peace Corps, though Malawi is always on my mind. That is surely a tribute to the Peace Corps. I do not believe Africa is a very different place for having played host to the Peace Corps . . . but America is quite a different place for having had so many returned Peace Corps Volunteers, and when they began joining the State Department and working in the embassies, these institutions were the better for it.'[2]

Although the Peace Corps is a government organization, many of the other volunteer groups that sprang up were not. The British Voluntary Service Overseas, the French *Volontaires du Progrès*, the German AGEH and *Dienste in Übersee*, Canadian University Service Overseas, the Australian Overseas Service Bureau and others were and remain NGOs. It is not so much the status of these organizations that matters, however, as the fact that they came into existence, and that they provided opportunities for a generation of young Europeans, North Americans, Japanese and Australians to see, and hopefully to understand something about the lives of people in countries hitherto accessible mainly through the pages of *National Geographic*.

It has been largely forgotten, but the volunteer-sending organizations owe their basic philosophy to cross-cultural European work camps that sprang up after World War I, and to an organization which developed branches throughout Europe and North America in the 1930s, Service Civil International.* In 1931, SCI's founder, Pierre Ceresole, spent several days with Mahatma Gandhi, who was returning to India following constitutional meetings in London. Ceresole was profoundly affected by Gandhi's practical attempts to advance the same sort of peaceful revolution advocated by SCI. Three years later, when Bihar was devastated by an earthquake, Ceresole and three companions went to India to help in the reconstruction effort. The four volunteers spent three years in Bihar, living, working and eating with the villagers, facing the same joys and hardships. Remarkable for their era, they were, in a sense, the first non-church Western volunteers to work in the South, long before volunteerism or even 'technical assistance' had been conceived and formalized.

Twenty years later, in the early 1950s, members of the Australian committee of World University Service, concerned about their country's negative 'white Australia' policy, devised a plan to send volunteers to teach in Indonesia. By 1953 the scheme was in operation:

---

*Known in Britain and the US as International Voluntary Service to avoid confusion with the governmental term 'civil service'.

the Australian Government provided the airfare, £50 and a bicycle. After that, living with Indonesian families and earning Indonesian salaries, they were on their own. The impact was electric. Indonesia's ambassador to Canberra said 'for the first time in our experience, and our experience includes many long years of European rule, white people have been ready and eager to live among us on our own standards of salary and living, to share family life with us, to become in truth real members of our community. This is indeed striking. Such a contribution is worth immeasurably more to us than the rupiahs which it saves our treasury.'[3]

The British Voluntary Service Overseas (VSO) was founded in 1957 as an explicit alternative to military service. Three years later, several Canadian efforts coalesced into what became known as Canadian University Service Overseas (CUSO). But it was the Peace Corps that gave the movement real impetus. John F. Kennedy, borrowing the idea from unsuccessful legislation drafted three years earlier by Hubert Humphrey, made the Peace Corps an election issue in 1960. Delayed one October evening by other engagements (about which history remains silent), he finally spoke at two in the morning to a crowd of students gathered on a lawn at the University of Wisconsin. 'How many of you are willing to spend ten years in Africa or Latin America or Asia,' he asked, 'working for the United States and working for freedom? How many of you who are going to be doctors are willing to spend your days in Ghana; technicians or engineers, how many of you are willing to spend your lives travelling around the world?'[4] Following the election, Kennedy made the Peace Corps one of his first Executive Orders, signing it into existence on 1 March 1961.

In the first 25 years of these organizations, some 10 000 Canadians, 20 000 British and 120 000 American volunteers served overseas. Their ranks were augmented by tens of thousands of Europeans and Japanese who joined them as newer organizations were founded. Thousands more served through a United Nations Volunteer Program, which recruited in the South as well as the North. As the years passed, more of the volunteers were mature, even retired professionals, but the majority in the early days were young idealists. They were often disparaged by home-grown activists who concentrated on what they saw as infinitely more important issues: desegregation, human rights, the Chicago riots, the student uprisings in Paris, the Prague Summer, Vietnam. The American campus radical, Tom Hayden, summed up the criticism when he dismissed the Peace Corps as a bunch of 4-H graduates. But to Paul Cowan, Freedom Rider, member of the radical Students for a Democratic Society and self-styled 'un-American', Hayden was too glib. 'I partly agreed,' Cowan wrote, 'but only partly. For the fact was that most of them stayed in their foreign villages for two

41

years. And too many of the self-proclaimed radicals I knew . . . remained in their rural towns or urban ghettoes for only a few months, or never tried to work with poor people at all. Actions seemed to me to be more important than attitudes: salvation by works a far more sensible doctrine than salvation by grace.'[5]

Theroux was right in saying the Peace Corps probably did more for America than it did for Africa. That is the enduring message of all returning volunteers. What the Peace Corps and its counterparts also built, were foundations for an entirely new kind of internationalism, one based on friendship and on direct, personal experience of development. Today, returned volunteers can be found in every walk of life: business, government, health and education services, politics. And many have remained in the field of international development. Nobody has done a survey, but it is safe to say that a significant proportion of the mid-level and senior staff in most bilateral development agencies, and many in the multilateral system, began their careers as volunteers. Perhaps more relevant to this book, many of the NGOs that emerged in the 1960s and 1970s were founded by former volunteers, and it is probably no exaggeration to say that half to three quarters of today's Northern NGO managers began their careers, like Paul Theroux, working in a clinic or a school, or as an extension agent in a place very unlike where they grew up.

The better mousetrap: intermediate technology[6]

For every problem there is a solution that is simple, direct and wrong.
H.L. Menken.

Fritz Schumacher led a life of reversals. German-born, educated at Oxford and Columbia, he was interned as an enemy alien in Britain during the war, and then became one of Britain's top economic planners. He was born a Protestant, was strongly influenced by Buddhism, but died a Catholic. He was employed for much of his working life by one the largest enterprises in Europe, but he is best remembered for a single book — about smallness. *Small is Beautiful*, first published in 1973 and translated into twelve languages, has sold over four million copies and remains a bestseller. A friend and confidant of the rich and powerful, Schumacher was consulted by Julius Nyerere, Pandit Nehru and Kenneth Kaunda. He went to the White House for tea with Jimmy Carter. Yet his greatest achievements were almost entirely on behalf of the poor.

Schumacher's adventure with small began unexceptionally in 1955, during a UN consultancy to Burma. Charged with advising the government on economic planning and fiscal policy, he was struck by the richness of Burmese culture, by the Buddhist religion and by the friendliness and dignity of people who were, in normal economic parlance, poor. He began to see that the 'economics of materialism', with which his professional life had been preoccupied, had limitations. And his report, focusing on the importance of rural development, spoke of the need to develop local expertise and self-reliance.

Later, participating in a series of seminars in India, he came into contact with some of the country's leading Gandhians, and in 1961 he began to articulate his first ideas on intermediate technology:

> Economic development is obviously impossible without the introduction of 'better methods', 'higher technology', 'improved equipment' . . . but all development, like all learning, is like a process of stretching. If you attempt to stretch too much, you get a rupture instead of a stretch . . . The only hope, I should hold, lies in a broadly based, decentralized crusade to support and improve the productive efforts of the people as they are struggling for their livelihoods now. Find out what they are doing and help them to do it better. Study their needs and help them to help themselves.[7]

Schumacher further refined his concept of relevant technologies for rural areas, and began to wrestle with the prohibitive cost of creating workplaces in capital-intensive factories. Some of his ideas were borrowed: small-scale rural industries were already a standard development tool in China, for example. And he was deeply influenced by Gandhi who had coined a phrase Schumacher often quoted: 'Production by the masses, not mass production'.

Much of what Schumacher wrote was strikingly new, however, especially to a Western school of development thought grounded in classical economics and theories of aggregate demand. In 1964, he presented a paper at Cambridge entitled 'Industrialization through Intermediate Technology' which was widely published and republished, and he began to develop a following of people who saw the relevance of his message. Rather than simply increasing aid flows, Schumacher argued that a change in direction was necessary, a change that would take aid agencies 'straight into battle' with the evils of poverty. This could be done by creating jobs in the areas where people live: the rural areas rather than cities. The workplaces would have to be cheap enough that developing countries could afford to create them in large numbers without unattainable levels of saving and imports. The employment should be in productive jobs requiring relatively simple production methods, producing goods for local consumption and relying to a large extent on local supplies of raw materials and finance. This could only be done, Schumacher, said, through a conscious effort to develop an 'intermediate technology'.

The task, he argued, was to establish a tolerable basis of existence for the majority by improving the productivity of traditional technologies, which were often in a state of stagnation or decay. Public reaction to his writing was overwhelming and positive. Letters and support flowed in, and in 1966, the Schumacher group incorporated itself as a non-profit company and a registered charity. They called themselves the Intermediate Technology Development Group.

When ITDG started, there were four characteristics of a technology that would make it 'appropriate' to a developing society: it would be small in scale so that it could fit into small market situations. It would be simple, so that sophisticated manufacturing skills, organization and finance would be unnecessary. It would not be capital intensive, and would therefore keep the cost per workplace down. And it would be non-violent. The non-violence of a technology was an essential part of its appropriateness: it should be completely under human control, it should not have unintended side-effects, it should not cause social or environmental disruption.

Over the years, the basic formula — small, simple, cheap, non-violent — attracted a surprisingly large volume of debate. Some observers insist on a clear distinction between 'appropriate technology', and 'intermediate technology'. Penicillin, for example, is very appropriate to the health needs it addresses worldwide, but it is hardly an intermediate technology. Likewise, the use of a satellite to predict hurricanes and cyclones is not an intermediate technology, but to people in the Pacific Islands, the Caribbean and the low-lying delta areas of Bangladesh, the warning that this sophisticated, expensive technology can provide is more than appropriate.

Intermediate technology is a relative term: a technology that stands somewhere between what is known — the traditional technology — and the modern. In Africa, animal traction, falling half way between the hoe and the tractor, may be an intermediate technology. In Asia, where animal traction is well developed, a power tiller might conceivably be the intermediate technology. But in some cases, neither of these examples may be appropriate. In Africa, the most appropriate advance on traditional slash and burn agriculture might be better seeds, the use of fertilizer, an improved hoe. In Asia, the power tiller might not be the most logical progression on animal traction. It might be a better plough, improved irrigation, better organization.

In 1966, the concepts of appropriate and intermediate technology were simply that, concepts. Ten years later there were an estimated five hundred organizations, groups and institutions with an appropriate technology focus, and by 1980 the number had doubled to a thousand.[8] The idea also spread quickly in the South. The University of Science and Technology in Kumasi, Ghana, established a

Technology Consultancy Centre in 1971. The University of Zimbabwe founded a similar institution in the early 1980s. Committees, groups and organizations were established in Zambia, Kenya and Tanzania. Two institutions were opened in Botswana, and there were dozens of others: the South Pacific Appropriate Technology Foundation, the *Centro Co-operativo Tecnico Industrial* in Honduras, and many in India.

Everywhere there were experiments with windmills, solar energy, latrines and energy-efficient stoves. Experimental pumps of every sort began to dot the yards behind workshops: pumps made of bamboo, wood, plastic; pumps powered by the sun, the wind, bicycles and oars. Small biogas plants producing methane from animal waste — a technology developed concurrently in India and China — began to appear throughout the Third World.

The widespread diffusion of technologies which seemed genuinely relevant, however, proved far more difficult than had been imagined. In retrospect, this is hardly surprising. The difficulties, however, fuelled a reaction in official development and academic communities. Quick to find fault, orthodox economists and development experts behaved like neo-Luddites, attacking AT on every point imaginable: technical grounds, economic, cultural, social and intellectual. Unlike the original Luddites, who smashed modern, job-reducing textile machinery in the nineteenth century, these attackers ignored modern, job-eliminating technology and assaulted innovations which sought to do the opposite. Some critics debunked the notion of 'technology choice', arguing that there is only one way of efficiently and economically pursuing an activity, only one readily available choice that makes sense in a given situation.[9] This ignored, however, one of the hallmarks of both the NGO and the intermediate technology movements: the rethinking and redefinition of 'what makes sense'.

Reflecting on the lessons of technology in history, Schumacher had argued that technology is both determined by, and is a result of factors within a society; it is rarely something that poor countries can order cold from a catalogue with hopes of instant success. Schumacher criticized the pathological inability of mainstream economists to think beyond quantitative growth. 'Instead of insisting on the primacy of qualitative distinctions, they simply substitute non-growth for growth, that is to say, one emptiness for another.'[10]

Since *Small is Beautiful* was published, there have been vast changes in technology, in raw materials, in production techniques, information systems and product development. In many ways, the gaps Schumacher sought to fill have become wider. But much has happened to revalidate his vision, and the messages contained in *Small is Beautiful*. The first is that the appropriate technology movement has matured, and has become more professional. Although weaknesses persist, there is a growing body of success and much greater sophistication in dealing with the societal and political obstacles which in the past have held progress back.

The second is a growing recognition in the North that big is not, of itself, better. Mass production and giant industries grew out of a particular approach to organization and out of ideas about the primacy of price and economies of scale. But there have always been dissenting views, some of them rediscovered and used to excellent advantage first by Japanese firms in the 1970s. The most successful Japanese companies, which by world standards are enormous, have focused clearly on the customer, on innovation and on close, personalized co-ordination between divisions, managers and the shop floor. But there is something else. An automobile has approximately 20 000 parts. The average Japanese car maker produces only 30 per cent of the parts itself, sub-contracting the rest to smaller firms. The average American car maker produces about half of its own requirements, and thus operates much larger and more complex plants. The story doesn't stop there. General Motors deals with 3500 sub-contractors, whereas Toyota deals with only 300. The difference between the complexity of the American network and the Japanese is as day is to night. But there is a further difference: Toyota's sub-contractors, with whom it is able to develop a very close, personalized relationship, in turn sub-contract much of their own work to a second tier of 5000 firms, which in turn deal with a further 20 000 smaller third- and fourth-tier firms.[11] 'Lean production' is based on the production of parts in smaller batches, and the 'just in time' concept focuses on arranging the flow of supplies so that a producer can live with smaller inventories. Smaller, in these cases, is better. And more profitable.

In the late 1980s one of the most striking examples of new industrial thinking could be found in the 'Third Italy', a region between the industrial heartland of the Italian north and the agricultural regions of the south. Characterized by a vast number of small firms, Emilia-Romagna has been one of the fastest growing of Italy's 20 regions. Its 350 000 registered firms have an average of only five employees each, and an estimated one-third of the work force is self-employed. And yet Emilia-Romagna has the highest per capita income in Italy and accounts for 10 per cent of the country's exports. With imports to the region accounting for only 4 per cent of the country's total, Emilia-Romagna contributes an international trade surplus of $5 billion to the Italian economy every year. Unlike California's high-tech Silicon Valley, the Emilia-Romagna workshops are largely devoted to low-technology industries in leather, textiles and automobile parts manufacture. The secret of their success lies not only in the smallness of the firms, but in their organization, in their productive associations and consortia, and in the fiscal, monetary and policy support they receive from government: all of which has implications for those seeking to develop industry in the South.[12]

A third factor which revalidates Schumacher's message is the growth of a vast informal sector in the South. Unorganized, disorganized, clandestine and usually illegal, the informal sector has until recently been neglected by aid agencies, denigrated by economists and harassed by officialdom. And yet an increasing number of studies reveal how widespread and how important it is. In most Third World cities, it represents as much as half the workforce; in Bombay it occupies a full 55 per cent of the labour force. In Peru it covers 47 per cent of the population on a permanent basis, accounts for 61 per cent of the person-hours worked, and contributes 38 per cent to the gross domestic product.[13] Actual numbers are probably even higher, as formal surveys often miss or understate secondary labour and the work of women.

Not only are these numbers high, they are getting higher, in both real and relative terms. Opportunities for work in agriculture are dropping. Labour-saving technologies reduced the Chinese agricultural workforce by 50 million people in the 1980s and the trend continues. The same trend is evident in India, and in Bangladesh, the agricultural sector is expected to absorb only 40 per cent of the additional labour force annually, although some estimates place its absorptive capacity at less than 20 per cent.[14]

The disaster looming behind these figures is compounded by other statistics which show that the formal sector is not creating jobs at a rate anywhere near the demand, and that the jobs it does create are as prohibitively expensive as they were when Schumacher wrote on the subject in the 1960s. Zimbabwe's 1986–90 National Development Plan, for example, forecast an increase in wage employment of 21 000 workers, with an expected investment of Z$1.4 billion. This put a staggering price tag of US$26 000 on each job.[15] At this rate, it would have cost over US$4 billion per annum to mop up the backlog, an amount equivalent to 90 per cent of the country's entire GNP. Needless to say, it didn't happen. In Kenya, estimates are similarly overwhelming. Even with continued economic growth and investment, it is estimated that only 1.4 million jobs can be created by the turn of the century, leaving approximately 40 per cent of the labour force, or 5.6 million people jobless.

If people are to work, there are three solutions. The first is that the cost per workplace in the formal sector will have to come down dramatically, as Schumacher said it must if chaos is to be avoided. The second is that the informal sector — of prime concern to many NGOs

— will have to expand to make room for large numbers of new entrants. This cannot be done if governments continue to ignore it, hound it and hide it behind tin sheet fences. The third is to recognize that for the majority of the poor, jobs are no longer, and probably never were, an answer. Most poor people have always survived by assembling livelihoods from a collection of activities that vary from season to season: backyard vegetable plots, poultry, wage labour, cottage industry.[16] All of these traditional or semi-traditional activities lend themselves more than ever to improvement, adaptation and expansion through the approaches developed by Schumacher, and to the small-scale, participatory approach he favoured.

There is a final phenomenon which revalidates Schumacher's philosophy: the overwhelming evidence that indiscriminate growth strategies have done little or nothing to reduce poverty. There are more poor people today than there have ever been, and the numbers show little sign of diminishing.

The environmentalists

And the fear of you and the dread of you shall be upon every beast of the earth, and upon every fowl of the air, upon all that moveth upon the earth, and upon all the fishes of the sea; into your hand are they delivered.

Genesis 9:2

When Rachel Carson's award-winning *Silent spring* appeared in 1962, the environmental movement as it is now known, had reached a watershed. Concern about industrial pollution, the disappearance of wildlife, damage to rivers, forests and farmland, of course, was not new. The industrial revolution had done as much to promote concern about the destruction of nature, as it had to promote interest in its beauty. The invention of lithography at the end of the eighteenth century had made possible the printing of books illustrating exotic flora and fauna, encouraging the study of natural sciences by both amateurs and professionals. It permitted the publication between 1827 and 1838 of Audubon's *The Birds of America*, which heightened interest in nature, and more especially in ornithology. The railroad, which despoiled much of the British countryside, also took Victorians away from the city to enjoy the beauty of nature. By the 1880s, interest in nature was such that the combined membership of British field clubs and natural history societies exceeded 100 000.[17]

Concern for animals was reflected in the 1824 creation of the Society for the Protection of Animals (later renamed the Society for the Prevention of Cruelty to Animals). The slaughter of birds for plumage on women's hats led to the foundation of several societies for the protection of birds. Concern for land use in Britain was reflected in the creation of the National Trust in 1895, charged with the preservation of both cultural and natural heritage. It was German forestry science that led to concern for, and action on the destruction of forests in both India and Australia in the latter half of the nineteenth century, and the establishment of early forest reserves in New Zealand and South Africa.

American environmentalism, spurred in part by the disappearance of vast forests in New England during the early nineteenth century, led to the creation of Yosemite National Park in California in 1864, and Yellowstone in 1872. Within 20 years, similar tracts of wilderness had been set aside for parkland in Canada, Australia and New Zealand. The creation of national parks, in fact, established one of the first debates in the environmental movement, between the protectionists and the conservationists. The former, including the founders of the Sierra Club in 1892, sought only to protect and preserve nature from predatory human inclinations. The conservationists, however, usually professionals, such as, zoologists, foresters, marine biologists — believed in the sustainable utilization of natural resources.

One of the earliest outcries of concern for endangered species had to do with big game in Africa, particularly the elephant. The slaughter of African animals reached epic proportions in the last two decades of the nineteenth century, accelerated by the advance of the railway, European settlement, and the advent of shooting parties, which in 1910 were estimated to have killed 10 000 animals in British East Africa alone.[18] Governmental concern led to the signing in 1900 of a Convention for the Preservation of Animals, Birds and Fish in Africa. The seven colonial powers controlling the continent were 'desirous of saving from indiscriminate slaughter, and of ensuring the preservation throughout their possessions in Africa, of the various forms of animal life existing in a wild state which are either useful to man or are harmless.'[19] Ironically, this limited notion of animal protection actually encouraged the further killing of lions, leopards, wild dogs and spotted hyena, all high on the 'vermin' list. Between 1924 and 1945, more than 320 000 animals were killed in southern Rhodesia alone in an anti-tsetse campaign.

The American Dustbowl caused soil conservation to rise suddenly on the global environmental agenda. Produced partly by drought but more by bad farming practice, 1.3 million square kilometres of the Great Plains were severely eroded between 1934 and 1937, devastating 16 states and adding to the economic and human havoc of the American depression. By then the need for an international conservation organization had been apparent for decades, but various half-hearted attempts had failed or had been halted by war. With the end of the Second World War, the international environmental agenda altered. The push for an international agency, pioneered by UNESCO and the governments of more than a dozen countries, had been advanced by the appearance of several books which presaged *The Silent Spring*. The titles, *Deserts on the March* by Paul Sears (1937), *The World's Hunger* by Frank Pearson and Floyd Harper (1945), and *Our Plundered Planet* by Fairfield Osborn (1948) give a sense of their message.

Complex marriage arrangements, a great deal of diplomatic intercourse, and a two-year gestation period finally produced a child. The International Union for the Conservation of Nature (IUCN) was founded in 1948, becoming the first truly international conservation agency. Its mandate was 'to provide leadership and promote a common approach for the world conservation movement in order to safeguard the integrity and diversity of the natural world, and to ensure that human use of natural resources is appropriate, sustainable and equitable.'[20] Compromising between the creation of a totally private organization and a member of the UN family, IUCN membership would be (and remains) open to national governments, governmental agencies and NGOs.*

IUCN's early years, however, were marked by limited innovation and low public interest. Focusing almost exclusively at first on nature protection, it found itself unable to raise enough money to finance even this limited mandate, and it was unable to encourage supposedly supportive state members to draw up basic lists of endangered species. Then, towards the end of the 1950s, things began to change, in part because wildlife conservationists were once again raising alarm about the future of the elephant, the rhinoceros, and the giraffe. By the time the winds of political change blew into African airspace, much of the damage had already been done. But conservationists, panic-stricken by nightmares about what might come next, began to mobilize. The African Wildlife Foundation, for one, was initiated by wealthy American conservationists (and sometime game hunters) to help offset the dangers they saw in African independence. The AWF's first newsletter in 1961 said that 'For better or for worse, the future of most of Africa's game country and the fate of its wildlife resources are in the hands of Africans themselves.' When the AWF

---

*The 1948 IUCN Mandate may be the first formal enshrinement of the idea of *sustainable development*. Unfortunately, this term has been so abused in recent years that it has come to mean just about everything, including the 'sustaining' of things as they are: consumption patterns, trading patterns, pollution patterns, and so on. The term will not be used much in this book, except in direct quotations.

said 'for better or for worse', it meant worse: '*In Tanganyika alone, the government recently ordered 100 per cent Africanisation of the game service by 1966!* (emphasis in the original).[21]

1961 was a good year for NGOs. In addition to the African Wildlife Foundation, it saw the birth of Amnesty International and the World Wildlife Fund (WWF).* WWF was established as a direct effort to raise money for IUCN and to popularize some of the issues with which IUCN was concerned. Largely a British initiative, the international headquarters of WWF was eventually located in Switzerland, and branches were soon set up throughout Europe, North America, and in later years, in India, Pakistan, Malaysia and South Africa. One of IUCN's major WWF-supported initiatives at the time, was something called the African Special Project, which aimed to encourage new African leaders to associate themselves with conservation and to understand — as a rather paternalistic issue of IUCN's *Bulletin* put it in 1961 — 'the virtue of living off the income of their natural resources, not the capital'.

The 1960s represent an environmental revolution. Hundreds of new organizations were formed, forcing older organizations to change, or to be left behind in more narrow, essentially charitable types of programming. The 'New Environmentalism' — more political, more dynamic, more anti-establishment — was fuelled by a variety of factors. Rachel Carson's book, which sold half a million copies in hard cover alone, took the issue, hitherto restricted to academia and science, forthrightly into the public realm. Atomic testing and fear of the toxic ingredients in nuclear fallout had become a major concern by the mid-1960s, and a series of disasters kept environmental anxiety in overdrive. The Japanese Minimata mercury poisoning scandal kept reappearing in newspapers regularly through the late 1960s. The collapse of a slag heap above the Welsh village of Aberfan killed 144 people in 1966, and the following year saw the first major oil spill when the *Torrey Canyon* struck a reef near Land's End, dumping 117 000 tons of crude oil into the sea. Scientific knowledge of the environment and the effects of industry and modernization was growing incrementally, and environmentalists benefited from crossovers with other movements of the 1960s: the anti-war movement, the civil rights movement, the women's movement, and the growth of an anti-industrial, anti-consumerist counter-culture.

No longer a quiet crisis, the environment became the subject of a series of apocalyptic new books: Paul Ehrlich's *The Population Bomb* in 1968, Barry Commoner's *The Closing Circle* in 1971, and the Club of

---

*Later *Worldwide Fund for Nature* except in the US and Canada, where the original name was retained.

Rome's doomsday scenario, *The Limits to Growth*, published in 1972. *The Limits to Growth*, which popularized the concept of non-renewable resources, eventually sold over ten million copies in 30 languages. Although many of the dire predictions contained in these studies have not come to pass, too many have: the depletion of global fish stocks; the limits of, and costs associated with the green revolution; the destructive effects of acid rain; and a stream of disasters associated with reckless and inadequately regulated industrial growth: Three Mile Island and Chernobyl, the wreck of the *Exxon Valdez*, the burning of the Kuwaiti oil fields, the Union Carbide disaster in Bhopal. More important than the precision of predictions, was an increasing recognition that the concept of exponential economic growth had real limits and contained real dangers, and that broad international strategies would be necessary if the obvious, present-day problems were to be dealt with effectively.

The United Nations Conference on the Human Environment, held in Stockholm in the summer of 1972, was one of the first international attempts to do this. Although in retrospect the impact of Stockholm may seem limited, it broke new ground in a number of ways. Attended by the representatives of 113 countries, it focused on the human aspects of environmental distress, and placed the concerns of Third World governments squarely on an environmental agenda that had hitherto been driven by Northern concerns. It had the effect of transforming environmentalism into a comprehensive global issue, one to be taken seriously by governments at a national policy level, rather than one fuelled (as was sometimes charged) by *ad hoc*, alarmist or unscientific debate. A new organization, the United Nations Environment Programme (UNEP), would be the means of carrying this forward. And finally, the presence of more than 400 voluntary agencies at Stockholm gave NGOs new legitimacy, and an access to policymakers that they had not enjoyed before.

The two decades between Stockholm and the 1992 UNCED Conference in Rio saw considerable change in the Northern environmental NGO scene. There was further growth in public concern about the environment. Between 1968 and 1984, membership in the Royal Society for Nature Conservation grew from 277 000 to more than two million, and between 1971 and 1994, membership in the Royal Society for the Protection of Birds grew by a factor of thirteen, exceeding the membership of the British Labour, Conservative and Liberal Democratic Parties combined. In the United States, the membership of the National Wildlife Federation doubled, and Sierra Club membership grew by more than 400 per cent.[22] Some of the older NGOs had reached a level of professionalism that made them an asset to, and an ally of governments and international development agencies. With the

1980 launch of its 'World Conservation Strategy', IUCN created the first broad platform for reconciling the protection of nature with sustainable economic development, a conceptual breakthrough for the environmental movement. The World Resources Institute, a Washington-based non-governmental policy and research organization, began publishing a massive 'guide to the global environment' in the mid-1980s, in conjunction with UNEP and UNDP. The World Conservation Monitoring Centre prepared two dozen biodiversity profiles of developing countries in the early 1990s, and IUCN worked with fifty countries in the South to prepare National Conservation Strategies before and after UNCED. Some of these — like the Pakistan Strategy, which was developed in close collaboration with NGOs, academics, the private sector and government — were adopted by governments as an important cornerstone of national planning.

There was also an increase in the number of organizations. One that emerged directly out of the Stockholm Conference was the London-based International Institute for Environment and Development (IIED). Although most were concerned solely or primarily with domestic issues, many developed a clear North-South agenda. By the time of UNCED in 1992, most knew that without addressing the human condition, environmental concerns, whether for biological diversity, the protection of wetlands or an endangered species, had little hope of success. This growing recognition was true of the 'light green' older organizations — IUCN, WWF, the Nature Conservancy, the Sierra Club — but it was even more true of a newer breed of 'darker green' Northern NGOs that began to emerge in the 1970s and 1980s.

Political, activist and sometimes confrontational, small or large, but often very effective, they are a type that has few parallels in the world of development NGOs. Friends of the Earth, for example, the outcome of controversy over political activism in the Sierra Club, led to the creation of a global network of more militant, autonomous national organizations in the 1970s. Greenpeace began as a Vancouver-based effort by other Sierra Club members to halt American nuclear testing in Alaska. Free of the Sierra Club, they bought an old boat, renamed it the *Greenpeace*, and with a small book about Indian myths for reading material, they set off for Alaska. The book was called *Warriors of the Rainbow*, and would give the name to Greenpeace vessels in the years to come. In the beginning, Greenpeace's only interest was nuclear testing. It was not until 1975 when the organization started to grow, that it began its direct confrontation with governments over whaling, sealing and the disposal of toxic waste. By the early 1990s, Greenpeace had become a major international NGO, with offices in two dozen countries and donor members numbering more than a million worldwide.

The Environmental Defense Fund grew out of a Carsonian anti-DDT campaign in the United States, and by 1990 had a staff of more than 90, half of whom were lawyers, scientists and economists.[23] EDF's international programme has focused on the damage done to the environment, and more particularly to poor people, by the large infrastructure projects of international financial institutions, most notably the World Bank. Building coalitions of Northern and Southern NGOs, the EDF became instrumental in drafting American environmental legislation, and in halting or changing some of the more reckless World Bank-financed projects: a massive Indonesian Transmigration Project, the Narmada Dam project in India, and the Polonoroeste Project, responsible for the devastation of vast areas of Brazilian rainforest and the lives of those dependent upon it.

Two other strands can be found in the environmental movement. One is a kind of 'New Age Environmentalism' which combines concern for the environment with a melange of spiritualism and mysticism. The other is the emergence of more radical activist organizations. Earth First!, Wild Earth and the Sea Shepherds are among those who find even the Greenpeace approach too tame. This brand of environmentalism has led to the sinking of Norwegian whaling vessels, the bombing of Canadian hydro-electric substations and even to assassinations in Italy.

There were other events between Stockholm and UNCED. 'Green' political parties, formed in some cases by an ageing 'sixties generation', contested national and local elections from Finland to New Zealand, with particular effectiveness as both parliamentary and extra-parliamentary opposition in Germany and Belgium. The World Commission on Environment and Development, known as the Brundtland Report, served notice in 1987 that 'the time has come for a marriage of economy and ecology, so that governments and their people can take responsibility not just for environmental damage, but for the policies that cause the damage.'[24]

Twenty years after Stockholm, 118 heads of government, 8000 official delegates, 9000 journalists and representatives of 3000 NGOs flew down to Rio for the United Nations Conference on Environment and Development (UNCED). More than 20 000 individuals from 171 countries attended the concurrent Global Forum.[25] For both environmental NGOs and development NGOs, Rio was the place to be in June of 1992. Brave words were spoken, broad, optimistic coalitions were formed, new charters and NGO manifestos were prepared and signed.

Perhaps, as Zhou Enlai once said about the significance of the French Revolution, it is too early to judge the Earth Summit. It is not too early, however, for Petra Kelly, founder of the German Green Party. Shortly before her death in 1992, she said, 'The Earth Summit has failed terribly. There has been no move towards democratization of the World Bank and the IMF. There has been no reduction of the debts the South owes Northern banks . . . protecting indigenous people living in rainforests across the world was not taken up . . . there has been no discussion about reducing affluence and saying simply that we can't go on doing what we've been doing. This is what has not happened at Rio.'[26]

Many, in fact, had predicted abject failure before the conference began. It certainly cost a lot. Indeed, its most tangible products, the non-binding Rio Declaration and Agenda 21, were rendered largely meaningless by the absence of cash, timetables, financial targets, and by the exclusion of important issues for the South, such as international terms of trade. Agenda 21 gave high priority to NGOs, in part because of their track record, in part because of the insistent role they had played in the lead-up to the conference. And no doubt for the same political, ideological and image-making reasons that caused development NGOs to be courted in other circles.

UNCED also had the effect, however, at least for a time, of drawing Northern environmental and development NGOs together onto common ground. Operating historically apart and gathering their support from incongruent constituencies, they have traditionally been wary of each other, and until the late 1980s, rarely co-operated in meaningful ways. Part of the problem is that professional environmentalists are drawn automatically to the green side of the NGO spectrum, leaving developmental NGOs largely bereft of experienced environmental talent. The same professional imbalance is found among the environmentalists. They may be well equipped to protect forests, wetlands and elephants, but they can be naively amateurish about the social, political and economic advancement of poor people living on poor land, and often living in apparent conflict with ideas of sustainable environment.*

The problem of territoriality is one thing. Like development NGOs, however, Northern environmental organizations are also highly competitive with one another. And they can be just as ideological, sanctimonious and egocentric as their developmental cousins. In his book about elephants and NGOs, *At the Hand of Man*, Raymond Bonner describes the hypocrisy and shortsightedness of some. In the early 1990s, many did their utmost to have the ivory trade banned, regardless of the impact this might have on people. In Botswana, Zimbabwe, South Africa and elsewhere, elephants were not an

---

*This divide, still pronounced in the North, is fading in the South where the relationship between human development and environmental protection is much better understood.

endangered species; their management was handled professionally and there were incomes to be made from limited 'culling'. More importantly, for villagers whose small farms, houses and livelihoods could be destroyed overnight by a single elephant, protection was essential. The Northern hysteria against killing elephants, however, provoked initially by the African Wildlife Foundation, became not only a lucrative crowd-pleaser for Northern NGOs, it forced organizations like WWF and IUCN — well aware of valid environmental and developmental reasons for herd management — to board the same bandwagon.

AWF doubled its membership in a single year as a result of its campaign for the ivory ban,[27] placing full-page ads in the *New York Times* in competition with others such as the International Wildlife Coalition which, in its own contribution to the *Times*, described an 'African chainsaw massacre'. A 1989 mailing to 50 000 people by WWF UK to fight the elephant 'slaughter' raised a bumper £300 000, and a second mailing brought in £200 000: more than double the response to pleas on behalf of the less emotive sea turtles and gorillas. In short, elephants were big business, regardless of good ecology, regardless of sustainable human development. Scientists, African governments, and the few NGOs that dared to resist the call for an ivory ban were labelled 'humaniacs'.

A journalist, Raymond Bonner is not shy of talking about human beings, and about a scene repeated daily in dozens of countries: impoverished people begging from tourists, selling their culture and their dignity. 'You feel sorry for them, but you also get angry because they won't leave you alone. As my wife and I hiked up the mountain to see the gorillas in Rwanda,' he says of a visit, well before the 1994 massacres, 'we were followed by children with dirty faces and torn clothes beseeching us to give them some food or money. When we returned many hours later, a larger number were waiting, their hands out.' The image was as powerful as anything they found among the gorillas. Years later, travelling with a Masai named Kasiaro, Bonner stopped at a lodge in Serengeti National Park. In the lobby, a Frankfurt Zoological Society poster caught Kasiaro's eye. 'Wild Dogs Need Your Help,' it said. 'Wild dogs are among the most endangered canids in the world, and are THE RAREST AND MOST ENDANGERED of the large carnivores in Serengeti'. Kasiaro read the poster and then said to Bonner, 'They care only about the animals; they say nothing about the people. They could have said there are also people, the Masai, who were living here for many years. They are living outside now and they are suffering. They don't have water. Even they need help. Not just the wild animals.'[28]

Elephants aside, it may be useful to think about the relative success some environmental NGOs have had in changing public attitudes, in building a broad membership and in gaining a strong public donor base for activities which often seem politically strident, confrontational, and research-oriented rather than strictly related to conservation. Why are these things so possible, and so well financed among environmental NGOs, when development education, research and campaigning are so fraught with stress and penury among the developmental NGOs?

One obvious reason is that the media, writers, environmental organizations and politicians have made the environment a domestic issue. People can see the problem with their own eyes, and can make the link between a disappearing rainforest in British Columbia, and one in Brazil. Environmentalism offers an alternative way of portraying the world to people who have become alienated from consumerism, industrialization and politics. But there are other, less attractive reasons. Regardless of the means used in supporting conservation — whether direct support to save the whales (or pandas or the Thai Jewel Thrush), whether research into the environmental policies of the World Bank, or confrontation at sea with the French Navy — Northern environmentalists generally have as an end objective nature, rather than people.

In the North, individuals have strong beliefs about why people are at war, jobless, orphaned or sick. They have strong attitudes about people who speak with different accents, whose habits or culture or religion or skin colour are different. They have no such problem with animals. A brown bear is as interesting as a polar bear. Conditioned by books and film from childhood, by Gerald Durrell, Jacques Cousteau, Marlon Perkins and *National Geographic*, people accept nature as natural, and can tolerate scenes of a lion bringing down a young wildebeest without condemning the United Nations for inaction. In nature, humans (often foreigners) are the only villain: burning, chopping, killing. Whaling, sealing and poaching are all bloody business; forestry is noisy, dirty and clearly destructive of natural beauty. A panda is just a panda, not a foreign panda with strange ideas and habits. It is an animal at one with its environment — not lazy, not producing too many offspring (any number is acceptable), not eating too much (as far as we know), not venal. It has no responsibility for its own situation. Our rose-coloured image of nature conforms perfectly with Mark Twain's observation that man is the only animal that blushes. Or needs to. Conservationists, as in the case of AWF and the ivory ban, play on all these attitudes. At their worst, they attack those seeking a compromise between people and nature, through 'sustainable development', as 'humaniacs'. At their best, most simply leave the human dimension out of their publicity material and fundraising.

Thoughtful Northern environmentalists, however, do see the limitations of, and are critical of the dominant growth model of development. This is taken by some critics as left-wing anti-capitalism. Rachel Carson, for example, was painted as a standard bearer for the 'left-wing academic brigade'.[29] Others, such as Friends of the Earth and Greenpeace, are assailed from the left: 'What neither of them has attacked in any serious sense is the nexus of state and commerce which leads to the practices they so ardently condemn.'[30]

A final difference between most Northern development NGOs and some of their most politically active environmental counterparts has to do with the heavy reliance of the former on government financial support. Government dependence breeds not only self-censorship, it can skew programming in directions favoured by the funder. It involves a selection process which cuts risk and controversy out of the herd at an early stage. But many environmental NGOs do take money from government and manage to criticize government policies at the same time. Unlike their development cousins, this was a primary *raison d'être* for many environmental NGOs, one that has remained front and centre. The fundamental goal was to change government policy, rather than to serve it; to advocate, rather than to be implementers of project-based 'assistance'.

Coming of age in Samoa and almost everywhere else

Perhaps the most significant problem facing Northern development NGOs by the mid-1980s was a severe identity crisis. The idea of actually sending in experts, volunteers or otherwise, to design and manage development projects started to change in the early 1970s. Oxfam had already begun to turn its attention away from missionary projects towards those managed by village communities; and later, to those developed and managed by upcoming new NGOs in Asia and Latin America. This was a radical concept in 1970 — providing support to a Third World NGO. But by 1990, the majority of Northern NGOs were working largely, if not exclusively with and through Southern NGOs, giving an enormous boost to young but vibrant home-grown movements throughout the South.

There were other changes in the 1970s. Some Northern NGOs did begin to see that project support was not enough. The conditions that made people poor were often beyond their own means to correct: the high price, or lack of access to seeds; bad government; skewed land ownership, inappropriate tax structures. The concept of 'conscientization' developed by the Brazilian, Paolo Freire, held that development could occur only through the growth of a public consciousness about the shortcomings of one's own society and political system. An essential part of the 'theology of liberation', it sought to 'empower' people to undertake their own development. Regarded as too radical by some Northern NGOs, the ideas behind conscientization, and the realization that village development was linked to global patterns of trade and industry led others into advocacy work, development education and political lobbying.

By the 1990s, those like CARE, Foster Parents Plan and World Vision that had remained largely 'operational' (devising and running their own overseas projects) were finding themselves the last of a fading, and somewhat expensive breed, the last cars on the lot with tailfins. On the other hand, those that simply provided support to Southern partner NGOs were being challenged to do more than act as babysitters and bank inspectors — junior clones of their own governmental benefactors. To make matters worse, as this identity crisis began to peak, it was becoming clear that the emperor of official development assistance itself had no clothes. Report after report on official aid scandals, misdirection and mismanagement peeled off the raiment, damaging public opinion and encouraging recession-plagued governments to retreat behind 'new' concepts of accountability, participation, and the role of 'civil society'. The implications for NGOs were to become enormous.

CHAPTER IV

Southern NGOs

This then, is our real job — the opportunity to work with our own people.

Saul Alinsky, 1946.

UNTIL ABOUT 1980, the most prominent non-governmental organizations operating in Africa, Asia, the Caribbean and Latin America, were foreign, rather than local — clearly operating outside their own communities and stretching the historical rationale for voluntary association to new dimensions. This is not to deny the importance of their contribution to education, health care, rural development and welfare. International NGOs were, through the 1960s and 1970s, at the forefront of developments in primary health care, credit for the asset-less, participatory approaches to development, the environment and the advancement of women. American foundations played a critical role in the reduction of malaria, yellow fever, cholera and hookworm, and in the development of high-yielding varieties of wheat and rice. CARE, Médecins sans Frontières, Oxfam and many others have acted as the world's conscience on human disaster, and have shouldered much of the responsibility for international relief activities.

There is a difference, however, between emergency assistance and development assistance. The need for the former is obvious, and if well handled, it will be finite in scope and time. Development assistance, however, when it is designed and managed by outsiders, often comes uninvited and, like The Man Who Came to Dinner, may not go home. It is arguable, in fact, that voluntarism does not travel well. International NGOs are an extension of the most basic elements of their society's altruism. But originating in a foreign country, they can hardly be described as an expression of local concern, either collective or individual. The strengths of international NGOs are legion. They have their handicaps as well: they must work in cultures and sometimes in languages other than their own. In addition to dealings with their own government, they must work with the governments of host countries. Communications, attitudes and working conditions vary greatly. Legitimacy may be a problem. Even those organizations that support local NGOs cannot avoid imposing their views of development, their priorities, and their bureaucratic requirements on the recipient. And northern NGOs that receive support from their own governments run the risk of becoming agents (or being seen as agents) of political or strategic, rather than humanitarian objectives.

Northern international development NGOs carry societal baggage as well. The wellspring of the American international NGO community is very different from that in Scandinavia. In Japan, many struggling modern NGOs emerge from a tradition of anti-government activity, while in Catholic countries such as Italy, voluntary activity has grown almost entirely out of the church, and from an alternative, anti-statist mentality, to which leftist anti-government views were later added. Recognition of variations in the Northern NGO heritage is important to an understanding of Southern NGOs. Even though some of the latter have been established with the help of Northern partners, they emerge from different traditions entirely: cultural, religious, ethnic, pro-government, anti-government, anti-statist, political, apolitical. Some are government-organized, and some, as in the post-Marcos Philippines, have been formed by politicians in order to cash in on sudden donor largesse. To view a Southern NGO community through a Northern lens, therefore — to assume for example, that Bolivian NGOs can or will behave like French NGOs in relation to government — could be an error with costly consequences for both the NGO and its supporter.

Voluntarism in the South

This is not to suggest that the basic foundations of Southern NGOs are different from those in the North. Altruism, conscience, fear, service,* self-interest and the organizing imperative all play a role. In the South as well as the North, the altruistic ethic has a long and honourable tradition dating back four millennia. Historically, this manifested itself in community-based welfare activities. During the colonial era, branches of larger metropolitan church and charitable organizations were planted or transplanted, and often flourished. Many, especially those that were mission-based, worked in education and health. In some cases they inspired local NGO development, either in imitation, or more often, as a defence against imported ideologies and religions. In Egypt, for example, there were

---

*'Service': In many countries it was once traditional for young men to enter government: either the military or the civil service. As these options became less appealing from a career point of view, and as the development movement began to take root, jobs in international development agencies, or the creation of home-grown versions became an alternative.

only two Islamic non-profit organizations before British occupation in 1882. The arrival of British mission organizations sparked not only a nationalist revival, but a sudden flowering of new Egyptian associations and organizations of all types.[1]

The same is true in Sri Lanka. The first Baptist Mission was founded in 1802, followed by the Wesleyan Missionary Society in 1814, the Church Missionary Society in 1818, and the YMCA in 1882. In reaction, a wide variety of local organizations sprang up. The Buddhist Theosophical Society was established in 1880, and the Mahabodi (Buddhist) Society ten years later. The Muslim Education Society was formed in 1880, the Young Men's Buddhist Association in 1897, and the Hindu Ramakrishna Mission in 1899.[2]

More profound developmental impact, however, is likely to be found in the recent emergence of an entirely new generation of Southern NGOs. The speed with which NGOs developed in the late 1970s and early 1980s becomes apparent in reading two of the most prominent books written about NGOs in the 1970s. With the exception of the co-operative movement, John Sommer's *Beyond Charity*, published in 1977, barely mentions Southern development institutions. Jørgen Lissner's groundbreaking book, *The Politics of Altruism*, published in the same year, misses them entirely.

It is in the South that the expression 'third sector' warrants further examination. 'Third', as in 'Third World' implies something residual or left over: third rate, and perhaps even lacking in legitimacy. In the South, however, familiar Northern concepts of sectors one and two — government and the private sector — lose their meaning and their lustre. Many governments in Africa and Asia are in a full state of rout, and throughout the South, the legitimacy of much government action is in question. The first sector's ability to provide basic social services is not, in most cases, expanding. And the weakness of the formal private sector is manifestly evident in the share of markets controlled by foreign investors and multinational corporations, and in the strength and size of the informal sector. In many countries, this informal sector — unregistered, unregulated businesses operating in black and grey markets — has become more important in job creation and service provision than the formal private sector.

In Pakistan, some 5000 active 'third sector' NGOs are registered with the Social Welfare Department and there are a further 21 000 registered co-operative societies. In 1992 there were 642 registered NGOs in Zimbabwe, and 110 in the Dominican Republic. A 1994 study found 4327 NGOs in Latin America and a further 5860 non-profit groups, the majority established after 1975. In Lebanon there are 1300 NGOs, and in Egypt 13 000. In Thailand there are over 12 000 registered foundations and associations, however the real number is probably more than double that. Even in China, where voluntary association has been strictly controlled, there are 181 000 registered social and 'mass' organizations that in many cases are indistinguishable from the small village organizations found in India or Pakistan.[3] More important than the size of the Southern NGO movement is the speed with which it has grown in recent years.

Many Southern NGOs have become large: larger in some cases than their Northern partners, and some have managed to combine altruism with advocacy and policy reform. AWARE in India, reaching over 2000 villages, had considerable impact during the 1980s on state government thinking about land tenure for tribals and scheduled castes. In Sri Lanka, Sarvodaya, covering a third of the country's villages, was one of the few national institutions, including government, that was able to function in all parts of the country during the civil war. The Aga Khan Rural Support Programme covers 80 per cent of the villages in Pakistan's Northern Areas with extension, technology transfer and credit facilities. Similar spinoff government-supported organizations have been developed in other provinces and at a national level.

The influence of Grameen Bank is legendary, not only in Bangladesh, but in other countries where the Grameen Trust provides technical assistance, training and startup grants.* At the beginning of 1995, the Bangladesh Rural Advancement Committee (BRAC) was operating 35 000 primary schools, with a 5 per cent dropout rate, compared with an 80 per cent dropout rate in government schools. BRAC's success has had a profound and positive influence on bilateral and multilateral donor agencies supporting government education projects in Bangladesh. In 1994, two BRAC staff were deputed to UNICEF in Kenya to help with planning, and the Government of Vietnam engaged BRAC to examine the feasibility of replicating some of its work there.

Similar comments on quality, quantity and impact could be made about scores of organizations throughout Asia and Latin America, and increasingly in Africa and the Caribbean. For each of them, there are at least two or three new NGOs coming up that show every sign of being able to reach similar levels of coverage and effectiveness. In many ways, these organizations represent the same phenomena, a generation or so after the independence of their countries, that de Tocqueville so admired in the United States of 1835. Far from being

---

*Grameen Bank is annoyed by its constant inclusion among NGO ranks. 'We are *not* an NGO,' says its founder, Mohammed Yunus. 'We are a *bank*.' Maybe, but not like any bank the average borrower sees. Grameen's success is derived from the fact that it has operated completely *unlike* most banks and that it derives its values, its methodologies and its legitimacy from the same wellsprings as the NGO community.

residual, the third sector in the South is one of the most vibrant areas of activity, experimentation and even of service delivery.

The beginning of a modern NGO movement

Some Southern NGOs began as an effort by middle-class professionals to deal with a particular emergency. Fazle Hassan Abed, an accountant, watched in dismay as his country, then East Pakistan, was devastated by flood and tidal wave, then by civil war and the exodus of ten million people across the borders into India. Perhaps he was thinking of an earlier disaster. 'When I was a boy', he recalls, 'there was a terrible earthquake in Morocco. I responded to an Oxfam appeal, sending the equivalent of perhaps a pound. In due course I received an acknowledgement and a brochure. But I was surprised to see that although Oxfam worked in many countries around the world, they did not work in mine. I wrote to ask why, and they said it was because there were no local organizations with which they could form a partnership.'[4] Not waiting for outsiders in 1972, Abed and his friends formed the Bangladesh Rural Advancement Committee, and established a reconstruction programme in a remote part of Sylhet District, where one out of five people had become refugees.

Gradually turning their efforts from reconstruction to long-term development, the BRAC workers soon attracted the attention of Northern NGOs that had also come to assist. One of their first major grants was received from the organization to which the young Abed had made his donation years before, Oxfam. If one good turn deserves another, Oxfam proved it: the fledgling BRAC received an initial grant of £161 000. There were perhaps four reasons for Oxfam making such a significant early contribution. One was that BRAC was doing effective and important work, and was doing so at a fraction of the costs usually incurred by external agencies. A second was that Oxfam had virtually no knowledge of Bangladesh. Off the beaten development track at that time, and largely ignored by development agencies before 1970, Bangladesh was both a new country and — for development agencies — an almost completely unknown part of the world. A third reason was that Oxfam, like so many other organizations, had raised vast sums for the relief of Bangladesh. Now the emergency was ending, and there seemed to be few ways to spend money effectively on reconstruction and human development. The new government had its hands full with bilateral donors. The church network that Oxfam worked with in many countries was tiny, and largely urban-based. And the provision of trucks, ferries and bridges — part of Oxfam's initial effort — did not directly address the immense and immediate needs of the country's poor.

64

BRAC and a small handful of other new Bangladeshi organizations provided a way out of the problem. But there was another reason for supporting organizations like BRAC. For several years, Oxfam's Asia Committee had been pushing the field staff to find and support 'indigenous agencies'.[5] Its traditional partners in India were either expatriate-led charities or church-related operations, and these hardly represented the social and economic fabric of the country, nor of the villages Oxfam sought to assist. The new approach, which had to function largely on trust, did not come easily. A 1964 grant of £35 000 to the Indian Red Cross had sparked the kind of debate that would rage within some hands-on Northern NGOs for the next three decades. Control, trust and fear of corruption would always be at the centre of the debate. In 1964, an Oxfam manager criticized the Red Cross decision, saying, 'The reputation of the Indian Red Cross is not very good and among foreign-based agencies there is much suspicion of the integrity of its distribution agents. For Oxfam to be using such a channel on such a scale at a time when the Indian papers are full of corruption stories scarcely enhances our reputation.'[6]

The policy was maintained, however, and one of the first real partnerships with a Southern development organization was formed in 1967 with the Sarva Seva Sangh, a Gandhian organization working with *harijans* (untouchables) in the rural areas of Bihar. In the same year, Oxfam made a small contribution in Tanzania to the Community Development Trust Fund, for well digging. This was followed the next year by a larger commitment of £31 000 for 233 more wells. In Brazil, Oxfam supported one of the first purely Brazilian NGOs working in community development. FASE (Federation of Organizations for Social and Educational Assistance) was a 1970 offshoot of Catholic Relief Services.

Although these first efforts did not always work smoothly, by the time Oxfam made its first grant to BRAC, the die had been cast. Throughout the 1970s, more and more Northern NGOs would reduce their own direct programming operations, seeking out and creating opportunities for the Southern NGOs that would now take up the development mantle. Like Sarva Seva Sangh, some were older organizations that became 'eligible' for support as the policies of Northern NGOs changed. Sarvodaya, founded in Sri Lanka in 1958, remained a largely volunteer-based organization until the need and the opportunities for expansion persuaded the leadership to begin a formalization process. Sarvodaya gained official charitable status in 1966, and in 1969 its founder, A.T. Ariyaratne, was awarded the Magsaysay Peace Award. This award, along with its first sizeable external grant, made in 1972 by the Dutch NGO, NOVIB, allowed the organization to build the infrastructure necessary to expand its work from a few hundred villages to thousands.

Some, like FASE, had their origins in the work of an external organization. Proshika in Bangladesh, for example, began as a CUSO project, without ambitions of autonomy, and without expecting to become a role model for others. Some have grown out of a national trauma. The civil war which gave birth to Bangladesh produced hundreds of informal village organizations where before only a handful existed. In the Philippines, the anti-Marcos movement legitimized the NGOs that were in its vanguard, and sparked the creation of hundreds more under the Aquino government. The same was true in Zimbabwe immediately after independence.

Organization is not a simple matter, however. It involves determination, money and risk. The passivity and social conflict among those who live on poor land in remote areas, are powerful deterrents to change. Poverty is not only a physical and economic condition. It weakens self-confidence and saps self-respect, leaving its victims fearful of authority and suspicious of outsiders. Organizing is therefore more difficult for the poor than it is for those who are better off. But Sithembiso Nyoni, founder of the Zimbabwean NGO, ORAP (Organization of Rural Associations for Progress), observes that rural people are not at the dawn of their history. 'They have memories of development failures, domination and manipulation from outside.'[7] Outsiders, with outside interests and complicated objectives, may present an opportunity, but they also represent both risk and threat for people living on the edge of economic desperation. Listening to people and working with them on *their* priorities is therefore an essential ingredient of successful change. This is not new, nor does it seem very radical, although one of its first and best proponents, Saul Alinsky, clearly saw the building of 'people's organizations' as a radical endeavour when he wrote about it half a century ago.

'Throughout the organizational period,' he wrote, 'many people and organizations will revert to avarice, individualistic opportunism, personal exploitation, and lack of faith.' Presaging Nyoni, he went on, 'It is not the people who must be judged but the circumstances that made them that way.'[8] Taking a leaf from Alinsky's teachings about organizing in the United States, or perhaps re-inventing his ideas from the ground up, ORAP was able to gain the confidence of villagers throughout Matabeleland, pulling more than five hundred groups into a loose federation in its first five years of operation. For ORAP, the key was the ability of its organizers to involve people not only in the planning and management of their own development efforts, but in the management of ORAP itself.

ORAP grew out of the euphoria of Zimbabwean independence. Other Southern NGOs have arisen out of direct conflict with the growth ethic that has gripped many Southern governments. Starting with small local protests against clear-cutting, tens of thousands of Brazilian rubber tappers organized themselves in the 1980s to fight their government and World Bank-financed plans to exploit and, in effect, destroy vast stretches of the Amazon rainforest. Emerging from generations of poverty and disorganization, the rubber tappers formed alliances among themselves, with other Brazilian institutions, and with some of the most effective Northern environmental NGOs. There was violence, murder and years of struggle. The rubber tappers' leader, Chico Mendes, was murdered in 1988 by a rancher. But the movement continued, eventually forcing the World Bank to repro-gramme part of its massive Brazilian loan portfolio, and compelling the Government of Brazil to create a new form of land tenure which would allow rubber tappers to manage and control at least some of their own future. As a result of the long and sometimes violent protest, fourteen extractive forest reserves had been created by 1992, covering almost three million hectares of tropical rainforest.[9] A further result was the creation of two institutions that would work to prevent further unregulated cutting, the *Conselho Nacional de Seringueros*, the rub-ber tappers' own organization, and the *Instituto de Estudos Ama-zônicos e Ambientais*, which seeks and maintains both national and international alliances.

The Brazilian rubber tappers and their mentors may have taken a lesson from the Chipko experience. The Chipko movement, which has spread from one end of the Indian Himalayas to the other, began rather unremarkably with the organization in 1960 of a workers' co-operative for skilled and semi-skilled construction workers in Chamoli District of Uttar Pradesh.[10] The co-operative, *Dasholi Gram Swarajya Mandal* (DGSM), bought forest rights from government to supply a small workshop that produced farm tools for local use. In the late 1960s, it also started an enterprise based on roots and herbs from the forest, in which turpentine was the main product. But for eight months in 1971–2, the DGSM factory was closed because the govern-ment would not give it allocations for wood or pine sap. As it turned out, however, there was a different policy for a sporting goods manu-facturer. This company had no difficulty in purchasing the rights to cut 300 ash trees in the area for its tennis racquet business.

When company loggers arrived to cut the trees, they found people — mainly women — forming themselves into a human barrier be-tween the trees and the saws. The women were employing Gandhi's strategy of *satyagraha*, or non violence. 'Chipko', which means 'hug-ging' in Hindi, had given birth to both an expression and a movement. Later in the year, villagers again prevented the company from cutting in another part of the district, and over the next five years they were responsible for ensuring that the state government banned tree-felling in an area covering thousands of square kilometres. In 1980, as a result of their efforts, the national government placed a fifteen-year ban on certain kinds of felling in the Himalayan forests of Uttar Pradesh, and the movement spread with equal success to half a dozen other states of India. Because of the awareness-building, the socialization and the politicization that occurred through the simple protection of trees, many of the women went on to form their own co-operatives, planting trees for fuel, fodder and as an anti-erosion device.

Chipko spawned dozens, if not hundreds of new self-help co-operatives and non-governmental organizations. Although some of these would lend themselves to international support, many did not, or did not require it. Support, however, is one thing; learning is another. Through the 1980s, Oxfam, IUCN and other organizations sponsored educational visits between Chipko villages and similar NGOs, co-operatives, and women's organizations in Nepal and Pakistan. While the outsiders learned that Chipko could not be transferred so easily to another setting, they found that training, drawing on the strengths of the community and reliance on indigenous species of plants and animals were key. For some of the Pakistanis, a 'hidden agenda' was also achieved: to build a nucleus of women professionals who could advance environmental activities in Pakistan.*

International NGOs

International NGOs — those without a strong national identity and with independent chapters in several countries — are a growing phenomenon. They are also the expression of a desire to reduce the North-South gap, particularly where communication, learning and development education are concerned. They include older organizations like the Catholic Church, the Red Cross and the Boy Scouts, but there are newer bodies which, though modest, have at their heart an international ideal which has eluded many larger organizations for generations. El Taller in Tunisia brings NGOs from the North, the South, the Arab World and Eastern Europe together, and serves as both a place and a platform for joint reflection, advocacy and research. Women's World Banking, is the only global network dealing with enterprise development, credit, and the economic participation of poor women.

---

*Several individuals on these tours went on to work with a range of new Pakistani NGOs, combining women's issues, economic development and environment. One of the Pakistani tour members, Aban Marker Kabraji, became IUCN's Pakistan Director, and co-ordinated the preparation, and later some of the implementation of the country's impressive National Conservation Strategy. Others went on to become prominent community development activists and senior managers in Pakistani NGOs.

Established in 1979, it builds banking services that by 1992 were supporting small entrepreneurs through 47 affiliates on five continents.

There is another kind of hybrid. A small number of NGOs have one foot in the North and one in the South. The Aga Khan Foundation, established in 1966, was originally an effort to draw together the different strands of an Ismaili support network of schools, clinics and hospitals in Asia and East Africa. By the early 1980s, however, it had expanded beyond its Ismaili confines, with a Head Office in Geneva and autonomous affiliates in Kenya, Tanzania, Bangladesh, India, Pakistan, Canada, Britain, the United States and Portugal. While money flows in the traditional southerly direction, members of the Foundation meet together as equals, debating, arguing, and moving easily between postings in both the North and the South. In addition to the support it now provides to a wide variety of Asian and African NGOs, the Aga Khan Foundation has established two additional independent members of the network, the Aga Khan Rural Support Programmes in India and Pakistan.

A variation on the AKF theme, the African Medical and Research Foundation was established in 1957 in Kenya by three expatriate doctors. Originally (and still) a flying doctor service, it became more, working in several countries of the region in training, environmental health, and research on malaria, trachoma and hydatid disease, a serious ailment produced by tapeworms. Because the needs AMREF sought to address were great, and because traditional support mechanisms were slow to respond, the organization's first Director General, Michael Wood, fell into the habit of making long fundraising trips to Europe. The cost in time and effort was high, and AMREF gradually developed a new approach in the 1960s and 1970s. It reversed the Northern NGO model, establishing branches in the North rather than the South: independent Northern support agencies in Britain, Canada, Norway (nine countries in all) whose main purpose was to raise money for AMREF's work in Africa.

The International Union for the Conservation of Nature offers yet another model. Preoccupied with a Northern-based emphasis on traditional conservation programmes until the early 1980s, it has since changed its programming emphasis dramatically, and has gradually become more reflective of Southern concerns about broadly based human development. By 1992, IUCN had 721 members, including 156 governments and government agencies and over 500 NGOs.

Ghana: sketch of an NGO community

Ghana is a microcosm of Southern NGO evolution.[11] There have probably been village self-help and welfare organizations in Ghana

69

for centuries, but the development of formally organized and registered non-governmental organizations is a relatively recent phenomenon. Before 1920, only one NGO was officially registered with the Ministry of Social Welfare and Community Development, in sharp contrast with India, for example, where the formal registration of NGOs began more than 130 years ago.

By 1960, the number of registered Ghanaian NGOs had grown to 10, and through the 1970s and 1980s the number expanded rapidly, rising to 350 by 1993. Of these, 20 were foreign, 120 operated in more than one community, and over 200 were community based. This is probably a vast understatement of village-based efforts, most of which are not registered. Like single-community NGOs anywhere, the Ghanaian variety may be welfare or development oriented; they may be registered or not; they may be well organized or loosely managed; they may have affiliations with larger groups or they may operate exclusively on their own. Most have no full-time paid workers. The Kalijiisa Multipurpose Co-operative is an example. Kalijiisa 'village' is actually a rural area of farmers and traditional blacksmiths in Ghana's far north. The villagers created an informal co-operative in 1972 and obtained government support, in the form of the use of a grader, to build a small reservoir. This was enlarged in 1986 with their own money. In 1987 they received a modest grant from USAID for a community building, and they were also introduced to an American support organization, the African Development Foundation.

ADF visited several times in the next three years, and eventually made a grant to upgrade the blacksmith facility and to provide mechanized food processing equipment that would provide the co-op with its own on-going income. Like most co-ops, Kalijiisa has a constitution, membership fees and a regular savings programme. A credit scheme was started in 1992. Although there are only 50 men and 75 women in the society, its services are open to all in the community and beyond. Unlike most Ghanaian co-ops, Kalijiisa survived Ghana's horrific economic traumas in the 1970s and 1980s, probably because of its blacksmithing, which has been the mainstay of the community for generations. The Chairman of the society says, 'We want to make a better life here so that our young people will not have to leave for the city.'

The multi-community NGO is a much newer phenomenon in Ghana. Some of these are welfare oriented, some have a strong religious thrust; but many today also have a vibrant developmental component. Most are small, and some have only one or two paid, full-time staff. Some are very new while others date from the 1960s and 1970s. An example is the Centre for the Development of People. CEDEP was founded in Kumasi in 1983 by a group of young professionals to assist co-operatives and grass-roots groups with technical, managerial and other forms of support. With very small grants from four European NGOs, and working entirely on a part-time voluntary basis, the group established a library and organized a series of seminars on women in development, co-operatives, evaluation, problem solving and project development. CEDEP produces a regular newsletter and general information flyers on subjects such as malaria, water, child labour and trees. In 1987, it was decided that if CEDEP was to become more relevant to the needs of the poor, full-time staff would be essential. In 1991, one of the founding members took the plunge. Despite the palpable commitment, drive and experience of the organization, however, CEDEP found donors stand-offish on the question of support for the institutional costs needed for a sustained takeoff. The most tangible support of this type was actually provided by the government, in the form of volunteers working in the National Service corps.

Ghanaian NGOs exhibit many of the same strengths and weaknesses as NGOs in other countries. On the plus side, they are innovative, and flexible; they work in difficult, hard-to-reach areas with the country's most vulnerable people. They focus on sectoral areas of greatest need: food security, public health, income generation, women's participation in development. They complement and supplement the efforts of government and international donor organizations. On the minus side, the Ghanaian NGO community is much younger than in many other African countries. Most organizations are small, and despite attempts at co-ordination, many remain professionally and geographically isolated. There is duplication and repetition. Sustainability is sometimes questionable.

The reasons for Ghana's late start are complex, but some are obvious. The first, perhaps, was the strong centralization of welfare services, health, education and rural development within government over the two decades following independence. The second was a noticeable absence of Northern NGOs throughout Ghana's most difficult years. The dozens of prominent Northern NGOs that have worked in Sahelian countries, Kenya, Botswana and Zimbabwe have played a major role in the fostering and financing of local counterparts over the past two decades. A third reason may be the absence of role models. In many Francophone African countries, in Latin America and throughout Asia, one or more large professional NGOs have emerged and serve as role models for others. This has so far not happened in Ghana.

A fourth reason is sociological: a high proportion of registered NGOs have been formed for welfare, rather than for development purposes. By definition, many are limited to a single group or community and have no interest in expansion. A final limiting factor may

71

have been church hegemony. The Catholic and Protestant Churches were very active in Ghana's education and health development for more than two generations, and in recent years they have become the mainstay of NGO rural development activities, especially in the North. While the churches have played a vital role in the development of Ghana, it could be argued that their strong presence and relatively good financial base has drawn away or even deflected many young people who might otherwise have created secular NGOs of the type found in other countries.

In the 1980s a number of factors combined to encourage change. There was a significantly improved climate for voluntary organizations after the arrival of the Rawlings Government in 1981. Another factor was the economy. The severe economic decline of the 1970s and early 1980s, a terrible drought in 1983, and the sudden expulsion of over a million Ghanaians from Nigeria the same year contributed to a perceived need for greater community and NGO activity. NGOs were also used by government and by some donor agencies as a means of reaching those hardest hit by the economic adjustment programmes of the mid- and late 1980s.

Because Ghanaian NGOs had a somewhat slower and later start than those in other countries, most arrive in a world of development issues, organizations and donors with much longer histories and with expectations based on two or three generations of trial and error. This gives them some advantages, but it creates special problems as well. Judith Thompson, Co-ordinator of an urban-based Ghanaian NGO, Integrated Social Development Centre (ISODEC), lists the most prominent of these as organizational, managerial and financial.[12]

Ghanaian NGOs usually begin with a clear social objective, but without a clear idea of the organizational structure necessary to support it. Having embarked on the programme or project, most discover that they have to establish a complete administrative system, dealing with finance, personnel, office management, monitoring and evaluation, and they must do so with limited skills and very limited money. Thompson observes that 'for many of us this is an uphill climb. We have been through an educational system which does not lay emphasis on training us to manage our time and finances. To add to that, we are operating in an unstructured atmosphere, unlike our colleagues in the North, and there are no blueprints for what we are doing.'

Many talented and committed young Ghanaians have joined the NGO movement over the past decade. Nevertheless, the NGO financial base is precarious and heavily project-biased, providing employees with little in the way of long-term security. For fresh graduates this may not be problematic, but for people starting families and thinking of

72

careers, it poses a genuine difficulty. The problem translates into one of continuity, memory and stability for the NGO community. Finding and keeping staff is one thing, but as Thompson says, 'the issue of developing their skills is the next task'. There are few training programmes in Ghana tailored specifically to the needs of NGOs. Thompson says that Ghanaian institutions specializing in the necessary skills training — personnel, finance, estate management, monitoring, evaluation and negotiation — 'hardly consider NGOs as organizations'.

Obtaining appropriate funding is a major problem for Ghanaian NGOs. Some require only small amounts, but find that donors are unable or unwilling to give them the time and attention necessary to understand the issues they are dealing with. Donors generally take a project approach with clearly defined and often rigid inputs, expectations and time lines. Recurrent costs are anathema, and all capital costs must be tied directly to the project at hand. 'Essentially,' Thompson says, 'these donors do not take NGOs in our part of the world very seriously. They think that our activities must be judged by the criteria that they are familiar with. Many of them have preconceived ideas about what the needs of the community are, and are only willing to finance projects which coincide with their beliefs.'

Ghana exhibits all the characteristics of the evolutionary stages of humanistic service described in Chapter II. Community-based voluntarism — small, village-level, self-help efforts — are by far the largest component of the 'NGO' community. Institutionalization can be seen in the formation of more formal, mainly non-membership organizations like CEDEP and ISODEC. Professionalization is evidenced in their struggles with strategy, money and management. The fourth stage, the welfare state, was a clear goal for Ghana's post-independence government, one eventually relegated to the scrap heap of poverty, mismanagement and structural adjustment.

Southern governments

Thompson also deals with the problems of working with government. The relationship between any government and its NGO community is likely to be complex and changeable.[13] It may depend on the level of responsibility that government itself takes for a particular area of welfare or social development. It may depend on the evolving nature and financial base of the NGO community, and on the level of comfort a government has with independent or semi-independent players entering traditional government territory. In the North, despite obvious weaknesses, competitive scrambles and the annoyance they can cause government, NGOs are generally regarded as a positive good. In some countries they are increasingly recognized as a necessity, as the state backs away from traditional responsibilities.

In many countries of the South, the state is not only backing away from these 'traditional' responsibilities, it has failed. Responsibility, however, is one thing, power is another. And few governments shed power enthusiastically. NGOs, therefore, increasingly competent, and increasingly expected to 'do more', are also encountering new levels of control and interference, just when the opposite should in theory be happening. Some governments and donor agencies even accuse NGOs of trying to 'crowd out' government.[14]

The climate for NGOs can be influenced by government in a variety of formal and informal ways. On the informal side, governments can foster what has become known as an 'enabling environment' through collaboration, consultation, assistance in co-ordination, and by sending positive messages to the media and to the public that NGOs have a beneficial and welcome role to play in development. On the formal side, the legal, regulatory and fiscal framework in which NGOs function will play a large part in their evolution or otherwise. Are registration and reporting requirements clear and simple? What tax and import concessions are provided? Are regulations applied in a fair and consistent manner? Is there a right of appeal? Governments can also go beyond the creation of a positive legal framework, assisting NGOs with money, or goods and services, and by making them eligible to carry out government contracts.

Unfortunately, these rather basic ideals sound facile when juxtaposed with reality. Professions of support for civil society, democracy and the right of association notwithstanding, the record in much of the South is dismal. Indonesia, for example, is a country caught between tradition and modernity, between poverty and affluence, between the demands of a complex ethnic heritage and the need for social stability and the rule of law. If the government finds itself between Scylla and Charybdis, Indonesian NGOs are surely caught between a rock and hard place. In addition to detailed but disorganized regulations which have long permitted the government to control NGOs one way or another, an omnibus 1985 Law on Social organizations gave government the authority to seize and close any organization threatening to upset domestic security. Tax exemptions for all NGOs were summarily abolished in 1994, and because registration procedures remain chaotic, only 1000 of the estimated 25 000 operational NGOs (*yayasans*) are actually legitimate.

In Thailand, despite lingering government nervousness in the wake of the mid-1970s revolutionary student movement, there is a relatively open, but complex legal framework into which NGOs must fit. In order to register, and registration is essential for an organization seeking financial support, an NGO must apply to one of four ministries under the provisions of up to five different parliamentary acts. It must also seek police clearance, and if it wants tax exemption, it must apply to the Revenue Department and provide a cash 'deposit guarantee' of as much as $20 000. Any organizations involved in income earning for self-support is automatically required to pay tax. One effect is that, of 12 000 Thai associations and foundations, only a handful have made it past the last hurdle to tax exemption.

The Indian Government's long and sometimes successful history of NGO manipulation includes various efforts at co-option with both carrot and stick. One of the most effective sticks is the Foreign Contributions Regulation Act. With a sweep of this far-reaching wand, almost any NGO dependent on external finances can find itself in a sudden financial free-fall. The carrot appears in the form of cash grants for rural development work from the Council for the Advancement of People's Action and Rural Technology (CAPART), formed to provide grants to NGOs. Praised by those it supports, and excoriated by those it does not, CAPART can be very political, and has the capacity to be both creative and selectively destructive.

In Bangladesh, the return to parliamentary democracy at the end of 1990 did not bring with it new space for NGOs. The NGO Affairs Bureau, set up under the previous military government, appeared to be the instigator of a well-organized anti-NGO campaign which, at its height in the summer of 1992, saw 53 anti-NGO newspaper articles and editorials, and the rigid enforcement of draconian foreign contributions regulations. These regulations required annual government approval for every project, and were effectively forcing many of the country's NGOs to a standstill. In the press, NGOs were attacked for mismanagement, corruption, foreign domination and anti-Islamic behaviour. Led by the Association of Development Agencies of Bangladesh (ADAB), NGOs solicited moral support from donors, Northern NGOs, politicians and writers, and were finally rewarded on the morning of 31 August 1992 with a letter ordering ADAB to close down. Donors complained. This, plus a massive dose of governmental ambiguity, may have produced the second letter that was received that day from the Prime Minister's office, cancelling the first. The NGO Affairs Bureau was reorganized and regulations were simplified. But considerable damage had already been done, and Bangladeshi NGOs, knowing that their detractors have neither seen the light nor disappeared, continue to look cautiously over a collective shoulder.

At the end of 1990, the Government of Sri Lanka established a Presidential Commission of Inquiry on NGOs. Ostensibly a general review, it was in fact a thinly veiled personal vendetta orchestrated by the President of the country against Sri Lanka's largest NGO, Sarvodaya. The story is a complex one, revolving around a long-standing rivalry between the President and Sarvodaya's founder. For more than two years, until he was assassinated in 1993, President Premadasa used the full weight of government against Sarvodaya. It was attacked on almost every ground conceivable: noise pollution (use of a generator when the power failed); air pollution (ostensibly overflowing toilets); corruption; selling babies abroad. It had land seized, a children's savings programme was closed and donors were intimidated. There were vicious and concerted attacks in the government press, seizure of new equipment at the port, death threats. Although the dogs of war were called off when a new President took office, Sarvodaya had been seriously destabilized, and a vivid lesson in the pervasiveness of state power had been delivered.

These Asian nightmares are familiar territory for NGOs in much of Africa, Latin America and the Caribbean. A prescient 1988 report on government–NGO relations in Mexico foretold the Chiapas uprising that began in 1994: 'The work of NGOs in Mexico in the rural sector and in particular with indigenous communities or refugee groups, for example in Chiapas, is often hampered by the bureaucracy of the Mexican state, not to mention resistance by local feudal chieftains, or *cacques* . . . The few small-scale development initiatives which are not within the direct purview of government organizations or parastatal institutions are carried out by local NGOs and groups which are often either unofficial or forced to operate without official status or approval: they work at the edge of legality.'[15]

If these problems demonstrate that Southern NGOs have a tougher row to hoe than their Northern counterparts, there is yet another issue in the government relationship. Apart from the fact that very few Southern governments provide direct financial support to NGOs, most also withhold the indirect support which Northern NGOs have come to expect from their governments. A 1994 study of Kenya, Uganda, Malawi and Zimbabwe found that while all governments exempt legitimate, registered NGOs from the payment of income tax, only Malawi provides any tax incentive for companies or individuals to make a charitable donation.* And exemption from customs duties, taken for granted by Northern NGOs when negotiating a government agreement in the South, are simply not permitted for most local organizations.[16]

Some of the problems Southern NGOs face in their dealings with government result from political anxieties, from apathy or simple bureaucratic bungling. And some are the result of legitimate governmental apprehension about the probity and effectiveness of NGOs, a genuine concern that amateurs, ideologues and development hustlers

---

*This problem is not unique to the South. Tax deductions for charitable donations are permitted in Germany, Hungary, Poland and all English-speaking OECD countries, but not in Japan, Scandinavia, France or Italy.

should not make things worse for the poor than they already are. By making procedures impossible to follow and difficult to implement, however, by scattering regulations through a rainbow of laws and codes, and by giving regulatory responsibility to a combination of different and often incompetent agencies, it can be argued that governments not only make life hell for the good, they defeat their own purpose in rooting out the bad.

If the suppression and harassment of NGOs in the late 1980s and early 1990s looks like a trend, there are signs of change. In Kenya, the government passed an NGO Co-ordination Act in 1990, recognizing the importance of NGOs in national development, but imposing what NGOs felt were severe and excessive restraints on their freedom to act. This was no doubt a reflection of governmental concern that organizations such as the Greenbelt Movement, sponsored by the National Council of Women, had become an international embarrassment to government in exposing and stopping its over-exploitation of natural resources. It may also have been a legitimate concern about regulation procedures and the appearance of bogus NGOs.

A common problem when governments examine NGO regulations is that they usually start to re-invent the wheel. Most of the things they attempt to restrict — fraud, theft, misrepresentation, poor worker safety and health, abuse of the minimum wage, currency manipulation — are already covered under existing civil, criminal and tax codes. There is no reason for inordinate NGO supervision, any more than there is for the private sector. Wrong-doing or infringements of charitable regulations, including fraud, giving support to insurgents and labour abuse, can all be apprehended if the normal rule of law is applied. The main concern should be to make any special regulations, like ensuring that legal and financial accountabilities are intact, clear, simple, and consistent.

In Kenya, after passage of the new act, a standing committee of NGOs was formed to lobby the government for change. Following two years of negotiations, the result was the passage of a new Private Voluntary Organizations Act which accepted many of the recommendations made by the committee. A further result was the creation of an NGO umbrella organization, the NGO Council, with membership of some 400 Kenyan and international NGOs.[17]

Similar attempts in 1994 to clamp down on NGOs in Pakistan resulted in much greater NGO awareness of policy issues, and in the creation of functional NGO support groups. Kenyan NGOs now have legislation that acknowledges and regulates their activities, but the question of arbitrary government control remains. As in Bangladesh, these examples demonstrate the fragility of NGO–government

77

relationships, but they also show that where an NGO community can come together to act with a united, concerted voice, it can achieve policy changes that will create more *space* and a more enabling environment for voluntary action.[18]

PART TWO

NGOs today

CHAPTER V

The pink elephant: empowerment and the status of women

A development process that shrinks and poisons the pie available to poor people, and then leaves women scrambling for a larger relative share, is not in women's interests.

Gita Sen and Caren Grown.

We not only want a piece of the pie, we also want to choose the flavour, and know how to make it ourselves.

Ela Bhatt.

THIS CHAPTER IS about women, and what NGOs have learned about one of the most over-worked words in the development lexicon: 'empowerment'. The discerning reader may have noticed that this word has been largely absent from the book up to now. This is because the concept of empowerment can be as unsettling as it is immodest: the idea that people with power can and will give it to people without. It is also because the word is so widely used by development organizations that it has become little more than hackneyed jargon. It is a word worth exploring in the context of women's development, however, not just because it means different things to different people, but because it is important, and because its application can mean different things to the people who are supposed to benefit from its application.

However, first a diversion: when Sharon Capeling-Alakija was Director of the United Nations Fund for Women, UNIFEM, she used to carry a piece of — what would you call it? — *cloth* in her purse. It was a small rectangle of dull white fabric, badly hemmed, to which had been sewn a crude pink elephant. This 'handicraft' had been produced by Liberian refugees in Ghana, in a 'training centre' where women, young and old, were hunched over sewing machines in the hope, probably the desperate hope, of finding some way out of their harsh lives and their dreadful poverty.

Capeling-Alakija carried the rather pathetic memento, not as a reminder of what women could do, but as a reminder and a demonstration to managers in aid agencies of what women were still being encouraged, even driven to do, by well-meaning but ultimately incompetent and destructive do-gooders. She carried this pink elephant, not in the early 1970s, before the term 'Women in Development' (WID) had been coined; not in the early 1980s when a distinction, 'Women *and* Development', had been produced; not even in the late 1980s, when 'Gender and Development' (GAD) began to analyse the problems of poor women in a broader and more political way. She picked up the elephant in the 1990s, after three World Conferences on women, a United Nations Year for women, a full United Nations decade for women; after the creation of women's bureaux, women's ministries, women's NGOs; after every development agency worthy of the name had practically signed an oath in blood that 'gender-sensitive' programming was at or near the top of its agenda, and that it would never again encourage women to sew pink elephants onto scraps of old bedsheet.

So here we have a mystery: was this pink elephant simply an aberration? Or did something go wrong between the 1975 International Women's Year Conference in Mexico, and the UN's Beijing World Conference on Women twenty years later?

If statistics are any guide, something certainly did go wrong. Or at least a lot of things did not get fixed. There have, of course, been advances: the life expectancy of women has increased. More women have access to education and the workplace. Child-bearing rates have fallen by as much as half. However, five hundred thousand women die every year from causes related to pregnancy and childbirth. Between 1970 and 1985, the number of illiterate women rose by 10 per cent, while the number of illiterate men rose by only 1 per cent. Women continue to be less well-nourished than men; family violence has stormed out of the closet, and we are beginning to recognize that 70 to 80 per cent of the world's 49 million refugees and displaced people are women or the children they have to care for. A shocking study in Bombay found that out of 8000 abortions, only one foetus was male, a fact not completely unconnected with the availability of sex-detecting ultra-sound.[1] These abortions, the infanticide and the simple neglect of girl children has led UNDP to estimate that as many as 100 million women are 'missing'.[2] Women continue to work longer days than men, and they continue to be paid less. Their long work day remains largely unrecorded in national statistics, and is therefore largely unrecognized: by planners, development organizations and by the families for whom they fetch water and wood, for whom they are producers and reproducers, and for whom they cook breakfast, lunch and dinner almost every day of the year (in the homes lucky enough to have three meals). The number of women-headed households, generally poorer than male-headed households, is increasing.

These inequities are not restricted to the developing world. As UNDP's 1994 Human Development Report put it, 'all countries treat women worse than men: unconscionable, after so many years of debate on gender equality, so many changes in national legislation and so many years of struggle'.[3] In fact new developments, many devised by the aid community between 1975 and 1995, have made the struggle more difficult. Rapid rates of population growth, long thought to be a major factor in impoverishment, led to the development in the 1960s and 1970s of simplistic birth-control programmes targeted heavily towards women. These programmes generally treated women as the objects of mass sterilization campaigns, or simply as consumers of pills, IUDs and operations that they were not expected to understand, and for which there was little follow-up. It was only after the 1974 Bucharest World Population Conference, that there was greater recognition of, or at least greater lip service paid to the need for a comprehensive approach to population: one which viewed family planning as part of a broader process of better health for women and children, better rural incomes, and improved legal and social status for women.

This 'recognition' notwithstanding, many Southern governments, encouraged by bilateral and multilateral donors, had no compunction over the next two decades about becoming directly involved in questions of reproduction and reproductive rights, about using both incentives for fewer children and, in the case of China's one-child family policy, radical disincentives against more. The question from a feminist point of view, after twenty years of costly debate and disappointing results for women, was a simple one, not unrelated to basic human rights. It was a question of personal choice and personal control. From the population expert's point of view, however, there is an older and more traditional sort of (male) question: if bureaucratic pressures and technocratic controls are relaxed, will women make the 'right' choice?

In their book *Development, crises and alternative visions: Third World women's perspectives*, Gita Sen and Caren Grown say that women well understand child bearing to be a social, and not a purely personal phenomenon.

> Nor do we deny that world population trends are likely to exert considerable pressure on resources and institutions by the end of this century. But our bodies have become a pawn in the struggles among states, religions, male heads of households, and private corporations. Programmes that do not take the interests of women into account are unlikely to succeed. More important, the requirements of a genuine, people-oriented development necessitate the acknowledgement of this fundamental need and right.[4]

Economic stabilization and the structural adjustment programmes of the 1980s and 1990s have been criticized in a variety of ways by a

83

wide cross-section of economists, UN agencies and NGOs.[5] In response, the World Bank asks two pertinent questions about structural adjustment. First, 'Would the poor have benefited from less adjustment? And to the extent that adjustment benefited the poor, could policy reforms have been designed differently to have benefited them more?'[6] The Bank's own answers, in a lengthy 1994 review of adjustment policies in Africa, basically ignore women, lumping all 'the poor' into a single category. This forgetfulness, this continuing unwillingness or inability to differentiate between the work of men and women, paid and unpaid, simply strengthens the hand of Bankbashers who see it as a reconfirmation of the 'invisibility' of women in the macro-economic policy bazaar. Certainly, the answer to the second question is *yes*, policy reforms could have been designed differently, and some changes, probably too little, too late, have been made. But for women, the first question — would they have benefited from less adjustment — should perhaps be re-worded: have they benefited in *any* way from adjustment?

Adjustment programmes aim at increased efficiency and greater productivity. By reducing government social sector expenditure in health, education and food subsidies, these programmes place greater burdens on women. Reduced health services take their first toll on women and children; the introduction of school fees results in higher dropout rates for girls than for boys. Government and donor programmes speak increasingly of 'people's participation', but this is often little more than a euphemism for unpaid labour, provided by women, in health projects, water users' groups, well-digging and maintenance, and almost any activity having to do with children, such as feeding programmes, pre-schools and immunization programmes.

The emphasis on tradeable crops and labour-intensive manufactured goods has drawn women increasingly into the farming of low-return cash crops and into jobs in export production zones where hours are long and wages are low. Taking work that men will not do because of the low wages, women run the risk of returning home to neglected children and marital conflict. And because the time required for household and community work has not been reduced, the 'double day' becomes longer.

Technological advance has also discriminated against women. Excluded from education, particularly science education, constrained from owning property, distanced from access to credit, information and extension agents, women have gained little, and have sometimes been displaced by new technology. When mechanized equipment became available for cassava grating in Nigeria in the 1960s, or for rice husking in Bangladesh in the early 1980s, men simply took over what had hitherto been viable income-generating work for women. Tractors,

84

rotor-tillers, even handpumps which are destined for use exclusively by women, are designed by, and tested on — men.

Types of intervention

The first, oldest and still most popular approach to programming for and by women is the welfare approach. 'Its purpose,' according to gender specialist Caroline Moser, 'is to bring women into development as better mothers. Women are seen as passive beneficiaries of development', and gender needs are addressed through top-down family planning programmes and handouts of food aid. USAID-sponsored feeding programmes managed by Lutheran World Relief, Catholic Relief Services and others are examples. 'Although welfare programmes for women have widened their scope considerably over the past decades,' Moser says, 'the underlying assumption is still that motherhood is the most important role for women in Third World development.'[7]

The 'equity approach', developed during the 1975–85 Women's Decade, was the original WID technique. It saw women as active participants in development and sought 'to meet strategic gender needs through direct state intervention, giving political and economic autonomy to women and reducing inequality with men.'[8] It dealt not only with the practical needs of women — water, health, better access to credit and technology — but also more important strategic needs, often institutional in nature, such as property ownership, family law and political equality. Attacked in its early years (by men, mainly) as an ethnocentric, Western feminist plot, the equity approach gave way to a less strident anti-poverty approach which focused mainly on the productive role of women in society.

Characterized by project interventions such as credit, the anti-poverty approach has been popular with NGOs and Northern donors because of its anodyne approach to power relations between men and women. Moser argues that the most predominant approach today is the 'efficiency approach', which aims to ensure more efficient and effective development through the contribution of women. 'Women's participation is equated with equity for women . . . [who] are seen primarily in terms of their capacity to compensate for declining social services by extending their working day.'[9] Health interventions, for example, are often targeted specifically at women. While many are welfare-oriented, some have equity as part of the objective. Economists, however, look at investments in health care for women as an efficiency issue. According to the World Bank, 'Spending on health is a productive investment: it can raise incomes, particularly among the poor, and it reduces the toll of human suffering from ill health . . .

85

Women need to be healthy to fulfil their roles as mothers and household managers. They have specific health needs, including protection against violence.'[10]

The different approaches — WID, WAD, GAD, equity, anti-poverty, efficiency — evolved mainly during the UN Decade for Women, during which three major global meetings were held: the first in 1975 in Mexico, the second in 1980 in Copenhagen, and the third in Nairobi in 1985. Each conference was attended by women's organizations from around the world, and each acted as a catalyst for the creation of new organizations. One of these was DAWN: Development Alternatives with Women for a New Era. An informal group of 22 women, many with NGO backgrounds and most from the South, DAWN held its first meeting in Bangalore in 1984. One of its first decisions was to produce a 'platform document' for circulation in the year before Nairobi, a document that would question the impact of development on the poor, and especially on women; one that would voice the urgent need for alternative development processes focusing on the basic survival needs of the poorest.

Types of organization

DAWN's platform document became a book: *Development, crises, and alternative visions: Third World women's perspectives*, written by Gita Sen and Caren Grown. Among other things, it provided a useful typology of Southern organizational approaches to women's issues. The first type, consistent with both Moser and Korten, are welfare organizations. These tend to be the larger, traditional service organizations that have existed in many countries for years. Some grew out of social reform or independence movements, but many retreated into a welfare approach when the primary goal was achieved. Often managed by middle- and upper-class women, they suffer from class bias, a top-down approach, and according to DAWN, 'they often lack a clear perspective or even understanding of gender subordination or its links to other forms of social and economic oppression'. Pink elephants on scraps of bedsheet are most likely to emanate from this sort of organization.

A second category are NGOs affiliated to political parties. These have obvious strengths, but they may be forced to subordinate gender issues to political solidarity and expediency. A third type is the worker-based organization. These may include formal trade unions and organizations of poor self-employed women, a type increasingly common in the South. Perhaps one of the best-known examples of the latter is SEWA, the Self-Employed Women's Association, formed in 1971 under the aegis of the Textile Labour Association, India's largest union of textile workers. The linkages between formal labour movements dominated by men, however, and an informal labour sector populated by women, can be fraught with problems — as SEWA and its leader, Ela Bhatt, discovered in the organization's early years.

SEWA's struggle for an independent voice came to a head in 1981, when Bhatt supported 'reservations', the protection of special positions in education and jobs for *harijans*, the untouchable caste from which so many poor women sprang. For SEWA, reservations symbolized empowerment rather than welfare. But for the Textile Labour Association, fighting to end the reservation system, Bhatt's position represented both indiscipline and grandstanding. It had been a dangerous period for the TLA, affiliated with a political faction that had broken away from Indira Gandhi's Congress Party. Gandhi's suspension of Parliament and her self-serving state of emergency had placed her enemies, like TLA, in peril. Time passed, however, and coincident with the end of the emergency, the TLA expelled SEWA, seizing its assets, severing all links and charging Bhatt with indiscipline. There was something else, however: 'I built a wall of poor women around TLA,' said its President, 'to protect us from Indiraji's attacks, but now that the emergency is over, we no longer need them.'[11]

The TLA may not have needed them, but Indian women did. SEWA and similar spinoff organizations have become one of the most vibrant aspects of the Indian NGO scene. In 1995, SEWA had 143 000 members and operated a women's bank with 41 000 savings accounts.

DAWN identifies a fourth type of organization, one that mushroomed during the 1975–85 period as a result of the foreign money and interest being showered on women. Many had no history or resource base other than the contract work they were able to undertake. While some evolved into participatory development organizations, others remained weak and dependent, basically dancing to a donor's tune. The cost extracted by such organizations from poor communities can be high. Take for example the scattered, poverty-stricken rural community of Darsano Charno, on the edge of the Thar Desert north-west of Karachi. At about the time DAWN was developing its typology, Darsano Charno was attempting to deal with its increasingly serious health problems. Elders had seen how other communities had formed village associations which could attract external assistance for tubewells and water tanks. So, deciding that the answer to their problems was a doctor, they registered the 'Darsano Charno Social Welfare Association' in 1984. They pooled their resources, and constructed the building that they were told was necessary to house an out-patient clinic and a maternal-child health centre.

After several setbacks, the government at last provided the services of a doctor for four hours a day. But the doctor was a man, and in a conservative Muslim area, this meant that women could not be treated. Because the women looked after the children, and because the distance for most was great, children were also not being treated.

Enter an international NGO, Pathfinder International, with a contract to execute a USAID family planning project. After several discussions with the village association, Pathfinder realized that the villagers were having trouble with basic problem identification: they had now decided that the answer to their health difficulties was an ambulance that could take the sick to Karachi. They also seemed to have little knowledge of development, no education or relevant training, and few of the things that they would need, such as staff, to qualify for a grant. Nevertheless, Pathfinder worked with them, and early in 1988, a very small project was put in place, involving the provision of a Lady Health Visitor, and training for teams of local men and women who would work in the surrounding areas on family planning and motivation.

Because the USAID project had to do with family planning, however, there was no money for medicine. Only birth control supplies. The LHV, therefore, could not treat women who came to the clinic with health complaints, nor could she treat their children. They had to be referred to the doctor in the adjacent room, the doctor who could not see them because he was a man. In June that year, the place looked like a scene from *The Good, the Bad and the Ugly* (or possibly *Catch 22*). Rocky, barren soil under a blazing sun. A silent clinic with a Lady Health Visitor sitting alone in an empty room, because now even the family planning supplies had run out. Flies are buzzing. Outside, seven men are complaining bitterly about joblessness, and wondering how they can get an ambulance. They show visitors the Pathfinder project document, written in English, a language they cannot read. It says that the project, which has no provision for self-generated income, is expected to become self-sufficient in three years.[12]

Economic empowerment: theory and practice

As it relates to NGOs, the literature on women, gender and development can be confusing. While there is no lack of theoretical writing, there is a glaring absence of substantive material on practical experiences, whether grass-roots, welfare, equity or empowerment-oriented. It is almost as though concrete activity has been sidelined in favour of theorizing and dialectic. This is not because there is no practical work being done. But it may be because work at the grass-roots level, regardless of orientation, approach or theory, has had very mixed results.

In 1984, Marilyn Carr reviewed more than fifty women's projects in two dozen countries, many of them developed by NGOs. The resulting book, *Blacksmith, baker, roofing-sheet maker*,[13] is almost unique in that it was a first of its kind, and seems not to have been widely repeated. Carr was looking for successful, innovative projects which recognized the triple role of women, which sought to reduce the double day, and which had empowered women either economically or societally. She found examples in traditional areas of food production, weaving and sewing, and in non-traditional areas: women making hospital equipment in Bangladesh, welders in Jamaica, sisal-cement roofing-sheet makers in Kenya.

At first glance and in isolation, many of the projects, submitted voluntarily for consideration by NGOs and donor agencies, look successful. But the majority suffered from serious and often very similar limitations. Most were small and isolated, frequently producing second-rate goods with limited consumer appeal. There was little evidence of depth or vertical integration in planning, and none of the projects seemed to have examined the possibilities of, or the need for, backward and forward linkages. Raw materials posed problems in several projects, and markets were an almost universal dilemma. Most projects exhibited 'a somewhat welfare, institutional or non-commercial approach to marketing. Sales outside the immediate neighbourhood are often dependent on special arrangements made by external agencies or on special sales outlets.'[14] Where prototype labour-saving machinery was introduced, as in the case of oil presses in West Africa or coconut graters in Guyana, little thought was given to how these would be manufactured, should the testing phase actually prove successful. Many projects were just plain dumb. A CUSO project in Tanzania sent electric sewing machines to a village many miles distant from the nearest power point — perhaps sparing the intended beneficiaries from the pink elephant syndrome.

Writing three years later, Sally Yudelman described a similar situation with regard to NGO activities in Latin America. Foreign NGOs 'pride themselves on their sensitivity to local cultures and their ability to work successfully at the community level. They do not want to be accused of cultural imperialism by tampering with sex roles.'[15] In Yudelman's sample, they tended to focus on women as home makers and to ignore their economic role. Where they did focus on income generation, the emphasis, among both foreign and domestic NGOs, was on traditional things like sewing and canning.

One could perhaps take cold comfort from the fact that many income-generation projects — not just those of NGOs, and not just those targeted towards women — suffer generically from the same failings. But it would not be entirely true. Women's projects suffer from particular problems of marginality within aid agencies, from poor financial support, inadequate staffing and low priority. Many are manageable only because they involve a heavy component of volunteer trainers and workers. Within Northern NGOs, part of the problem has to do with 'symbolic policy' and ambivalent institutional attempts to create meaningful gender awareness, an eager but sometimes hollow '*Ich bin ein feminist*' approach. In Oxfam, for example, the Gender and Development Unit (GADU) has been called 'the moan and groan unit'. One staff member said that 'When GADU started, many people laughed; one or two called us lesbians, dikes: that is no longer acceptable. Now the most difficult problem is one of people pretending they agree.' A Christian Aid staff member said the same thing: 'The fact that people pay lip service to the rhetoric of gender does not mean they necessarily take on the issues in practice.'[16]

Even if a gender policy, backed by sound analysis, is in place, there are further roadblocks. The irony in attempting to discern alternatives for women is that many potential options are closed off in the very early years of a woman's life. In far too many countries girls receive less care and attention than boys. Their food intake is lower and their health is poorer. For those women who do obtain an education, gender stereotyping is no less prevalent in the South than it has been in the North. In Ghana, for example, by the end of secondary school, 12 per cent of girls have opted for physics, chemistry and biology courses, and only 5 per cent are enrolled in mathematics. At university the imbalance continues: female enrolment in science faculties ranges from a low of 1 to a high of only 22 per cent. Mid-level Ghanaian technical schools have a one per cent female enrolment.[17] The upshot is that women, whose needs are often greater than those of men, face development challenges with fewer skills, less education and little spare time. And they often do so pregnant and in poor health.

There are, perhaps, three broad strategic approaches to income generation for women.[18] The first, programming strategies based on a geographical area, usually encompasses a range of activities such as credit, marketing assistance, basic education, skills development and health programmes. The second, sector-focused strategies, deal with a particular industry or occupational area. The third, a function-based approach, could also be called the 'missing piece' approach, because it focuses on a particular constraint which, when removed, is expected to allow beneficiaries to advance.

The missing piece

The most common 'missing piece' strategy for women today relates to credit, although there are others such as health or specialized approaches to education. Lack of credit, however, especially for the poorest, is increasingly seen as the major stumbling block to genuine, sustained income enhancement. Among the proponents of credit, there is a school of purists who would limit external involvement to the barest minimum. This 'minimalist' approach suggests that credit *alone* is the missing piece in the development puzzle, and that little else should be offered. Stripped-down credit programmes offer very limited training, no extension services, and no investment advice. This is essentially how SEWA, the Working Women's Forum (WWF) of Madras, and the Grameen Bank in Bangladesh began. And as these organizations and others like them have grown to significant scales of operation, evidence shows that the approach can work, especially for women.

A relatively small minimalist project may help to illustrate the approach better than the more established ones. Throughout the 1980s in Kenya, CARE operated a comprehensive, area-based approach to income generation for women in one of the country's poorest districts.[19] The programme began with a goat-rearing project and gradually expanded into training and the provision of grants for the promotion of agri-business, horticulture, bee-keeping and other small enterprises. But an internal review in 1988 confirmed what CARE already knew: most of the efforts were both unprofitable and, therefore, patently unsustainable. Searching for a solution, CARE turned to the stripped-down credit model, adding only training in basic book-keeping.

The approach was simple. A women's group would approach CARE for assistance. After careful scrutiny and basic training for five elected group members, CARE would give the group a two-year loan of about KSh20 000 ($800). Interest was set at 12 per cent. The fund was then managed by the group, usually on a consensus basis, making loans to individual members at rates of interest established by the group itself, ranging between 5 and 20 per cent a month. Loans could not exceed KSh2000 ($80) and each borrower had to have three guarantors.

Although new and relatively small, by 1990 the CARE programme found itself with the same sort of results as larger organizations like SEWA and Grameen Bank. Despite the high rates of interest charged by the groups to their members, on-time repayment rates were in the neighbourhood of 95 per cent. Perhaps more important was the discovery that most borrowers were making healthy profits on their loans. Many groups, in fact, replaced or even exceeded the amount of the original CARE fund within the two-year framework. Apart from such obvious successes, the minimalist approach also proved to be inexpensive, easily replicable, and it required little in the way of

91

technical assistance. Moreover, it was capable of reaching large numbers of poor women.*

A superficial glance, therefore, seems to bear out minimalist claims that the availability of credit, with limited training and technical support, can enable women to increase their incomes, and more importantly, can enable them to move into newer and more profitable lines of work, becoming in some cases, microentrepreneurs themselves.[20]

A more rigorous examination reveals that this is only partially true. As with other organizations, virtually all the CARE loans were for trading. The women, many of whom were already petty traders, simply took their loan down the road to the first big town where they purchased maize, sorghum, soap or clothes. They then returned home to sell at whatever mark-up the traffic would bear. This approach can be particularly successful in a district where village market economies are weak and where the availability of capital is stunted. The project proved, as have many others, that poor women can be good credit risks. They were increasing their incomes and building a savings cushion. But there was little or no value-added in what they were doing, no increase in productivity, no reduced dependence on external sources of supply. And to assume that there are many opportunities where poor women can quickly repay a loan which costs between 5 and 20 per cent per month, and make a profit, is to live in a technicolour dreamland.

Women borrowers assuredly make the best of their loans, but without help, the value-added may be limited, and their endeavours may well be limited to the narrow confines of the world in which they are generally restricted. This is why so many never get beyond traditional handicrafts, food processing and petty trade. It would be a very unusual individual who could create a job or even a meaningful increase in income for herself with a $100 loan. This is confirmed by statistics from Grameen Bank, where efforts to develop new investment opportunities have been limited and mainly unsuccessful. This may be, in part, because the Bank firmly believes that 'the borrower knows best'. Over 90 per cent of the Bank's 1992 loans were made to women, yet more than 70 per cent were for a limited number of traditional activities: mainly milk cows, paddy husking and cattle fattening. One study found that after ten years of borrowing, about half the members' families were no longer living in poverty, a remarkable achievement. As for moving on to higher value-added activities, however, success was less marked.[21]

Without tried investment opportunities based on sound technical information *and knowledge* (there is a difference), minimalist credit programmes for women will probably result in either slow or minimal improvements.

---

*By June, 1994, the total loan portfolio had grown to KSh9.9 million (US$214 000), reaching 245 groups and about 6000 women.

A sectoral approach

Genuine productive and meaningful income generation for poor women remains an extremely difficult proposition. In Bangladesh, approximately 70 per cent of landless rural women are directly or indirectly involved in poultry, each keeping, on average, two or three birds. Most chickens survive by scavenging, and are fed on household waste and crop residue. Each bird produces about 40 to 60 eggs a year, far less than both demand and need. Because of the scavenging regime and poor or non-existent veterinary services, the average mortality rate of village birds is as high as 40 per cent.[22]

BRAC, the Bangladesh Rural Advancement Committee, realized that by reducing the high death rate in birds, by improving the local breed, and by providing a technical support package, an effective economic programme for poor landless women was possible. An experimental poultry programme was started in 1979, based initially on cockerel exchange and on the distribution of hatching eggs. The effort failed because the mortality rate of the 'improved' chickens was even higher than for the local variety. As a result, BRAC started training women in vaccination. This resulted in a reduction of the death rate to 20 per cent — in a controlled environment. But it was recognized that if the project was to be removed from its protected, experimental confines, it needed a variety of support mechanisms: backward and forward linkages: training, management, and a supply system for chicks and vaccines.

In 1983, BRAC's tested model was ready for implementation. BRAC staff were responsible for group formation, motivation, training and credit support to group members. Government officers were responsible for the supply of vaccine and day-old chicks. The model, largely successful, covered what BRAC thought was the whole process. The BRAC system began with the chick rearer (all poultry workers are women) who each took 300 baby chicks for two months. Then came the 'key rearer' who took one cock and ten hens. A 'poultry worker' provided vaccination services and an egg collector, obviously, collected eggs. Each worker was provided with training, a loan facility and the necessary equipment: a medical kit, for example, in the case of the vaccinator. Each became part of a commercial chain where services or chickens were bought and sold — from each other, not BRAC. The vaccinator, for example, responsible for a thousand birds, earns about two US cents per vaccination.

In the early 1990s, however, BRAC found that the commercial poultry feed necessary for hybrid chickens was adding disproportionately to the cost of production. BRAC began to experiment and found that a cheap, viable product could be made from locally available fish meal, oil cake, oyster shell, and a commercial premix of vitamins and minerals. Poultry feed centres were gradually established in each programme area, creating both jobs and a decentralized supply. Day-old chicks presented another problem. Commercial hatcheries were both expensive and, ultimately, unable to keep pace with the BRAC demand. After experimentation with a heat-generation technique based on the use of rice husks instead of electricity, five small hatcheries were developed, each capable of producing a thousand chicks a month.

By 1992, there were over 65 000 women involved in the programme, but that was only the beginning. By the turn of the century, BRAC expects to have over 300 000 women involved in its poultry operations, each in relatively simple, discrete activities, but operating in what has already become a very sophisticated, village-based industry.[23]

Much of what made BRAC's poultry project successful would apply to any project, whether for men or women. But there are important lessons that relate specifically to women. First, the targeted sector, in this case poultry, should have large numbers of poor women already in it. In the BRAC example, one reason for success was that chickens were not new to women. Secondly, there should be a strong market for the product. And third, there should be government recognition of the sector's importance in order to promote supportive policy measures. For sustainable success, it may be necessary to build — and to keep building — follow-up activities which recognize changing market dynamics. Above all, of course, the activity must be profitable, with a realistic calculation of profit, including the opportunity cost of the enterprise, and the possibility or even likelihood that some of the income will be appropriated by a male family member.

This approach can be further subdivided. Marilyn Carr suggests four distinctions.[24] The first is increased productivity of known or existing work through improved technologies, techniques and supporting services. A second is increased access to previously unavailable opportunities: through co-operatives, credit or technological change. A third approach involves the development of existing skills to produce new products or modified traditional products. And finally, a fourth involves new skills for new products or modified traditional products. Each sub-division suggests different complexities in training, institutional development and technological assistance.

The BRAC poultry project cuts across several of Carr's categories. It provides skills that modify a 'traditional product'. It includes new technologies (better chicks, feed, vaccine), substantial organization, new support services and access to credit. And there is a strong demand for a product (chickens and eggs) that women already know.

Marty Chen offers a similar example from India, where traditionally women have responsibility for the care and feeding of milk animals, and for the processing of milk products.[25] In the 1970s and 1980s, aiming to integrate women into the national dairy programme, a number of NGOs and government bodies in the State of Andhra Pradesh began to develop all-women dairy co-operatives, training female extension workers and technical staff, and providing credit. By 1988, there were 23 000 active members in 400 women's dairy co-operatives and a further 73 000 in mixed co-operatives. In addition to improved income levels, the programmes gave women recognition and leverage (i.e. empowerment) at a policy level. And although these numbers are small in relation to the estimated 74 million Indian women engaged in dairying, the Andhra Pradesh success shows other organizations and other states what the potential may be.

Empowerment revisited

So far this chapter has dealt mainly with gender theory and with questions of economic empowerment. Despite the problems of getting it right, however, economic empowerment is not the same thing as the social empowerment that correctly preoccupies much of the women's movement. The former may be a precursor to the latter; alone it is not likely to be enough. But for many in the development business, there is a problem. Researchers and academics can and do play an important role in creating development theory, and in prodding, shaping and criticizing the way it is applied. In the women's movement, they have provided intellectual credibility and space that was not there two decades ago. And unlike more general development theory, the intellectual leadership of the women's movement has shifted South, encouraged, rather than discouraged, by strong feminist writers and thinkers in the North. But researchers and academics are usually one step removed from the reality of the programming efforts which affect the lives of ordinary people. In the women's movement, it may be that theory has moved two steps away from the reality of poor women's lives, with much greater effort being applied to dialectic and analysis than to application.

When the WID/WAD/GAD debates move into the arena of social empowerment, they become reminiscent of the language used to describe participatory development: complex, esoteric, confusing and — for many well-intentioned people — inaccessible. And without solid experience to back it, without careful application and comprehensible evaluation, it becomes an intimidating Rubic's Cube of theoretical jargon.[26] It is especially intimidating for men who work in the development business — the very people who need to understand it most.

One of the best articulations of 'the empowerment approach' to women and development comes from Sara Longwe, who tackles the concept head-on.[27] For her, the empowerment model recognizes the triple role of women as reproducers, as producers and as community managers, but it distinguishes between issues like food production, which are the common concern of men and women everywhere, and the ways in which a particular food-related intervention may impinge on a woman's day, her role in the family, and her role in the community.

Longwe breaks women's development into a hierarchy of five criteria. The first and most basic has to do with welfare: the relative welfare between women and men. The second relates to access: do women have access, on an equal basis with men, to land, labour, credit, and so on. The third has to do with conscientization: an 'understanding of the difference between sex roles and gender roles, and that the latter are cultural and can be changed . . . a belief in sexual equality'. The fourth criterion is participation. 'Equality of participation means involving women . . . in the same proportion in decision-making bodies as their proportion in the community'. And the fifth criterion is control: 'equality of control over the distribution of benefits', a balance of control between men and women so that neither side is in a position of dominance or subordination.

This rather liberating definition means that even a very simple project aiming to provide relief to a community in distress could well meet all these criteria. And a credit project for women, with a 98 per cent recovery rate, might meet the second criterion alone: access to resources. In such a project there might be nothing in the way of *relative* change between men and women in welfare; there may have been no conscientization, no participation, and husbands may well take all the money earned by their wives. It is an analysis which can shine a rather different and important light on accepted wisdom, on ways to assess project proposals, and ways to evaluate projects in progress.

It can also liberate organizations from the idea that all projects for women must in some way be tied to health, 'mothering' or income generation. There is, in fact, a wide range of promising 'empowerment' projects that have little to do with economics. Sistren, a Jamaican theatre group of working-class women has for almost two decades helped women and men examine gender issues through the medium of entertainment, drama, and even humour. Women's groups in India are leading the struggle to reduce alcoholism and to stop the sale of liquor in their villages, in order to reduce family violence and to improve the economic position of their families. In East Africa, 'family life education' projects deal with questions of mutual respect and conflict resolution, not only between men and women, but between generations. Legal reform and the simple creation of greater protection and 'space' for women can lay the groundwork for other kinds of empowerment. Brazilian 'women's police stations' and special Bangladesh bank branches for women are examples.

Empowerment, in both its social and its economic manifestations, is the essential core of any activity that is serious about improving the lot of women. Competence — including the business skills necessary for successful income generation projects, including institutional commitment, learning, remembering and the dissemination of practical lessons: these are what gives life to the idea of empowerment, and meaning to the word. Until more of these rather simple lessons can be absorbed by development organizations, and until gender theory becomes more accessible and more user-friendly, the movement is likely to suffer from practical weakness that can only limit its theoretical strengths and its political gains. Stand by for more pink elephants.

CHAPTER VI

Disasters: some came running

We must recognize that . . . we have failed in our response to the agony of Rwanda, and thus have acquiesced in the continued loss of human lives. Our readiness and our capacity for action have been demonstrated to be inadequate at best, and deplorable at worst, owing to the absence of collective political will.

Boutros Boutros-Ghali[1].

WE ARRIVE NOW at the first of several of the great intersections that confront non-governmental organizations. At first, this one looks familiar. A terrible disaster: drought perhaps. Flood. Cyclone. War. Reporters fly in. Screaming headlines. Exhausted relief workers on the television news; a smokey camp in the background, crowded with refugees. An appeal for help; money arrives; food is sent. Reporters depart. Story over.

It seems like rather standard fare, the sort of thing that has become commonplace since the 1960s: 'just another disaster'. Most disaster stories, however, do not end with the departure of the reporters. They may drag on for years. Often the television news is only the beginning of a logistical, political and human nightmare, a horror that can be understood only by those who have lived through one. But there is a bigger story. For NGOs the emergencies fuelled by the Cold War — Cambodia, the Central American wars, Angola, Ethiopia — were the beginning of an even bigger nightmare. The disasters that scar the 'new world order' test the very limits of altruism, drawing NGO leaders into heated political controversy and their front-line workers more and more frequently into dangerous, unfriendly fire. The financial, political and developmental implications of the increasingly terrible disasters that seem to mark the world have been enormous for NGOs, raising profound questions that go to the root of what they are, what they do, and who they answer to.

What is a disaster?

Over the past decade it has become clear — in places like Ethiopia, the Sudan and Cambodia, that the old idea of a disaster as a disconnected event, separate from 'normal' life and distinct from the standard processes of development, is often wrong. In fact it may be wrong most of the time. Bangladesh, for example, is a country prone to flooding. Every year, as much as half the land surface is covered with water. This has been a fact of life since the Ganges-Brahmaputra delta was formed. Flooding brings silt which regenerates the land after the monsoon, and it fills the rivers and ponds with fish. People have found ways to live with it by building roads, villages and home-steads above the normal flood level. But poverty and crowding have pushed more and more people into fringe areas, and onto low-lying, newly formed *char* land in the far south. This land was never safe, and an unusually high flood or a cyclone — also not a new or unforeseen phenomenon — can become a major killer.

The tropical storms and hurricanes that wreak havoc in the Carib-bean and the Pacific every few years tend not to wreak much havoc on well-built homes. It is the people who live in shacks, in unpro-tected and unsafe areas — exposed low-lying land, and on hillsides susceptible to erosion and mudslide — who are most vulnerable to such events. Lima, the capital of Peru, is located on the cusp of two tectonic plates, and as a result is highly vulnerable to seismic activity. Three major earthquakes and hundreds of smaller ones have taken place in Lima in this century. Rural poverty and urban-based growth policies in Peru have led to a major demographic shift over the past fifty years, which has resulted in two thirds of the country's popu-lation living in cities and towns. Lima, which alone holds one-third of the Peruvian population, grew from 650 000 in 1940 to 6.4 million in 1992. In the city core, and in residential areas constructed according to building codes and zoning by-laws, the streets are wide and buildings incorporate anti-seismic technologies. But rapid growth has pushed hundreds of thousands of people into completely unregulated inner-city slums and onto the hilly scrubland at the edges of the city. Of all the housing in Lima in 1982, 43 per cent had been constructed by the 'informal sector', without permission, without adequate health and sanitation facilities, and without regard for safety.[2] Here is a disaster waiting to happen.

Add to this sort of vulnerability a combination of bad agricultural and environmental policies, fragile economies based on the export of crops like sugar, cotton, jute, sisal or cocoa, whose prices keep falling, and political instability will not be far behind. Aid projects can add to the burden. Careless, even reckless mega-projects have led to long-term environmental damage and to the mass migration of people into urban slums. Egypt's Aswan High Dam, opened in 1970, may have improved flood control, irrigation and electric power generation, but it also polluted drinking water, contributed to the spread of bilharzia, and killed off the country's sardine fishery. The Kainji Dam in Nigeria halved fishing on the River Niger and reduced harvests from traditional floodplain agriculture. Between 1979 and 1985, 40 World Bank-financed projects for agriculture and hydro-electric power development resulted in the forced resettlement of 600 000 people in 27 countries, with devastating consequences for their health and livelihoods.[3] That many of these people end up in the slums of Lagos, Accra, Dhaka and Lima is not surprising.

Are mega-projects which add to the vulnerability of the poor a thing of the past? Hardly. China's Three Gorges Dam Project, which promised to be the world's largest-ever power development project, was shelved in the late 1980s because of protest from Chinese and international environmentalists, and because aid donors were embarrassed by the hard-hitting, well-documented critiques they and environmental NGOs produced.[4] The project was dusted off again in 1992, however, and an official ground-breaking ceremony was held in 1994, putting the international community on notice that one of the greatest engineering projects of all time, one that might involve as much as $3 billion worth of machinery and equipment contracts and $5 billion in overseas financing, would soon be calling for tenders. The Three Gorges Dams, scheduled for completion in 2009, will put a lake on top of two cities, 140 towns, 4500 villages and 30 000 hectares of farmland. Resettlement, not a great humanitarian success in other Chinese projects, will be required of more than a million people.[5]

The ecological marginalization of people fosters another kind of vulnerability and builds a potential for political violence. During the 1970s and 1980s, landlessness and poverty in the Philippines caused thousands of families to move into the hills, where property rights were unclear. Deforestation and erosion were the primary and most tangible products. And because the poor remained poor, they became ready recruits for the New People's Army, the National Democratic Front, and a war of insurgency. For more than a generation, the Government of South Africa pushed poor people into agriculturally unproductive, ecologically fragile 'homelands' like Ciskei, where the population density was more than forty times higher than in the surrounding Cape Province. The result was an uncontrollable out-migration to city slums and an upsurge in violence. In the southern highlands of Peru, the *Sendero Luminoso*, a brutal guerilla movement, found willing recruits among people in the same predicament. The population density on what was already poor land grew by 50 per cent between 1940 and 1980, while the availability of farm land fell to one-fifth of a hectare per capita.[6] In the absence of offsetting opportunities, political destabilization was likely, if not inevitable.

The story may be getting ahead of itself here, except to demonstrate that the distinction once made between natural and man-made* disasters is not as simple as might be thought from reading a newspaper. The examples given here also demonstrate that the distinction between 'sudden', 'creeping' and 'chronic' disasters is one filled with ambiguity and broad areas of greyness. Were the 1984 Union Carbide disaster in Bhopal or the Chernobyl meltdown man-made or natural? In their immediate confines, they were obviously man-made; but it was wind that put them into the league of mega-disasters. The Ethiopian drought of 1984–6 was natural, but what turned it into a disaster was a witches' brew of bad economic policies and a slow, inadequate response when the problem was recognized. Although the Ethiopian disaster may have seemed rather 'sudden' to the world's press, it had been creeping up for ten years. And looking at Ethiopia a decade after Bob Geldof and the popular music industry became involved, the disaster would appear to have become rather chronic.

Democracy has a good deal to do with preventing disasters like the one that has afflicted Ethiopia for two decades. India, which has a free and vibrant press, has had no famine since independence, despite severe food shortages in 1967, 1973, 1979, and 1987. Harvard economist Amartya Sen, who has written extensively about food and poverty, observes that 'there has never been a famine in any country that's been a democracy with a relatively free press. I know of no exception. It applies to very poor countries with democratic systems as well as rich ones'. But in the absence of a free press, Sen says, 'it's amazing how ignorant and immune from pressure the government can be'.[7]

Biafra, Bangladesh and Cambodia

The world's best-known international NGOs and a host of smaller ones were formed first and only to deal with emergencies. The Red Cross was a product of the wars of Italian unification. Save the Children followed the First World War, Foster Parents Plan was created as a response to the Spanish Civil War, and the International Rescue Committee was formed in 1933 by Albert Einstein and others to help refugees fleeing from Nazi Germany. Oxfam was established to deal with the Greek famine of 1943. CARE was a response to needs in Europe after the Second World War, World Vision was a product of Korea, while Médecins sans Frontières and Concern emerged from Biafra and the tumultuous birth of Bangladesh. Much of the church

---

*'Man-made': although not a politically correct expression, in this context it is technically correct.

effort in the South has been relief oriented, resulting in the creation of other large NGOs: the Adventist Development and Relief Agency, Catholic Relief Services, the Lutheran World Federation.

When the initial disaster these agencies sought to address was over, each faced a choice: to disband or to continue. Many had started their efforts in Europe, and with the independence movement, they logically turned their attention south. Most also moved away from disaster relief into development programming. While they retained a capacity to deal with emergencies, the logic was, and remains, that it is better and cheaper to deal with the underlying causes of the poverty and vulnerability that contribute to disaster, than it is to wait until a situation is out of control.

Situations do get out of control, however. Perhaps the first great modern disaster challenge for NGOs began in the south-east corner of Nigeria in 1967. The Nigerian Federation was an awkward hybrid, a patchwork of vastly different historical, cultural and economic realities. Ethnically, there were dozens of distinct groups and languages, but the country was dominated by three: the Yoruba in the west, the Hausa in the north, and the Ibo in the east. An Ibo-led coup in 1966 was the spark that began a conflagration. Two horrific pogroms in the North resulted in the deaths of at least 30 000 Ibos, and by the end of the year, a million people living in Nigeria's Ibo diaspora began flooding back to their eastern homeland.

A second murderous coup, this time led by northerners, further destabilized a tenuous political situation, and a Federal Government decision to divide the country's four regions into a dozen states suddenly became a political watershed. Fearing destruction of the predominantly Ibo-populated Eastern Region as a power block, the Region's Military Governor, Colonel Odumegwu Ojukwu, announced its secession from the Federation in May, 1967, thus beginning the short, violent life of the Republic of Biafra.

The Nigerian Government anticipated a brief police action. But a combination of bungling, lengthy supply lines and fierce Biafran resistance turned the effort into a siege which, by the Spring of 1968, was becoming a crisis of starvation. Initially, UNICEF and the International Committee of the Red Cross (ICRC) were able to fly food and drugs to Biafra, supplying the same amounts to the Nigerian side as well.*

---

*The ICRC, which seeks to act as an intermediary between belligerents, and to provide protection and assistance to victims, is a private Swiss organization, legally and financially independent of the League of Red Cross Societies, and from national Red Cross, Red Crescent and Red Lion and Sun Societies. UNICEF is not a relief agency, but it does have a unique mandate to operate in countries that are not recognized by the United Nations.

Impartiality was the watchword, as both organizations, dependent upon governments for their survival, required the permission and goodwill of the Nigerian Government to continue. The permission and goodwill, however, did not last. The UN, still reeling from a disastrous experience only four years earlier in the former Belgian Congo, was unprepared to involve itself in another 'internal' African affair, and in the end it never did play a role of any importance. The ICRC saw itself as the best possible co-ordinator for urgently needed relief flights into the besieged enclave, and managed to persuade first Oxfam and then a number of Church organizations to wait until it could obtain Federal Government approval.

By August, 1968, however, three months after the ICRC had itself issued an urgent 'S.O.S. Biafra Alert', nothing had happened. The ICRC had become embroiled in negotiations with the Nigerian and British Governments, both of which hoped and believed the war would end within a few weeks. They also believed that any relief might serve to prolong the war, and so blocking the ICRC became a matter of policy. As with UNICEF and Oxfam, the churches had at first been willing to wait for an ICRC airlift. But as time dragged on, their frustration and anger grew. Tens of thousands of people were starving to death. Finally, tired of waiting, they began their own airlift from the Portuguese Island of São Tomé. Known as Jointchurchaid, the airlift brought together 33 European and North American church agencies.

The ICRC airlift ultimately began in September, but from the outset, strenuous efforts were made by the Nigerian Government to derail it: pressing irresolute Western governments to withhold money; tying the UN and its ambivalent Secretary General in legalistic knots; persuading the newly independent government of Equatorial Guinea (where the ICRC airlift originated) to halt flights; and finally, in June 1969, shooting down a Red Cross plane. ICRC flights, which carried food and medicine from a dozen national Red Cross societies, Protestant church organizations, Oxfam, CARE, UNICEF and Save the Children, were immediately suspended. Months of futile negotiations ensued, during which ICRC became more and more deeply entangled in legal technicalities and debates about the finer points of national sovereignty. Their planes never flew to Biafra again.

Unreported at the time, a completely different approach to the conflict had been developed by the American Friends Service Committee — the Quakers. In 1963 they had established a programme to bring new and potential West African leaders together to find African solutions to African problems. When the war began, they were able to make contact with both sides, meeting regularly with both leaders and acting as the only emissary trusted by both sides throughout the war.[8]

Meanwhile, Jointchurchaid, never doubting the righteousness of its cause and unfettered by legal niceties, continued flying, except for brief occasions when the only remaining airstrip was temporarily bombed out of action. For the churches it was a matter of conscience, and one of very real human need. Estimates of the death toll from starvation rose as high as 25 000 a day, and the word 'genocide', not as loosely used then as it is today, became a common characterization of events in the editorial pages of newspapers around the world. In the end, of the 7800 relief flights into Biafra, 5310 were operated by Jointchurchaid, providing 66 000 tons of food and supplies, valued at an estimated $116 million.[9] It was a historical feat rivalled in volume only by the Berlin airlift, and it is probably still unrivalled anywhere for bravery.

The airlift and the broader relief effort was also something else. It was an act of unfortunate and profound folly. It prolonged the war for 18 months, because the relief agencies believed, incorrectly as it turned out, that an unrestrained Nigerian Government would unleash a final genocidal bloodbath against Ibos, should Biafra collapse. This was a willing suspension of disbelief. By mid-1968, half of the Eastern Region, along with a large number of Ibos, had been liberated. Large areas of the Midwest State, liberated in the early days of the war, were also Ibo-speaking. There had been no massacres in any of these areas.

A great deal of post-war effort went into refuting the charge that the churches and NGOs prolonged the war. Because if it is true, they must also have prolonged the suffering, contributing to the deaths of 180 000 people or more. This is a conservative estimate, based on a calculation of 10 000 deaths per month for the 18 months of the war that followed the start of the airlift, which coincided with the lowest ebb of the Biafran military effort.[10] It is also a rather terrible charge, one that deserves explanation. After all, 'Could a small amount of relief food, spread so thinly, really have buoyed the war effort?' A senior CARE field worker asked this question, and answered it: 'Almost certainly not.'[11]

Former Biafrans disagree. Writing after the war, N.U. Akpan, head of Biafra's civil service said, 'The efforts of the relief agencies did in fact help prolong the war'.[12] In that appalling summer of 1968, Biafra's military fortunes had reached a low point that was not paralleled again until the last days of the war. The food situation was terrible and the military predicament was worse. Onitsha, Port Harcourt, Calabar and the capital, Enugu, had all fallen to rapidly advancing Nigerian forces. Little stood between Biafra and total defeat. Explaining how Biafra survived this period, Odumegwu Ojukwu later cited three factors: Biafra's logistical advantage, operating in a small enclave with a good network of paved roads; the long supply lines faced by the advancing Nigerians; and the financial assistance he was receiving from the relief agencies. 'The only source of income available to Biafra was the hard currency spent by the churches for yams and *gari*. That's all. At this stage we had no loans or anything else. It wasn't much, but it was enough to sustain us.'[13]

Ojukwu was referring to the massive doses of hard currency he needed for weapons, the hard currency made available by relief agencies through their purchase of goods and services inside Biafra. By 1969, when the war was in its second year, the price of *gari* and cassava flour, still produced in great quantity by Biafran farmers, had increased in price almost 36 times. Although the Biafran pound was worthless, relief agencies still exchanged hard currency at the official rate established before the war. As long as they accepted this rate — and it never changed — they contributed directly to the Biafran war chest. For example the World Council of Churches representative in Orlu, one of ten Biafran provinces, reported local purchases worth $140 000 a month in November, 1968. A German agency reported spending $1.25 million up to October, 1968.[14] In addition to purchases, most distribution costs were borne by relief agencies. Nordchurchaid, for example, spent $50 000 renting cars and trucks in August 1969 alone. The living costs of 100 ICRC staff and several hundred church workers added to the expenditure. And before September 1968, the British and Irish Catholic Churches alone spent more than $400 000 on special projects, to build clinics, hospitals and camp facilities.[15]

Relief flights contributed several thousand dollars a day in landing fees, despite the fact that the agencies had practically built the single Biafran airstrip. They had flown in 30 000 square feet of aluminium planking, had built feeder roads and parking aprons, provided landing lights, radio equipment, a standby generator and a direction finder.[16] At fifteen to twenty flights a night in 1968, Uli Airstrip was the busiest airport in Africa after Johannesburg. In all, the best estimate of the cost of the relief effort is $250 million.[17] If as little as 15 per cent of this was spent inside Biafra, it would have provided the regime with as much foreign exchange as was spent by Nigeria on arms throughout the war.[18] Such a figure does not take into account the hard currency with which Biafra started the war, nor does it include the direct provision of money and arms supplied by France, Portugal and other countries with a stake in seeing Nigeria collapse.

While the rapid escalation of relief activities helped Biafra to survive the late summer and early autumn of 1968, it essentially transformed a potential country into little more than an object of pity. Interpreted largely through the eyes of relief agencies, Biafra became a humanitarian problem rather than a political problem, excusing the UN and virtually every Western government from direct involvement. Unlike the spate of rapid diplomatic recognitions that followed the political breakup of the Soviet Union and Yugoslavia two decades later, the emphasis on Biafra's suffering, used by the relief agencies for fund-raising purposes, perhaps damaged its chances for recognition and for the international political support that might really have saved it.

Second time lucky: Bangladesh

Chagrined perhaps by their inaction in Nigeria, United Nations agencies virtually tripped over themselves five months after the collapse of Biafra in rushing support, both appropriate and inappropriate, to the victims of a Peruvian earthquake. Only six months after that, a devastating cyclone, with attendant tidal wave, flooding, massive death and dislocation, struck East Pakistan. NGOs and United Nations agencies moved in and had started to pick up some of the pieces when the Pakistan army began its murderous crackdown on Bengali nationalists. This fomented a full-fledged revolt, retaliatory military action against civilians, starvation, a massive exodus of refugees and finally, a war with India. Because NGOs were already there when the fighting broke out, dealing with the havoc created by the cyclone, they were well placed to assist victims of the civil strife. More importantly, they carried the story of Pakistani military atrocities to the outside world. Nigerian Head of State Yakubu Gowon, knowing what this might mean, wrote to Pakistan's military ruler, Yahya Khan, warning him to get rid of the NGOs if he wanted to keep his country together.[19] He did neither, and eight months after it began, East Pakistan was transformed into the world's newest, and poorest, nation: Bangladesh.

As in Nigeria, UN agencies made themselves scarce for much of the trouble, removing most of their staff from Dhaka just before the military crackdown in March, 1971. A small relief presence was maintained, but it was not until December, when ten million Bengalis had crossed into India and the Indian army had crossed the border going the other way, that the UN General Assembly became involved. It adopted a polite resolution calling on India and Pakistan to cease hostilities so there could be an early voluntary return of the refugees. It was polite, and it was futile. The matter was settled more quickly and more decisively than the General Assembly would have had it — on the battlefield.

The first two years of Bangladesh were a high point for NGOs, UN agencies and the Red Cross. War damage was estimated at $1200 million, crops had not been planted, and the infrastructure of a badly underdeveloped country was virtually destroyed. More than a hundred international NGOs set up offices in Dhaka, providing emergency supplies, development assistance and infrastructural support for the bridges, roads and communications networks that had been damaged or destroyed during the war. Oxfam provided ferries to replace those that had been sunk, and the Red Cross operated a helicopter service, carrying medical personnel and supplies to remote island areas. UNICEF and a dozen NGOs ran feeding programmes; CARE built houses; and a massive, redemptory United Nations relief operation known as UNROB operated a national radio communications network, a small fleet of aircraft, and a large fleet of mini-bulkers to ferry food to the port of Chittagong from the world's largest freighter, the *Manhattan*, sitting just offshore in the Bay of Bengal.

In retrospect, it may seem that there were too many white cars and jeeps loaded with expatriates (and not very many Bangladeshis), that too many outsiders provided too much relief, too uncritically. But it was a time of great need and tremendous energy, and after Biafra, where many of these same relief workers had cut their teeth, questioning motives and techniques was not the fashionable thing that it became in later years.[20]

Bangladesh was perhaps the beginning of a recognition that major emergencies were likely to be a continuing phenomenon. As the war in Vietnam began to wind down, many foresaw the need for massive relief and reconstruction efforts throughout Indochina. Although their timing was off, they were not wrong. In the interim, UNICEF established an emergency operations unit in 1971, and a year later a United Nations Disaster Relief Office (UNDRO) was created. During the 1970s, emergency units were created throughout the UN system: in FAO, UNHCR, WHO, the World Food Programme and the Pan-American Health Organization. But the lacklustre performance of many of these institutions, especially of the World Food Programme during the Sahelian drought of 1974, served only to strengthen the reputation of NGOs.

UN agencies suffered from the sluggish bureaucracy that can accompany any large organization. Worse, however, their mandates were often uncertain and they were entirely dependent upon the goodwill and largesse of their members. These members are national governments, and if they want to delay, block or otherwise hamper a United Nations operation, there are dozens of arrows in their quiver that can do it. A simple lack of money, imposed almost entirely by governments, has fuelled a thousand media attacks on UN 'incompetence'.

Take, for example, Angola, where the civil war which began in 1974 was still raging two decades later. Six UN agencies along with 45 international and 41 local NGOs, heavily supported financially by UN agencies, were working on an increasingly difficult situation at the end of 1993. An estimated 3.3 million people were dependent on emergency food aid as a result of the war, and as many as a thousand people, mainly children, were dying every month. In May 1993, a consolidated UN appeal for $226 million was made on behalf of its own agencies and the NGOs. Governments responded immediately, but with pledges of only $70 million. Worse, four months later, less than $20 million had actually been received. In the end, less than half the requirements were met, and in the case of UNICEF, only a quarter of what had been asked for was received.[21]

Cambodia: year zero

The Cambodian holocaust, which took the lives of millions of people between 1969 and 1989, which scarred an entire generation, and which dragged interminably on, was caused directly, and was generously sustained, by mid-century superpower psychosis. The Khmer Rouge buildup and its eventual takeover of Cambodia in 1975 may have looked like a sideshow during the Vietnam War, but what followed was not. Between 1969 and 1973 as many as a million died; under the Khmer Rouge another one to two million were murdered or starved to death. In a single decade, one third of all Cambodians died from unnatural causes. The murderous Khmer Rouge reign was finally halted by a Vietnamese invasion in 1979. Astonishingly, however, the West, fearing a new game of Vietnamese dominoes, gave artificial respiration to the moribund Khmer Rouge, propping the body up for years in the Cambodian seat at the United Nations, and denying both bilateral and multilateral assistance to the devastated country until the Vietnamese pullout in 1989.

Unlike NGOs, which can move more quickly and which are not always concerned with legal technicalities, UN agencies are hampered by their inability to go to the media with complaints about member states. This was exemplified in spades when the Cambodian crisis finally came to a head in 1979. Because the Pol Pot regime had been allowed to occupy the Cambodian seat at the UN, only two multilateral agencies had access to the country: ICRC and UNICEF. As in Biafra, however, these two organizations had to please a government that had understandable political concerns, not least of which was the fact that much of the Khmer Rouge army had fled to refugee camps in Thailand, where ICRC and UNICEF, among others, were already providing assistance.*

---

*This concern was not diminished by a meeting between Kurt Waldheim and Ieng Sary, the former Khmer Rouge foreign minister, who thanked the Secretary General for the assistance ICRC and UNICEF were providing to his people on the Thai-Cambodia border.

Ten years earlier, Oxfam had been diverted from direct action in Biafra by ICRC and UNICEF, and so it was no longer willing to be put off by their promises that they could and would act. Following its own field visits, Oxfam went to the media in September 1979 with an exposé of the horrors that Cambodia had experienced. It predicted the starvation of 2.2 million people if immediate aid was not forthcoming. Despite charges that it was aiding and abetting Vietnamese aggression, Oxfam managed to send in two relief flights that month, and early the following month it accomplished something much more dramatic. Guy Stringer, Oxfam's Deputy Director, flew to Singapore, chartered a barge, filled it with food, seeds and agricultural equipment, and, standing on the bridge of an appropriately named tug, *Asiatic Success*, had it towed 640 nautical miles to the port of Kompong Som.[22] It was a spectacular start to an odd arrangement, in which a consortium of NGOs, led by Oxfam, filled an aid vacuum created by the Cold War. More than that, however, Oxfam and other NGOs continued to speak out about the on-going neglect of Cambodia and the preposterous seating of the Khmer Rouge at the United Nations.* In 1982, Oxfam published a booklet on the subject, *The poverty of diplomacy,* and in 1986, 20 NGOs formed a consortium to campaign for an end to the aid embargo, publishing another critique, *Punishing the poor.*

The ICRC and UNICEF were eventually able to start operations, and bilateral support was provided from a range of communist countries as well as from Scandinavia, France and others. But the NGO work started first, and it was significant. Worldwide, the NGO effort generally represents about 10 per cent of official development assistance,[23] but in Cambodia, in the critical years between 1979 and 1988, it made up an estimated 30 per cent.[24]

The NGO effort to assist Cambodians was not without controversy. While only a handful of NGOs operated within Cambodia before 1988,** a virtual army rushed to the Cambodian border in north-east Thailand, where upwards of 600 000 starving refugees and displaced persons were crowded into camps that would continue to fester through the 1980s. At the end of 1979, there were 30 international

---

*The US, Britain and other western nations said the matter was simply one of credentials, although credentials had not been an issue for Bangladesh following the 1971 Indian invasion, nor for Uganda after the 1979 Tanzanian invasion.
**There were about 13 during the initial emergency, rising to 19 by 1987, some supported by consortia in their home countries. The biggest were Oxfam, representing several members of the Oxfam family; Lutheran World Service and a variety of Catholic agencies, sometimes working independently, and sometimes under the auspices of Coopération Internationale pour le Développement et la Solidarité (CIDSE), a Catholic co-ordinating body.

109

NGOs operating in the border area, and a year later there were nearly 60. The need to help the refugees could not be denied, but there were more cynical motives behind some of the money that became available. The United States and Thailand had a particular interest in destabilizing the Vietnamese occupation of Cambodia, and half a million or so refugees helped to do this. Some of the refugees were Khmer Rouge cadres, housed in special camps where, with international care and feeding, they lived to fight another day.

However, this was perhaps not the worst of it. The border operation revealed all the imbalances and weaknesses of international relief efforts. The border operation was significantly better financed than most refugee operations, receiving three times per capita what later went to Afghan refugees and eight times what went to refugees in western Somalia.[25] Despite the level of effort, inappropriate types of assistance were rampant. Any relief operation is bound to have its share of junk and stupidity: Go-Slim Soup to Somalia; outdated baby food to a Honduran refugee camp, laxatives to Nicaragua, custard powder and pickled vegetables to Biafra, vacation tents that blew away in Costa Rica, and then blew away again in Peru.[26] But there were other problems. Among them, UNHCR, UNICEF and ICRC sought to co-ordinate a relief effort heavily dominated by feeding programmes, with all the attendant logistical requirements. Up to then, none of them had ever dealt with a programme of this magnitude.

Although mistakes were made, by the end of 1979, UNICEF and the ICRC were delivering 2500 tons of food to the border every week. Many of the NGOs, however, had no relief experience whatsoever. Almost worse in some respects, many assumed that experience of Africa or Bangladesh was an adequate qualification for work with Cambodians in Thailand. What they brought, an ability to move food and give injections, was not enough. Relief workers have to be able to understand the sociological implications of what they do, as well as the psychological and political ramifications. They must be able to communicate with the victims of disaster in a way that recognizes them as real people, with real lives, real homes, real memories and fears, and real talents. In many cases, refugees and displaced people begin to develop a coping strategy long before the relief agency arrives, and they can assist the relief effort in a multitude of ways, not least because they alone have an understanding of the trauma they have been through.

The involvement of Southern NGOs in disaster relief is badly documented. While there is no lack of historical data, books, newspaper accounts and fundraising material on the work of Northern NGOs, their Southern counterparts usually get left out of the story. This is partly because in some countries they have been suppressed, or because in others they are a relatively recent phenomenon. In Cambodia, for example, the first national development NGO, Khmera, was not formed until 1991. But it is also because many of the resources, at least until the 1980s, were controlled by Northern NGOs who, although perhaps working through a local institution, tended to control both events and publicity. Publicity notwithstanding, the European churches certainly could not have worked in Biafra without local counterparts. The same was true in Ethiopia and in Eritrea and Tigray, where local institutions — quasi NGOs created by the liberation movegments — made virtually all of the decisions about who would handle relief, and how.

Local NGO and church organizations were especially prominent during the natural and man-made disasters of the 1980s in El Salvador, Nicaragua and Guatemala, and many external NGOs could not have functioned without them. Much of the emergency assistance following the Bangladesh floods of 1988 was handled exclusively by Bangladeshi NGOs, many of whom had by that time outstripped their Northern counterparts in terms of capacity and effectiveness. While the bravery and dedication of international NGO workers cannot be faulted, it is often their Southern counterparts who take the greatest risk. When CARE and MSF workers were threatened by Hutu militia in Zairean refugee camps, they could withdraw. But 30 Zairean Boy Scouts, helping to collect dead bodies in Katale Camp, could not. They were hog-tied and slaughtered by refugees.[27]

The invisibility of Southern NGOs remains, however. Some of the most prominent studies of the Cambodian refugee situation in Northeast Thailand make no mention of local NGOs beyond the Thai Red Cross.[28] Raymond Cournoyer, who had worked for Oxfam in the Bengali refugee camps of India, in newly independent Bangladesh and in Mali during the Sahelian drought, saw old mistakes being repeated in Thailand. 'In the Kao I Dang refugee camp you had all those dispensaries, one CRS, one International Red Cross, one Quaker, one Mennonite . . . all separate. And the refugees had nothing to do apart from eating, sleeping and gossiping; they were kept in an unproductive refugee situation.'[29] He was bemused by ineffectual attempts to impose order on food handouts. On one occasion, a truck bearing sweetened milk, vegetables and two foreigners arrived. Heads of families in that section of the camp were called together and made to sit on their haunches in a straight line while one of the foreigners explained, in English, how the distribution would be carried out. 'It was the same farce I had seen so many times in the camps in Calcutta. After the careful explanation, the two foreigners were surrounded by people, all pushing and shoving. And in the end, the foreigners simply gave up and walked away, and left the damned stuff there for people to fight over.'

As Director of CUSO's Asia programme, Cournoyer and his colleagues had good contacts with Thai NGOs. And because CUSO had no emergency experience, it could look at the camps from a slightly different perspective. After discussions with UNHCR, which was desperate for assistance from any organization with a management capacity, CUSO agreed to take responsibility for the 45-acre Kab Cherng holding centre, a smallish facility for 8500 people, 56 per cent of whom were women, and 35 per cent children. To its surprise, CUSO discovered that Thai villagers in the neighbourhood were in some cases worse off than the refugees, so camp health facilities were opened to them as well.

In Kab Cherng, the work was done almost exclusively by Thais, working for Thai organizations. The Community-Based Emergency Relief Services handled food distribution, camp maintenance and sanitation. Education was handled by two NGOs, under-five activities were managed by Friends For All Children Foundation, and Mahidol University administered medical and nutritional programmes. Teachers to run the schools were found among the refugees, Cambodian medical personnel helped in clinics, potters made cisterns to collect rainwater from roofs.

People were helped, but Kab Cherng was a relatively small operation in the general scheme of things. The most lasting impact was probably felt by the Thai NGOs, who not only worked together for the first time, but who developed the confidence to institutionalize their relationship in a larger project outside the camps when the emergency was over. Over the next decade, the North-east Thailand Project became a demonstration of how Thais, when given the challenge and the opportunity, could band together to work effectively in a poor area largely ignored by the international development establishment. Eventually a new Thai NGO was established, the NET Foundation, institutionalizing a development approach that had started as an *ad hoc* relief programme.

Similar things have happened elsewhere. The creation of cereal banks in Burkina Faso was an outcome of the drought and relief efforts of the early 1970s. The first cereal banks were started by a Burkinabé NGO, the *Fondation Nationale pour le Développement et la Solidarité* (FONADES), as investments in village-based food security. The idea has since become widespread, with support from Northern NGOs, UNDP and bilateral donors. In 1976, Guatemala was struck by a powerful earthquake which killed 23 000 people and left a million people homeless. Joyabaj in north-eastern Guatemala was particularly hard-hit, and became the focus of attention for seven members of the International Save the Children Alliance. Pooling their resources, they created an alliance — an *alianza* — with a unified management team to focus first on housing and reconstruction, and later on longer-term development. Today, *Alianza para Desarrollo Juvenil Comunitario de Guatemala* is a registered national organization with its own long-term development programmes.[30]

The generic lesson of the cereal banks, Alianza and Kab Cherng is one that some NGOs later learned and applied in Somalia, out of necessity, after the withdrawal of the ill-fated UN military operation. Between 1991 and 1992, as many as half a million Somalis, mainly children, died of disease and starvation resulting from conflict. Angry American journalist P.J. O'Rourke sat amidst the horror and shambles of Somalia at one of its lowest ebbs and wrote, 'It's all well and good to talk about what can be done to end famine in general. But what can be done about famine specifically? About this famine in particular? About a place as screwed up as Somalia? What the fucking goddam hell do you do?'[31]

Maybe the answer is that *you* cannot do as much as you would like or think possible. Futility notwithstanding, some of the aid efforts of those years and, more importantly, the efforts of Somalis themselves, still bore fruit. Despite an absence of government, or perhaps because of an absence of government, many refugees returned home, and farmers planted again. Feeding programmes were phased out. Away from Mogadishu, and away from the television cameras, NGOs, UNHCR, ICRC and Somalian organizations such as the Red Crescent, started clinics, immunization programmes and veterinary services. Despite the uncertainty caused by on-going clan warfare, Somalis began rebuilding their houses, they re-established primary schools and they began integrating NGO primary health care programmes with community-supported, self-financing schemes that they had developed for themselves.[32]

So what in fact, are the priorities in sickening places like the Rwandan refugee camps in Zaire, or on the Cambodian border in Thailand: food? Medical assistance? Organization for training and skill development? Repatriation? The answers are sometimes determined not by objective need, but by what an organization can sell to its donors at home, or by what a bilateral agency, possibly driven by political concerns, will pay for. Major disputes can erupt over the issue of priorities. Such a dispute arose over rice seed and what became known as the 'land bridge' between Thailand and Cambodia. In 1979, only a quarter of Cambodia's rice fields were planted, resulting in the food crisis of 1980. It was clear that if rice was not planted in 1980, the situation would become much worse in 1981. Seeing a rather simple solution, CARE made a proposal to UNICEF: instead of providing only food to the thousands of people travelling to the border, provide seed. In March, CARE ran an experimental programme, sending 400 tons of seed across the border. Impressed with the apparent success, it purchased an additional 1500 tons, and was followed by a small American church organization, World Relief, which bought 1300 tons using a UNICEF grant. After that, although USAID made $2 million available to pay for the 100 000 tons of seed needed, UNICEF and ICRC slowed the operation down.

Both still wanted to demonstrate their neutrality to the Phnom Penh Government, and feared that USAID money on the border would compromise them politically. Neither wanted the land bridge to jeopardize their relief work inside Cambodia. They were also wary of creating a 'magnet' at the border, and there were concerns about seed varieties, packaging, and the need for care in handling seeds that had been treated with pesticide. Frustrated and angry, and seeing only the need and the opportunity on its own doorstep, World Relief denounced ICRC relentlessly in the press, calling it a 'too little, too late' agency that prevented the serious, like World Relief, for example, from getting on with 'saving lives and saving a nation from destruction'.[33]

In the end, 22 000 tons were distributed in time for planting, and the effort is regarded by some as the most important success of the border relief effort. Conceived and carried out almost entirely by NGOs, the rice seed programme took the western part of Cambodia a long way towards adequate food production that year. More importantly, it involved Cambodians in their own survival and was the beginning of an end to dependence on food aid.

During the first year of the emergency, NGOs provided between 20 and 25 per cent of the relief assistance on the border, either from their own coffers, or with money provided by other donors. After 1982, operations were co-ordinated by the United Nations Border Relief Operation (UNBRO), until 1991 the biggest *ad hoc* organization ever established by the United Nations. In some ways, UNBRO began to change the way many NGOs looked at relief. Originally, it was something they undertook almost exclusively with their own finances. By the early 1980s, however, they found themselves becoming increasingly attractive to bilateral and multilateral organizations as delivery mechanisms. Government financial support for NGO relief operations, handled in an improvised and sometimes covert way during the Biafran airlift, had become much more pronounced by the mid-1980s. UNBRO, which co-ordinated assistance to 'displaced persons' camps on the border, confirmed it. Towards the end of the operation, it was providing 90–100 per cent of all NGO funding, and UNHCR, which handled the 'holding centres', provided between 30 and 90 per cent, depending on the NGO and the activity it was carrying out.[34]

114

The same thing began to happen elsewhere. In 1981, UNHCR asked CARE (at the insistence of USAID) to take over the co-ordination of food logistics between Mogadishu and 35 camps of displaced Somalis. 'We had never intended to get into that kind of activity,' said CARE's President, Wallace Campbell, 'but in retrospect it was a logical way to make good use of the skills and expertise CARE people had built up over many years.'[35] Three years later in Ethiopia, NGOs (including the ICRC) were directly involved in the distribution of 60 to 70 per cent of all emergency food aid, the bulk of it derived from western governments and UN agencies. And in Eritrea and Tigray, NGOs were probably involved in handling more than 90 per cent of the relief assistance.[36]

Lesson 1: The brutality of nations

The most damning indictment that emerges from the major disasters of our era is that many were caused by governments. And govern-ments could have done something to prevent, stop or at least mitigate almost every one, whether natural or man-made. This indictment is levelled at both Southern and Northern governments which, in a ma-cabre set of gavottes and murderous game-playing, have inadver-tently or deliberately conspired to deprive millions of people of their homes, their livelihoods, their dignity, their humanity, and far too often, their lives. These dances and games have been variously la-belled: 'The Cold War', 'National Sovereignty', 'Political Will' (or lack thereof), 'The Domino Theory', and the 'New World Order'. Most of them have been characterized by high degrees of brutality, myopia, self-interest and — not too strong a word — murder.

The British Government's unrelenting manipulation of the Inter-national Committee of the Red Cross (ICRC) during the worst days of the Biafran War, and its covert but eager supply of arms to the Nigerian Government is mirrored almost precisely a quarter century later by the French supply of arms, aid, diplomatic succour and troops to the genocidal Hutu regime in Rwanda. President Nixon's deliberate 'tilt' towards a Pakistani Government that was engaged in one of history's most brutal attempts to crush a nationalist uprising was not based on support for Pakistan's national integrity. It was based solely on Pakistan's usefulness to the United States during those months as a broker for Henry Kissinger's secret efforts to open an American dia-logue with China.

The million (or so) Bengalis who died, and the ten million who fled across the borders into India in 1971, were mirrored eight years later in Afghanistan, after the Soviet invasion of 1979. The ensuing civil war and the internationalization of the crisis by Western governments —

primarily the United States — led to the exodus of between five and six million people into Iran and Pakistan, *almost 40 per cent of the country's entire population.* Between 1978 and 1989, an estimated 1.3 million people died, of whom 60 per cent were civilians.[37]

Repeated requests from the Government of Ethiopia in 1983 for emergency food aid were largely ignored by Western governments, inured to what they believed, or chose to believe was exaggeration by a brutal, pro-Soviet regime. The US and Britain had stopped their own bilateral assistance and managed to spike various forms of multilateral assistance as well, ignoring the pleas for assistance until their noses were rubbed in a disaster that eventually drove a million people from their homes. It also took the lives of something between five hundred thousand and a million Ethiopians. The Cold War had left Somalia fractured and destabilized when a drought occurred only a few years later. The first appeal from the Government of Somalia to USAID for emergency drought assistance was made in February, 1987. The appeal, which the Somalian Government costed at $750 000 for aid to an estimated 880 000 people, was dismissed as alarmist.[38] Stonewalling, bickering over numbers, and the active deterrence of other donors by USAID marked the following months, and set the stage for Somalia's long downward slide into anarchy and death. Between 1989 and 1992, Canada alone spent more than 1300 times in Somalia what the Somalian Government had requested of USAID in 1987: more than Canada spent in a year in all the rest of Africa. And when Canada finally scurried away with the others, there was little to show for the effort.[39]

Lesson 2: Competition, co-ordination and evaluation

Competition between NGOs for the hearts and minds of donors is not new. But as the years passed, with the advent of more and more NGOs, with a growing need for development money and an increasing number of disasters, and with a prolonged recession in the early 1990s, competition has increased. There are certainly admirable examples of efforts to co-ordinate fundraising appeals. A joint Disaster Relief Agency was created by Dutch NGOs in 1993. Similar arrangements, usually of an *ad hoc* nature, have been tried in other countries. The Disasters Emergency Committee (DEC) in Britain has seven participating organizations,* and between 1966 and 1993 they ran 35 joint appeals. But getting into the DEC is extremely difficult, and other organizations with legitimate field operations are unable to benefit.

---

*Red Cross, CAFOD, Christian Aid, Oxfam, Save the Children, ActionAid and Help the Aged.

Some do better on their own anyway. World Vision, regarded by other NGOs as something of a maverick because of its evangelical roots and orientation, has one of the most powerful fundraising machines in the business. Its fundraising messages rely heavily on images of disaster, and as a result, it has often been accused of thriving on the pornography of poverty. In fundraising terms, it is the fourteenth largest fundraising charity in the United States, and at $209 million in private donor support in 1993, it was by far the most successful one operating internationally.* In Canada, Australia and New Zealand, World Vision raises more money than all other NGOs in those countries combined, and it has established a good foothold in Britain and mainland Europe. Like World Vision, Médecins sans Frontières, another fast-growing swashbuckler, has been accused of using short-term 'starving baby' tactics to raise money, regardless of the damage this might do to longer-term development understanding among donors. Bernard Kouchner, MSF's founder and later Minister for Development Co-operation and Humanitarian Action in the Government of France, endorsed *la loi du tapage* (the law of hype) in his 1986 book, *Charité business*. He argued that it is 'necessary to popularize misfortunes and make use of feelings of remorse'.[40]

Disaster appeals are well known within NGOs as building blocks for longer-term donor relationships. Many organizations with absolutely no disaster experience or qualifications, therefore, have begun taking to the newspapers with advertisements for relief work. In July 1994, at the height of the Rwandan massacres and the exodus to Zaire, Match International, a small Canadian women's development organization, went into competition with the Canadian branches of the Red Cross, CARE, Oxfam and World Vision. While people were dropping dead of starvation on the road to Goma, it aimed to 'supply kerosene stoves to stop the destruction of forests by refugees seeking fuel'. More cynical perhaps, the American Jewish Joint Distribution Committee and the African-American Institute, neither with any serious African relief capacity or experience, took out an emotive, full-page advertisement in the *New York Times* appealing for money: 'The power to snatch life from the jaws of death rests in your hands'.[41]

NGO co-ordination in the field is a different sort of problem. When governments do it, as was the case in Nicaragua during the 1980s, NGOs can lose their independence of action. They can become instruments of government policy, and they can become involved in the delivery of politicized and wrong-headed assistance. Jointchurchaid in Biafra was probably one of the most impressive examples of NGO

---

*Small by comparison, CARE raised $48.2 million in 1993, and Save the Children US raised $41.1 million (Source: *Chronicle of Philanthropy*, 1 November 1994)

self-coordination. There have been other examples: in Somalia, Ethiopia, Angola, and in the Oxfam Cambodia consortium of 1979–80. There are, however, horror stories about inept and costly competition. In 1980 there were 37 foreign agencies working in the Kao I Dang refugee camp in Thailand, one frequently visited by foreign journalists and politicians, and therefore important to fundraising. Cambodia historian William Shawcross acknowledged the thousands of lives saved in Kao I Dang, but he observed that 'the level of medical care offered there in early 1980 was probably higher than that which could be obtained by any ordinary peasant or city dweller anywhere in South-east Asia or most of the Third World. (One ICRC delegate worked out that there were more medical teams on the border than in four African countries combined.)'[42] In a large Rwandan refugee camp in Goma, Zaire, there were 83 operational NGOs at the end of 1994, and some 170 international NGOs were registered in Kigali.

The problem of field co-ordination is not restricted to NGOs. Bilateral donors are often the worst instigators of competition and miscoordination, and there are 16 different UN agencies with a mandate to work in relief and emergency situations. Until a smaller number are *effectively* mandated and adequately funded to co-ordinate relief operations, including the gathering of up-to-date information and the development of a rapid response mechanism, these problems will remain. Perhaps the time is at last ripe for the establishment of a standby UN police force that can be deployed quickly in order to avoid the spectacle of the Secretary General begging members of the General Assembly for troops.*

Somehow too, a longer-term development perspective must be maintained, perhaps by requiring the active involvement of *development* agencies in relief efforts. Learning would have to be part of the new mandate. Evaluation of relief work is poor, usually little more than lists of what was provided. The same mistakes are therefore made over and over again: the same scrambles, the same problems of inadequate or inappropriate supplies, the same sort of highly dedicated but often inexperienced relief workers trying to figure out what to do.

Lesson 3: Independence and the continuum

Ironically, many of the larger Northern NGOs that began with relief as their main purpose, have returned to it as an increasingly important

---

*In January 1995, the Secretary General appealed to sixty nations for peacekeepers to deal with lawlessness in Zaire's Rwandan refugee camps. Every one of them said no.

part of their work, in part because of support from UN agencies. But the move to greater reliance on NGOs is not limited to the UN. In the Netherlands, official emergency aid channelled through NGOs increased by 150 per cent between 1990 and 1992, and the Foreign Ministry says that 'Dutch NGOs, which have a relatively limited operational capacity at present, have a duty to strengthen this capacity'.[43] British refugee and disaster relief, programmed mainly through UN agencies and the Red Cross in the early 1980s, is increasingly channelled through British NGOs, and by the early 1990s, 75 per cent of British food aid was going the same way. Over 40 per cent of SIDA spending on emergencies and refugees in 1992–3 was channelled through Swedish NGOs, an amount representing roughly half of what was available in matching grants for their development programmes. In Australia, 1993–4 financial support to NGOs for emergencies and refugees represented almost 40 per cent of all financing available to NGOs from all government sources. And in 1991 the European Commission provided three times more to NGOs for food, emergencies and refugees than it did for development.[44]

NGOs have demonstrated that they can be a fast and comparatively efficient means of responding to emergencies. As happens with any large new injection of cash, however, the growing use of NGOs has enlarged the problems as well as the opportunities. Government support provided on concessional and even cost-plus terms can be a powerful magnet, especially when money for development programmes is shrinking, and when the administrative procedures for getting emergency funds are less demanding. Increased fundraising competition for development work can also persuade an NGO to emphasize disaster appeals. In order to establish itself in Australia, for example, CARE has since 1987 devoted itself almost entirely to emergency appeals. The two biggest British NGOs, Oxfam and Save the Children, saw their private donor income increase in the early 1990s only because of emergency appeals.

A further danger is that some NGOs will become little more than contractors for governments and UN agencies. The greater the level of financial dependence, the more fragile the degree of independence. NGOs might do well to recall Henry Kissinger's 1976 comment: 'Disaster relief is becoming increasingly a major instrument of our foreign policy'.[45]

More money from some sources, particularly UN agencies, does offer the possibility, however, of better co-ordination. And it has done something else. Some NGOs have recognized that with greater funding comes greater responsibility. More care must be taken in the way emergency assistance is provided and portrayed. To that end, eight of the oldest and largest NGO networks have developed a self-policing code of conduct for implementing disaster relief.* The Code says that the humanitarian imperative comes first, that aid should not be used to further a particular political or religious standpoint, and that signatories should not act as instruments of government. It also calls for greater involvement of, and respect for beneficiaries, especially in the way they are represented in fundraising and media campaigns.

However, more money and a code of conduct are only part of the sea change that is taking place for NGOs. The rapid growth in emergency budgets has altered thinking about the relationship between relief and development. There is a great deal of important new writing about the need for a more comprehensive approach to security, human rights and vulnerability. There is recognition of a 'continuum' between relief, rehabilitation and development, and of the need to de-isolate emergencies, placing them within a much broader historical and economic context.

On the ground, there are some basic lessons that have been learned over the years. They may not always be applied. They may not, in fact, be applied very often, but some important ones are contained the findings of a Harvard University International Relief and Development Project, and they are worth quoting:

o Both relief and development programmes should be more concerned with increasing local capacities and reducing vulnerabilities than with providing goods, services or technical assistance. In fact, goods, services or technical assistance should be provided only insofar as they support sustainable development by increasing local capacities and reducing local vulnerabilities.
o The way that such resources are transferred must be held to the same test.
o Programming must not be solely preoccupied with meeting urgent physical and material needs, but must integrate such needs into efforts that address the social, organizational, motivational and attitudinal elements of the situation as well.[46]

Today, calls for mapping, early warning, disaster preparedness and prevention abound. But so far, studies and exhortation have done little for Liberia or Sri Lanka, and the dozen or more tragic disasters that have flared in places like Tajikistan, Chechnya, Sierra Leone, Gaza, Zaire, Central America and the former Yugoslavia.

And they did nothing for Rwanda, a country beset by land shortage, poverty and generations of ethnic tension. In the early 1990s, in the

---

*The groups included ICRC and the Red Cross and Red Crescent Societies, Caritas Internationalis, Catholic Relief Services, the International Save the Children Alliance, the Lutheran World Federation, Oxfam and the World Council of Churches.

midst of growing political and ethnic chaos, France generously supplied its faltering government with weapons, rocket launchers, helicopter parts and even troops. Rwanda was a tinderbox, and everybody knew it. David Waller wrote a book about it: *Rwanda: Which way now?*[47] In 1992, NGOs such as Human Rights Watch and Amnesty International began warning of impending disaster. A 1993 UN human rights report said, 'There is a certain élite which, in order to cling to power, is continuing to fuel ethnic hatred.'[48] Although there were internationally assisted peace talks, most of the recommendations made in these reports were never implemented.

When the massacres began early in April 1994, there were 1700 UN peacekeeping troops in Rwanda, there to bolster a peace accord signed the year before. Because the force was inadequate to deal with the 'sudden' problem that arose, the UN Security Council was faced with the choice of doing more, or doing less. Fifteen days after the butchery began, it chose the latter option, cutting the force to 270 personnel. The murder rate skyrocketed. In May, UN Secretary General Boutros Boutros-Ghali asked the Security Council to sanction more troops, and this time they agreed. But there was precious little action. Member governments were — how can one describe it? — slow to respond. Nothing happened in May, or June or July. An almost hysterical flock of NGOs, trying to cope with the 10 000 refugees crossing the borders into Zaire, Tanzania and Burundi *every hour*, demanded action. And they denounced the UN to every passing journalist (of whom there were plenty). Once again, the UN took the blame for the knots and procrastination imposed on it by its member governments; the same members paying for pious research into disaster preparedness, mapping, human rights and conflict resolution. During the last half of 1994, the Rwandan crisis cost the international community $700 million, roughly double what Rwanda had received in development assistance in 1992, and many times more than it would have cost to send UN troops when the massacres began.

In fact, as the share of emergency expenditure that goes to NGOs has increased, there has been little apparent action on preparedness, prevention or 'the continuum'. 'Apparent', however, may be an important word. That something cannot be seen does not negate its existence. International and local NGOs, along with hundreds of community-based organizations, played an important role in the peaceful conclusion to decades of South African strife. External political lobbying by anti-apartheid groups and internal pressure from a vast number of organizations, small and large, helped first to lay the groundwork for negotiation, and then to ensure that negotiations would be productive. NGOs and church organizations are given credit for important contributions to the political resolution of Central

121

America's civil wars during the 1980s.[49] Unsung, NGOs and UN agencies are at work in other places — elsewhere in Africa, in the Middle East, the Balkans, the Caucasus, Central America — struggling with conflict resolution, working in camps, and on indirect measures to prevent incipient disasters from occurring, and from reoccurring.

Lesson 4: Politics

There are other lessons to be drawn from NGO emergency work. Despite great efforts on the part of most NGOs to appear neutral or 'apolitical' during the Cold War, the record reveals something different. In most of the major disasters of the past two decades, NGOs have repeatedly provided relief, succour, foreign exchange and legitimacy — often on an accidental but sometimes deliberate basis — to combatants. This was true in Biafra, and in the support provided by the Oxfam consortium to the Vietnam-backed Cambodian regime. It was true in the choices made by NGOs in whether to work inside Ethiopia or with the Tigray and Eritrean liberation groups. It was true in Central America. Sometimes NGOs have — unwittingly or in the name of a greater good — provided protection for thugs and killers: the Khmer Rouge and Hutu murderers in the refugee camps of Thailand and Zaire. In Somalia, the first guinea-pig of new-world-order humanitarian intervention, they ignored corruption and extortion, paid protection money to warlords, encouraged and mostly applauded massive foreign military intervention, and then many of them ran away with the armies of the world when the guinea-pig died.[50]

At the time, and in retrospect, much of this was understandable. But the British organization, African Rights, questions the new, expansive humanitarian role that NGOs have taken on. It believes that whenever there is a clash between the charitable imperative on one hand, and on the other, principles of justice, rights, conflict resolution and advocacy, fundraising NGOs will always go with the charitable imperative. They will submerge and sometimes subvert more important questions which in the long run might reduce the need for charity. 'The mistakes may have been made in good faith, but they must be acknowledged openly. To pretend that mandates do not conflict, and that humanitarianism can provide a political and human rights programme, would be a dangerous dishonesty.' African Rights calls for an evaluation of the NGO role: not a standard evaluation dealing with efficiency, the continuum and problems of co-ordination, but 'a thorough-going examination of the entire [range of] principles on which responses to political emergencies are mounted . . . The enlargement of a charitable mandate into areas of lobbying and advocacy on political and human rights issues is a major step with enormous implications. A commitment to human rights cannot be picked up and set down at will: the watchword for any human rights activism is consistency'.[51]

The downstream effects of the changes facing NGOs in emergency situations — new and more political roles, greater physical danger, huge injections of money, raised expectations and increased pressure on development budgets — seem so far to be only peripheral concerns for NGOs, UN agencies and bilateral donors. NGOs are mostly too busy to notice that they are becoming caught, sometimes to their short-term financial benefit, between powerful competing institutional and political demands. They are unclear on how to balance delivery and advocacy. There is a very good possibility that they may simply be a convenient way for the international system to let itself off the hook of responsibility. The overall impact of these changes on the scope, direction and purpose of voluntary action for development has already been enormous, and it is not likely to diminish.

Today, war is a thing that takes place mainly in the Third World. The Stockholm International Peace Research Institute calculates that 40 million people died between 1945 and 1992, in 165 major armed conflicts.[52] During this entire period, not a single person was ever charged or tried by an international body for war crimes. (This may be changing, however. In 1993 and 1994 the UN created war crimes tribunals to deal with atrocities in both Rwanda and former Yugoslavia. Resisted by many governments, the tribunals' early work was financed to a large extent by non-governmental institutions: the Soros and MacArthur Foundations, and their greatest encouragement came from NGOs like Human Rights Watch and Médecins sans Frontières.)

In 1974 there were 2.4 million refugees. By 1984 the number had risen to 10.5 million. In 1993 there were 23 million refugees, plus 26 million 'internally displaced' people, like those in the camps of Angola, Somalia and the Sudan. The total, therefore, was a staggering 49 million, more people than live in Switzerland, Belgium, the Netherlands, Austria and all of Scandinavia combined. Most of these people are in the South. Half are children, most of the adults are women, and as many as half receive no assistance at all. The total US Government assistance for disaster relief was less than $12 million in 1964. By 1991 it had risen to $1.2 billion, and had cost over $6 billion in the previous 25 years. American NGOs, which spent less than a million dollars on relief in 1964, spent more than five hundred times that much over the next 25 years.[53]

After a visit to Moscow in 1919, American journalist Lincoln Steffens said, 'I have seen the future, and it works'. It didn't, actually. And it still doesn't.

CHAPTER VII

Mixed messages: NGOs and the Northern public

God down, Devil up in French survey

PARIS (Reuter) — Belief in God is declining, but belief in the devil is rising in France, an opinion poll on religious attitudes showed Wednesday. The CSA Institute poll for *Le Monde* newspaper found 61 per cent of French people believed more or less in God, compared with 66 per cent eight years ago. Thirty-four per cent said they believe in the devil, up from 24 per cent in 1986.[1]

ALTHOUGH 'STRAW POLLS' began almost two centuries ago, public opinion polling has become very big business in the past three decades. Most widely used by political parties and private sector firms to test ideas, products and attitudes, it has become increasingly popular among governmental and some non-governmental development organizations as a means of investigating public attitudes towards development assistance.

Here is what ten years of polls told the Canadian International Development Agency (CIDA) about Canadian attitudes in 1994:

○ support for government spending on foreign aid remained fairly stable from 1979 to 1983, rose sharply in the mid-1980s, and has been declining since then;
○ since 1991, more Canadians have chosen aid for emergencies over aid for long-term development when asked which they believe it is most important for Canada to provide;
○ the majority of Canadians are neutral in their opinions on aid. They do not think of aid very often, do not feel it has an impact on them, and do not consider themselves part of any global community. Two out of five Canadians are neutrals who tend to support aid, and one out of five are neutrals who tend to oppose it.[2]

Similar sorts of findings were reported throughout Europe and North America in the late 1980s and early 1990s. Public support for development assistance dropped from 85 per cent in Norway in 1986 to 77 per cent in 1990. In Sweden, traditionally high support had plummeted by 1991 to only 56 per cent among the important 25–34 age group. A 1993 opinion poll in the United States found that American support for economic assistance to other countries had declined since 1986, and that 'Americans do not view foreign aid, given its track record, as warranting continued support . . . The public does not have confidence that aid is helping to improve conditions in other countries or reaching the people it is intended to reach.'[3] It is generally received wisdom that recession, aid fatigue and compassion fatigue have taken a disastrous toll on public support, and that as a result, in some of the more extreme scenarios, development assistance as we know it may not survive.

The 'sky is falling' school of public affairs is not new, at least in the development community. A 1983 report observed darkly that 'the climate for aid is deteriorating'.[4] As far back as 1969, the Pearson Commission Report stated that 'public support for development is now flagging. In some of the rich countries its feasibility, even its very purpose, is in question. The climate surrounding foreign aid programmes is heavy with disillusion and distrust . . . we have reached a point of crisis.'

Public opinion: roadkill on the Infobahn

The trends of downward public support in Norway, Sweden, Canada and the United States cited above are worth examining in closer detail. In each case, the 'downward trend' is debatable, transitory, or it is actually false. By 1993, for example, support for development assistance in Norway had rebounded from its 1990 drop, and had returned to the all-time 1985 high level of 85 per cent. In other words, public support for development assistance in Norway was never higher. In Sweden, the decline that began in 1988 reversed itself three years later, and the 25–34 age group that had registered only 56 per cent positive in 1991, had become 72 per cent positive by 1994. While Canadian polls show that support has fluctuated over the years, the 1993 level was almost precisely what it was in 1979.[5]

The 1993 US poll is particularly interesting, because there were, in fact, two polls conducted at almost the same time by different firms, both using questions and comparative data derived from an earlier 1986 poll. Both the new polls used the same techniques, the same probability sampling, and both claimed to vary in their findings by plus or minus three per cent. But they emerged with quite different findings. One found a lack of public confidence, and concluded that 'Americans do not view foreign aid . . . as warranting continued support', while the other, conducted only three months later, found that 'Despite Americans' domestic concerns, they strongly favour assistance to other nations'. A 1995 poll found 80 per cent in favour of aid to countries in genuine need. When informed of actual spending levels on aid, a strong majority favoured maintaining or increasing it.[6]

125

In the European Community, the results of three consistent and comparable opinion polls (1983, 1987 and 1991) are revealing: in 1991, 80 per cent of European respondents — considerably more than in earlier years — considered it important or even very important to '[help] poor countries in Africa, South America, Asia, etc . . .'. Further, 86 per cent of Europeans were 'For (very much, or to some extent) helping Third World countries'.[7] Responding to a 1994 Swiss poll, 78 per cent said that aid should remain the same or be increased, a slight improvement over 1984; while in Japan the trend moved the other way by 2 per cent between 1991 and 1992, but remained over 80 per cent. In Australia, 73 per cent approve of aid, and only 11 per cent disapprove.[8]

Aid agency fatigue

Even though public opinion seems generally supportive of development assistance, there are reasons for concern. Professional pollsters are the first to decry the weakness, abuse and limitations of public polling. While polling offers a simple and cost-effective way to learn what a cross-section of the public thinks on an issue, polls can be wrong. They are also open to rampant abuse and misinterpretation. Depending on the context, the words used, how questions are phrased and whether information is provided in advance, opinions can be badly skewed (or easily manipulated) on any emotive issue: capital punishment, abortion, sex education in schools, immigration, gun control. A 1985 *Los Angeles Times* survey found that when Americans were asked whether the country is now spending 'too little', 'too much' or 'the right amount' on 'assistance to the poor', there was a ten to one view that too little was being spent. When the same question was asked about 'welfare' spending, 42 per cent said spending was too high.[9]

Manipulation notwithstanding, can it be concluded from the evidence that we have reached 'the point of crisis' in public support that Pearson described in 1969? Despite fairly good evidence to the contrary, there is a persistent, strong, and perhaps irrational sense in many parts of the aid establishment that we have. Why? It may be that the crisis, and the climate that is heavy with disillusion and distrust actually lies *within* aid agencies, and does not extend as far into public opinion as is thought. Examples of the crisis within the aid establishment can be found in the United States, where a wide variety of respected pro-aid NGO and advocacy groups began calling in the late 1980s and early 1990s for a fundamental overhaul, and in some cases, the complete abolition of USAID because of the subversion of its aims and objectives to political and commercial interests.[10] A detailed 1993 interview-study of senior Canadian development executives found the community 'marked by pessimism and despair' over budget cuts, politicization and the rise of commercial priorities.[11] Speaking at the 1995 World Summit for Social Development in Copenhagen, Richard Jolly, Acting Director of UNICEF said, 'We should cut through the cynicism and despair which at times seems to entangle the corridors of this conference'.[12] Rather than public aid fatigue, there is strong evidence of an 'aid administration fatigue'. *The Reality of Aid 94*, a joint NGO review of development assistance, says that 'among politicians and commentators, there appears to be a lack of confidence in aid, which translates itself into nervousness about asserting the needs of the poor overseas in a time of austerity at home.'[13]

Several factors may be contributing to this 'aid administration fatigue':

○ the chronic inability of committed aid managers to de-link official development assistance from commercial and political interests; a concomitant inability among aid agencies to focus on human priority concerns;
○ criticism of the commercialization and politicization of aid from governments and people in the South, the very people it is supposed to help;
○ failure of the infrastructure, capital-intensive and 'integrated development' approaches of the 1960s and 1970s; divisive internal debates over structural adjustment in the 1980s and 1990s;
○ the decline of many Southern economies and the collapse of some;
○ deep and discouraging cuts to many aid budgets in the 1990s (FINNIDA was slashed by 62 per cent between 1991 and 1993, and Italian aid was reduced by 26 per cent in 1993. Canadian aid will fall from 0.5 per cent of GNP in 1988 to a projected 0.3 per cent by 1997);
○ a declining level of direct control and involvement because of the increasing use of consulting firms, commercial executing agencies and NGOs;
○ a public belief, strongly expressed in most opinion polls in Europe and North America that national governments are not the most useful or effective means of channelling development assistance to the Third World (this is discussed further, below);
○ the 'greying' of aid management. The phenomenal growth through the 1960s and early 1970s of bilateral, multilateral and non-governmental organizations slowed in the 1980s, and the 1990s have been marked in many by severe 'down-sizing'. Individuals who entered the field in the 1960s and 1970s have reached the top, and will not move on until they retire, which for most will be well into the next century. There are fewer and fewer opportunities for

young, enthusiastic managers. 'Age', the poet observed, 'makes a winter in the heart, an autumn in the mind.'

Donations: another measure of opinion

There are not many other trustworthy measures of public support for international development assistance, but a tangible one has to do with donations to NGOs. Donations are made consciously by individuals, over and above the taxes they contribute to official development assistance. Trustworthy statistics on national giving to NGOs are problematic, however there is at least comparative consistency over time in OECD figures. Between 1985 and 1993, bilateral aid disbursements rose by 68 per cent. During the same period, NGO spending rose by 103 per cent. More recent statistics, however, show an even greater spread in the rate of growth: between 1990 and 1993, bilateral disbursements grew barely 4 per cent, while NGO disbursements rose by almost 24 per cent.[14] The general trend, therefore, was one of continuous and relative growth over a decade.

Some of the largest Northern NGOs are actually growing both consistently and rapidly. The private Canadian cash income of World Vision Canada rose 25 per cent between 1991 and 1994. Christian Children's Fund grew 43 per cent in New Zealand between 1994 and 1995. In Japan, Foster Parents Plan grew by 25 per cent between 1991 and 1992, and in the Netherlands, between 1986 and 1991, the same organization grew by 104 per cent. In Britain, ActionAid had a 15 per cent increase between 1992 and 1993; Christian Aid grew 46 per cent between 1991 and 1992. Plan International grew from a worldwide income of $144 million in 1990, to $207 million in 1994, a 44 per cent increase. Although its income for emergencies tends to fluctuate wildly, Save the Children grew from £56 million in 1991 to £100 million in 1992, a 79 per cent increase.[15] In fact among all British charities, the biggest gain — 20 per cent after adjustment for inflation — was registered by the international agencies. Religious missionary work was next (at 7 per cent), while arts, environment and animal protection lagged far behind.[16]

In the United States, the first six NGOs (listed alphabetically) in the 1993 InterAction Directory recorded average growth rates in private donor income of 28.9 per cent between 1990 and 1991.* Some of the larger NGOs such as SCF(US), World Vision and Childreach were relatively flat, but CARE donations rose 27 per cent between 1991 and 1993, and Oxfam America had an increase of 15.6 per cent between 1990 and 1991.[17]

---

*These were ACCION, Adventist Development and Relief Agency, the African-American Institute, AMREF, Africare and the Aga Khan Foundation.

128

It is not difficult to find holes in such statistics. Many of the organizations mentioned are heavily engaged in emergency relief work, and there were, during the years cited, a wide variety of major disaster appeals. This does not in any way validate the 'aid fatigue' argument, however. Quite the opposite, in fact, it demonstrates that humanitarian appeals, at least, have not lost ground. The same is not true for those many NGOs not involved with relief work that *have* experienced falling income in recent years. This may be for reasons that have nothing to do with 'aid fatigue':

o the genuine impact of recession. This may have some effect on donor giving, but not necessarily on attitudes;
o government cutbacks and the growing need for welfare assistance at home. Again, this may affect donor giving, but not necessarily attitudes. As noted above, it is certainly not the case in Britain;
o the ever-increasing number of NGOs has made fundraising more difficult. Growth of the 'pie' may be outpacing inflation, but it must be divided among more organizations: 1600 NGOs in OECD Member countries in 1980, and well over 3000 in 1993.[18] If donors are moving increasingly towards 'name-brand NGOs' like Save the Children, Médecins sans Frontières and Oxfam (as their growing income seems to indicate in several countries), the problem may well be aid *agency* fatigue, rather than aid fatigue. A 1992 British Social Attitudes Survey found that 'three-quarters of those questioned agreed that it is difficult to decide where to give, because there are too many charities'.[19]
o donors to international NGOs (and international NGOs themselves) are being drawn more and more towards emergencies. Hence the obvious and sometimes remarkable growth of organizations with emergency appeals. This may well lead to a decline for those working only in longer-term development, but it does not indicate a decline in support for international assistance;
o the increasing fundraising sophistication and growing international media presence of larger 'transnational NGOs' such as CARE, Médecins sans Frontières, World Vision, and Plan International is drawing donors away from smaller organizations. Smaller NGOs may be mistaking a loss of market share for 'aid fatigue'.

The quality of support

General public support for development assistance is probably high, even surprisingly high. And pessimism in the aid community notwithstanding, public opinion does not appear to be undergoing any profound downward shifts. There are, however, a number of serious

129

concerns about the *quality* of public opinion. Daniel Yankelovich argues that public judgement is a much more useful concept. A prominent American pollster, Yankelovich defines public judgement to mean a particular form of public opinion that exhibits '(1) more thoughtfulness, more weighing of alternatives, more genuine engagement with the issue, more taking into account a wide variety of factors than ordinary public opinion as measured in public opinion polls, and (2) more emphasis on the normative, valuing, ethical side of questions than on the factual, informational side.'[20]

If more public opinion polls investigated the knowledge levels on which people base an opinion, the need for Yankelovich's distinction would be obvious. In the few cases where they do, the results are depressing. A 1993 Lou Harris poll discovered that Americans know within a few percentage points how much the federal government spends on social security, medicare and defence. But for some reason, people believe that 20 per cent of government spending goes to foreign aid, a figure more than twenty times the actual amount.[21] The problem persists: a 1995 University of Maryland poll found that 75 per cent of Americans believed the US to be spending 'too much' on foreign aid. Most thought that aid consumed about 18 per cent of the budget. When questioned further, they said that a reduction to three per cent — triple the actual figure — would be too severe. But when they were told the actual amount, many still stubbornly favoured a cut.[22]

All questions relating to whether the aid budget is too high, too low, or 'just right', become tainted by this sort of dumbness. In 1994, the Times Mirror Centre for People and the Press conducted a comprehensive, 10 000-person international survey, on opinions about the media in eight countries: the United States, Canada, Mexico, Britain, France, Germany, Italy and Spain. It found that knowledge of current events varied tremendously, but for those concerned about public awareness, there were disturbing results. Three-quarters of British respondents could not say who Boutros Boutros-Ghali was. In France, almost half could not say what ethnic group had surrounded Sarajevo. Of five questions, 37 per cent of the American respondents got all five wrong. One of the questions was 'Who is the President of Russia?'[23]

Many polls show that the public does not trust government agencies, and there is a high rate of scepticism about whether aid actually reaches those in need. In Canada, roughly 80 per cent believe Canadian aid to be effective, but oddly, 81 per cent believe that most aid sent to poor countries never gets to the people who most need it.[24] (This sort of contradiction occurs in virtually every poll.) While beliefs about the positive effects of aid are relatively strong in the United States, only 18 per cent believe that the US Government does the best job in delivering it. In 1993, a remarkable 47 per cent favoured the

United Nations, and 16 per cent favoured NGOs.[25] In a Canadian poll, 52 per cent said that aid should be channelled mostly through NGOs, with 38 per cent favouring government.[26] A broad 1991 European poll showed that 41 per cent believed the most useful aid to Third World countries was being provided by the UN and its agencies. Nineteen per cent believed that NGOs were most effective, while only 8 per cent cited their national government.[27]

What all this demonstrates is that the knowledge base around development issues is extremely low, that people in most countries do not understand 'development', and would rather provide assistance for emergencies than for long-term development assistance. It also shows that trust in government programmes is universally low, a rather dangerous statistic for the health of official development assistance.

The meaning of public opinion

Daniel Yankelovich believes that there is a three-stage process involved in moving from ill-informed and dangerously fickle 'mass opinion' to something resembling the more thoughtful 'public judgement' upon which democracy, in an ideal world, should be based. The first stage is one of 'consciousness-raising'. Consciousness-raising, he says, is more than simple awareness, it is a blend of increased awareness with concern and readiness for action, as can be seen in the women's movement, the environmental movement, or responses to the danger of AIDS. There are usually a number of serious obstacles to genuine consciousness-raising. One highly variable factor is time: some things take longer than others. The modern women's movement has taken more than a century to get to its present position, while consciousness-raising on AIDS took less than a decade. Another factor is the 'cogency of events'. Nothing advances consciousness-raising as forcefully as events that dramatize the issue. Other factors include the perceived applicability of the issue to one's self, the concreteness and clarity of the issue, the credibility of information sources, and the quantity of information the issue receives.

Yankelovich calls his second stage, 'working through'. Sometimes this is relatively easy, often it is not. And the result may depend upon how the consciousness-raising was carried out. 'Working through' means, essentially, that attitudes must change along with overt behaviour. An issue will be poorly launched into stage two if:

o people do not understand what the possibilities for action are;
o if they are given insufficient and inadequate choice;
o if they do not grasp what the consequences of the various choices would be;

131

o if their attention is diverted away from an issue before they have a chance to come to grips with it;
o if they are given contradictory information about it;
o or if they believe those who propose the action are acting in bad faith.[28]

The problem in moving from stages one to two on an issue has to do with the way news is reported. The media are masters at raising public levels of anxiety on issues, but journalists move from one problem to the next as if their only purpose was to report bad news. Political leadership is another problem. Increasingly, leaders look like followers, attempting to find out what the public thinks on an issue before taking action or expressing an opinion of their own. Yankelovich gives an American example which could apply to almost any country where development co-operation is concerned (the actual issue has been replaced with an 'x'):

> In a democracy, the function of the leadership is to alert the public to the existence of any serious threat, define it, develop a strategy (or alternative strategies) for dealing with it, and seek to mobilize and focus the energies of the people to meet it. One of the principal reasons for America's failure of political will in confronting the 'x' challenge is that America's leadership has not presented the public with realistic choices, and on occasion has actually created obstacles deflecting the public from working through the issue.[29]

Much of the necessary 'working through' on important issues is given over to 'experts', and public opinion is either manipulated or ignored. The public's frame of reference can be a partial substitute for knowledge, however. If *values* are resolved correctly, technical solutions will follow. There is an obvious opportunity here for development co-operation, because all opinion polls from all countries show a very strong public desire to help when people elsewhere are in trouble.

Stage Three, 'resolution', may be extremely difficult, because it involves cognitive, emotional and moral resolution, a clarification of thinking and a recognition of the ways in which other issues relate to the subject in question. It requires an ability to grasp and accept the consequences of the available choices, and to 'do the right thing' despite the personal costs or sacrifices that may be involved.

The media

A commonly asked question in many opinion polls has to do with a person's source of information. Not surprisingly, in most countries television is the most important source of information on the Third

132

World and development issues. There is almost no doubt, however, that television in particular and the media in general are doing an inadequate job of consciousness-raising. That the media concentrate on disaster and bad news is not news. What is more problematic is their preoccupation with quantitative data rather than qualitative analysis of the context in which an event takes place.

Hemingway once wrote about his career as a journalist: 'After I finished high school I went to Kansas City and worked on a paper. It was regular newspaper work. Who shot whom? Who broke into what? Where? When? How? But never why, not really why?'[30] The situation has not improved. With the closure in recent years of more and more foreign news bureaux, with the increased reliance on television news wholesalers and wire services, and with increased commercial competition for viewer audiences, much news about the Third World has become authorless, anchorless and impossible to understand or follow. It is, as ITN editor Nik Gowing says, random, fickle and incomplete. Somalia became big news well before the US/UN invasion, while Angola and the Sudan, with similar scales of misery, did not. Liberia was an on-going, low-level news story for years, while Sierra Leone next door, with a situation arguably as bad, if not worse, was almost never reported. Rwanda, hot news in the summer of 1994, was flickering only dimly on the media radar by the end of the year, despite a continuing human disaster.

A ten-year study of foreign news coverage on US network television concluded that between the mid-1970s and the mid-1980s, when television basically replaced radio and the print media as the primary source of public information, and when the technology became available to access international stories faster and cheaper, there was no marked increase in foreign news coverage.[31] A ten-year study of Third World coverage in the New York *Times* and the Chicago *Tribune* found that conflicts dominated the news and that there was a stereotyped bias against the South which fostered 'images of Third World nations as political systems rife with conflict'.[32] A two-month 1992 analysis of ten French newspapers and journals, and the 8 p.m. news bulletins of the two major television stations, found the same thing. Although there were obviously differences between outlets, the image of the South was, globally, negative: it was portrayed as a largely abstract and almost singular society, prone to war, famine, disease and natural disaster. The most common stories, derived almost exclusively from Northern observers, dealt with 'the incompetence of [the South's] governments, the misery and submission of its peoples, the assistance needed by its children, the corruption of its administration'.[33]

In 1979, Mort Rosenblum, a seasoned Associated Press foreign correspondent, wrote that there was a crowning irony to the poverty of

133

international news reporting: 'Producers and consumers both want better coverage. And coverage could be improved, almost easily, at no added cost. To do better, we need not crowd out domestic news, or the juicy scandals and comics which help sell newspapers . . . But since few consumers know how easy it is to make themselves heard, there is little change.'[34] Editors and executives take silence as tacit approval, he said, and could easily be persuaded to include more and better coverage if pressured to do so by readers. Fifteen years later, with a lot more experience and a stint as Editor of the *International Herald Tribune* behind him, Rosenblum was asking the same question: 'Who stole the news?' And his advice was the same. 'We can get the news back, with little fuss and no more money than we are already spending. But we have to decide to do it. Readers must say what they want. Correspondents must provide it. And then, if editors open the gates, the rest will follow.'[35] No one will open a bureau in Utopia, he warns, but concerted audience influence can work.

Today, added to the problems identified by journalists themselves, there are two new trends: a major blurring of the line between news and entertainment, and the populism of television news. Along with many others, communications specialist Daniel Hallin decries the fact that news in North America and elsewhere is increasingly reduced to tiny 'soundbites', and to what is becoming known as 'trash television': tabloid 'news programmes' and talk shows, such as *Oprah!* or *Larry King Live*, which may feature transvestites and diets one night, and the President of the United States the next.[36] While Yankelovich puts much of the onus (and hope) on the media to raise consciousness and assist in the 'working through' of important issues, Hallin says this is virtually impossible, at least as far as the American News media are concerned:

> Discussions of the media and public policy are traditionally dosed with exhortations to the media to provide the public with more and better information, 'an informed and active public being essential to a vigorous democracy' (as the saying goes) . . . [but] the problem with American news media [lies] with the fact that the major relation of political communication has become a relation of seller and consumer . . . The modern mass media cannot play the role of sparking active public participation in deciding the direction of public policy. I use the word *cannot* deliberately. Individual journalists . . . can certainly from time to time break out of the focus on technique and strategy to raise the direction of public policy as an issue . . . But all of this must remain within relatively narrow limits; the anti-political tendencies . . . are deeply rooted in the structure and professional ideology of the American news media.[37]

He concludes by saying 'To the extent that life is to be breathed into the public sphere of liberal capitalist societies, the initiative must come from outside the [media] institutions now dominating that sphere'. Like Rosenblum, Hallin puts his faith in the public: in citizen's organizations.

NGOs to the rescue

Northern NGOs relate to the public in two principal ways: through fundraising, and through development education and campaigning. Although for most NGOs these are very distinct types of activity, they are basically two sides of the same coin. Within the development community, NGOs are regarded as one of the best hopes for improved public information and better education on development issues. In fact in many countries they are virtually the only purveyors of thoughtful development education.

It may come as something of a surprise, therefore, to both supporters and critics of NGOs, to learn how limited the spread of their information services actually seems. When asked about sources of information, most respondents in most opinion polls put television first, newspapers second, and radio third. Of course people have many sources of information, including books, school, friends and relatives, the government. As a primary source of information, however, NGOs appear relatively low on most scales. In the European Community, only 11 per cent of those polled give NGOs as a source of information. Churches are listed as a source of information by 13 per cent of Europeans.[38] Polling done by NGOs themselves is usually carefully guarded for fundraising purposes, but two representative examples are of interest. A 1989 British Harris Poll conducted for ActionAid found, surprisingly, that only 3 per cent of respondents received their information about poor countries from NGOs (and a further 3 per cent from churches). Another British survey, carried out for World Vision in 1993, found that NGO advertising accounted for 12 per cent, and other information from charities for a further 4 per cent. Churches were mentioned by 7 per cent.[39]

These rather uneven numbers may underestimate NGO impact. First, respondents are naming what they *believe* to be their primary source of information. In all countries, however, information leaflets (with a 7 per cent response factor in Europe) and TV fundraisers (13 per cent in Canada) would be almost exclusively NGO-produced. Many television documentaries and magazine stories (with a 25 per cent response factor in Europe and Canada) focus on NGOs. Many television and newspaper news stories are also generated by or are about NGO activities.

The fundraising coin

By far the greatest NGO investment in public communication is in fundraising, a subject of contention among Northern NGOs for years. The debate usually revolves around what has become known as 'the pornography of poverty': the use of starving babies and other emotive imagery to coax, cajole and bludgeon donations from a guilt-ridden Northern public. The argument is not that starving babies don't exist, but that such pictures, repeated year after year, create an image of horror and helplessness that far outweighs reality. This is generally recognized by most NGOs to be counter-productive in terms of creating understanding and awareness for longer-term development assistance. In 1987, Oxfam and the European Community sponsored a report on 'Images of Africa' which showed beyond doubt that negative images had contributed to a stereotype of a doomed and helpless continent, whose own people were unable to help themselves.[40]

A further problem relates to child sponsorship, a form of fundraising that has proven exceptionally successful for many organizations, including World Vision, Plan International, Christian Children's Fund and others. Widely debated in the early 1980s,[41] child sponsorship is criticized because helping one identifiable person can cause divisions and can exacerbate inequality in a community. Direct correspondence with a child is very expensive, and it can raise high expectations while maintaining a sense of aid and dependence. Although most child sponsorship agencies now target communities in their field work as much as the child, the child remains the publicity anchor, and projects are therefore smaller, more parochial and are often less cost-effective than others. And the high administrative cost remains. Despite the criticism (e.g. the 1993 UNDP *Human development report*), child sponsorship continues to grow. Plan International grew from 200 000 child sponsorships in 1982, to 720 000 in 1994. In 1982, World Vision supported 270 000 children worldwide; by 1993 there were more than a million on the roster, 516 000 supported from the United States alone.[42] In the same period, the income of Christian Children's Fund grew from $40 million to $112 million.

Charged with everything from exploitation to racism (usually by Southern NGOs), many successful Northern NGOs began to change their imagery in the 1980s. Some NGO communities subsequently developed codes of ethics which dealt with the question of images. For example in Australia, members of ACFOA, the NGO co-ordinating agency, undertake to 'respect the dignity of recipient communities in advertising, audiovisuals, written materials and presentations'.[43] In the United States, InterAction requires that a member's 'communications shall respect the dignity, values, history, religion and culture of the people served by the programmes. They shall neither minimize nor overstate the human and material needs of those whom they assist'.[44] Similar codes have been developed in other countries.

The problem with most of the codes is that there are no sanctions, and violators are rarely, if ever, challenged. With increased competition in a tough economic climate, at a time marked by an escalation in emergencies and disasters, evidence of the temptation to return to what works in advertising can be found almost daily in newspapers and on television. Even more cautious NGOs have discovered that they can have their cake and eat it too. It is no longer so necessary to *pay* for starving baby advertising, because if a disaster becomes bad enough, the media will provide publicity for free. Visiting journalists, no longer resident in Africa, for example, and therefore unfamiliar with the context, regularly seek out the local representatives of Redd Barna, Oxfam or CARE to get their stories.

In 1969 a British fundraising consultant provided a formula for dealing with the public: *babies.* 'Show babies,' he said, 'all the time show babies and more babies.' The advice, by and large, seems to have been adopted.[45]

Development education: the other side of the coin

The greatest tension for the thoughtful Northern NGO today lies in the attempt to balance fundraising messages for a public most easily moved by short-term disaster appeals, with recognition that longer-term development depends on the willingness of that same public to support difficult and costly structural change. This is a tension between the 'appeal' of helplessness and antipathy towards empowerment; between concern for children and indifference towards parents; between the provision of food and the creation of jobs; between aid and trade; between charity, as some NGOs say quite clearly, and justice.

Inevitably, the 'balance' almost always tips heavily in favour of fundraising. In 1993, the US Bread for the World Institute interviewed media and public relations directors of the twenty five largest American charities dealing with international development, hunger and poverty. The Institute found that these organizations, with budgets totalling $3 billion, were spending approximately 0.25 per cent of their budgets on what might be called development education. Of this, only 12 per cent was being devoted to advocacy or influencing specific hunger legislation.[46]

Development education is not new. It began in many countries in the 1950s and 1960s, and over the years has undergone a variety of transitions. Today there is a broad spectrum of 'Dev Ed' organizations,

137

some large, some small, working in the formal education system, with churches, organized labour, with media and cultural institutions, taking development messages into the school, the workplace and the home. Development education began in most places with basic information about the South, and about development assistance. Gradually, in the 1970s and 1980s, it grew into a more mature form of pedagogy, encouraging critical analysis, reflection and action on the information that was being provided, not unlike what Yankelovich calls 'working through'. From the beginning, some NGOs took development education a step further, moving into campaigning and advocacy on issues related to the scale and focus of official development assistance, and into more political issues such as the independence struggles in Southern Africa, human rights, racism, immigration and the environment.

Increasingly, Southern NGOs have urged their Northern partners to devote greater energies to an activist style of development education, to reorient their activities and to attack, for example, the 'policies of their governments, corporations and multilateral institutions . . . which adversely affect the quality of life and political and economic independence' of the South.[47] This wording, from a 1986 declaration of African NGOs meeting at the UN Special Session on Africa, is neither unique, nor is it unusually strident. At a large 1987 NGO gathering in London, the message was the same, as it was in a 1989 'Manila Declaration', at an Arusha meeting the same year, and at many North-South gatherings since.

The problem can create serious tension within NGOs. Staff criticize senior management and trustees for unrealistically limiting development education budgets, and for undue timidity. On the other hand, some NGOs have come under serious fire from the media, politicians and the public for being anti-government, anti-capitalist, even pro-revolutionary. The Charity Commissioners for England and Wales are notorious throughout the international NGO world for their policing of British NGO campaigns and development education. Some governments, in particular the United States, are expressly forbidden from supporting activities which might be considered propaganda or lobbying, even in support of government positions. Under such circumstances, an NGO would therefore be unable to lobby in favour, for example, of an aid budget increase (or against a decrease). While not forbidden in other countries, lobbying, campaigning and advocacy are often only barely tolerated. And because many NGOs today are heavily reliant on their government for a high proportion of their income, there is inevitably a measure of self-censorship, even where government financial support for development education is not explicitly involved.

Most individuals writing about development education and campaigning list the more notable successes:

o a code of conduct for the marketing of baby milk;
o the drafting of an international essential drugs list;
o the removal of certain trade restrictions;
o the creation of an emergency EC food reserve;
o the imposition of sanctions against Rhodesia and South Africa.[48]

British NGOs have campaigned successfully, twice in the past decade, to prevent cuts to the aid budget. NGO-run alternative trading organizations like Tearfund, Oxfam Trading and the Max Havelaar Coffee sales in Belgium and Holland give both a practical and a commercial dimension to development education. The Swiss NGO Coalition school service, the International Broadcasting Trust in Britain, the 'One World Campaign' in Canada and the 'Africa Alive' campaign in Australia are all evidence of successful NGO initiative and innovation.

Where the quality of development education, rather than the breadth of its reach, has been emphasized in evaluation, there are other positive signs. A detailed 1993 evaluation of a ten-year USAID-NGO programme found that 'audience members for DevEd programmes learn, believe and do things they didn't before. And, compared with the general American public, DevEd audiences have much stronger support for foreign assistance and understanding of the US stake in the Third World'.[49] Similar findings, though not perhaps as scientific, are available in other countries.

There is, nevertheless, a paucity — almost a fear in the development education community — of serious evaluation. One examination of the subject says that 'Grassroots development education in Europe is healthy and vigorous . . . activities are based upon the premise that people *are* concerned about global issues, *have* imbibed information . . . The general standard of planning, target-setting and evaluation is increasing.' But, it asks, 'How far are we going to be pushed down this [evaluation] road? How many NGDOs are asking questions of how effective their work is, not with a view to *improving* it but, perhaps, with a view to cutting back on it?'[50]

This not uncommon defensiveness has to do with a constant refrain from government agencies: has public opinion improved?* A more appropriate question might be this: How can deeply ingrained public attitudes be expected to change when they are reinforced every day in a variety of ways by television, the print media, and by

---

*Like Laurence Olivier in *Marathon Man*, torturing Dustin Hoffman in order to get an answer to the question, 'Is it safe?'

NGO fundraising messages which governments tacitly encourage through the provision of uncritical matching grants?

Just as pollsters criticize polling and journalists are often the most trenchant critics of the media, NGO managers can be the most critical of failings in development education. Citing an NGO-commissioned opinion poll, a senior Canadian NGO manager observes that even NGOs with the highest public credibility have a major problem communicating with the public. The report noted that the public find their terminology incomprehensible, and that NGOs have an attitude that is 'patronizing, self-righteous, joyless and defensive'.

He went on to say:

> A 1988 report commissioned by CIDA on public education strategy identified a broad range of strategic problems in the development community's approach to public education, including a lack of critical mass, no perspective, a fragmented approach involving a number of messages and methods, absence of leadership and planning by CIDA, the inability of DevEd groups to popularize the development message, and counterproductive procedural tensions between CIDA and the NGOs. Despite some progress, most of these problems remain today (1994). A final strategic issue for the development community is the lack of human and financial resources devoted to public education. To put this in perspective, the development community as a whole spends less on public education on development issues than Labatt's brewers spend on marketing beer.'[51]

Funding for development education: no coins in the fountain

Private donor support for development education is severely limited. If long-term development loses out to disaster appeals in general NGO fundraising, development education is a virtual non-starter. Larger NGOs can afford to divert a small percentage of their general income into education, but organizations that have been expressly established for development education purposes live with short institutional horizons and extremely small budgets. Underpaid, their staff are often young returned-volunteers, or committed part-timers who work long hours with meagre resources. The generic development education centre, whether in Australia, Japan, North America or Europe, has almost exactly the same cramped, threadbare look to it.

Government support for development education can only be described as ambivalent at best. NGOs are at times critical of official aid programmes, which some governments believe undermines general public support. And it makes them nervous about feeding the mouth that bites. Many governments manage their own programmes with the formal school system (e.g. Japan, Netherlands, Norway, Sweden, Australia), and each has an information department which produces reports, studies, evaluations and in some cases, films and videos. The co-financing of television productions made by independent producers is becoming a more common means of 'leveraging' tight information budgets, and of surmounting the media's fear of government 'propaganda'. The budgets for these endeavours, however, are tiny in relation to the task. In Sweden, SIDA's 1994 information budget represented roughly 0.1 per cent of its overall annual budget. CIDA spends about 0.5 per cent on public information or, in real terms, less than World Vision spends on fundraising in Australia.[52]

A handful of governments have given serious attention to co-financing NGO development education: Austria, the Netherlands and Canada devote about 0.5 per cent of their official development assistance to this purpose. Denmark and Finland devote about 0.2 per cent, while Germany, Australia and Switzerland spend roughly 0.1 per cent. Japanese, Italian, Spanish, British and American spending on development education is minimal. The British Government explains its position this way: 'It is . . . considered unethical in the United Kingdom for the government to finance pressure groups or to use public money to advocate policies which are not already approved by Parliament. At the same time, the British education system is very jealous of its professional independence and does not want any outside interference.'[53] In 1994, the Government of France allocated one franc towards co-financing NGO development education for every 45 000 francs it spent on ODA. In percentage terms, the number looks like this: 0.002 per cent.[54]

Prologue to a tragedy?

James Madison, the fourth President of the United States, said after his time in office that 'a popular government without popular information, or the means of acquiring it, is but a prologue to a farce or a tragedy, or perhaps both'. In the end, perhaps public understanding about other people and about development assistance doesn't matter. But if James Madison and the countless others who have written about democracy are correct, this is probably a dangerous assumption. Dangerous, not in the sense that aid budgets may be cut, but dangerous in the sense that if people in Northern democracies are unequipped to deal with the biggest, and most integrated global challenge of the coming century — poverty and its increasingly terrible manifestations — they are bound to deal with them badly.

In discussing successful consciousness raising on important issues like the women's movement, the environment and AIDS, Daniel Yankelovich identifies the following six crucial factors that could be applied to the development field.

Time variability. The environmental movement was able to move towards resolution after a consciousness-raising period of about thirty years. For AIDS, the process took less than a decade. North-South charity dates from the days of Wilberforce and the anti-slavery movement two hundred years ago. It has gone through starving babies in the Congo a century ago, starving babies in China half a century ago, and the starving babies of our time in Biafra, Ethiopia, Somalia and Rwanda. Little seems to have changed. The more complex *development* movement is much younger: roughly 35 or 40 years old. But it too is old enough to have made more headway than is the case.

Cogency of events. Nothing advances consciousness raising as powerfully as events that dramatize the issue. Unfortunately, the events that dramatize development issues are usually portrayed in the media (and by most NGOs) as a series of disconnected tragedies, having little to do with each other or with the North. They can be variously assigned to mismanagement, corruption, or natural events beyond the control or responsibility of ordinary people elsewhere. Most have so far led only to 'simple' solutions and temporary measures: unpredictable aid programmes, peacekeeping and charity. The public knows little about people's efforts to help themselves, little about the fact that Third World loan repayments outstrip aid budgets which, in any case, are a pitifully small part of government expenditure.

Perceived applicability to self. Today, the women's movement has direct applicability to a large majority of people in the North: men, women and families as a whole. People understand it in clear, personal terms. Around AIDS and some environmental issues, personal relevance has been fundamental to the creation of a readiness to grapple with solutions. Although development assistance is occasionally justified from a commercial self-interest point of view, or from a 'global village' perspective, it remains distant from the lives of most people in the North. Speaking of development, President Kennedy said, 'A rising tide will float all boats.' The public has not been told that all boats are at risk in the gathering storm.

Concreteness and clarity. Development messages from the media, from NGOs and from government agencies are confusing, self-serving, contradictory and more often than not, negative. Complex issues have been made more complex by fragmenting the message and packaging it in jargon.

Credibility. Lack of credibility is a serious detriment to consciousness-raising. Most opinion polls show that governments have especially low credibility where development assistance is concerned. Although NGOs survive on, and exist because of public donations, the giving public is not the same as the entire public. Questions about NGO credibility as a source of information show that they too have believability problems.[55] Television and other media, with all the failings described above, come out well on top in most surveys.

Publicity. In order to arouse concern for action, people must be aware of the issue. Messages must be clear and unambiguous, and quantity is an essential feature, both in getting the message across, and in reinforcing it. Where quantity is concerned, public messages on development are virtually non-existent compared with the bad news provided by the media and self-serving NGO fundraising.

Questions about public information can perhaps be distilled further: will I read it? Do I believe it? How long will I remember it? Does it move me to do anything differently?

It is perhaps important to make a distinction, in case it is not clear enough yet, between people's support for their government's efforts, and for development assistance in general. When people are critical of government, this is not the same as opposing foreign aid. The high levels of public support for the United Nations throughout Europe and the US can be seen as evidence of this. Nor should a lack of public understanding be mistaken for a lack of public concern or values. Perhaps if there was greater cogency and clarity within aid programmes, and less emphasis on the commercial and political interests that characterize so many, credibility would rise. In short, the problem is more fundamental than choosing the right words and images in order to 'sell' development assistance as it is now practised.

Is this the winter of discontent, or can it be the spring of hope? As a way of dealing with the problems of public support, some recommend much more spending on information and development education. The 1994 UNDP Human Development Report, for example, recommends that two per cent of official development assistance — about $1 billion per annum — should be earmarked for communication and development education, for greater work in the formal education system and with the media, 'not to mislead or manipulate public opinion, but to fulfil the duty of accountability'.[56] This would probably help, because there is almost nowhere to go but up.

Some place their faith in the coming 'information superhighway', the 'infobahn'. They believe that the disintegration of mass audiences and mass media will encourage like-minded people to seek out unfiltered news. The public will be better informed because there will be 150 television channels to choose from instead of three or four. There may well be one or two or even six channels dealing

143

with development issues. News from the South will no longer be so heavily controlled. Much more of it will flow directly into homes at the viewer's discretion, rather than at the discretion of editors and gatekeepers in commercially driven networks.

This may well be true. But there is also the spectre of an Elvis Channel and an Oprah Channel. This solution suggests that television (or computers, or virtual reality or some other technology) is the answer. It ignores the failure of previous silver bullets, like the elusive 'peace dividend'. It ignores the fact that discerning readers and viewers already have access to reasonable sources of cogent and coherent information, and that even though there are already thirty or forty television channels in most North American homes, one American in four cannot identify Boutros Boutros-Ghali and half cannot name the President of Russia.[57] It also ignores the fact that society somehow came to at least partial grips with environmental issues in 30 years and AIDS in only five, without an information superhighway.

In truth, the answers lie well beyond the scope of this book. They also lie well beyond the scope and mandate of government aid agencies, and beyond the power of a fragmented, charity-bound NGO community. The glimmer of one sort of partial answer can perhaps be found in a footnote to an organization that grew out of the American pop-singer aid effort of the 1980s, USA for Africa. Like Band Aid and Live Aid in Britain, USA for Africa started with a song, 'We are the world', designed to raise money for the Ethiopian famine. Between 1985 and 1990 when it began to wind down, USA For Africa raised over $96 million, channelling much of it through American NGOs, and about a quarter through African NGOs. Fatime N'Diaye, director of a consortium of Senegalese NGOs, believes that USA for Africa, as well as Band Aid/Live Aid, missed an opportunity to create a network of Northern NGOs that could have reduced fundraising competition, that could have worked in less paternalistic ways than it did with Southern NGOs, and which might have had a broader impact on public thinking in the North.[58]

Reducing competition and the babble of voices is an aim of the National Committee for Development Education (NCO) in the Netherlands. Financed entirely by government, but managed by a council of NGO representatives, it divides its budget ($9 million in 1994) between support for the educational activities of Dutch NGOs and programmes of its own. Another kind of potential can perhaps be found in the 'alternative funds' and community foundations that began in the United States in the 1970s. These are amalgams which consolidate the giving of family foundations, bequests, corporate and individual donors around specific themes. Sometimes they are small and community based, as with the Community Foundation of Ottawa-Carleton which, by the end of its first seven years had created an endowment of C$5 million, and was supporting local causes to the tune of about C$300 000 annually. Others, such as the Bread and Roses Community Fund in Philadelphia, the San Francisco Vanguard Foundation or the Amalgamated Rich Folks Fund (wisely re-named the Council on National Priorities), support innovation, alternatives and social activism, in ways that welfare organizations, dependent on what they perceive public attitudes to be, cannot or will not.

Perhaps the most interesting British fundraising phenomenon in recent years is Comic Relief, the public persona of an organization called Charity Projects, which began in 1985. By 1991 it had become twentieth among the big fundraising organizations, raising just over £19 million. Charity Projects 'was set up to create new money, make grants and raise awareness of the issues it funds'. Being the brainchild of a number of British comedians, it takes a light-hearted approach to a difficult subject, but does so with integrity and a high degree of professionalism. Of its grants, one-third are made in the UK, and two-thirds in Africa, mainly through British NGOs. Of the African spending, one-quarter is designated for emergency assistance, and three-quarters for development efforts. Its development spending in 1991–2 was £6.4 million, making it about half as large as the British Government as a grant-making body for NGO development projects in Africa.

In the end, however, fundraising co-ordination and more effective development education are only a small part of a bigger picture. No doubt unaware of the views of James Madison, Mark Gearan, President Clinton's Communications Director, observed that citing public opinion to justify a foreign policy decision was only 'an additive to bolster an argument. Public opinion,' he said, 'is not that important'.[59] But what if it won't *bolster* an argument? What if a potential decision is *un*popular? What about 'the chronic ailment of democracy: the craving for short-term popularity'?[60] If Gearan is correct, or even if he is only partly correct, it places a great deal of the onus for dealing with the pressing issues of international development squarely on the shoulders of governments and their leaders. Galbraith agrees: 'What is needed to save and to protect, to ensure against suffering and further unpleasant consequence, is not in any way obscure. Nor would the resulting action be unpleasant. There would be a challenge to the present mood of contentment with its angry resentment of any intrusion, but, in the longer run, the general feeling of well-being would be deepened . . . No one should be misled. The central requirement cannot be escaped: almost every action that would remedy and reassure involves the relationship between the citizen and the state.'[61]

Such action — action to remedy and reassure — would inevitably include a recognition in trading relationships and aid programmes that development is much more than a short-term sideline; an admission that if problems are to be solved, the effort will have to be much greater. This will require uncommon national and international leadership, leadership that can rise above, or at least make workable bargains with short-term economic and political self-interest. It will require leadership that can inspire ordinary people as well as the media, that can draw many more constituencies into the task and obtain their support rather than their animosity. It requires leadership that itself understands and can convey the message that long-term self-interest lies in long-term disaster prevention, rather than short-term crisis management.

It requires leadership that has faith in what NGOs, hundreds of opinion polls and simple common sense tell governments about people throughout the industrialized world: that they do care, that they want to help, and that they will make sacrifices if they understand them to be in the genuine interest of a better and more secure life for their children.

CHAPTER VIII

Management, memory and money

*Planners want to retain the stability that planning brings to an organiza-
tion, planning's main contribution, while enabling it to respond quickly to
external changes in the environment, planning's main nemesis.*

Henry Mintzberg.

TODAY, DEVELOPMENT NGOs spend an estimated $7–$10 billion annually,[1] about as much as the gross domestic products of Zimbabwe,
Nepal and Tanzania combined. In volume, this compares favourably
with the $55 billion in overall official development assistance pro-
vided by OECD member governments in 1993. But NGOs live with a
level of financial insecurity that would quickly bankrupt the average
private sector firm. Criticized by governments for lack of professionalism, NGOs are then accused of bureaucratization when they do
professionalize.

Professionalism: brother can you paradigm?

'Professionalism' is yet another word, especially when applied to
NGOs, that has been ruined by the development community. A 'professional', according to the dictionary, is one who is extremely competent
in a job. 'Professionalism', therefore, is the combined methods, character and status of a professional. The push to make NGOs 'more professional' is not a new phenomenon, but as NGOs have grown in size, and
as they have become more beholden to governments for their income,
the pressure to conform to external images of professionalism has
grown. The 'logical framework analysis' (LFA) was introduced to American NGOs by USAID in the early 1970s as a means of developing
greater precision in goals, objectives, inputs, outputs and 'objectively
verifiable indicators' of achievement. Over the next twenty years it
became the tool most favoured by Northern governments in organizing
their own bilateral projects, and in ensuring that NGOs, at least when
working on larger government-assisted projects, conformed to their
own 'professional' management standards and techniques.

The LFA has endured as a specific instrument, and other management techniques have overflowed the boundaries of the business

community, spilling into both government and non-governmental organizations. 'Management by objectives', the 'planning-programming-budgeting system', strategic planning, stakeholder analysis, mission-based management and other techniques have been urged on and accepted by NGOs to varying degrees over the past two decades. None has proved very satisfactory, perhaps because development works to a certain extent in a political economy, rather than a market economy. In addition, much development work, like some industries, is highly 'emergent', requiring flexibility and constant adjustment. A company producing only one thing may be well suited for blueprint planning, but companies with changing products, operating in volatile markets, are not.

Careful and 'professional' planning has not been a panacea for the private sector any more than it has for NGOs. Henry Mintzberg, an iconoclastic management expert, has examined planning and strategy formation in a wide range of private and public sector firms:

> We found strategy making to be a complex, interactive and evolutionary process, best described as one of adaptive learning. Strategic change was found to be uneven and unpredictable, with major strategies often remaining relatively stable for long periods of time, sometimes decades, and then suddenly undergoing massive change. The process was often significantly emergent, especially when the organization faced unpredicted shifts in the environment . . . Indeed, strategies appeared in all kinds of strange ways in the organizations studied. Many of the most important seemed to grow from the 'grass roots' (much as weeds that might appear in a garden are later found to bear useful fruit) rather than all having to be imposed from the top down, in 'hothouse' style.[2]

This is as true for NGOs as it is for business. Gradually, however, a distinct — or at least a distinctive-looking school of thought on NGO management has emerged. In the 1980s, established writers like management doyen Peter Drucker began to turn their attention to the voluntary sector. Universities and training institutes developed special programmes for NGO management: the London School of Economics, the Asian Institute of Management, the Manitoba Institute of Management. In Britain, a group of former NGO managers established the International NGO Training and Research Centre (INTRAC) in 1991, to deal specifically with organizations working in international relief and development. In the 1970s, specialized books began to dot the expanding management rack in bookstores: Philip Kotler's *Marketing for nonprofit organizations* (1975), Richard Cyert's *The management of non-profit organizations*, (1975), *Managing nonprofit organizations* by Borst and Montana (1977), Charles

148

Handy's *Understanding voluntary organizations* (1988) and Drucker's *Managing the non-profit organization* (1990). Jossey-Bass, a California publisher, has in recent years produced an entire line of books on NGO leadership and management.

Many of these compare and contrast the non-profit sector with business. How important is the absence of a profit motive? Are commitment and values an adequate substitute for 'the bottom line'? What is the nature and effect of competition (or lack thereof) in the non-profit world? How does (or should) leadership in NGOs differ from that in business or government? How can an NGO retain the traditional hallmarks of flexibility, responsiveness and innovation, and still meet basic norms of planning, budgeting and reporting? Does the absence of shareholders and paid board members make NGOs less responsible? Less accountable? Less well managed?

In a way, some of these questions, which have generated papers, books, workshops and even entire management institutions, are red herrings. Certainly the 'bottom line' for Toyota is important, the most important thing about staying alive. But a favourable bottom line is not achieved by making shoddy products. Drive, commitment and values all have a place in the company. And while departmental managers may be evaluated on their ability to work within projected time frames and established budgets, the keeper of the Toyota plant's library in Georgetown Kentucky is no more driven by the profit motive than a data processor at Christian Aid in London.

Without any competition, of course, an automobile manufacturer might not be so concerned about quality and price. The status quo in the European and North American automobile industries received a rude shock in the 1970s and 1980s when the entry of Japanese car makers forced a radical rethink about quality, customer preference and price. Competition among Northern NGOs is no less real. New entrants, more sophisticated fundraising techniques, mergers and the growth of transnational NGOs like World Vision, Plan International and Médecins sans Frontières have made competition even more intense during the 1990s. Similar competition exists in the South, both for the attention of Northern donors and for government approval.

A major difference between the private sector and non-profits lies in the nature of accountability. Technically, Toyota is accountable to its board of directors and its shareholders, not unlike an NGO which is accountable to its board of directors and membership. But in reality, Toyota is accountable first and foremost to its customers. If they buy a lot of Corollas, the shareholders and the board will be happy, because the bottom line will presumably look good. The problem for NGOs is that the 'customer' is more diffuse. Every NGO pays at least nominal lip service to the notion that its primary

149

accountability is to 'the beneficiary'. But most behave very differently. Most Northern NGOs tailor their appearance and their public messages entirely to suit the donor. Comparing the direct mail messages of Oxfam, Save the Children and a dozen others, it would seem, in fact, that their fundraisers all went to the same school.*

Accountability to larger donors, especially government, has led NGOs to other hoops, mainly in an effort to get, and to demonstrate good management and efficiency. The result has been a degree of useful 'professionalization': mission statements, personnel policies and procedures, budget and performance reviews, computerized accounting, external audits. This is true of both Northern and Southern NGOs.

Accountability to board and membership, however, is an area of particular weakness for many NGOs, especially in the South. Unpaid, many NGO trustees are content to be supportive, and sometimes to assist with fundraising. Often chosen for their name or reputation, many have little time to devote to the policy, management and financial questions for which they are technically responsible. They will attend meetings and act in a supportive manner, but they may be unwilling or unable to ask deep, potentially embarrassing questions. Many assume that someone else is taking care of issues which they do not fully understand. If they are elected by a broad membership to 'represent' a particular constituency, the tendency is worse. Prone to factional interests, they may fail to take responsibility for the organization as a whole. In the end, as a general rule, the executive director and the senior staff of most NGOs propose and control three-quarters of the agenda, and influence or even control the outcome of most decisions.

In the South, the phenomenon is even more pronounced. Because the modern NGO movement is very young, many of today's Southern NGOs are still headed by their founder. Most founders are remarkable individuals possessing equal amounts of charisma, energy, political savvy and a strong, value-based commitment to development. Sometimes alone, sometimes with a small group of like-minded individuals, they have created living, breathing institutions where none existed before. Faced with enormous challenges, however, few were interested in creating boards of directors that would challenge or block them.

---

*The letter should never exceed two pages. The words and the paragraphs should be short, the messages simple. There should be a name and description of a particular person, preferably a child. A project should be described and reference should be made to the remarkable things that can be done for a pittance. The Executive Director or a celebrity should appear to 'sign' the letter, so the signature must be printed in blue ink. A post script should always be added, possibly in blue-ink handwriting, to further 'personalize' the letter.

The result, as these organizations mature, is a pronounced demonstration of what might be called the 'guru syndrome': the ageing, charismatic leader who, two or three decades on, still runs the organization by personal fiat, sometimes as though it were still small, sometimes as though it were a family enterprise, rarely challenged by staff and seldom checked by trustees. Many of India's Gandhian organizations withered in the 1950s and 1960s for precisely this reason. There is a worse example of what the guru syndrome can do: the Dutch NGO, NOVIB, discovered in 1994 that one of its major Indian partners had been keeping two sets of accounts, audited by different accountants, possibly in an effort to build an endowment. The deception, which may have involved several million dollars over more than a decade, was possible only because a powerful leader at the core of the Indian NGO was essentially and effectively unaccountable, and was therefore able to conceal the fact for years.

The guru syndrome, of course, is not peculiar to the South. Nor is it peculiar to the non-profit organization. Henry Ford personified the problem in the company he formed, built and then nearly destroyed. Much of the German and American co-operative movement a century ago collapsed when the first wave of leaders retired or died off. While the most prominent of today's Northern NGOs have survived several leadership tests, the future is not clear for Southern NGOs. Will they be one-generation operations, or will they be able to institutionalize their management in such a way that an orderly succession can take place when the founder disappears? Survival will be most likely among those that have built and encouraged a broad and independent-minded accountability structure.

Oversight and overheads

'Oversight' is an interesting word, because it has two meanings that seem almost diametrically opposed. In its most common usage, an oversight is an omission or mistake. Less common, but frequently used by the US Government, oversight can also mean supervision, as in 'overseer'. Where NGO overheads are concerned, oversight in both its meanings is apt.

Overheads are a thorny subject for most NGOs because of the powerful public myth that development should be cheap. An NGO with high overheads or administrative costs is thought to be squandering donor money. In its sixth annual ranking of the hundred largest American charities, the widely read magazine, *Money*, offered only one criterion in judging what it called 'the winners': the cost of administration. The International Rescue Committee came first because its overheads were only 7.7 per cent. The Mennonite Central Committee

151

and Save the Children came second and third, with 11.8 and 17.9 per cent respectively.[3]

Overheads of 15 per cent are the most the average NGO will admit to, although the general reality is probably higher. But true overheads for most NGOs are almost impossible to determine for a variety of reasons. One is that many costs which might in the private sector be charged to overhead — the Executive Director's salary, for example — may be apportioned to projects because of work he or she does when travelling in the field. Most NGOs assign as much of their central cost as possible to projects, in order to give the appearance of low overheads. (This practice, by the way, is not unique to NGOs. It is a hallowed tradition in government, UN agencies and other multilateral institutions.)

Another factor that makes overheads indecipherable is a paucity of industry standards on accounting. One NGO may apportion 80 per cent of headquarters costs to projects, while another may assign only 50 per cent. A particular problem has to do with 'in-kind' donations. For example World Vision's 1993 cash income in the United States was $173 million. According to its annual report, its fundraising expenses were $31.9 million, or about 18 per cent. But World Vision also had $84.7 million worth of 'gifts in kind'. By including the value of these in the income statement, fundraising was pushed down to 12.3 per cent.[4]

This point is not raised to suggest that there are no costs associated with obtaining and managing in-kind donations. It does raise questions about how they are valued, however. The question is particularly pertinent where in-kind costs are a significant proportion of an organization's income. In the United States, USAID commodities are usually valued according to government guidelines, but beyond that, there are few norms. In 1991, non-government in-kind income represented 90 per cent of the 'spending' of the AmeriCares Foundation. It was 73 per cent for Christian Relief Services, and 79 per cent for Feed the Children.[5] The following year, however, state and federal regulators began to examine in-kind donations more carefully, and discovered that several organizations had inflated the value of commodities. One of them was Feed the Children, which made its calculations based on retail rather than wholesale prices. As a result of negative publicity, Feed the Children revised its 1991 figures, reducing the value of in-kind donations from $86.3 million, to $61 million. This had the effect of boosting the cost of its fundraising and administration by 30 per cent.[6] The change brought it more into line with guidelines issued by the Association of Evangelical Relief and Development Organizations, guidelines which discourage the use of retail pricing, and which recommend discounting when a product is impaired or nearing its expiry date. The guide-lines, however, developed to forestall greater government regula-tion, worked in this case only when government action became imminent.

More dramatic subterfuge was used by World Vision Germany to give the appearance of low overheads in the late 1980s. Although it was stated that more than 80 per cent of money raised in Germany went overseas, this was not the complete picture. Money was indeed transferred overseas, either to a World Vision account in Singapore, or to World Vision International Headquarters in California for onward transmission. 'Onward transmission' usually meant that money went first to one of three regional offices, then to country offices in the South. At each stage, there were probably deductions for local admin-istration. More upsetting for donors to World Vision Germany, however, was the fact that a hefty proportion was transferred back to Germany, to a marketing company responsible for promoting World Vision in Germany, Austria and Switzerland. Although World Vision Germany could show low overheads in its own books, the reality was significantly different. In the end, according to former employees and consultants, less than half the money raised ever reached the ultimate country of destination.[7]

As in the case of World Vision Germany, high overheads may well have to do with the increasing cost of running sophisticated fundrais-ing and advertising departments aimed at maintaining or expanding an organization's market share. The Dutch version of Médecins sans Frontières, for example, *Artsen zonder Grenzen*, spent 37 per cent of its 1991 gift income on publicity and fundraising.[8] Higher costs are certainly a characteristic of child sponsorship agencies like World Vision, Plan International and Save the Children US, which calculates administration ('independent cost recovery') at 28.5 per cent.[9] World Vision Australia recorded 32 per cent of its gross 1991 income as fundraising and administration.[10]

Of course a good fundraising year can make overheads work the other way. In 1991, the combined publicity, fundraising, administra-tion and education costs of Save the Children UK represented 14 per cent of total income. The organization's phenomenal growth in the following year (a 77 per cent increase in income) brought these costs, which did not change significantly in real terms, down to less than 10 per cent.[11]

The colour of money

Fundraising has become big (and expensive) business. While volun-teers are important to NGOs, they are virtually absent from the pages of the various trade publications devoted to fundraising. The British magazine, *Professional fundraising*, a glossy example, is packed with advertisements from companies seeking to work with charitable organizations. The range is enormous: advertising agencies, direct marketing companies, event management firms, legal services, printers, firms specializing in 'prospect' research, public relations, telephone fundraising and how to get information into doctors' waiting rooms.

Some companies specialize in promotional gifts: golf umbrellas, pens, lighters, key rings, rulers, pencils, badges, calculators, t-shirts, caps, balloons, signs, banners, stickers, coffee mugs, collection boxes, Christmas cards, calendars and mail order catalogues. There is a wide range of computer software with clever names like *The raiser's edge* (for Windows), 'the ultimate fundraising application for the '90s and beyond'. There are others: *Alms* (for DOS and Windows), *Fund master*, *Donorbase gold* and *Donorbase easy*.

In the increasingly competitive world of fundraising, new ideas are constantly being tested and refined: balls, dinners, walks, film premières and the like. Will-making is one of several sensitive areas that are regarded as potential gold mines if they can be tapped tastefully. The British Law Society estimates that only 31 per cent of British adults have made a will, and 58 per cent of existing wills are probably out of date. The Law Society organized 'Make a will week' in 1994, aimed at increasing its own business more than anything else. But some charities saw it as a potential bonanza, running their own campaigns at the same time, sending out kits on how to make a will, and how to leave money specifically to them. Some companies specialize in legacies for charities. The London firm of Smee and Ford advertises itself as the 'Willbusters: legacies — who you gonna call?'

Affinity cards were a clever invention of the 1980s. Banks, credit unions and building societies issue their Visa, Mastercard and other credit cards in the name of a particular charity, contributing a small percentage of each purchase to the organization in question. The Midland Bank's affinity card, for example, raised over £1 million between 1990 and 1994 for the National Trust. The Royal National Lifeboat Institution, one of 250 charities, clubs and universities with Royal Bank of Scotland affinity cards, generated 15 000 dedicated cardholders in the mid-1990s. A Leeds Building Society affinity card supports the Imperial Cancer Research Fund, the British Heart Foundation and MENCAP, an organization working with the mentally handicapped. In 1994, this card, then six years old, entered the *Guinness book of records* as the most successful to date. Deducting 20 pence from every hundred pounds spent, it raised £5 million for its beneficiaries. (This, of course, was good for the bank as well.)

'Direct mail' is the professional term for what most people know as 'junk mail'. Names are usually 'rented' from the subscription lists of magazines, or from other commercial mail registers. Some charitable organizations rent their lists to others, although always through a professional third-party firm that will ensure no more than one-time access to a name and address. The efforts to find out whether subscribers to *National Geographic* are better givers than those who subscribe to *Architectural Digest, Soldier of Fortune,* or *The National Lampoon* are the stuff of brain surgery. So complex is the business, that it has been fine-tuned into a broad range of highly complex disciplines: targeting, market segmentation, random selection, and esoteric specialities such as 'de-duplication', 'angel-dusting', 'leapfrogging' and something called 'promiscuity'.

Often a mail campaign includes a gimmick or a gift: address labels in the name of the potential donor, an extremely low-value banknote from Bolivia or Pakistan, or a small pack of greeting cards. These are known in the trade as 'teasers'. For its 1993 Christmas campaign, the British Salvation Army designed a teaser campaign to raise money for the elderly homeless. Many live outdoors under cardboard, and so the Salvation Army printed its appeal on stiff cardboard, combining the first mailing, or 'donor prompt' with a door-to-door collection and a second prompt a couple of weeks later. The campaign raised half a million pounds and came in with an 'income to cost ratio' of 5.1:1. The campaign won a Silver Award for Innovation in the 1994 British Professional Fundraising Awards.[12]

Telephone fundraising is a relatively new technique. A group of people, sometimes volunteers working at home, but more likely employees of a specialist firm, work the telephone book, much the way direct mail companies use the postal service. The cost can be high because lists must be prepared, special equipment rented or purchased, computers set up to log the data, and callers paid. The phenomenon, maddening for the person who picks up the phone, appears — at least temporarily — to be a winner. In the early 1990s, ActionAid adapted it to the solicitation of corporate donations, for approaching potential volunteers and for general donor communication. ActionAid's telephone marketing was so successful, in fact, that it set up a commercial telephone fundraising consulting firm in order to earn additional income for the organization. 'ActionAid's success bears testimony to our unique approach,' says their National Telephone Team advertisement. 'We invest heavily in training to ensure our callers are skilled in speaking with sensitivity, care and knowledge. We take pride in the fact that our complaint levels are consistently low . . .'

Another approach is the establishment of commercial trading companies which can channel profits to a charity. Some of these 'alternative trading organizations' (ATO) purchase goods from producers' groups overseas; some rely heavily on the sale of greeting cards. Some, like the Intermediate Technology Development Group, the World Wide Fund for Nature and Help the Aged sell mainly through catalogues, while others have wholesale or storefront operations.

In 1988, the Max Havelaar Foundation began purchasing coffee from producers, packaging and selling it through commercial outlets in the Netherlands and elsewhere in Europe. Rather than the 80 cents growers were receiving through normal channels, the Max Havelaar Foundation paid $1.12 to $1.26 a pound. By the end of 1994, Max Havelaar coffee had captured a small but not insignificant portion of the Dutch market: 3000 of the 126 000 tons marketed annually.[13]

There are many others contributing to the estimated annual ATO turnover of $300–400 million: Transfair International in Germany, Italy and elsewhere, Trade Aid in New Zealand, the Fairtrade Foundation in Britain, Equal Exchange in the US, and Fair TradeMark Canada. While some buy and resell products, others simply offer a label to manufacturers with good labour or environmental practices. The 'Rugmark' label, for example, identifies Indian rugs that are not manufactured by indentured children.

In Britain, there are an estimated 5000 'charity shops' selling used clothing, books, handicrafts and selected commodities like coffee and tea from the South. At the end of 1993, about 840 of these were Oxfam shops, and 160 belonged to Save the Children. The economics of catalogue operations and charity shops are mixed. For some it is justified more by the publicity and the market created for Southern goods, than by the profit. The average weekly turnover in an Oxfam shop in 1993 was £1200 a week, and for Save the Children it was only £302 — far less than the average retailer would need to stay in business. One reason for survival, however, is lower costs. Run mainly by volunteers, the net profit margin for Oxfam is about 32 per cent, and for Save the Children it is 43 per cent. In 1993, Oxfam turned a handsome profit of £17 million on income of £52 million, and Save the Children showed a profit of £1.8 million on a turnover of only £6 million.[14]

In all this, principled NGOs face a genuine dilemma. Financial independence and security are essential to good management. Development is not cheap or fast or easy. Donors want professionally run operations, but professional fundraisers, accountants, managers and field workers are real people, with families, obligations and choices. Better management does not result from paying amateurs more money, nor does it result from paying professionals half the going rate. Worker burnout, a common occurrence in NGOs, results from worker overload. In the end, all work and no pay makes Jack look for another job. It is, to use another useful cliché, penny-wise and pound-foolish. NGOs should not be on the leading edge of salary norms, but if they fall too far behind, the resulting amateurism and inexperience may well lead to even greater long-term administrative costs, or to reduced effectiveness.

There is another important aspect to the general question of money and overheads, one that any private sector producer understands intimately: overheads vary. The overheads in an insurance company are very different from overheads in a glass factory. The overheads of an airline are likely to be different from the overheads in a bank. They may be higher or lower, depending on scale, innovation and, of course, on efficiency. Parents rarely ask what the overheads are when they send an offspring to university. Nobody asks what Mazda's overheads are, as compared with BMW. Donors rarely question overheads in domestic charities dealing with cancer or heart disease. But for some reason, it has become fashionable to expect 'low' overheads of international NGOs, without ever considering whether child sponsorship is generically more costly than a community development programme based on savings and credit, or whether a relatively consistent, plannable activity like sending volunteers is less or more cost-effective than an almost unplannable emergency operation in a war zone.

Part of the problem is that there are few public evaluations available, no real industry standards, no comparisons between child sponsorship agencies, no clear benchmarks for well-drilling, rural credit or immunization, much less for more intangible things like 'empowerment'. And between activities there are few comparisons. With careful study, it may be possible to determine levels of efficiency, but efficiency only deals with the question of doing something right. Doing the right thing — an effectiveness issue — is another question entirely. Without industry standards, without benchmarks, comparisons, transparency, and a regulatory framework that helps donors to make educated choices, unscrupulous NGOs can flourish. And scrupulous NGOs are likely to continue to face irrational pressures which do little to advance effectiveness, efficiency or professionalism.

Evaluation: who wants to know?

Good leadership and sound management, however they are described, are a precursor to, but not a proxy for good work. One of the odd things about most NGOs, explained only in part by the overhead problem, is their lack of attention to evaluation. In order to be effective, development must be knowledge-based. Knowing what works, and why, is essential to success. Knowing what does not work is

157

equally important. Knowledge involves awareness, memory and the familiarity that develops with experience and learning, particularly true at an institutional level. The inability to learn and remember is a widespread failing of the development community as a whole. Among NGOs it is a particular problem, however, because there are few reasons to disseminate the positive lessons of development, and many more powerful reasons to conceal and forget the negative ones.

The problem relates to both advertising and expectations, those of both the public at large and governments. NGOs pride themselves on their ability to reach the poorest quickly, effectively and efficiently. This sort of message was appropriate in the 1960s, when much NGO work was relief oriented, and it is still true in emergency work today. NGO 'advertising' has remained the same, however, despite the complexities of development work. It still emphasizes speed, effectiveness and efficiency.

Development is rarely speedy or simple, however; certainly it is not as speedy and simple as fundraising messages imply. Working with poor people who have few assets and who live on marginal land, NGOs know that effectiveness and efficiency in human development is not nearly as straightforward as the building of dams, roads and bridges. Having promised the donor too much, however, and caught in the low overhead snare, the NGO is trapped. If income is to be maintained, success stories are essential. These are often exaggerated, while failures are downplayed or camouflaged. Open evaluation, a perilous business, therefore, is avoided as much as possible.

Governments, on the other hand, channelling more and more money through NGOs, do want to know how effective and how efficient they are. So in the absence of acceptable NGO self-evaluation, governments have increasingly insisted on external evaluations of their own devising. There are three basic problems with these evaluations. The first is that most are designed by the donor agency as control and justification mechanisms, rather than as tools for learning or for disseminating findings. The second is that in the absence of baseline data and comparative benchmarks, many are highly subjective, relying heavily on the intuition and experience of the evaluator, rather than on performance in relation to objectives. A third is that increasingly, the entire NGO is becoming subject to evaluation, rather than the project or the component being supported by government. The result is that in return for a modest investment, a government agency may be able to exert considerable influence over the entire work and direction of the NGO, insisting on more rigorous future homage to logical framework analyses and the like.

For NGOs concerned about these issues, one major solution presents itself: to focus on the 'why' of evaluation rather than the 'how'. In other words, evaluation should be treated first and foremost as a learning exercise. This implies that findings must be made available so they can be debated, acted upon, and used by others. This can be done through participatory methods such as the Rapid and Participatory Rural Appraisal techniques developed at the University of Sussex and the International Institute for Environment and Development (IIED). Or it can be done in more formal and traditional ways by external evaluators. It means, however, that the implied financial threat that seems to accompany failure must be removed. In other words, as much distance should be placed between evaluation and financial decisions as possible. This may seem like a contradiction in logic, but it is not intended to absolve NGOs from responsibility for preventable errors and inefficiencies. On the contrary, if done well over time, this approach to evaluation could help to ensure that the preventable becomes more predictable, and therefore more avoidable. If the learning function is performed well, then the other major purpose of evaluation — reassuring the donor — will take place of its own accord.

Results: dealing with effectiveness

Before any of this can take place intelligently, however, the tyranny of the logical framework and other blueprint-based management approaches must be addressed.[15] The standard LFA and most project proposals are based almost exclusively on inputs or activities, and on outputs, rather than results. Teacher training may be given, but it may not be used in the classroom. A well may be dug and a pump installed, but the buckets used to carry the water home may be dirty. The results in these cases will differ markedly from what was intended.

Results have always been important to NGOs, but their planning mechanisms and those of bilateral agencies have always been somewhat vague on the question of ultimate results, and more particularly on how to measure them. Evaluation exercises inevitably return to broadly stated goals and objectives for their terms of reference, and too often discover that there are no baseline indicators or, worse, no prior agreement as to how or when the results might be measured. Evaluations tend to focus, therefore, on activities and specific outputs for detail, and on sketchy evidence of achievement in relation to broader project goals.

A particular problem, measurement aside, is that predicting results is not the same as achieving results. Attempts to predict measurable qualitative results, and even quantitative results, can lead back to a rigid blueprint and what Brinkerhoff calls the 'empty behaviour' of oversimplification and false quantification.[16] Results, therefore, need to be articulated in a variety of ways, sometimes through proxies:

159

- Learning results (e.g. is oral rehydration training remembered?)
- Results related to capacity-building, empowerment and sustainability (e.g. the improved capacity of farmers to produce food; the increased capacity of women to add to family income; the increased capacity of a partner organization to act independently of its sponsoring agency).
- Efficiency results (e.g. doing more with the same inputs; reduced costs; economies of scale; experiments with user fees; self-financing credit programmes).
- Effectiveness results (e.g. can reduced child mortality be measured and correlated with a training programme? How many job trainees actually have jobs? How many small enterprises have improved productivity or income levels?)

Using LFA-type language, a results-based education project in Ecuador might look like this:

- Goals: broad statements of intent; the basic result the project aims to achieve (e.g. an improved education system in Ecuador).
- Objectives: specific statements of purpose, expressing a desired end (e.g. to upgrade teacher education; to improve school textbooks).
- Inputs: the activities and resources applied to the project (e.g. money, technical assistance for curriculum development, scholarships for teacher trainers; a mobile resource centre).
- Outputs: the goods produced or services performed (e.g. the number of teachers trained; the number of textbooks revised).
- Results: the benefits, or otherwise, flowing from the project (i.e. an improved education system in Ecuador).

The immediate challenge will be to develop and agree on indicators of what an improved education system in Ecuador might look like. Three or four obvious indicators flow from this hypothetical example:

- a certain percentage of the teachers trained are actually working in Ecuador as teachers;
- they remember and are using the teaching methods that they were taught;
- the new textbooks are being used;
- the teachers and the textbooks are effective (use of proxies such as improved pass rates; lower dropout rates; improved cognitive skills in students).

Although this approach seems relatively straightforward, it will undoubtedly prove less so when discussed with the people responsible for implementing the project. It will become obvious to them, for example, that results-based indicators will or should form the basis for future evaluation, and must therefore be very carefully thought through. Expectations may very well have to be reduced, which, given the unrealistic promises of so many past projects, is not a bad thing.

Two other issues emerge. The first has to do with time. Things may take longer than anticipated, through no fault of the planners. And in this example, improved cognitive skills, lower dropout rates and better pass rates may not be measurable until a year or so after the training has been completed and the textbooks printed. In some projects, the most important results may not be visible for two, five or even more years. Standard donor-oriented mid-term reviews and end-of-project evaluations, therefore, have to take this into consideration if project implementors are expected to work towards long-term results in short-term financial arrangements.

The second issue has to do with risk. Risks are traditionally characterized in LFAs as vague 'assumptions', such as 'the inputs are available as planned'. But there are usually other, unforeseen risks: the partner organization collapses; inflation wrecks the budget; the government unilaterally alters all teacher education.

Given increasing levels of uncertainty, complexity and risk in all development work, management writer Dennis Rondinelli believes that it has become more difficult and complex to state goals and objectives precisely, because development problems are not well defined or understood. 'Solutions' are not always clear or easily transferable, the impacts of interventions cannot always be predicted, and the objectives of multiple participants and stakeholders in a project are not always consistent.[17] It has also become more difficult to assess the feasibility of an intervention because the understanding of the problem is rarely complete at the outset. Under conditions of complexity and uncertainty, it is increasingly difficult to keep the design and implementation phases separate, because activities have to be adjusted as they are carried out, and as more is learned about people and conditions. And it has become more difficult to apply standard appraisal criteria because implementation is frequently not under an NGO's direct control.

There are various ways of dealing with this. One is to undertake activities which minimize risk. Risk avoidance, however — a pandemic within bilateral and multilateral development organizations — is counter-productive. Without risk-taking, Paul Theroux would never have gone to Malawi, Ela Bhatt would never have started SEWA, there would be no Oxfam, no appropriate technology, no Greenpeace. Real development, based, as it is, upon change, is inherently risky.

Rondinelli suggests an alterative to risk avoidance. Rather than applying ever more rigid and inflexible controls and monitoring

161

techniques, he suggests that experiments should be viewed as such, and that the lessons of failure should be 'learned' and absorbed along with the successes. One way of profiling and balancing the risk element in a portfolio of activities, is to categorize them as to their degree of experimentation. The most risky will be experimental projects which are needed when little is known about beneficiaries, their problems or the most effective means of setting objectives. Such activities can be kept relatively small and on a fairly tight leash.

Pilot projects are less risky. They test the results of experiments under a greater variety of conditions, and make sense when the problem is well-defined and when something has been learned from earlier experimental efforts. Demonstration projects are larger still, and may have longer time frames. They are used to show the effectiveness and to increase the acceptability of new methods, techniques and forms of behaviour on a broader scale. Less risky than experiments and pilots, demonstration projects still need innovative and creative management in order to gain acceptance for new ways of doing things. Replication or production projects evolve from experiments, pilots and demonstration projects. These will take place when most uncertainties and unknowns have been dealt with.

Institutional results

Achieving results in projects is one thing, but institutional performance is often a very different matter. The whole can sometimes be considerably less than the sum of the parts, as those worried about NGO contracting often proclaim. Some of the best American cars of the 1930s, Cord, Deusenberg, Pierce-Arrow, were made by companies that failed. Conversely, some of the most efficient governments of this century have wreaked untold havoc on their citizens.

Staff, trustees, donors and volunteers all want to know how well an organization is doing in relation to its values, its mission, and its broad objectives. A serious problem in answering such questions, the attempt to narrow the gap between vision and reality, is that an organiztion's vision is often stated in vague and unassailably virtuous terms, terms that do not lend themselves to measurement and evaluation. In fact the mission statement is often vague because there are so many different stakeholders in an organization that specifics appropriate to one would not suit another. Trustees, for example, are most likely to be concerned that the organization is engaged in activities that give it legitimacy, that create pride in its work. Managers, on the other hand, will be judged on the basis of their efficiencies, their capacity to solve problems, and to balance the allocation of resources between the vigorously competing demands of, say, the fundraising and development education departments. Beneficiaries, however, (and institutional donors), are most likely to be interested in standards of performance in programme delivery, which may emphasize the short run, rather than the long run that is of most concern to trustees.

A number of tools have been developed in recent years to help NGOs deal with the institutional tradeoffs between legitimacy and management, between the competing demands of funders and beneficiaries. One is The Drucker Foundation's Self-Assessment Tool, which borrows from Peter Drucker's work in the private sector, and places heavy emphasis on an organization's 'product' and 'customer'. Customers include beneficiaries as well as 'supporting customers': volunteers, donors, trustees and staff. The Self-Assessment Tool uses multi-stakeholder exercises to make organizations confront and resolve competing customer demands.[18]

Another tool is the 'social audit', pioneered in Britain three decades ago, and currently enjoying a revival in both the private and the nonprofit sectors. One example is the Ethical Accounting Statement, a public, multi-stakeholder account of a company's operations. Versions have been developed by the Copenhagen Business School and have been adopted by companies as diverse as the SBN Bank in Scandinavia, and a popular American ice-cream maker, Ben and Jerry's. A London-based research and lobbying NGO, the New Economics Foundation, has taken the social audit further, introducing concepts of comparison, regularity, public disclosure, and the need for external validation by outsiders with no vested interest in the outcome. One of their first social audits was conducted on behalf of Traidcraft, a public limited company that buys goods produced by Southern NGOs, co-operatives and small producers in the South for resale in Britain. Traidcraft's 1992 turnover was about £6 million. Its objectives are based on the idea of a fair return to suppliers, and on the concept of establishing 'a just trading system which expresses the principles of love and justice fundamental to the Christian faith'.

The social audit conducted by the New Economics Foundation involved individuals from business schools, corporate responsibility campaigning and research organizations, as well as representatives of Traidcraft's shareholders, suppliers and staff. The result was a published document which discussed the organization from the perspective of suppliers, staff, shareholders and customers. It addressed markup and profit, environmental issues, staff salaries and training, tradeoffs between price and commitment, and shareholder involvement.

The process involved the full range of Traidcraft's stakeholders, and while it dealt with accountability on financial matters, it also investigated questions of effectiveness and performance in relation

163

to the organization's *social* aims and objectives. It had the benefits of a participatory process, but it was managed by outside professionals who ultimately took responsibility for the final report, signing it just as a financial auditor would. As a published document, the social audit tells more about Traidcraft in fourteen pages than the average external evaluation would about another organization in ten times the space.[19]

Still in an evolutionary stage, the social audit does begin to address in new ways, and perhaps to narrow, gaps between vision and reality, between efficiency and effectiveness. It has been adopted by organizations as diverse as The Body Shop, a large cosmetics company, by community businesses in Scotland, and by Shared Earth in York. While perhaps not appropriate for all settings and all types of organization, the social audit provides relief for thirsty travellers seeking responsible and comprehensive mechanisms for dealing with the broader issues of accountability. Accountability, the achilles heel of the NGO movement as a whole, will be a recurring theme in the remaining chapters of this book.

PART THREE

Now the trumpet

CHAPTER IX

Dependence and independence in the contracting era

You must know this law of culture: two civilizations cannot really know and understand one another well. You will start going deaf and blind. You will be content in your own civilization . . . but signals from the other civilization will be as incomprehensible to you as if they had been sent by the inhabitants of Venus.

Ryszard Kapuściński, *The Emperor.*

The day of the contract

DESPITE FREQUENTLY REPEATED reassurance that NGO independence is reasonably intact, the fact is that Northern NGOs have stumbled into a contracting era without appearing to have noticed it.[1] It began rather innocuously in 1962, when Germany introduced a programme of financial support for its NGOs. In the decade after that, 'matching grant' programmes were developed throughout OECD member countries. Some remained relatively simple, as in Britain and New Zealand, matching the cash provided by an NGO on a dollar-for-dollar and on a project-by-project basis. These arrangements were essentially responsive in nature, with government asking only basic questions about budgets and timing, and almost never seeking any sort of evaluation. Gradually, as the number of NGOs and projects grew, variations began to develop. Throughout the North, 'block grants', 'frame agreements' and 'institutional funding' became more common, with three-, four- and five-year time horizons. Today, the size of these responsive programmes varies from minuscule (about 0.1 per cent of official development assistance in Japan; 0.2 per cent in the US) to small (1 per cent in Australia, 1.5 per cent in Britain). Some are more generous (about 4.5 per cent in Canada; 5.3 per cent in Norway), while others are relatively large (7 per cent in the Netherlands; over 10 per cent in Germany).[2]

Governments provide financial support to NGOs in other ways. Tax relief is one, and the authority to issue receipts to donors for income tax deductions is another. The value of this privilege — common in most English-speaking countries as well as in Germany, Hungary and Poland — is rarely computed for international NGOs. In 1991, however, Australia calculated the value at A$19.5 million. This had the net effect of increasing the government's cash contribution to NGOs by more than 32 per cent.[3]

One way of looking at the responsive programmes is to view them as 'entitlements': money *owed* to NGOs because of the good work they do and because of the public support they demonstrate through their ability to raise independent income in the form of donations. The concept of entitlement is one with deep roots in the philosophy of social welfare. It is based on the premise that the state owes its citizens certain social benefits and protection. But the concept of unquestioned entitlement is changing. Governments throughout Europe and North America have been 'down-sizing' and 'contracting out' for more than a decade, placing heavy new burdens on non-profit organizations in all walks of life. Although criticisms have not prompted the elimination of entitlements in Western societies, they have frequently justified the imposition of conditions and reciprocal obligations on the part of beneficiaries.[4]

The word 'subsidy' is perhaps more apt than 'entitlement' in describing 'responsive' support programmes. An entitlement is a right; a subsidy is a privilege. Subsidies too, seldom occur without reciprocal obligations, sometimes called 'strings'. During the 1970s, many responsive government programmes prohibited the use of their money in places like Cuba or South Africa (including support for liberation movements). During the 1980s, Cambodia and Vietnam were on several banned lists. The British Overseas Development Administration says that 70 per cent of its support to block-grant agencies must be spent in its 45 preferred countries. While not an overwhelmingly unreasonable restriction at first glance, it does pose some difficulties for British NGOs, because large parts of Latin America and Francophone Africa are thus excluded.

NGOs for windows

In recent years, growth in matching grant programmes has tended to slow or stagnate, while other funding mechanisms for NGOs have gradually taken up the slack. In the case of American NGOs, food aid and support for freight costs is the largest, representing 31 per cent of all government support to NGOs in 1991.* Throughout OECD

---

*'Programme grants' represented 51 per cent of the total, but these were not matching grants as the term is commonly understood. They may include a contribution from the NGO, but they are negotiated overseas with the resident USAID mission on the basis of its own country priorities. A project may originate with the NGO, or with USAID, and no pre-set budget is set aside for NGOs. Programme grants in 1992 totalled more than $300 million, as compared with only $18 million in the responsive matching grant programme.

countries in the 1980s, governments created other special financial 'windows' (or 'spigots' as they are sometimes called in the US) — for AIDS, Women in Development (WID), democracy and emergencies — and special country initiatives — Southern Africa, the Philippines, Cambodia. Sometimes these funds are created as a direct response to NGO pressure. Usually they are offered on highly concessional terms, frequently on a 100 per cent basis.

Governmental influence on choice is often benign. Most WID money, for example, has aims, objectives and criteria that few NGOs would contest. Sometimes NGOs have helped draft the terms of reference for such funds. But the cumulative effect can be large. An NGO may use the bulk of its private income to 'draw down' money from windows with the most favourable terms. In the end, it may have little left for countries or activities which were once on its own priority list. The extent of government encroachment into both the sectoral and geographical programming of NGOs can be seen in the creation of Australian windows: of all government support to Australian NGOs, only 30 per cent in 1993–4 was fully 'responsive'. Another 26 per cent was designated for special geographical areas, 37 per cent was for emergencies and refugees, while other money was set aside for women, AIDS and other government priorities.[5] The danger for NGOs can be seen in the Canadian situation, where in the 1980s and 1990s CIDA established more than a dozen different country-specific and sectoral NGO windows in addition to the basic NGO programme. Two of these actually became legally incorporated NGOs, but none were spared when CIDA changed its mind about the usefulness of windows and slammed them all shut without warning in 1995. Even the most responsive donor programmes can pull NGOs in the general direction of governmental priorities, but the windows phenomenon clearly serves to reduce initiative and to make NGOs more compliant with government priorities.

As noted in Chapter VI, in recent years there have been major changes in the financing of NGOs for emergencies, refugee work and the provision of food aid. In the Netherlands it grew by 150 per cent between 1990 and 1992. Seventy five per cent of Britain's food aid is handled by British NGOs, and more than 40 per cent of SIDA spending on emergencies and refugees in 1992–3 was channelled through Swedish NGOs: roughly half of what was available in matching grants for development programmes. Sixty per cent of all USAID emergency spending was programmed through NGOs in 1992–3.[6]

These statistics begin to make the notion of low NGO dependency on government and the concept of a hands-off matching arrangement look a little threadbare. Although some countries such as Britain attempt to keep the ratio of government support to NGO funds for NGO development activities below 50 per cent, others like Sweden and Norway will provide 80 per cent for development projects, and up to 100 per cent for emergencies. Like their counterparts in many other countries, the average Norwegian and Swedish NGO, therefore, has a very high level of financial dependency on government.

Norwegian and Swedish NGOs explain that government support must be seen within the context of Scandinavian corporatism, and that high subsidies — entitlements, perhaps — do not rob an organization of its independent voice, nor of its ability to criticize government, should the need arise. This claim must be set against the rule that some Scandinavian NGOs have established, to restrict government income to 50 per cent of the total. These organizations believe that there *is* such a thing as 'too much'; that there is a point beyond which independence of voice and independence of action become muted. Similar concerns can be found in other countries. In Britain, Oxfam restricts its government income to 20 per cent of the total, while Oxfam America and the American Friends Service Committee take no money from government whatsoever.*

In the South, there is no need to create 'windows'; the damage is done by the simple setting of donor 'priorities'. A generous donor with an interest in children or family planning or social forestry will draw small NGOs, and sometimes big ones, like a magnet. There are probably hundreds of Southern NGOs that have been formed simply because there was a strong donor interest in a particular type of activity, and there are many more whose aims and objectives have become skewed in the direction of donor priorities. This is bound to continue until there is generic support for NGOs and their own priorities, and until Southern NGOs are able to develop their own independent financial base.

Public service contractors

In 1990, David Korten wrote about something he called 'public service contractors'. These are organizations that 'are driven by market considerations more than by values, and therefore are more like businesses than voluntary organizations'.[7] In coining the terminology, Korten identified a problem and held a useful mirror up to the NGO community. A public service contractor (PSC), he said, is likely to be

---

*It could be argued, however, that this is not really adequate protection: if Oxfam's charitable status were suspended for, say, political activities contravening government regulations, its public support could be seriously affected. This small-donor dependency can contribute as much to self-censorship as can a cash dependency on government.

well managed, efficient, and probably quite large, hence its attractive-ness to a donor. Going beyond Korten, it could be said that the PSC does the bidding of others: running, for example, donor-supplied feeding programmes. The PSC is an executing agency. Increasingly dependent on contracts to maintain its infrastructure, it gradually be-comes an easily manipulated, cost-effective surrogate for govern-ments struggling with concepts of neo-liberalism, down-sizing and privatization. It has made a Faustian bargain which may allow it to thrive, but its soul has been compromised.

This sort of bogeyman haunts the discussions of NGOs and re-searchers alike. The writing about public service contractors is usually polite, but when people talk about them, they do so with disdain.[8] Korten outlines the pressures that drive NGOs towards public service contracts:

o the fatigue of constantly existing at the margin of financial survival and the attraction of donor funding;
o the strain faced by more activist NGOs who must constantly fight established interests, values and practices;
o the difficulty of maintaining value consensus and commitment as the organization grows;
o a sense of moral obligation to provide job security for paid staff;
o the belief that contracting will bring greater funding and make it possible for the organization to do more of those things it feels are truly important; and,
o the pressure from donors to 'professionalize'.

These are all very real problems that senior NGO managers face on a daily basis, problems that inevitably require judicious and not infre-quent compromise. In his writing, Korten was perhaps most exercised about American NGOs that receive support from USAID. The US Government's hands-off, responsive matching grant programme is tiny: $18 million in 1992, or about 1.4 per cent of all government support to NGOs. Most NGOs dealing with USAID, therefore, must in some way fall into line behind the aims and objectives of official American development assistance. Those handling food aid often do so in a big way. Food and freight represented 62 per cent of the income of the Adventist Development and Relief Agency in 1991, and the figure for Catholic Relief Services was 57 per cent. For Lutheran World Service it was 43 per cent, and for CARE, 41 per cent.[9] Contract-ing of this type and magnitude is uncommon in Scandinavia, Britain and Germany. But it is a growing phenomenon in Canada and Italy, and it has created a dependency in Switzerland that far outstrips the American scene. Swiss NGOs raise only 14 per cent of their income from the Swiss public. The balance — all from government — has a matching grant component. But contracts for the execution of Swiss Government programmes account for 70 per cent of government 'support' to NGOs.[10]

Ratios notwithstanding, to suggest that contracting is somehow irreconcilable with the holding of values is illogical. The problem is not contracts, but what an NGO agrees to do under the terms of a contract. In an ideal world, there would be considerable congruence between the objectives of NGOs and government development agencies. Where there is no threat to an NGO's values or direction, where it understands the terms and conditions and where, ideally, it has been involved in developing the terms of reference, the 'danger' in taking a contract should be low. In fact, contracting offers several advantages to both the NGO and the aid agency that are often glossed over in the rush to warn of falling sky.

For the donor agency there are several possible advantages. Because many have limited capacities of their own, contracting an NGO can expand a donor's poverty-oriented programming. The private sector does not have the capacity to do this. Further, the donor does not have to expend great time and energy administering such projects because the executing agency — the NGO — is a development institution with its own infrastructure at home and overseas. If it is so inclined, a donor can learn from the NGO experience. And by cultivating an NGO, the donor is also building a broader support base for itself through the NGO's public support base. This is not often the case with private sector firms.

The contract mechanism provides certain disciplines that are absent in a grant situation. These can be a mixed blessing, but many NGOs welcome the clarity of expectations and the finite time frame that a contract offers. For the donor, a contract does the same. It can also instill the 'professionalism' and accountability that many believe is lacking, or at least is not clearly visible in standard NGO activities.

The sky is falling

Contracts become problematic when they deflect NGOs from their own agenda, when compromises are not judicious, and when the NGO becomes little more than an entrepreneur; when it will, or must, take any kind of contract in order to stay afloat, bowing to donor-specified terms and conditions, and suffering the indignity of donor-led evaluations. The biggest risk for an NGO today lies in broad ideological changes in thinking about development, about development assistance, about the role of the state and the role of civil society. For example, the damage done to the poor by structural adjustment programmes has caused donors to develop programmes intended to mitigate the worst effects of these. In Ghana in the mid-1980s, donors initiated a Programme of Actions to Mitigate the Social Costs of Adjustment (PAMSCAD). Much of the money was channelled through the Ghanaian NGO community. Eight local and international NGOs, including ActionAid and World Vision, were involved in implementing the Programme to Alleviate Poverty and the Social Cost of Adjustment (PAPSCA) in Uganda. And two hundred NGOs, 80 per cent of them local, were involved in implementing three thousand projects connected with the Bolivian Emergency Social Fund (ESF).[11]

The World Bank and the Government of Sri Lanka were the prime movers behind the 1991 creation of the $87.5 million Janasaviya Trust Fund (JTF), established as an anti-poverty programme with a large NGO-support component. Many good projects were financed by the JTF, but damage was also done. Caught between unprincipled Sri Lankan politicians and micro-managers in Washington, the JTF sometimes became a parody of the models, like Grameen Bank, that it sought to emulate.[12]

In cases such as these a question may be asked: are participating NGOs being used as band-aids to cover up deep wounds? Or are they providing badly needed first aid? The answer is probably a little of both, but it is a fine point which avoids the bigger question. If the contract prevents an NGO from speaking out about what it sees as the cause of the wound, then one of the principle *raisons d'être* behind the creation of independent associations will have been lost.

There is no longer any doubt that the contracting ethos has weakened domestic non-profit organizations in many countries. In Britain it has damaged the advocacy work of NGOs in two ways. The money available for advocacy has been reduced because of what one NGO worker calls the overwhelming pressures 'on management and other staff time of meeting the demands of the contract culture'. But there is another problem which strikes at the essence of what non-governmental organizations are all about: 'NGOs cannot afford to campaign as before if, in doing so, they now place at risk their capacity to win contracts for services or to have their grant-aid renewed.'[13]

In *Nonprofits for hire: the welfare state in the age of contracting*, Smith and Lipsky deal with the declining independence and voice of domestic American organizations. Like ancient Greek mariners, a high proportion have been lured by the siren's song of government money onto the rocky shoals of compliance, homogenization and bureaucratization. While there may be a degree of reciprocity between government and NGO in a contracting regime, this is not at all the same as 'partnership'. Smith and Lipsky point out that most contracting structures are sponsored and directed by a relatively powerful agent. 'Just as the hegemonic nation — the United States in the post-war period, or Britain at an earlier time — bends the behaviour of nominally independent nations toward its way of doing things according to its preferred economic, political and social systems, so government gradually influences the behaviour of independent non-profit contractors to accept its practices and preferred policies.'[14] The result in the United States is that the 'ideal marriage' between government and non-profits, bringing together the best of both worlds, has turned into a confused and expensive mess that satisfies few except those with vested interests. It has led to overweening government intervention in NGO affairs, it has stifled initiative, silenced voice and created widespread NGO destabilization.

Peter Drucker perhaps says it most clearly: 'To be able to perform, an organization must be autonomous. Legally it may be a government agency, as are Europe's railways, America's state universities, or Japan's leading radio and television network, NHK. Yet in actual operation, these organizations must be able to "do their own thing". If they are used to carry out "government policy", they immediately stop performing.'[15]

Crowding out the state

After a discussion about the increasing dependence of NGOs on governments, it may seem odd to reverse the debate, and to raise the concern that NGOs may be 'crowding out the state' in some parts of the developing world. Odd, maybe, but there is a strong feeling that the increased bilateral and multilateral financing of NGOs poses a threat to Southern governments. John Clark says that some governments see it as 'the erosion of their sovereignty; the increasing execution of state functions by staff who are answerable not to them but to foreign governments; the diversion of some of their most skilled labour from government to 'non-government' service; and the gradual takeover by foreign influence, culture and values.'[16]

Ironically, it is when governments are weak and defensive that they are most fearful and critical of NGOs. It might be helpful, therefore, to segregate these charges and to examine them more carefully. The appropriation of 'state functions' by NGOs, for example (schools, hospitals, immunization programmes), occurs most noticeably where the state does not or cannot provide these functions. Sometimes this is the product of a historical division of labour: mission hospitals, for example, having been established before there was government capacity. In many instances, however, NGOs have stepped in where government services have fallen into disrepair.

More often than not, in such cases NGOs have been encouraged by governments to complement and to supplement what have been called, with considerable historical inaccuracy, 'state functions'.

NGOs, for example, supply a third or more of all clinical health care in Cameroon, Ghana, Malawi, Uganda and Zambia. They provide more than 10 per cent in Indonesia and India, and they own a quarter of the health facilities in Bolivia's three largest cities. In Brazil, a single NGO has more than 47 000 community health workers providing health care and training in nutrition, prenatal care, breast-feeding, immunization and the management of diarrhoea. As far as efficiency is concerned, NGOs often get more mileage from their investments than governments. A doctor in a Ugandan mission hospital treats five times more patients in a day than one working in a government hospital, and mission hospital nurses handle twice as many patients.[17] Far from being resented, in most cases these services are supported financially by government. In Zimbabwe, government subventions to mission hospitals grew by more than 500 per cent between 1981 and 1991, representing almost 10 per cent of the budget of the Ministry of Health.[18] Similar sorts of statistics could be cited in the provision of education and welfare services. With structural adjustment programmes and greater 'privatization', numbers like these are not growing smaller.

In these examples, NGOs are not usurping state or government authority, they are simply doing what NGOs have always done — they are providing services where there are none. This is sometimes called 'gap filling'. But unlike the early years of independence in Africa and Asia, many of these gaps are widening into canyons that are unlikely to narrow in the near future. When governments collapse, disappear or simply walk away, as they have in Somalia, Ethiopia and elsewhere, NGOs have usually been the first, and sometimes the only ones, apart from bandits, to step into the breach. This is not 'supplanting' government.

The effect of foreign influence, culture and values is a legitimate concern. Zimbabwean writer Yash Tandon accuses Europeans in general and NGOs in particular, of 'universalizing their value systems'. Unfortunately he and others tend to assign almost as much influence to NGOs as to those whose business truly is the transfer of culture: Warner, Bertelsmann, Thorn-EMI, Phillips (which owns Polygram), Matsushita (which owns MCA) and Sony (which seems to own Hollywood). If there are concerns about the universalizing of value systems in Zimbabwe, consider Japan, where 50 per cent of popular music sales are in English; or Germany, where the figure is 80 per cent.[19] Less mundane than popular music, Tandon's cultural charge sheet against NGOs includes the imposition of 'gender awareness', and concern with human rights and the environment. 'Amnesty International and Africa Watch are the best illustrations of the universalists. They imagine that there are certain principles of human rights that are universally valid for all time and place, and they forget that these rights, in their own countries, were products of intense struggle . . .'[20] If he attacked the cloying paternalism and righteousness with which some NGOs coat these issues, Tandon might have a more valid argument. But Europeans are not alone in having struggled for rights. Africans have had rather more intense struggles in recent years, and many of these struggles were, and still are being supported by NGOs, both African and foreign. And by individuals within these organizations who take very great personal risks.

In the late 1970s, a Liberian NGO, Susuku, was 'filling gaps' in the fields of agriculture and education. Susuku had been founded by young Liberians, mainly recent university graduates, who wanted to do for themselves what foreign NGOs and aid agencies had been doing up to then. One of the Susuku leaders, Siapha Kamara, taught adult literacy programmes in the evening. Like many NGOs with an agenda based on social justice, Susuku leaders talked about other things in their literacy classes. Such as social justice. One of Kamara's pupils was a young army sergeant named Samuel Doe. Later, after Doe had shot his way into the Presidential mansion and established himself as Head of State, he called Kamara in for a private discussion about social justice. When the discussion was over, Kamara lay bleeding and unconscious on the presidential carpet. It was only through the efforts of the Catholic Church and NOVIB that he was eventually released. A re-arrest warrant had been issued the same day, however, so Kamara went straight from prison to the airport and escaped, on a ticket provided by a foreign NGO.[21] While Yash Tandon has a point, Siapha Kamara, for one, might agree that there actually *are* principles of human rights that are universally valid for all time and place. In the hundreds and thousands of untold stories like his, Northern and Southern NGOs have managed, sometimes together, to make at least a little headway against the tyranny that, until recently, only governments have been capable of.

On less emotive ground, a variety of writers have begun to suggest that NGOs can weaken both governments and civil society because of their weak accountability, the taking of contracts from governmental donor agencies or the disempowering of existing, community-based organizations.[22] UNDP's 1993 Human Development Report suggested that NGOs 'could "crowd out" governments' by offering better salaries. It cited cases in Mozambique and Uganda and predicted that this problem was 'likely to continue'.[23] Other writers have gone further, accusing NGOs of trying to replace the state entirely. A frequently stated view is that 'NGOs cannot replace the state, for they have no legitimacy, authority or sovereignty, and crucially, are self-selected and thus not accountable'.[24]

It is hard to know where to start with all this. True, NGOs may be weak in the areas of legitimacy, authority, sovereignty and account-ability. But it is perhaps worth noting that the private sector has these exact same problems. In fact many governments, both historically and currently, are also weak in the areas of 'legitimacy, authority and sovereignty'. Far too many are 'self-selected and are thus not account-able'. Even the state has lost its sanctity — in Yugoslavia, Czechoslo-vakia, the Soviet Union and Ethiopia for example — not because of NGO intrusion, but because of government failure.

The salary question: yes, in many cases, NGOs probably do pay more than government. In several countries this would not be hard to do. Some governments have trouble paying any salaries: Zaire is a frequently cited case. The Government of Jamaica found itself unable to pay agreed retroactive salary raises in 1994. Structural adjustment had eaten so deeply into the exchequer that payment was postponed until 1995. But the question of high NGO costs and high NGO life-styles remains. It had become such an issue in Bangladesh by 1990, that a senior government official was asked to uncover the facts. He discovered that individuals in the upper echelons of the civil service received substantially higher salaries than their NGO counterparts, while in the field, NGO workers were slightly better off. Unlike gov-ernment personnel, however, NGO staff worked long hours and had virtually no job security.[25]

For NGOs there is often a different problem associated with salaries. Despite the UNDP worry that NGOs might 'crowd out government', it is UN agencies that are the most generically guilty, worldwide, of luring trained personnel away from NGOs, and from Southern governments.

On the charge of weakening government at a political level, it is true that in some cases, NGOs have acted in an overtly political man-ner. Their anti-apartheid efforts are a good example. They have gone as far as supporting breakaway rebel regimes, as in the case of Biafra, Eritrea and Tigray. In Afghanistan NGO support for anti-government *Mujahuddin* refugees (and militants) far outweighed the NGO effort to relieve suffering within Afghanistan. With the exceptions of Biafra and possibly South Africa, however, the NGO impact on national or even international politics has been modest. This is not to deny the role played by local NGOs in the downfall of the Ershad regime in Bangladesh, or the Marcos Government in the Philippines. But in these instances, there was a very broad canvas, one on which NGOs were relatively small brush strokes. In the end, there were massive public demonstrations of disaffection, along with a critical collapse in support from religious and business leaders, and from the armed forces. Despite their significant endeavours in Ethiopia, Somalia or pre-Sandinista Nicaragua, NGOs can hardly be said to have weakened civil society, the government or the state. This was done almost single-handedly and with great effectiveness by the governments of the day themselves, with a blend of brutality and official foreign assistance: Soviet, Western, multilateral; whatever came to hand.*

In addition to the charge of weakening government structures by what they *do*, NGOs are sometimes accused of weakening government structures by ignoring them. Mozambique is a case in point, 'a classic case study,' said one observer writing in 1993, 'of the reluctance of many international NGOs to support government services rather than running their own programmes in an un-coordinated way in different parts of the country.'[26] True, perhaps. But it is also a classic case of once burned, twice shy. The Government of Mozambique banned NGO health activities in 1975, believing itself to be the most appropriate and capable delivery mechanism. It was wrong. Uganda provides another example of the same thing. Idi Amin's brutal 1973 expulsion of the Asian community, which included teachers and doctors working in non-governmental institutions, was quietly reversed by the Museveni Government in the early 1990s when the Aga Khan Education Service was invited to return and resuscitate its (ruined) schools.

Independence and accountability

There *is* a problem, however. By default, in many countries, NGOs are picking up the pieces that governments have dropped, or never did hold. They are being encouraged or permitted to do so, sometimes reluctantly, by Southern governments. Vaguely stated fears about NGOs 'crowding out the state' and the creation of parallel delivery systems are in fact legitimate worries about the collapse of basic government administrative systems, and concern for their revival rather than the creation of substitutes.

Reacting to growing transfers of bilateral and multilateral support to NGOs, Southern governments ask valid questions about NGO accountability. NGOs, not unlike private business and government, are notoriously opaque in their decision-making, funding and evaluation. Because they can apparently 'deliver the goods', they have become attractive to the official development community. But contracts and greater financial support have resulted in 'reciprocal obligations'. In the process, Northern NGOs have lost a great deal of the independence and autonomy they once had. By failing to develop their own accountabilities, they have become increasingly answerable to

---

*A rhetorical question: if it could be proven that local NGOs actually *had* played a significant role in the destabilization of the non-democratic and widely reviled Marcos, Ershad, Mengistu or (fill in the blank) regimes, would this have been a bad thing?

government for their priorities, their management practises and their approach to advocacy. Southern NGOs risk the same loss of accountability, handing it not to their governments, many of which would love to take it on, but to outsiders.

Dependencies, of course, are not always one-way. In the North, official development assistance owes at least part of its existence in many countries to the public support base created by NGOs. NGO campaigns in Canada in 1990, in Australia in 1991, in Britain in 1992, and Sweden in 1993 are only examples of the many times NGOs have gone to the public in order to preserve the official development assistance budget. Although in the 1990s cuts have been widespread, NGOs may have been instrumental in mitigating or reducing the worst of them.

There is another dependency: government agencies have, as in Switzerland, become increasingly reliant upon NGOs for much of their poverty programming, and in many countries for more than half of their support to refugees, food aid and emergency programming. This dependency is under-reported in aid statistics, but it is unlikely to diminish, given the general retreat by government aid agencies from a hands-on role. In the South, many governments rely heavily on NGOs for important aspects of health, education and welfare delivery. These dependencies offer new challenges and new opportunities for NGOs, and will no doubt add further pressure to conform with government priorities.

The debate about NGO independence and accountability goes to the core of the discussion about what a voluntary organization is. The questions that arise from interaction with the state are not new, and the answers are, to a large degree, situational. A long-forgotten 1973 report stated the fundamentals of the current problem well, citing three issues in over-dependence on government:

> It places tremendous constraints on [NGOs'] freedom to be assertive in determining what they feel they ought to be engaged in, thus relegating them to the posture of 'hired guns' rather than independent thinkers and doers. It also creates apprehension that availability of government money may have a lulling effect, to the extent that personnel are no longer able to make independent assessments of whether they have sacrificed agency integrity or are indeed continuing to act in good conscience. Finally, it frustrates their attempts to make a contribution to the fundamental analysis and debate about the nature of the development process.[27]

For NGOs, independence is an issue of abiding importance. It should also be an issue of importance for governments. But independence is a relative term, one heavily nuanced by history, money, politics and situational relationships. Independence does not mean licence. Nor does it mean that NGOs can act without reference to government, government plans or government regulations. In some cases, as with clinical health care in Africa, there is a long-standing partnership between government and non-governmental agencies. In other situations, NGOs and government seem to be in a perpetual state of antagonism. In the end, each organization must struggle to strike an appropriate balance between autonomy and engagement with government, between prejudice against government on the one hand, and the real danger of co-option on the other.

Part of the difficulty in managing change is that individuals in most government agencies are not charged with nurturing the independence of NGOs. If anything, they are responsible for ensuring that NGOs conform to government rules and regulations, for ensuring that risks are minimized. In the end, the issue for those NGOs that receive government support may not be whether the dependency ratio is 10 per cent or 50 per cent or 80 per cent. This is as much an indication of financial vulnerability as anything else. The real issues are twofold. First, does the NGO in question see itself as something more than a 'hired gun'? If so, can it broaden its accountabilities, make them transparent and effective, and thus reduce donor inroads? Although its budget may come from government, a school, for example, has many accountabilities that restrict excessive government intrusion: students, parents, the parents' association, the teachers' union, employers that will hire the graduates, the local community. For NGOs, new or improved accountabilities might include beneficiaries, small donors and other partner organizations, as well as more open approaches to monitoring and self-evaluation.

The second issue has to do with how much governments respect and value the independence of voluntary organizations: whether they see NGOs as an important part of civil society, or simply as inexpensive executing agencies, working in places they themselves cannot reach. One study correctly notes that NGOs, just like governments, have institutional interests to protect, conflicting internal views to reconcile, and the difficult task of striving for organizational coherence while remaining responsive to a multitude of needs and pressures.

> Their freedom to function implies that NGOs can do what governments cannot, ought not, or will not do: supporting human rights, for example, or working in politically 'difficult' areas . . . or asking questions about the impact of large-scale projects on the environment. But the *will* to do so derives not from some formalistic assertion of autonomy, nor even from independence from government money, but from a vision of development rooted in values and choices. It is this willingness to explore alternatives and to experiment with new initiatives which makes NGO autonomy valuable and worth protecting.[28]

CHAPTER X

Partners

*If I knew for certain that a man was coming to my house with the
conscious design of doing me good, I should run for my life.*
                                        Henry Thoreau, *Walden*, 1854.

WHEN NORTHERN NGOs began their operations in the South, some
worked with governments. Church organizations tended to work
through missionaries. But most did everything themselves. They set
up schools and clinics, they designed agriculture projects, they
formed groups, trained adults, sent in extension workers. They operated income generation projects. Local people were hired as administrators, clerks, sometimes as managers. But essentially, development
was something conceived, managed and paid for by outsiders. In the
1960s and well into the 1970s, from Gaberone to Khartoum, from
Quito to Port Moresby, virtually every NGO office and every project
featured a profusion of pink faces.

For some Northern NGOs, this is still the case, but their number is
declining. The change, described in Chapters III and IV, began with
the rise of a new generation of NGOs in the South. What started as a
trickle in the early 1970s became a flood in the 1980s, heralding a
profound shift in the character of the Northern NGO. No longer innovators, many became facilitators. No longer implementers, they became catalysts, trainers, sources of money, technical support, and
sometimes partners in advocacy around issues such as structural adjustment. The North-South relationship became one of *partnership*,
founded on common values and goals, and on principles of self-
reliant, people-centred development.

The British NGO, War on Want, is typical. In the mid-1990s, it
defined its mission this way:

> War on Want's support for social and economic projects in Third World
> countries is based on a *partnership* with democratic local organizations
> who are working for change at grass-roots level in their countries. It has
> been our long-held belief that it is our *project partners* who are best
> placed to determine the needs of the people they represent. War on
> Want, therefore, works with a wide range of organizations: NGOs,
> trade unions, popular organizations, women's groups . . . The type of

work War on Want supports is diverse, but always the long-term aim of our project partners is to find ways to remove the obstructions to social and economic development of the communities and groups they work with. Most of the work that War on Want supports is looking at the long-term, towards finding paths of development which will provide a basis for change.[1]

With few modifications, this language — goals, purposes and mission statements — would be interchangeable among a thousand Northern NGOs. In operationalizing such partnerships, there is an attempt on the part of the Northern and the Southern organization to match institutional principles, values and ideologies. Emphasis is placed on concepts of mutual trust, respect and equality, and there are efforts to construct a degree of reciprocity in decision-making, evaluation and matters of accountability.

That, of course, is the ideal. And where it works well, it probably *is* ideal. There is evidence, however, that it does not always work quite this way. In fact the gap between rhetoric and reality is often so large that bilateral agencies can drive a bulldozer through it. And increasingly, they do.

In the summer of 1984, Sarvodaya, Sri Lanka's largest NGO, had partnership arrangements with almost two dozen Northern organizations: non-governmental, bilateral and multilateral. They included two Oxfams (UK and America), NOVIB, Helvetas, ITDG, the Friedrich Naumann Stiftung, USAID, CIDA, NORAD and UNICEF. All financed projects of a particular geographical or thematic nature, usually with short life-expectancies and often with severe restrictions on administrative costs. Although it worked in 5000 villages and had an annual budget of almost $3 million, Sarvodaya was in the maddening position of not knowing at the beginning of each financial year, or at any other point in time, how much money would be available for the next thirty days. Senior staff spent significant proportions of their time writing proposals, reports and enquiries; travelling to Europe and North America in search of money: engaged in the imprecise but all-important job of dealing with the donors. On one momentous occasion, an overworked Sarvodaya clerk reported to Oxfam on the wrong project. The return telex, perhaps understandably, was an icy blast from the North.[2]

A similar situation prevailed at the same time in East Africa, where AMREF was running a variety of regional health programmes covering rural areas in Kenya, Uganda, Somalia and Tanzania. In 1969, before the 'partnership' era, AMREF had a budget of 1.6 million Kenyan shillings. By 1987, with 600 employees and a fleet of flying doctors, its income had risen one hundred fold, to KSh163 million, almost $10 million. That year, 64 different donors provided AMREF with a total of 106 grants for some 50 projects. Among Southern NGOs, this was probably a record, something that would have been beyond AMREF's wildest dreams even a decade earlier. But over the years, the dream had become a reality. And then the reality became a nightmare.

Co-ordination and reporting alone required a staff of dozens, filling out applications, tailoring each to particular donor interests, dealing with the different quarterly and annual reporting requirements of each, trying to anticipate what their representatives would want to see when they arrived, as they always did every year, if not more frequently. As with Sarvodaya, donors often refused to pay for administrative costs, and few were interested in anything that looked like a recurrent expenditure. 'Recurrent cost is the money required to maintain an investment facility, such as the Family Health Unit at AMREF, and to operate its annual activities,' said a USAID evaluation. 'This is the cost donors are most reluctant to fund because there is no specific time when its funding will end. If USAID decides to fund the CSD project in South Nyanza . . . USAID and AMREF should work closely to ensure that the recurrent cost problem will not arise at the end of the project.'[3]

How? 'Self-sufficiency' is a term that was replaced in the late 1980s by 'sustainable'. When it refers to money, as it often does, this expression usually flies straight into Never-Neverland. Northern NGOs have no self-sustaining income except the goodwill of donors and the occasional small endowment. Southern NGOs are even more strapped for cash. A number have invested in money-earning schemes. AMREF's Aviation Department was at the time self-financing, and the organization earned an additional $1.3 million from a printing and book distribution unit. Sarvodaya too had a handful of income-earning units. But if one could assume a return of 15 per cent on investment (a big assumption for a non-profit organization), Sarvodaya would have required a capital fund of $35 million in 1984, and a lot of business acumen, in order to earn what the donors were giving. When faced with this sort of calculation, the average donor will stop talking about self-financing. But the idea lurks, and the vocabulary of sustainability waits in the shallows, playing crocodile to the recipient's springbok.

Most Southern NGOs deal with this problem in one of three ways. The first is to dream along with the donor. In 1977, A.T. Ariyaratne, the founder of Sarvodaya, said he expected the organization to be financially self-reliant by 1985.[4] Given the level of investment required, this was (and, many years later, remains) a dream. The second way is to find a new donor when the old one runs out of money and interest. This is problematic, because Northern NGOs tend not to favour second-hand projects. They want to be 'catalysts', 'innovators',

'ground-breakers'. The Southern NGO, therefore, has to find inge-
nious ways to redraft or remix its project portfolio, proposing newer
lessons to be learned and newer ground to be broken. A third technique is to simply damn the torpedoes and hope for the best. Although it knew that its overheads on a large CIDA-financed project in
1983 were 26 per cent, AMREF accepted 20 per cent and wound up
subsidizing the project to the tune of $300 000 — money that had to
be squeezed out of other income that it did not have.

Like Sarvodaya, AMREF never knew from one day to the next what
its cash-flow situation would be. It took grave chances, pre-financing
projects or second phases before receiving donor approval. All donors, and all Southern NGOs know that this is wrong. But in the real
world, where future success may depend on a decision to do something today — to hire someone who is available *now*, for example —
action is required. Life does not work on a donor project cycle; clinics
and schools cannot close because the critical fax has not arrived from
Rugby, Zeist, or Norwalk Connecticut. Crops must be planted on time,
not later: for poor farmers there *is* no later. So the NGO goes ahead
and pre-finances the project, using money sent by another donor for
something else. If and when the grant is approved, there is usually a
caveat: despite a delay which may have been caused entirely by the
donor, retroactive payments are not allowed. That is the immediate
past. For the immediate future, donors may restrict advances to as
little as 90 days. But because the donor is often slower with paper-
work than the recipient (who, after all, has everything to gain from
alacrity), 90 days is seldom enough. A still greater proportion of front-
end money is therefore required.

For the larger Southern NGO, some of this is especially problematic, because many have outstripped the capacity of Northern NGOs
to keep up with them financially. While needs, opportunities and
capacities in the South have been growing, the financial capacity of
the older Northern NGOs to support Southern growth has slowed.
One opening for new money has been through the continuing proliferation of smaller NGOs in the North. But dealing with them means
that Southern NGOs must build a larger and larger portfolio of small
projects, with all the overheads and frustrations that are entailed. Or
they must begin to look towards the larger amounts of money available from bilateral and multilateral agencies. This too has drawbacks.
Large Southern NGOs tend to have a holistic approach to development, and they may have an integrated programme which includes
elements of education, income generation and agriculture together.
Some donors, such as UNICEF or UNIFEM have specific and restricted
mandates, financing only activities relating to children or women.
Others have a tendency to chase very similar rainbows across the

184

South, seeking the most innovative-looking, poverty-alleviating activities possible: micro-credit, the environment, population. They want segregated projects, with clear aims and objectives, time frames of two or three years, and a good deal of reference to the idea of sustainability. Some activities, like curative health care, are very far down the average donor's list of priorities. Understandably enough, however, curative health is at the very top of a sick person's priority list. And unless sick people can be made well, they are unlikely to listen attentively to an NGO preaching nutrition, population control or the benefits of preventive health care. Finding money for such essentials can be problematic, and many Southern NGOs have found themselves with first-rate budgets for secondary priorities, and with little or nothing for what they really want to do.

Every Southern NGO has a donor-related horror story to tell, like Sarvodaya's reporting to Oxfam on the wrong project. For AMREF it was a mistake in a $1.2 million financial claim to GTZ in Germany. Two months after the submission, a query arrived from Europe. Not an earth-shattering query, but one that held up the entire claim until an answer could be provided. AMREF ate up all its financial reserves, spent almost all the advances it had received from other agencies for other projects, and went to the bank for an overdraft. In countries like Kenya, however, where credit is tight, overdrafts tend to be small, even for a good customer. AMREF's covered about 14 days of operating costs, and in the end, salaries had to be thinned out to deal with the delay.

These phenomena are common for Southern NGOs: donor 'cherry-picking', treating NGOs like a buffet lunch, taking what they like and leaving the rest; unclear priorities; frequently changing personnel; a refusal to countenance overheads or income-earning investments; delays in decision-making; delays in sending money.* The result is not a *strengthening* of Southern NGOs; it is a life of constant apprehension and a process that contributes to destabilization. And it is not *partnership*; it is the same old paternalism the South started to know when Portuguese navigators first sailed down the coast of West Africa.

Supplicants, of course, can't be overly picky, and many Southern NGOs have chosen to bear the problem in silence, attempting to make the best deal possible under the circumstances. Some have done very well. In recent years, however, there has been a growing chorus of complaint and criticism. In India, Kamla Bhasin observes that 'although we have been using the word partnership for a long

---

*Ultimately, there may be only three things a Northern donor must be able to do in a timely fashion: (1) raise the money, (2) write the cheque, and (3) post it. A surprising number fail at more than one.

time . . . project implementation has been the main thrust, and funding the main link. And with one partner giving funds and another receiving them, all the inequalities enter the relationship.'[5] Honor Ford-Smith, writing about the experience of a Jamaican NGO, says that Northern donors 'have an enormous amount of power. They are able to shape the lives of the organizations they support, not simply because they fund them, but also because of the processes and disciplines they require the organizations to become involved in. The term "partner" only obscures what remains a very real power relation. The egalitarian label does not change reality.'[6] And in Zimbabwe, Yash Tandon says that 'foreign NGOs are a secretive lot. We do not know much about them . . . We know little about how their heart beats in Europe or America or Canada . . . they work with such secrecy and opaqueness that it is right for an African to be suspicious about them.'[7]

In 1992, Carmen Malena went to Kenya and Zimbabwe to see what NGOs there had to say about their partnerships with Northern NGOs. She returned with disturbing news. She found that African NGOs were much less happy with arrangements than Northern NGOs had made out. The definition of 'mutual' goals tended to be a one-way thing. Their articulation, often tortuously developed in the North, was frequently accepted without demur in the South 'for fear of losing funds'. Few Southern NGOs 'would openly express ideological difference with Northern donors'.[8] Communication revolved almost exclusively around project administration and execution, and most important decisions were made by project selection committees and boards far away in the North. Questions relating to money and accountability remained uni-directional, with enormous amounts of time spent in the South dealing with demands from the North for reports and evaluations. At a conference in Bulawayo, Southern NGOs concluded that 'in effect, more time is spent in accounting to Northern partners than in actually applying one's mind, judgement and energies to the work at hand.'[9]

Enter the bilaterals

By the mid-1980s, a handful of bilateral agencies had begun to provide sizeable support directly to Southern NGOs, rather than through their own national NGOs. There were good reasons for this. One was that Southern NGOs were asking for it. Dealing with one or two large donors, regardless of the problems that might ensue, was infinitely preferable to the confusion of working with a dozen small ones. Only a handful of Northern NGOs have been willing or able to provide Southern NGOs with money that would allow them to scale up significantly. Without the financing that direct support from government donors could provide, most large, well-known Southern NGOs would never have reached their present size and capacity.

Many Southern NGOs did not find the distinction between Northern NGOs and Northern governments to be as profound as did Northern NGOs. In any case, many Northern NGOs were acting largely as brokers for their government's money; they often passed on their government's rules and regulations intact, but removed ten or fifteen per cent of the cash for their own administration. Larger Southern NGOs, burned by 'partnerships' to which they felt no loyalty, did not require the services of a Northern NGO as chaperone, gatekeeper or babysitter. Many felt quite capable of dealing with governmental donors: perhaps more so than Northern NGOs.

In addition to requests from Southern NGOs, there were other reasons for direct support. It allowed a bilateral agency to get a first-hand look at grass-roots, poverty-oriented activities; it offered a learning experience that was not always available by supporting Northern NGOs as intermediaries. It allowed the bilateral to take direct credit for a poverty project in the pages of its annual report. It also provided a number of other attractions: Southern NGOs were more cost-effective and were usually easier to deal with than Southern governments, not least because the gap between rhetoric and action was smaller. When the idea of 'strengthening civil society' came into vogue in the early 1990s, direct funding fitted neatly into that slot, and it also coincided nicely with the idea that the Southern state should, like the Northern state, retrench, downsize and privatize.

There are, of course, problems. By the late 1980s, 'direct funding' had become a regular practice for USAID and the bilateral agencies of Canada, Norway and Sweden. Britain, France, Switzerland and Japan had dabbled, but remained ambivalent. In some countries, Northern NGOs saw nothing incompatible with the idea of a Southern NGO 'graduating' from NGO to government support. This view is particularly prevalent in Scandinavia, where Swedish and Norwegian NGOs are reasonably relaxed about their own relations with government. In Commonwealth countries there tends to be greater concern. British, Canadian and Australian NGOs see the thin edge of a wedge when government poaches on their territory. If the rhetoric is stripped off many NGO-to-NGO 'partnerships', what remains is mostly money. Direct funding, therefore, poses a direct threat to the very *raison d'être* of many Northern NGOs.

While this may seem a rather selfish concern, there are reasons for taking it seriously. Northern NGOs are an important interface between the citizens of industrialized countries, the problems of development, and the people of the South. NGOs build a Northern constituency for development assistance, and they can explain development issues to individuals at home, to politicians and to the news media, in ways that government cannot. Actively contributing to a diminution of their role could, in the long run, damage the entire aid effort, and the support needed to sustain it. Direct funding also reverses the idea of 'contracting-out'; it involves the Northern state in a *new* enterprise, one that it is usually not well equipped to handle.* Most bilaterals have limited experience of Southern NGOs, and because economies of scale are essential, they are likely to avoid small and mid-size NGOs in favour of the biggest. They are also likely to attract and to support organizations that fit their ideal of good management. In the end, quality may lose out to size and polish.

Some writers suggest that direct funding can contribute to the weakening of civil society.[10] This can happen in two ways. First, making NGOs in one country beholden and answerable to governments in another cannot be terribly healthy, no matter how benign the relationship. Secondly, by making NGOs part of a *bilateral* aid programme, a donor automatically involves them in a government-to-government relationship. This may well open the Southern NGO to the scrutiny of its own government: not necessarily bad in theory, but in practice, risky. And it does something more insidious. By redirecting money from a government programme towards an NGO, a bilateral agency makes a value judgement about effectiveness and efficiency. Unless the host government agrees with the decision — and this would take a fair degree of understanding and generosity — the donor may well place the object of its affection into direct competition with its own government.

The result, very evident in countries like Bangladesh, Sri Lanka, Pakistan and Indonesia, where direct funding has been growing for a decade, is increasing government angst about NGOs. This manifests itself in the imposition of draconian rules and regulations, political invective and government-inspired media attacks on the probity, legitimacy and accountability of organizations which, in other countries, would be seen as champions of development. In the long run, this may not be an entirely bad thing. While the process can be very difficult for NGOs, it may be an essential and inevitable stage for any country working through the roles and potentials of both government and non-governmental organizations.

---

*This is not always true. Bilateral and multilateral organizations can and do hire knowledgeable and experienced local staff, many with good NGO backgrounds. A 1994 study (Lewis, Sobhan and Jonsson, p.44) found that the SIDA mission in Bangladesh was more knowledgeable and had a far more subtle understanding of Bangladeshi NGOs than many Swedish NGOs.

Damage limitation

Larger Southern NGOs have dealt with some of the problems inherent in managing a variety of donors by forming consortia. The consortium approach to financial assistance is not new to bilateral and multilateral organizations, but until the mid-1980s, it had rarely been applied to a Southern NGO. In 1986 in Sri Lanka, four of Sarvodaya's larger donors (NOVIB, CIDA, NORAD, and ITDG acting on behalf of the British Overseas Development Administration) agreed to work together on a co-ordinated financial approach. After a basic agreement had been reached, Sarvodaya presented them with the first comprehensive, multi-year plan and budget that had been possible in its full 25 years of existence. Each donor agreed to support a percentage, rather than a particular set of activities. What resulted, after some give and take, was a 'balanced budget', one with agreed activities and costs, and a clear indication of where support would come from. For the first time in its history, Sarvodaya could start to focus on activities rather than money, and at least on the mid-term rather than tomorrow.

A donor-appointed 'monitoring team' visited from time to time, providing technical assistance and acting as a buffer between donor concerns and the Sarvodaya reality. From the donor point of view, it was a success. There was much greater transparency; instead of reports on peripheral projects, each donor saw the organization in its entirety. The donor's administrative workload, risk and exposure were reduced, while the burden on Sarvodaya of multiple applications, reports and evaluations had dropped to a single set of exercises. It worked. Following the Sarvodaya lead, in subsequent years donor consortia were formed for a host of Southern NGOs: AKRSP in Pakistan, AMREF in Kenya, AWARE and others in India, Proshika, Grameen Bank and BRAC in Bangladesh.

Steinbeck warned about the inherent flaw in any form of giving, however: 'The most overrated virtue on our shoddy list of virtues, is that of giving'. A selfish pleasure, 'it builds up the ego of the giver, makes him superior and higher and larger than the receiver'. While consortia may have reduced the financial and paper burdens on NGOs, they have not always solved the matter of donor ego. The BRAC consortium, established in 1988, started going awry within two or three years. There were ever-increasing numbers of appraisals, evaluations and monitoring missions, each one looking more and more like bank inspections and dealing with ever greater minutiae. There was no specific problem. In fact *this* was the problem: evaluators were too positive, and donors insisted on digging deeper and pushing harder. In one case, representatives of eight donor agencies debated whether or not BRAC should invest a small amount of money to investigate external markets for the silk produced in its sericulture project. In a project employing poor rural women, BRAC had by then more than doubled the tonnage of silk produced in Bangladesh, and local markets were becoming saturated. For reasons known best to donors, the donor consortium objected to the study.

On a broader level, there were other dangers. Donors can unwittingly attempt to tip scales that have been delicately balanced over time, differing with each other as well as BRAC. Donors may have different priorities entirely, some stressing institution building, participation, gender equity and empowerment — usually without cost calculations — while others may demand detailed, mathematically sound cost-effectiveness. The contradictory messages and demands culminate in a hurried semi-annual meeting, attended by ever-changing representatives from Britain, Norway, Canada. At such meetings or shortly before, they are confronted with the growing stack of studies they themselves have commissioned, and by the need to balance various head office and embassy concerns that may have to remain unspoken.

One donor, seemingly well-informed on a particular issue, wants a special study. The others defer, uncertain of the implications, and because, after all, more information can't be a bad thing. The studies, concerns and demands mount. Because so much is at stake, BRAC acquiesces. Ultimately, it is a repetition of the approach common to bilateral and multilateral decision-making: donors using the clout of their money to delay, to block, to insist, to push, and sometimes to entice: in short, to do the opposite of what has, in the past, allowed the NGO to mature and succeed.

Ultimately, BRAC and its donors have been able to make the consortium work. Sarvodaya, however, one of the first Southern NGOs off the mark with a consortium, did not fare so well. According to one observer, the donors quickly 'established their own performance reviews based on approaches and indicators that were neither institutionalized within the organization, nor necessarily consistent with Sarvodaya's aims . . . the role of the consortium extended quickly beyond that of merely co-ordinating the multi-source aid programme, evolving into a strategy development group which carried the weight of being the primary, and by now necessary, consolidated source of income. The 'monitoring team' financed by the consortium and comprising entirely non-Sri Lankan consultants, acted effectively as a policy unit, developing proposals on the back of their review missions.'[11] A senior Sarvodaya worker put it more succinctly: 'evaluators, consultants and donors literally took over the policy and decision-making functions, trying to convert Sarvodaya into a mere delivery mechanism'[12]: in other words, what many Northern NGOs had already become.

The greatest risk for any NGO in forming a donor consortium had come to pass for Sarvodaya. It had become transparent, and when it did, the donors did not like everything they saw. They made suggestions. When the suggestions were ignored, they became recommendations, and then they were included in grant documents as requirements. By 1988, Sarvodaya had probably touched 5000 of Sri Lanka's 24 000 villages in one way or another. But much of the activity was ephemeral, based on one-off work camps and group meetings to discuss Sarvodaya's ideals of sharing, peace and co-operative village life. The consortium provided money to consolidate these activities in the 2000 most active villages, and to establish concrete health, nutrition and income generating activities. More concerned about the spread of its message than specific development efforts, however, Sarvodaya kept growing, even as donor money began to flag.[13] Failing to receive the kind of satisfaction it expected, the consortium finally placed conditions on its support, conditions that Sarvodaya either would not or could not meet. According to a 1994 Sarvodaya publication, 'donor representatives from ODA and NOVIB dominated the last two Donor Consortium Meetings and dictated terms.'[14] As a result of Sarvodaya's inability to comply with the terms of agreements it had signed, NOVIB finally cut its support dramatically. CIDA reduced its commitment and ODA all but withdrew. Sarvodaya began the 1994 financial year as it had in all the years before 1986: without a clear commitment of donor support. Rather sadly, it concluded that the consortium 'now simply does not work'. Obviously, the consortium had concluded the same about Sarvodaya.

Playing with puppies

With BRAC in Bangladesh, donor incursions were successfully warded off in a variety of ways. First, BRAC was extremely careful in its agreements, and rarely undertook to do anything it could not accomplish. Its planning and budgeting were impeccable, and its finance department was probably computerized before some of the donors were. Its reports were available on time, providing all the information required, and more. It 'sold' things that donors could readily understand and measure: primary schools, pass rates, the acceptance of graduates into the formal secondary system. It had self-financing savings and credit operations; tens of thousands of jobs for women in sericulture; a multi-million dollar handicraft marketing operation that aimed to become self-financing, and did. BRAC's own evaluations were usually better than anything the donors could mount, which is partly why donors kept fielding more and more missions, like a new schoolteacher trying to stay one lesson ahead of the class.

With Sarvodaya it was different. Although Sarvodaya had many of the social and economic activities of the standard NGO — training, health, credit — it was a *movement*. 'Sarvodaya Shramadana' means the awakening of all in society. The Sarvodaya mission 'is to create a new social order based on the values of truth, non-violence and self denial, and governed by the ideals of participatory democracy.' This mission manifested itself in ways that were sometimes amenable to donors, and sometimes in ways that were completely incomprehensible. The confusion made a clash between two very different institutional cultures inevitable. Donors *said* they accepted the vision, but what they paid for were the more tangible things that could be inscribed in a logical framework analysis. There was another problem. 'Sarvodaya management personnel tried their very best,' said a senior official, 'to improve on administrative and financial management, monitoring and reporting systems,' but they were 'not well equipped in modern business management techniques, monitoring systems and reporting, like the laptop computer-carrying, flying consultants' who produced 'dozens of recommendations and reports without visiting the rural areas'.[15] This plaintive and inaccurate explanation for administrative weakness would perhaps suffice in a project of a few thousand dollars, but between 1986 and 1994 when these words were written, Sarvodaya received more than $20 million from the consortium. In Jamaica there is a saying: 'Play with puppy, puppy lick your face'. Sarvodaya had played, and the puppy licked.*

Some want to use you; some want to be used by you

At the end of most project evaluation forms, there is a place for 'lessons learned'. Lessons tend to be situational, however. What is right for one time and place, is not always right for another. And lessons, of course, are only learned if they are remembered and applied to future behaviour. There is no real evidence in either of these cases that the quality of direct government funding to BRAC or Sarvodaya was better or worse than would have been the case had it been provided through NGOs. In fact there were NGOs involved in both consortia. Would Northern NGOs alone have done better? The question does not really arise, as both consortia were formed precisely because Northern NGOs could no longer keep up with Sarvodaya and BRAC. And in any case, the Northern NGO *modus operandi* had helped to push both BRAC and Sarvodaya towards larger donors and simpler procedures. Problems of the sort faced by AMREF over recurrent costs were solved. Working together, donors

---

*Perhaps it was more a case of lying down with dogs and getting badly mauled.

were able to modify their individual, often rigid rules, and they were able to accept that building an institution is a long-term prospect. In both cases, donors were prepared to invest money in activities that could help build long-term financial sustainability. For Sarvodaya, they provided assistance for direct, income-earning ventures: metal workshops, furniture manufacture, a printing press. BRAC's large revolving loan fund, capitalized by donors in the form of grants, became the basis for a self-financing approach which should see donor dependency drop significantly by the turn of the century.

The accountabilities of Southern NGOs are much more complex than those of Northern NGOs. Northern NGOs deal primarily with trustees, government agencies, the media and a myriad of uncritical individuals making small gifts. Southern NGOs must also deal with public perception, if not donations. They must contend with a sometimes hostile media, and a government which may run hot one day and cold the next. They have a monstrous management problem in dealing with a plethora of sophisticated, bureaucratic Northern donors, each with different aims and objectives, and each with different administrative requirements. And they have a particular accountability that Northern NGOs and donor agencies can sidestep: people. A Southern NGO is directly responsible, face to face, for what happens to the people it has encouraged to attend classes, to save money and take loans, to change jobs and farming practices, to alter old habits and accustomed ways.

Like Northern NGOs beguiled by government money, Southern NGOs have been seduced by money from the North, NGO and otherwise. The potential for local philanthropy has been largely ignored, and in the rush to grow, many organizations have willingly, if not eagerly, made themselves both available and accountable to Northern donors. Few Southern NGOs have yet developed mechanisms to make their different accountabilities effective, to spread them in ways that can provide protection and, more importantly, create inducements for better and more responsible practices. Like their Northern counterparts, Southern NGOs are competitive. Despite the many coalitions and shared activities, at their core they too are a secretive lot. It is not always clear how their hearts beat. They too work with secrecy and opaqueness. And like Northern NGOs, they too have institutional interests to protect, conflicting internal views to reconcile, and the difficult task of building organizational coherence while remaining responsive to a multitude of needs and pressures.

Patrons and clients, or friends?

At its worst, Northern interaction with Southern NGOs is little more than a patron-client relationship, one of vertical rather than horizontal ties. It is one of asymmetric obligations, what one writer has called 'lopsided friendships'.[16] These vertical relations — clientelism — can undermine the potential for important horizontal relationships, for the creation of interactive and mutually supportive networks of local organizations. Vertical relationships can also create rivalries between local organizations vying for the attention of donors. And ultimately, any relationship based on one-way financial dependency runs the danger of mutual exploitation and dishonesty.

The business of receiving is as difficult as that of giving. Neither can be done well if they are done lightly or quickly. Both require as much clarity and openness as possible, but clarity and openness do not emerge from reports, or at two-hour meetings around a bargaining table. They are the product of time, and of personal and institutional commitment. Expectations on both sides must be clear, and must be as unclouded by jargon and rhetoric as possible. Accountabilities, whatever they are, must be understood and formally acknowledged. For those serious about helping the poor to help themselves, and about building the institutions that are required as intermediaries, a message: this is not a place for amateurs. Large government agencies wishing to support Southern NGOs should not entrust the task to junior desk officers and the youngest third secretary in their embassies. Ways must be found to bring mature, thoughtful NGO experience into the arrangement. And a warning: if Southern NGOs are treated only as inexpensive delivery mechanisms for bilateral and multilateral assistance, they are likely to be damaged in the process.

Southern human rights organizations tend to get along a lot better with their Northern counterparts than development NGOs, because functionally they share more intellectual common ground. Money, and accounting for money, are not the basis for their relationships. In fact money may not enter into the equation at all. Between Northern and Southern development NGOs, there is certainly scope for changing the terms of engagement, but only if both parties to an agreement can find ways to complement each other as *development* organizations, with greater focus on goals and work than on structures and reports. Northern NGOs that believe in the language of partnership must find ways to make alliances that can have a life outside the financial relationship. This could mean reverse evaluations. NOVIB once invited some of its Southern partners to evaluate NOVIB, and IUCN has engaged Southern NGOs as evaluation consultants. Such an idea could be elaborated in different ways: Peruvian NGOs might institute an evaluation of the Belgian NGO scene. Or recipients of assistance from Radda Barnen in one country (or several) might institute an evaluation of the donor. If this sort of thing could be institutionalized, and if the impetus for it came from the South, a radical change in the reality of partnerships might take place quite quickly.

Another possibility might be reciprocal board placements, or the election of people from the South to the boards of Northern NGOs. Some Northern organizations — as diverse as IIED, CUSO, WWF and World Vision — have done this for years, and despite the risk of paternalism, have made it work. NOVIB's 'Guest at Your Table' programme is essentially a joint fundraising effort, with Southern partner organizations meeting donor groups in the Netherlands, and contributing material for newsletters. Katalysis, a small American NGO, has used virtually all of these techniques with its five partner organizations in Central America. Not only are its programming results positive, the relationship between Katalysis and its partners is excellent: when a single place as a Katalysis partner became available in Guatemala, 20 Guatemalan NGOs applied.[17]

Moving from a project relationship to long-term programme support can also make a difference. The Swiss NGO, Helvetas, makes a general commitment to a Southern partner for ten years, and provides assurance that at least one or two years' notice will be given before a pullout, regardless of how emotional a debate might become. This is extremely helpful to recipients in managing their finances responsibly.

In Latin America, a consortium of Southern NGOs has created a different kind of mechanism that moves the locus of decision-making about money away from the North entirely. Based in Costa Rica, FOLADE (the Latin American Development Fund) was created in 1993 by 16 NGOs in 14 countries to systematize and protect a financial base for economic development. Supported financially by its own member agencies and by external donors, FOLADE lends money or provides bank guarantees for its members' projects. But it does much more: it serves as a data bank, it provides information on technical assistance and training, and it carries out risk analysis, evaluation and auditing services. In effect, FOLADE becomes the intermediary between North and South, placing important aspects of learning, control and responsibility precisely where it should be.

A final note on partnership: some principles of partnership have been addressed in the codes of conduct created by many national groupings of NGOs. But few of these are binding, and most concern themselves only with what NGOs should do. Governments, the North-South connection, and principles of appropriate funding practice are generally absent. In 1995, following a lengthy process of drafting and consultation with NGOs and governments in the North and the South, the London-based Commonwealth Foundation produced the first comprehensive document to address many of these broader issues: *NGOs: Definitions and Guidelines for Good Policy and Practice.* In time, if endorsed by NGO communities and governments, this document could become a useful and important international code of conduct.

Ultimately, partnership means investing in the capacity of Southern NGOs, and in their independence: not just the jargon of independence, but the concrete reality of independence. This means coming to serious grips with ideas about self-generating income, endowments, the development of local philanthropy and the building of regulatory environments that are conducive to these things. It also means a reapportioning between those seriously committed to partnership of decision-making, evaluation and, perhaps most importantly, responsibility.

CHAPTER XI

Act globally: the rise of the transnational NGO

A Company for carrying on an undertaking of Great Advantage, but no one [is] to know what it is.

The South Sea Company Prospectus, 1711.

SOME OF TODAY'S best-known Northern NGOs began as wartime or post-war relief efforts. Gradually they grew beyond the crisis they were created to deal with, becoming large, multifaceted organizations with programmes in scores of countries on every continent. Save the Children began in Britain after the First World War; Foster Parents Plan (now Plan International) began as a response to the Spanish Civil War. The Christian Children's Fund began in China in 1938. Oxfam was established to provide assistance during the Greek famine of 1943. CARE sent its first food packages to war-ravaged France in the spring of 1946. World Vision was the creation of an American missionary in Korea.

In subsequent years, thousands of NGOs sprang up in Europe, North America, Japan and Australasia to deal with relief and development problems in the South. But these, and a handful of relative newcomers, such as Médecins sans Frontières, dominate the scene in terms of their size, and in terms of the messages they provide to their supporters at home about development issues and developing countries. Collectively, their budgets probably total $1.5 billion. World Vision raises more private money in the US than any other international relief and development agency. In Canada, Australia and New Zealand, it raises more than all other development NGOs in each of those countries combined. In Britain, Save the Children and Oxfam together raised almost 30 per cent more in 1992 than the combined donor income of all charities devoted to the blind, heart disease, leukaemia and multiple sclerosis. In the US, the combined cash and kind 1991 income of CARE, Save the Children and World Vision was US$520 million. These larger organizations, 'transnational NGOs', are emerging as a distinct class of organization, very different from other Northern NGOs, and quite different from what has generally been thought of as an international NGO.*

The term 'transnational' has connotations. A transnational corporation (TNC) is one which is registered, and which operates in several countries at once. By providing a package of resources — investment funds, managerial, technical and entrepreneurial skills — TNCs have contributed to both the visible and the invisible growth of world trade through increased income flows in profits, interest and dividends. For shareholders, their greatest asset is their ability to move capital quickly in response to national conditions, and their general lack of accountability to any particular national government. Criticized for the stimulation of inappropriate consumption patterns and the production, through capital-intensive technologies, of inappropriate products, TNCs exert considerable political and economic leverage over Southern labour and Southern governments, often damaging or suppressing local entrepreneurship with their superior knowledge, global contacts, support services and, through transfer pricing, their ability to raise and lower costs to suit local tax situations.

Fundraising *sans frontières*

Oxfam UK began its Northern trans-border operations in the early 1960s, with the establishment of Oxfam Canada. Although legally incorporated in Canada, the new organization was supported with cash and personnel sent from Britain, the idea being that once it was up and running, its Canadian fundraising income would repay the investment and be channelled through Oxford.[1] During the mid-1960s, Oxfam UK invested £60 000 in the establishment of the new branch, and within a few years was being amply repaid. By 1970, Oxfam Canada had sent £1.2 million overseas, of which half was channelled directly through Oxford.[2] Two decades later, Community

---

*The generally accepted description of an international development NGO (INGO) is one with affiliated member organizations legally incorporated in several countries, with a headquarters whose location has little relationship to the sources of its income. To qualify for grants from bilateral and multilateral funding agencies, such organizations usually comprise a mix of Southern and Northern affiliates (e.g. the International Committee of the Red Cross, International Planned Parenthood Association, the World Council of Indigenous People). AMREF, with headquarters in Kenya and affiliated but independent fundraising operations in Britain, Italy, Canada and elsewhere, is a variation on this theme. A further variation is found in organizations such as El Taller in Tunisia, or Worldview International Foundation, with headquarters in Colombo and programmes in Africa and Asia. Although both have strong Northern connections, they have been deliberately headquartered in the South and draw their *raison d'être* from an international and largely Southern membership.

Aid Abroad, the Australian Oxfam affiliate, did the same thing, investing money in the creation of an Oxfam New Zealand. In 1993–4, Oxfam New Zealand's net return on the CAA investment was NZ$335 000. The Oxfam start-ups in Canada and New Zealand have many parallels in Europe, Japan and Australia. World Vision US sponsored the Canadian branch, which in turn begat the Australian body, which then begat World Vision New Zealand. CARE established a very successful Canadian fundraising branch in the late 1940s, and the payoff was, in business terms, phenomenal. CARE Canada's 1994 income (in cash and kind) was C$75.3 million.[3]

Similar CARE investments were made in the early 1980s in Germany, Norway, Italy and France, and later Austria, Denmark and Japan. Not all performed as well, but in the late 1980s, the British effort stood out. By 1992, CARE Britain was raising £17.6 million, £11.6 million of it derived from government sources.[4] A 1987 start-up investment from CARE International proved hugely successful in Australia. By 1992, the new affiliate was reporting income in cash and kind of A$17.3 million, and had already become the third largest NGO recipient of Australian Government assistance.[5] A relative newcomer, the French NGO Médecins sans Frontières, had more than half a dozen national affiliates within a decade of its start-up in 1979.

World Vision, with 3670 field staff, and 1700 staff in 20 offices in Europe, North America and elsewhere, demonstrates even more spectacular growth, spending US$261 million worldwide in 1993.[6] In Canada alone, between 1987 and 1992, its total revenue from individuals, corporations and government rose by 121 per cent to a total of C$81.3 million: all in Canadian cash contributions. By 1994 the figure had reached C$95.7 million.[7] In Australia, World Vision raised A$66.9 million in 1991, an increase of almost 20 per cent over the previous year. The support it received from the Australian Government was more than double that of the next largest NGO. In New Zealand, World Vision raised NZ$20 million in 1994, four times more than the next largest NGO and more than all the rest combined.[8] World Vision has not been successful everywhere. The Irish Confederation of NGOs for Overseas Development (CONGOD) made an issue out of their arrival in Ireland in 1988, instigating a national debate over the problems associated with child sponsorship. National television coverage and a lawsuit by World Vision against an established Irish NGO, Trocaire, damaged the start-up effort, and in the end, World Vision never established a serious toe-hold.[9]

That the transnational NGO is big should come as no surprise, although the pace of growth *is* surprising, especially during a recessionary period when the income of other NGOs was stagnating or reversing. Some of the reasons for this growth are perhaps obvious;

199

others are not. With the exception of Plan International, most trans-nationals devote a significant part of their fundraising effort and their programme expenditure to emergencies. In recent years this has proved to be the most important way for the very biggest fundraising NGOs, for example, SCF UK and Oxfam UK, to maintain and expand their market share. It has also proved to be the most successful way for newcomers to enter established markets. In its start-up fundrais-ing in the late 1980s and early 1990s, CARE Australia focused exten-sively on refugee and emergency situations, rapidly surpassing more established organizations such as Austcare, UNICEF and SCF Australia.

Some of the transnationals have perfected and thrived on child sponsorship as a fundraising tool, and as a programming approach. It has proved to be one of the most enduring success stories in NGO fundraising. Despite widespread criticism from the NGO community at large (and unfavourable mention in the 1993 UNDP *Human de-velopment report*), child sponsorship shows no sign of flagging and has allowed more recent entrants into the field, like Feed the Children, to grow very rapidly. It is the bedrock of several of the older organiza-tions (Save the Children USA and some other SCF affiliates, World Vision, Plan International) and has been the key to their expansion into new countries. In Japan, for example, where the tradition of charitable giving is weak, 'Foster Plan Japan' became in ten years one of the biggest and fastest-growing fundraisers in the country, support-ing 62 000 foster children and families in 1994, as many as the UK and Germany combined.[10] The income of *Stichting Foster Parents Plan Nederland*, grew from Dfl 54 million to Dfl 110 million between 1986 and 1991.[11] By 1994, almost 40 per cent of Plan's worldwide child sponsorships were being financed from Holland alone.

Obviously, larger NGOs can afford the best consultants and man-agerial talent, as well as the newest and most effective fundraising methods. They have large workforces which mean that gaps can be filled relatively easily and emergencies answered quickly. They can afford 'luxuries' such as research, policy and publicity departments, things which are beyond the capacity of many smaller organizations. They can also absorb mistakes, poor investments and political ruc-tions in a way that smaller organizations cannot.

Most transnational NGOs work in scores of countries in Asia, Latin America and Africa. They not only look large and professional, they usually *are* large and professional. This makes them attractive to the individual donor, but it sometimes also makes them essential to bi-lateral and multilateral donor agencies. Almost 40 per cent of all US Government food aid channelled through NGOs in 1991 went to CARE, for example. When an emergency erupts in the Horn of Africa,

200

Haiti or Bangladesh, it is usually organizations like this that have the infrastructure and the experience to deal with it. While many NGOs may be involved in an emergency situation, the bulk of the money from the general public, and from governments and UN agencies flows through six or eight of these transnational organizations and their affiliates.

Perhaps as important from a financial point of view, whenever a new funding window opens in a bilateral agency, the transnational will have (or can soon make) programmes to suit the criterion: generic issues, such as human rights, the environment, democracy or women in development; and special geographical interests, such as Southern Africa or the Philippines.

'Transfer pricing'

The term 'transfer pricing' is used here for dramatic effect rather than precise accuracy. NGO variations, however, are not entirely dissimilar from what prevails in the corporate sector. One of the most glaring examples, described in Chapter VIII, was the international manipulation of money by World Vision Germany in the 1980s in order to make overheads seem lower than they were. A more common variation might be called 'transfer programming'. An established British, French or American NGO opening a fundraising office in a new country can demonstrate very quickly that it is a viable, going concern, because it already has field operations that can be 'transferred' into new brochures and fundraising programmes. This, and hiring Danes, say, can make a French organization like Médecins sans Frontières look very Danish, very quickly. Japan has been viewed as a potential gold mine in this regard. Starting in the mid-1980s, affiliates of CARE, Save the Children, World Vision and Plan International were established in Tokyo or Osaka. World Vision has been very successful raising money in Taiwan, and Christian Children's Fund has done the same in Korea and Taiwan: the precursor, perhaps, of a broader transnational fundraising trend in the South.

Transfer programming builds rapid credibility with donors and government agencies, but it also helps the newly established organization find prestigious local directors and 'star' patrons. Singers, movie stars, royalty and retired politicians are much more likely to associate themselves with a large, well-known international organization than with smaller, lesser known agencies. Taking a lesson from UNICEF's experience with Audrey Hepburn, Danny Kaye and Peter Ustinov, several transnationals have gone after the stars. Princess Anne has been extremely helpful and visible as President of SCF UK. Médecins sans Frontières roped in Yves Montand, Raymond Aron and Jean-Paul

Sartre in its early years. And CARE Australia's Chairperson, former Prime Minister Malcolm Fraser, was invaluable in establishing the organization's *bona fides* with the Australian public and with Australian officialdom. Sally Strothers, a minor American television actress in the 1970s, made a memorable comeback for Christian Children's Fund in some of the most cloying advertisements ever shown on US and Canadian television.

Another variation on transfer pricing is the 'transfer emergency'. Unlike smaller organizations, the transnational NGO can demonstrate quickly and effectively to several constituencies at once that its people are 'on the ground', responding to an emergency. CARE, for example, demonstrated simultaneously to television audiences in Britain, the United States, Canada and Australia that it was operational only days after the 1992 disaster 'broke' in Somalia — simply by changing the face and the accent in front of the camera. World Vision Hong Kong sent cameras, on behalf of WV International, to the 1993 Chinese flood disaster. Oxfams in Canada, the United States and elsewhere have benefited repeatedly from the international media publicity earned by Oxfam UK workers in Bangladesh, Ethiopia and Rwanda. SCF could be New Zealand's 'eyes and ears of the world' in Somalia, Rwanda, the Sudan, even though most of the New Zealand organization's money went to support projects designed and managed entirely by the British mother house. This, plus economies of scale and access to increasingly sophisticated communications technology give such organizations considerable advantage over the lone German or French NGO operating on its own, regardless of the quality of its work.*

'Transfer grant-matching' is another advantage available to the astute transnational NGO. Most Northern governments provide matching grants based partially on an NGO's domestic fundraising. The terms and conditions of the matching formulae vary greatly, from less than 50 per cent to more than 90 per cent. In Sweden where ratios are generous and competition is low, an American NGO, say, need only open an office in Stockholm, invest (perhaps heavily) in fundraising, and then apply for a matching grant. This practice is becoming especially fashionable in Europe with the advent of the European Community and increasingly blurred national borders.

A final type of transfer might be called 'transfer politics'. When the politics of an NGO's home government make programming difficult

---

*Sometimes the different branches of a transnational NGO do act very independently, however, *adding* to the plethora of agencies. In the early 1990s there were four Oxfams in Mozambique (UK, US, Australia and Canada), three SCFs (Norway, UK and US) and three MSFs (Belgium, France, Holland).

in a particular location, other affiliates can come to the rescue. A good example was Washington's attempt to isolate the Sandinista regime in Nicaragua during the 1980s. Rather than closing down the programmes initiated and managed by CARE USA, the organization was able to call on CARE Canada to step in and take over.

Like transnational corporations, transnational NGOs can support each other with 'transfer financial assistance'. When a transnational affiliate has financial difficulties, the others (or headquarters) are able to provide assistance of a type that is completely unavailable to most other NGOs. Popular legend in CARE USA has it that the HQ loaned CARE Canada $200 000 in the mid-1970s, to underwrite new fundraising campaigns and to achieve greater autonomy.[12] In fact, after 30 years of sending Canadian dollars (millions of them) across the world's longest undefended border, the newly independent CARE Canada found that the price of liberty was a bank account stripped of all but $80 000, and a paper liability of $120 000 attached to an undepreciated computer and other used equipment. Two years later, when CARE USA faced a liquidity problem, it was CARE Canada that came to the rescue with a genuine cash loan. When CARE Britain faced a major cash-flow crisis in 1994, it was the turn of CARE USA to provide a financial rescue package, estimated at a million dollars. In a variation on this theme, and a possible sign of things to come, World Vision Hong Kong raises money directly from the Canadian Chinese community, and World Vision Korea maintains an office in Los Angeles.

These characteristics and techniques are used to varying degree and effect. The impact can be dramatic. Plan International, for example, raised less than US$30 million in cash in the United States in 1994. In the same year, it raised over US$80 million in the Netherlands. On a per capita basis, this represents about ten cents per person in the US, and US$5.26 in Holland. Similar calculations show that World Vision raised less than a dollar per head in the United States in 1991, approximately US$1.50 in Australia, US$1.78 in Canada, and US$3.00 in New Zealand.[13] With differentials like these, it is little wonder that new markets are so aggressively tackled.

Managing globally

In addition to the webs and connections that have helped make them large, transnationals share a number of other common features. Some have shallow programming roots overseas. Once the confident purveyors of development projects which they designed, managed and evaluated themselves, most smaller Northern NGOs have shifted ground to make room for, and provide support to the growing number of competent and effective Southern NGOs. Surprisingly, however, of the major transnational NGOs, only the Oxfam group and some Save the Children affiliates work closely with Southern NGOs. World Vision, CARE, Plan International and some members of the International Save the Children Alliance have, in fact, tended to reinforce and reconfirm the 1960s approach, continuing to devise, manage and evaluate their own projects directly.

Alan Fowler observes that NGOs 'seldom make sufficient distinction between different types of decentralization or fully appreciate the consequences associated with each'. He notes three distinct types of decentralization:

o deconcentration: responsibilities move outwards and downwards within the organization, but the distribution of authority does not similarly change;
o delegation: both responsibility and the concomitant authority to make decisions are moved down to lower levels;
o devolution: responsibilities and associated authority are transferred to (semi)-autonomous organizations, i.e. to entities that are often legally separate, and in any event are not under the direct control of the organization that is decentralizing.[14]

Most transnational NGOs have by and large moved to full devolution in the North, while in the South the model remains one of deconcentration — or delegation at most — and mainly to expatriate rather than local managers.

The original idea of an 'Oxfam International', with shared programmes and field staff, was all but dead by 1974, with a completely independent Oxfam America, and an independent Oxfam Canada that had spun off an even more independent Oxfam Quebec. The same sort of move occurred within CARE at approximately the same time. In the words of one of the American founders, 'Canadian leaders, itching a bit about directions from New York, felt they should be something more than a field office for CARE, like our offices in Boston, Washington, Los Angeles, Seattle and other US cities.' He added a late-blooming insight: 'Canada, after all, was a sovereign independent country.'[15]

CARE International was formed in 1980, with a headquarters in Paris serving as clearing house and an international forum for its national affiliates. Relations between these affiliates and their connection to overseas programmes vary. Some have become 'lead agencies', taking primary responsibility for certain overall country programmes. CARE Australia is lead agency for Cambodia, for example, while CARE Canada has prime responsibility for co-ordinating all CARE International activities in Kenya, Indonesia, Angola and other countries. Most country programmes continue to be run and staffed by CARE USA, while other affiliates such as CARE Britain contribute money and staff to general field operations, or take on fully fledged projects for which they can raise money in their own country.

Oxfam UK went through a major self-examination in the early 1990s, rethinking its aims, objectives and programming strategies. One of the key outcomes was an intention to convert it from a British organization to one that is 'more European and more truly international'.* The first step in this direction was the inclusion of Ireland in the name 'Oxfam UKI'. The next was greater co-ordination with Oxfam Belgique. In 1994, an unusual but perhaps portentous programming partnership was struck with NOVIB, the largest secular Dutch NGO. And as part of a wider potential expansion, test Oxfam shops were opened in Germany, France and Italy. Some of this had to do with strategic positioning in the rapidly evolving European political scene, part with a recognition that pursuing independent programming and policies could be counter-productive. An internal Oxfam document observed that problems could arise if more than one Oxfam were to pursue its own independent programme in the same country. 'Furthermore, communications and media increasingly cross international boundaries, thus making necessary a consistent message from organizations with the same name. There is also a concern that the development of new Oxfams, whether from South or North, could further increase the fragmentation of Oxfam's programme and message.'

The re-creation of an Oxfam International and the idea of coming closer together, however, coincided with a move in the opposite direction in India. There, the idea of an independent Oxfam India has been the subject of discussion and debate for several years. Some feel that India, a country with its own fundraising capacity and with no shortage of top-level development administrators, should hardly have to justify itself to British decision-makers based in Oxford.

Receptivity among Northern Oxfams was half-hearted, however, conflicting perhaps with the idea of a tighter family of institutions, operating, albeit, with a much more decentralized management system. Further arguments (in Oxford) against Indian independence included market surveys which purported to show that as a purely

---

*The other Oxfam affiliates are Oxfam Canada, Oxfam Quebec (merged in 1993 with the Organisation Canadienne pour la Solidarité et le Développement), Oxfam Belgique, Oxfam America, Community Aid Abroad (Australia), Oxfam Hong Kong and Oxfam New Zealand.

domestic organization, Oxfam India would lose some of the credibility and clout that are necessary in advocacy programmes. This seemingly important institutional debate, in an agency which pioneered support to Southern NGOs, warranted only five lines on the second to last page of the 1992 official 50th anniversary history of the organization.[16] CARE too, busy creating chapters throughout the North, has no place yet for Southern affiliates. Stated concerns include the potential for diminished accountability, weakened programme quality, the danger of corruption, and the need for protection of the CARE name.* There is also a direct equation that is made between having money, and having the right to spend it one's self. Sometimes the equation is stretched further, linking the possession of money to the possession of knowledge.

Although overall planning and control of World Vision International is exercised from the organization's headquarters in Monrovia, California, World Vision has probably devolved more than other transnationals. Head office staff numbers fell dramatically, from almost 500 in 1989 to fewer than 150 in 1994. The organization is responsible to an 86-person council, elected from advisory councils and boards elsewhere, and is more or less equally divided in make-up between North and South. The Board is made up of representatives from World Vision operations worldwide. Roughly half of the Southern operations, including Thailand, India, Kenya, Tanzania and Zimbabwe, have been recognized in a category which includes provision for a local advisory council or Board of Directors, and eligibility for representatives to serve on the international Council and Board. The International Save the Children Alliance (ISCA) is a looser grouping of 24 organizations holding similar aims and objectives. Collectively they support a small secretariat in Geneva for liaison with the EC, UN agencies and other NGO bodies. The secretariat also co-ordinates information between member agencies and carries out an advocacy function on issues related to the rights and welfare of children. Its 1993 budget was US$365 000.

The ISCA 'family' of organizations,** which had a 1993 combined spending power of $317 million, is the loosest of the coalitions.

---

*Corruption, of course, is not a monopoly of the South. Lou Samia, the chief financial officer and later Executive Director of CARE US, went to prison in the early 1980s for embezzling $116 000. In 1995, William Aramony, former President of the United Way of America, was convicted on 25 counts of fraud, conspiracy and money laundering, crimes that cost the charity almost $600 000.

**Includes Redd Barna (Norway), Radda Barnen (Sweden) and Red Barnet (Denmark) with combined fundraising power of $100 million in 1991. SCF US total 1991 income was valued at $97 million, of which roughly $40m was related to food donated by the US government. SCF UK 1992 income was £100m (of which £15.5m in kind), up from £56m in 1991.

206

A unique feature of the SCF grouping is that nine of the 24 affiliates are Southern organizations, with Southern Boards, staff and programmes. SCF, in fact, is one of the few transnationals to have encouraged, or even to have allowed Southern affiliates.* Several of these were fostered by SCF US in the late 1970s and early 1980s, but there is a degree of apathy towards them elsewhere in the network. SCF US, unlike SCF UK, is based heavily on child sponsorship, and actually created many of the Southern member organizations so they could become SCF *agents*. A seemingly progressive thing to do at the time, the creation of Southern branches was also administratively cheaper than running a field office, and they reduced SCF's direct liability in the country. As 'independent' organizations, the new affiliates also had the possibility of raising money from individual donors in their own countries, as well as from other donor agencies operating there.

Discussions within most transnationals about the creation of such affiliates are usually negative (as with CARE or the Oxfam India Trust). Trust and control are the central issues, often disguised in euphemisms about such things as protection of the name, or an aversion to the creation of dependency. In the case of ISCA, the entire combined budgets of all nine Southern affiliates in 1991 was US$3.12 million, only 3 per cent of SCF US expenditure that year, and 1 per cent of the combined income of the SCF Alliance. The overall burden of the Southern affiliates on the Alliance was rather small, therefore. With regard to dependency, the Southern affiliates have reduced their initial heavy reliance upon SCF US, but dependence clearly remains: if not on SCF US, then on other Northern agencies. This is hardly surprising. All NGOs are dependent upon others for most, if not all of their income. SCF US, for example, received over 47 per cent of its 1991 income from the US Government, in cash, food and freight reimbursements.[17]

In addition to the dependency issue, there is an independence issue. Many of the Southern ISCA members have started developing aims, objectives and programmes that do not always coincide with those of SCF. Some have become more welfare-oriented, and some have moved away from the SCF child orientation. One way of counteracting this has been the institution of 'co-operation agreements' between SCF US and Southern members of the alliance. These are complex legal documents which essentially require the Southern NGO to comply 'in all respects . . . with the standards of service adopted by Save the Children . . . without limitation'. This sort of arrangement does not represent a devolution in organizational terms;

---

*Southern affiliates now exist in the Dominican Republic, Egypt, Lesotho, Malawi, Mauritius, Mexico, Korea, Tunisia and Guatemala.

rather it is a binding contractual arrangement with a fee for services. It is not a contribution to the aims and objectives of the Southern organization, and it has little to do with the concept of partnership that is so common to NGO publicity, SCF included.

Staffing: the Oreo syndrome

Bringing people from recipient Southern countries into the senior management of the transnational NGO has generally not been much of an issue, mainly because in most it has not been seriously considered. When it comes to staffing, most do not see themselves as international organizations, but as British, American, Swedish or Australian first. SCF UK is proud of the fact that its several thousand overseas employees are largely citizens of the countries in which they work. But most of the top management positions continue to be held by expatriates, mainly British. This, the organization feels, is a matter of responsibility and accountability to the small donors who provide the bulk of the organization's income.*

A 1992 study of CARE staffing patterns found that although the organization had internationalized, 'international' had a visibly pale face. At that time CARE certainly had thousands of Asian, African and Latin American staff. But the most critical decision-making posts, those of country director, assistant country director and field representative, were held mainly by what Africans refer to politely as 'Europeans'. Of 165 such positions, all but 22 were held by Northerners. Of the individuals filling the remaining positions, only two or three had actually risen above the temporary field representative status to which CARE had assigned them, usually in the most difficult of disaster situations.[18] After about six decades in the business, Save the Children US had moved a bit further than CARE towards internationalizing its upper ranks overseas, with three out of 27 country directors in 1993 holding Southern passports.

Plan International is the corporate body which co-ordinates money collected by nine Northern Foster Parent Plan member organizations. In the mid-1980s, the International Board of Directors decided that the preponderance of Americans with international staffing status (68 per cent in 1983–4) had to be changed. Plan went beyond the original intent of the Board, which was aimed largely at a greater reflection of their own national diversity. By mid-1993, there were 175 individuals

---

*As with shareholders in transnational corporations, however, the individual donor exercises virtually no influence over a transnational NGO apart from the actual donation. Donors are rarely, if ever, canvassed on their attitudes towards or ideas about development, programming, staffing, evaluation or anything else.

in the category, of whom only 47 per cent were from the North. Bringing more Southerners into senior international ranks was part of a major reorganization and decentralization effort. By the mid-1990s, international salaries and benefits were all on the same scale. It was an expensive proposition, but in Plan's view, the changes led to more responsive programming, better staff management, and better in-country contacts and government relations, especially in times of political difficulty, when local directors become invaluable. Other changes were afoot as well: reflecting the fact that more than half its global income was European in origin, Plan moved its headquarters from Rhode Island to London in 1994, and expanded fundraising operations into France.

The transnational impact

Undoubtedly, transnationals are setting new standards of professionalism for NGOs and for governmental agencies in some areas of endeavour. The effective delivery and programming of food aid is one. It is certainly the case in emergencies and refugee situations. Transnationals can move quickly; they have decades of relevant experience; they have a core of professionals who are willing to take serious personal risks and who know what to do in an emergency. Some are carving out particular niches. CARE has developed a well-deserved reputation in logistics; Oxfam has built considerable expertise in the provision of water supplies in emergency situations. Médecins sans Frontières has obvious expertise in the health field.

In development work, however, the transnationals have considerably less, and probably declining, impact. The most innovative and influential work on participatory development today, on job creation, on the environment, on rural banking, on women in development, on human rights, on matters of sustainability is being done by Southern NGOs, not by fully operational Northern agencies. In 1993, the Overseas Development Institute published a four-volume study of the impact of NGOs on agricultural development. It examined 70 projects in 18 countries of Asia, Latin America and Africa. Although several Northern NGOs working in consort with Southern counterparts were discussed, most of the successful projects were designed and carried out by Southern NGOs. The only transnational to find its way into the study was CARE.[19]   The 1994 UNICEF *State of the world's children* Report provides another indicator: of 137 references in the report, the only source material from a transnational NGO was a single document produced by Oxfam UK. Although NGOs were obviously the subject of some discussion in the World Bank's 1990 *World development report* on poverty, none of the 261 references in the bibliography can be traced directly to a transnational. And of the 394 bibliographical references in the 1993 *World development report* on health, only one flows directly from a transnational (SCF UK).

This criticism may be unfair. If the World Bank and UNICEF refuse to consider the experience and findings of NGOs, it is not necessarily the fault of NGOs. And in truth, very few other NGOs are cited in these studies. The broader point is that transnational NGOs have the staff, the history, the experience and the mandate for considerably greater direct impact than others, on general development theory, policy and practice. Some Oxfam members have made a pointed effort to do this, through campaigns and a wide variety of publications and research documents. The first institutional expression of Oxfam International, in fact, beyond a one-person office, was the opening of a Washington bureau. Its purpose is not to seek World Bank contracts, but to work on policy-related issues with the international financial institutions and UN agencies.

SCF UK has taken a similar approach on issues relating to the rights of the child, and in encouraging international research on the more generic role of NGOs in development. World Vision, CARE, Plan and Médecins sans Frontières are highly visible in their fundraising, but are otherwise largely absent from public consciousness. Part of the problem is will, part has to do with the nature of their income. Unlike single-issue transnationals such as Amnesty International, or environmental organizations like Greenpeace and Friends of the Earth, development agencies by and large have donors rather than members who are committed to the cause. And many of these donors, wooed by pictures of children and promises of success, have little interest in broader issues of human rights, world trade and structural adjustment.

Will the transnationals crowd out other Northern NGOs? It is already happening in the case of emergencies, and there can be little doubt that they are eating into the 'development' income of smaller one-country NGOs. There is so much fundraising competition, and so few ways to learn about which NGO is effective, that individuals considering a donation simply go with the household names: those seen every night on the news from the latest famine, cyclone or war zone. In the end, neither the market nor the need can justify or support the proliferation of tiny Northern NGOs, each trying to be special, different, more effective, more efficient, more unique than the rest. Few are amenable to mergers or even to shared programming and administration. Yet new lookalike agencies appear every year. Some of the hardier ones will undoubtedly survive, either because they adopt some of the techniques of the transnationals, or because they develop special expertise and carve out new niches in

210

development education or fundraising.* But some will surely vanish, victims of their unwillingness to join with like-minded organizations, or victims of the increasingly sophisticated fundraising techniques of the transnationals. Others will be reduced to boutique NGOs — which is how many of them began — filling very particular niches and appealing to small or specialized donor constituencies.

The impact of the transnationals on public attitudes in the North is hard to gauge. Some, such as Oxfam UK and SCF UK have active and internationally respected development education and campaigning programmes, but even they have doubts about their impact. Michael Edwards, Head of SCF UK's Information and Research Unit, sees four problems: an overall absence of clear strategy, a failure to build strong alliances, a failure to develop alternatives to current orthodoxies, and the dilemma of relations with donors.[20] For most of the others, however, development education is so small that it rarely warrants a line item in the annual report. Many have thrived on the pictures they purvey of starvation and of desperate children, a formula they are reluctant to tamper with.

Smile, and the world smiles with you

There is another kind of non-governmental transnationalism, one of networks and alliances: partnerships of like-minded organizations, forming to work together on particular issues, constantly disbanding and reforming to suit the context. The new vocabulary might call these 'virtual transnationals', but the concept is not new. The peace and anti-apartheid movements are examples from other decades. More recent ones include the Third World Network, Global Exchange, Civicus — a 'world alliance for citizen participation' — and groups linked by modem to global computer networks. Richard Falk talks of a 'globalization from below', the emergence of 'a transnational activism that started to become important for social movements during the 1980s': the environment, human rights, women's movements. 'Amnesty International and Greenpeace are emblematic of this transnational militancy with an identity, itself evolving and being self-transformed.'[21] Among NGOs, there is a tendency to accentuate the positive, and to place great hope in a vaguely defined but optimistic future. NGOs acknowledge the size of the problems they tackle, but there is always light at the end of the tunnel. People

---

*A somewhat unlikely but not unsuccessful transnationalizing NGO is the British Voluntary Service Overseas, which began recruiting and fundraising in Ireland and Holland in the late 1980s and, despite an apparently saturated field of five volunteer-sending organizations in Canada, set up an operation there in 1993.

are motivated by success, not failure. Optimism, in any case, is part of human nature.

Optimism is not always helpful as a guide, however. Sometimes the light at the end of the tunnel is an on-coming train. Caution, therefore, and the occasional reality-check may reveal the need for different tactics and different views about how to organize one's affairs. In one of the last interviews before her suicide, Petra Kelly, founder of the German Green Party said, 'When I look at the alternative movement I can say, "Well yes, there is still a small hope that some day, we'll break through"'. But she, for one, was not optimistic. 'It was supposed to be our decade', she said. 'At the moment it seems we have lost the battle. We are all hanging in, but we don't seem to have much influence any more.'[22]

This chapter may have over-stretched the analogy between the transnational NGO and the transnational corporation. The point was not really to liken one with the other, but to discuss the arrival of a new type of organization with specific characteristics that make it different from other NGOs. Transnational NGOs, of course, do not all operate in the same fashion. Some of the national bodies are very much like independent NGOs in, say, the Netherlands or Italy. Unlike transnational corporations, they rarely move staff between their Northern affiliates. A *dictat* from the international headquarters would most likely be ignored. Some have sent reasonably healthy roots into the societies of their own countries. And while many of the affiliates may be excellent performers, some are not, and the international 'head office' can usually do little about it.

Ultimately, what emerges from the evidence, is that some transnationals have traded long-term development impact for growth, short-term child sponsorship and emergency donors; that they may have hitched their cart to an old horse while those around them are trading in their buggy whips. This is not to deny the very genuine commitment of their workers to development. But at a corporate level, many actually do bear an uncanny resemblance to transnational corporations in their opportunistic (some might say human) behaviour. Like many transnational corporations, they have maximized growth through the successful international manipulation of pricing, marketing and product. Unlike most transnational corporations, however, they have a serious weakness, an odd one, considering their line of business: where policy, management and control are concerned, 'international' really means 'north'. South of the Mason-Dixon Development Line, 'international' rarely seems to apply.

Transnational NGOs have done something else, however. They have demonstrated that there is an enormous amount of goodwill in the North, and that even in the harsh, self-interested 1990s, the pool of people willing to try to understand, and to do what they can to help the South can be greatly expanded. The transnational success may flow partly from questionable fundraising tactics and sophisticated advertising. But it is also the product of a vacuum. Because despite the thousands of other NGOs raising money and awareness in the North, and, despite impressive growth, international giving remains — in relative terms — resolutely at the bottom of the Northern donor's priority list. Donations for international assistance represent 13 per cent of total giving in Britain, but only three per cent in Canada and one per cent in the United States. The transnational NGOs are moving into this vacuum, gaining world-class status in television news coverage of disasters, and brand-name recognition in fundraising appeals. The continued existence of hundreds of small, self-centred, unconnected organizations in the wider NGO community only makes the growth of the transnational NGO phenomenon more certain.

CHAPTER XII

Democracy, participation and the rights stuff

> *No one pretends that democracy is perfect or all wise. Indeed, it has been said that democracy is the worst form of government except all those other forms that have been tried from time to time.*
>
> Winston Churchill.

AT THE BEGINNING of the Third Development Decade (the 1980s, for those who are losing count), before the word 'governance' had crept into everyday development discourse, before human rights had climbed down off the United Nations Charter and into official aid policy, before people began speaking of, and recommending 'democracy' as an important element of development, there was something called the 'Cold War'.

This cold war required (or permitted) Western governments, official aid agencies and multilateral institutions such as the World Bank to look ingenuously downwind on issues of governance, human rights and democracy. The cold war condoned and encouraged private investment, as well as official or unofficial economic and military backing for Portuguese wars in Africa, for repressive governments in South Vietnam, South Korea and South Africa, for any number of Latin American dictatorships, and for dozens of one-party African states with life presidents who were dependent upon military life support systems. It can perhaps now be suggested that the lionizing of undemocratic but ideologically friendly regimes in countries such as Kenya, Brazil and the Philippines actually worked *against* human rights and helped to damage democracy in ways that cannot yet be properly assessed. Western support, explicit or implicit, during the takeoff period in the careers of Jean Bedel Bokassa, Anastasio Somoza and Augusto Pinochet did nothing to further democracy and human rights in the countries which they subsequently terrorized and defiled. On a visit to Manila, Vice President George Bush told Ferdinand Marcos, 'We love your adherence to democratic principle and to the democratic process.'[1]

Western fear of communism's 'evil empire' permitted and sometimes encouraged monsters to flourish. An example of the myopia which forbade mention of governance, democracy and human rights, can be found in the World Bank's 1981 report, *Accelerated development in Sub-Saharan Africa: an agenda for action*. The report

214

discussed, in detail, the economic crisis that existed in Africa at the time. It spoke of the new priorities and policy adjustments that would be required, and about the 'persistence of special constraints'. This euphemism — 'special constraints' — was as close as the report got to the political questions that would come to dominate the policy agenda by the end of the decade. The report spoke timidly of the 'political fragility' which had 'forced the post-independence leadership to give especially high priority to short-term political objectives'.[2] Although it conceded that enormous efforts had been made 'to adapt organizational and administrative arrangements' to the African setting, it acknowledged that the 'mammoth undertaking' remained unfinished. This seminal report on the state of African development made no mention, did not even hint that the mammoth undertaking in adapting 'administrative arrangements' would soon be urged on Africa by donors using aid as a blunt weapon. Governments would be forced to hold multi-party elections; basic human rights would become an aid issue; and governments would be obliged to start transferring some of their authority to a phenomenon that would soar on the development agenda during the Fourth Development Decade, 'civil society'.

Within ten years of the Bank's report, everything had changed. The cold war evaporated in the gale of popular revolutions that spread through eastern Europe. A similar uprising had already ended the regime of Ferdinand Marcos in the Philippines, and the Government of South Africa, which had already given up Namibia, was beginning to plan for majority rule. For the first time in decades, multi-party elections were held in Kenya, Zambia, Benin, Cameroon and Togo, and the military handed over to elected civilian governments in Uruguay, Argentina, Chile and Haiti.

However, elections, flawed and limited as many of them seemed to be, were only a part of the change. The World Bank, emboldened by a neo-conservative war on political correctness, now fearlessly attributed Africa's problems, *inter alia*, to a 'crisis in governance', and said that a systematic effort was required 'to build a pluralistic institutional structure, a determination to respect the rule of law, and vigorous protection of the freedom of the press and human rights'.[3] The United Nations Development Program, which had rarely pronounced on such subjects during the 1960s and 1970s — the heyday of development assistance — published a 'Human Freedom Index' in its 1991 *Human development report*. Asking if there was a correlation between human freedom and human development, the report said that although causality remained unclear, 'countries that rank high on one indicator also tend to rank high on the other'.[4] It then classified 88 countries, according to 40 'freedom indicators'.[5] These included the freedoms of travel and association, free media, independent courts,

215

the right to free, open and prompt trial, freedom from torture and the right to religion, gender equality and citizenship. Sweden and Denmark scored highest, with 38 out of a possible 40 points. Thirty-one other countries, including, for example, Papua New Guinea, Argentina, Senegal and Jamaica received a passing grade of 20 points or more. The rest became contenders in an ugly contest, with 15 scoring 5 points or less. Romania and Libya tied with one point each, and Iraq, already the bad boy of the Middle East, received zero.

International concern about these issues may have seemed novel as the 1980s unfolded, but there were precedents. Jimmy Carter, for one, had made respect for human rights and democracy a cornerstone of his presidency between 1977 and 1981. Although implementation fell short of rhetoric, Carter helped to legitimize the issues, and to pave a way for the full flowering of concern that would be unleashed as communism withered, and as donors realized, or began to admit, that good development does not usually flow from bad government.*

Concepts of democracy and human rights, of course, predate Jimmy Carter. 'Democracy', which entered the English language in the sixteenth century, had its birth in Athens some 2500 years ago. Most Western school children know this. Some also know about the 1688 English Bill of Rights, the 1789 French Declaration of Rights, and the concern about tyranny enshrined in the American Declaration of Independence. These codes centred primarily on the nation state. Following the Second World War, a more 'universalist' approach emerged. The first example of this was the 1945 United Nations Charter, under which the UN was to 'promote universal respect for, and observance of human rights and fundamental freedoms for all'. Human rights were more fully defined in the Universal Declaration of Human Rights, adopted by the United Nations General Assembly in 1948 without dissent (but when the General Assembly was one quarter its present size). Further reaffirmations include the 1950 European Convention on Human Rights, the 1975 Helsinki Accords, and the 1981 African Charter on People's and Human Rights.

Democracy

After 2500 years of refinement, there is surprisingly little consensus on what 'democracy' actually means. One-party states, 'people's

---

*Governance: Donors have skirted suggestions that a recipient country might possibly have a bad government by avoiding the word *government* altogether. The stress on *governance* makes the whole exercise more anodyne, having less to do with specific cases of venality, corruption and tyranny, and more to do with the clinical aspects of managing or *governing* in a wise and humane fashion.

democracies', socialists, capitalists, liberal democrats, republics and constitutional monarchies all claim, often vigorously, to be democracies. The first of three major variants on the theme was the one invented in ancient Greece. In direct democracy, citizens participate individually in governance and decision making. The second variant, representative democracy, is based on the concept of individuals elected to a legislature. There they represent their constituents within the framework of a constitution or the rule of law. It is the rule of law and the ability to limit arbitrary decision-making which create stability and trust between government and the governed.

A third variant, 'one-party democracy', allows voters to choose between candidates who work within the superstructure of a single party. Disparaged by Western political scientists in the post-Soviet era (and discredited by an army of one-party politicians who have used it mainly for personal gain), one-party democracy does have a legitimate pedigree. Schmitz and Gillies point out that 'few theorists of development have paid much attention to the problems of ethnic diversity and other deep cultural cleavages which make a unifying democratic consensus so difficult to achieve in many Third World countries'.[6] Once the heavy administrative hand of colonialism was lifted, newly installed parliamentary democracies began to demonstrate their fragility, falling like ninepins before a rush of demagogues, revolutionary reformers and military takeovers.

Schmitz and Gillies suggest that a more appropriate model might be found in the 'consociational democracies' of Europe, a form of government practised in countries that are deeply divided along religious, ethnic or racial lines. The result may be a federal arrangement or one in which decision-making, appointments and spending are allocated along proportional lines according to the country's ethnic or religious makeup. Variations are found in Switzerland, Belgium, Canada and Israel, and the approach has been tried with varying degrees of success in Austria, the Netherlands and Malaysia. Its shortcomings, however, can be seen in pre-war Lebanon, pre- and post-Biafran Nigeria, post-Tito Yugoslavia and in post-Soviet Russia. These are, or were, formal examples of consociational government. But the concept works in less formal ways in dozens of other countries. Schmitz and Gillies point out that, 'consociationalism, with its pluralistic methods of gradual consensus-building, seems to be more in keeping with pre-western traditions in many developing states than the . . . Westminster model of one-party government versus 'loyal' opposition.'[7]

They may well be right. Multi-party elections, urged in very non-democratic fashion by donor countries on Nicaragua, Kenya, Zambia, Benin and others in the late 1980s and early 1990s have not always resulted in appreciably better 'governance', nor have they heralded a major improvement in human rights. Nor is it clear that this crop of elected governments will survive longer or better than their forebears, who assumed power from colonial governments in the 1950s and 1960s.

While multi-party elections can certainly contribute to better and more accountable government, democracy is more than an election every few years. Democracy, respect for human rights and good government are all tightly interwoven; they include principles of legitimacy, accountability and participation, and they include the notion of quality in standards of management. The basic elements of a democratic political system include:

○ *Legitimacy:* a system of government that relies on the consent of the governed; where the means exist to change governments and policies; where government has respect for and can enforce constitutional order and the rule of law; where the judiciary is independent of the political process.*

○ *Accountability:* a government that is accountable to the citizenry for its policies and actions between elections, ensured through the freedom of association, freedom of the press, and the freedom to dissent.

○ *Participation:* a government that permits and encourages citizens to take advantage of opportunities and rights. Pluralism and tolerance for diversity are encouraged, and the means exist to solve conflict peacefully; participation and accountability are developed through the encouragement of a robust and independent civil society: non-governmental associations based upon public rather than private goals.

○ *Competence:* a government with effective, honest and transparent civilian institutions that have the ability to formulate and implement policy and to deliver essential services effectively.

Civil society

There are implications for NGOs in all of these categories. Some were foreseen by Alexis de Tocqueville when he wrote *Democracy in America* a century and a half ago: 'Among the laws that rule human

---

*This brief, essentially liberal-democratic definition of legitimacy is not all there is to say on the subject. Historically, the legitimacy of the leader or the government was an outcome of several things. Values, tradition and ideology — such as belief in the divine right of kings — were one set of factors. These were reinforced or undermined by the quality of the leader's 'product', such as patronage, peace, and a healthy economy. And a third was the threat of force, required in increasing proportions as the quality of values and product declined.

218

societies, there is one that seems more precise and clear than all others. If men are to remain civilized or become so, the art of associating together must grow and improve in the same ratio in which the equality of condition is increased.' He also noted the direct connection between democracy, associations and the media: 'Only a newspaper can put the same thought before a thousand readers . . . hardly any democratic association can carry on without a newspaper.'[8]

The importance of an association-based civil society finds supporters in unlikely places. Lenin saw the associations of civil society as transmission lines between people and state (and therefore as instruments to be carefully designed and managed by the party). Antonio Gramsci, leader of the Italian Communist Party in the 1920s, saw them as a key element in the building and maintaining of a nation's political consensus and social mindset. While these associations were problematic for Gramsci when they supported the domination of one class over another, they were significant in a revolutionary sense because they could also be used to bring people together around other experiences, and around new ways of thinking.

Ironically, conservatives see the organizations of civil society in much the same way. George Will, writing about the Russian political crisis of March 1993, observed that 'every day brings a thickening of civil society, those private institutions of consensual association and empowerment that enable society to flourish independent of, and if necessary in opposition to, the state.'[9]

Concern about civil society grew by leaps and bounds in the early 1990s, but mainly among donor agencies and NGOs, rather than political scientists (who mostly knew it was there all along). A conceptual product of the Enlightenment, 'civil societies' are those governed by the rule of law and held together not so much by blood and ethnicity as by institutions of common interest. By the early 1990s, fuelled as much by changes in Eastern Europe as by concern for the South, the expression 'civil society' had found its way into major policy papers of almost every donor agency, and had become a topic of concern among NGOs in legitimizing their role. As one aid agency puts it:

> Simply stated, civil society is, together with the state and market, one of the three 'spheres' that interface in the making of democratic societies. Civil society is the sphere in which social movements become organized. The organizations of civil society, which represent many diverse and sometimes contradictory social interests . . . include church-related groups, trade unions, co-operatives, service organizations, community groups and youth organizations, as well as academic institutions and others.[10]

In much of the South, and especially in Africa, there is another dimension to civil society. What the aid agency definitions describe is a set of institutions that have evolved organically in the West: a series of formal, structured and regulated institutions that operate under the rule of law in a richly varied associational culture. Alan Fowler argues that in much of Africa, civil society is differently configured. 'The material base in African countries is dualistic, comprising both risk-averse family subsistence and capitalist-oriented elements that coexist and interact with each other, but seldom on an equal basis.'[11] African respect for collective rights must also coexist with the individualism of modern economies. This adds to the dualism, as do ethnicity and flourishing informal economies.

So much time is currently devoted to defining civil society, that sight of its importance is sometimes lost. Legitimacy, accountability, participation and governmental competence are all given as reasons for encouraging it, but empirical evidence of the link between traditions of association on the one hand, and development on the other is generally weak. Of theory there is no lack, but evidence of correlation and causality tends to be patchy, contradictory and sometimes seems like wishful thinking.

In a twenty-year study of civic traditions in modern Italy, Robert Putnam approached the topic more scientifically. In an effort to discover the reasons behind the great differences in government effectiveness, economic performance and social development between regions in the north and the south of the country, he and his colleagues conducted several waves of investigation between 1970 and 1989. They surveyed regional councillors and community leaders, they conducted institutional case studies and mass surveys, they analysed all regional legislation over a 14-year period, and they sifted ten centuries of regional history.

What they found was striking. The strong associational life in several northern regions such as Emilia-Romagna was clearly and unambiguously responsible for good government, and was a factor in the development of a strong economy. Its historical and present-day absence in southern regions has led to weak government and to societies based on paternalism, exploitation, corruption and poverty.[12] The Putnam study bears out what Michael Ignatieff says about civil society:

> It is in the institutions of civil society . . . that the leadership of a democratic society is trained and recruited . . . It is civil society in tandem with the state that tames the market. Without a strong civil society, there cannot be a debate about what kind of market to have, what portion of its surplus should be put to the use of present and future generations . . . Without a free and robust civil society, market capitalism must inevitably turn into mafia capitalism . . . Without civil society, democracy remains an empty shell.[13]

Participation

Like many over-worked words in the development lexicon, 'participation' has been devalued by a myriad of self-serving interpretations. In liberal theory, participation is regarded as an important element of responsive, democratic government. It promotes equality by providing a voice for ordinary people and by involving them in decision-making. Transparency and responsibility in government are advanced through dissemination of the information required to make informed choices. Accepted in recent years by most bilateral and multilateral aid agencies as an essential part of effective development, it is sadly — and more often than not — treated either as a simple cure-all, or as a new bottle into which old wine must be carefully decanted.

'Popular participation' means a process by which people, especially the disadvantaged, are informed of and involved in the implementation or benefits of a development activity. More importantly, however, it suggests that people can and should exercise influence over, and ultimately take responsibility for things which affect their lives. The objectives of popular participation may be limited or extensive. They may include increased beneficiary capacity, improved effectiveness, greater project efficiency and the financial participation of beneficiaries in the project. 'Empowerment' may also be an objective: the organization of bonded labourers to demand and acquire their legal rights; the economic empowerment of the landless through access to credit; the social empowerment of women through changes in laws of inheritance, or the effective application of laws dealing with family violence.

Participation can be fostered through a variety of mechanisms. Extension agents, government departments and large development agencies can all encourage and initiate participation at different levels. The concept of 'community development', for example, was a cornerstone of India's first Five Year Plan in 1951. The draft plan was widely circulated for public discussion, a process reflecting the view that extensive public consultation is an essential part of the social process in a democracy. By 1960, community development had become the basis of national, regional or localized programmes in dozens of countries in Africa, Asia and Latin America. Comprising both economic and political objectives, it was based on the idea that the process involved in achieving a goal was often an important part of the objective.

Expectations of community development were high, however. Too high, as it turned out, for governments and aid agencies alike. Community development failed to meet political and economic expectations; its economic results and the institutions that grew from it were often stolen or co-opted by local élites. And most worrying for some governments and aid agencies, community development habitually fostered unsatisfiable demands and annoying criticism from below. By the late 1960s, attention had turned away from participatory community development towards the siren's call of growth: green revolutions, the transfer of capital-intensive technology, heavy industry and modernization.

Development theory, however, is a bit like the circle game: the painted ponies go 'round and 'round. Today, perhaps more aware than a decade ago that women, the poorest, the disabled, indigenous people and sometimes whole countries have been bypassed by the growth model of development, participation has been rediscovered by governments and donor agencies. The demands and criticisms from below are now unselfishly regarded as a key element of both development and good governance. In a 1992 study on the causes and consequences of poverty, IFAD said that 'organized demands upon governments and, through them, upon external agencies and private commercial bodies, focus resources where they are needed and reduce the unequal exchange characteristic of economic relationships between the élite and the rural poor.'[14] The World Bank, more cautious than most, observed the same year that 'rigorous empirical evidence is scant but nevertheless positive about the benefits of participation to development effectiveness'.[15] The Bank had good reason for expressing caution about popular participation, because whenever participation rears its head in a Bank project, the Bank tends to get a black eye.

Take for example, the Flood Action Plan (FAP) in Bangladesh. In an effort to mitigate the worst flood disasters, a Bank-led, multi-donor, multi-billion dollar plan was conceived after the very severe floods of 1988. Through a system of embankments, diversions and barrages, the FAP was designed to put an end once and for all to the chronic disasters that seem to plague the country. NGOs, however, were critical, and gradually they put together a familiar-looking NGO protest network which donors dismissed in the traditional donor manner as being little more than ill-informed, knee-jerk reaction. NGOs, however, were reflecting what they heard in the villages, where normal flooding is essential to agriculture and fishing.

Studies of one project component, the FAP Compartmentalization Project in Tangail, record a dialogue of the deaf. Villagers, having experienced the ill-effects of badly planned flood protection projects in the past, were ambivalent, if not hostile to the new project. In previous flood-protection interventions, sluice gates quickly silted up, exacerbating floods, damaging fishing and resulting eventually in destructive waterlogging. Villagers wanted assurance in the new project that

222

adequate provision would be made for proper maintenance. This, they were told, was *their* responsibility: part of the 'new' approach to participatory development. It was, in fact, the old approach to infrastructure development: hardware without software; projects hastily designed and implemented by engineers — often outsiders — with little more than vague hopes about maintenance and follow-up.[16]

The 1993 UNDP *Human development report* was more effusive about the benefits of participation than the Bank: 'People's participation is becoming the central issue of our time. The democratic transition in many developing countries, the collapse of many socialist regimes, and the worldwide emergence of people's organizations: these are all part of a historic change, not just isolated events . . . [Participation] can become a source of tremendous vitality and innovation for the creation of new and more just societies.'[17]

Although there are possibilities for putting participation into action in government projects, it is the NGO community through which most bilateral and multilateral agencies choose to apply participation, and from which most take their lessons. There are good reasons for this. One is that NGOs have a head start as well as some natural advantages. The community development work of Northern NGOs in the 1960s relied heavily on participation. Although the names changed and the techniques varied, participation did not go away. In the 1970s, Paulo Freire's 'conscientization' came into vogue, and towards the end of the decade, Northern NGOs began to devolve hands-on programming to their fast-emerging Southern counterparts. Apart from their historical advantage, most NGOs — whether Northern or Southern, large or community-based — work directly with the poor, usually in rural areas far from the embassies and government offices of the capital city. Because many have based their interventions on participation, and on respect for local traditions and technologies, they have gathered a reasonable amount of what the Bank might call 'empirical evidence of success'.

Sarvodaya, for example, became one of the largest NGOs in Asia, basing its self-help *shramadana* philosophy on traditional Sri Lankan and Buddhist concepts of social development, strengthening the village as a social entity and building on prevailing cultural patterns and value systems, rather than on imported models. Sarvodaya took its name from a loosely structured society formed in India in 1948, the *Sarvodaya Samaj*, or society for the welfare of all. Based on the teachings of Gandhi, its village workers were expected to wear *khadi*, the home-spun cloth that symbolized self-reliance, and to help villages become self-contained and self-supporting.

The Aga Khan Rural Support Programme in Pakistan starts with a series of 'dialogues' between organizers and villagers. Meetings are held outdoors so that the entire village can hear and comment on what is being said: not unlike the way the Greeks did it 2500 years ago. Thousands of primary schools operated by the Bangladesh Rural Advancement Committee function efficiently where others have failed because the teacher is recruited from the village and is responsible to a parents' committee which provides land and equipment, and which helps schedule the school day and the annual school calendar. The Orangi Pilot Project, operating in one of Karachi's worst slums, is centred almost entirely on self-help for the purpose of constructing low-cost sanitation systems. In the decade following its 1980 start-up, OPP involved 28 000 families in the construction of 131 kilometres of underground sewerage and 28 000 latrines. It built schools and initiated economic programmes for women. The cost, more than a million dollars, was almost entirely financed by those who lived in the slum.

Examples like these and a thousand smaller ones have helped demonstrate the continuing validity of participation. Tom Dichter, an American NGO specialist, observes that although the concept is a deeply serious one, participation is not rocket science. 'When the reams of paper on the subject are put aside, development professionals . . . know how to foster it:

○ help people reflect on their own condition;
○ speak their language;
○ live with (or at least spend time with) them;
○ take their interests and values into account;
○ respect them as individuals;
○ find ways to get them to have a stake;
○ train them;
○ create appropriate award structures;
○ pay attention to detail;
○ take adequate time;
○ do your homework.'[18]

Certainly this is not rocket science. Chairman Mao said something along the same lines: 'go to the people; live among them, learn from them'. But talk is cheap, and as Mao discovered, it is not as easy as it sounds. Nor would everyone agree on the list. First, it has mainly to do with how outsiders foster, create and manage participation, in something of their own devising. This is at least a partial contradiction in terms. The list describes the role of a catalyst, without suggesting the limits to what outsiders should and should not do, or how far they can go as agents of change. 'Speak their language' covers a multitude of challenges having to do not only with linguistics, but with culture, style, values and power.

The list does not address the limitations imposed on the development process by the culture of funding agencies. Participatory planning takes time, often a lot of time. It could perhaps be likened to a front-end business cost. Manufacturers know that without adequate market analysis, product testing and factory retooling, a seemingly good idea can lead to bankruptcy. NGOs, restricted to low overheads, have little money of their own for project development and the sort of feasibility analysis that would include real consultation and participation. And the governmental benefactors of NGOs rarely provide it either. Participation, therefore, tends to be a cottage industry that is difficult to replicate or scale up.

Blueprint planning, 'logical' framework analysis, target-based budgets and the project cycle favoured by most large donor agencies (and copied by many Northern NGOs) impose a rigidity on the implementation process that also works against the reflection and adjustment that are inherent aspects of real community participation. And donor reporting requirements are usually inimical to a participatory approach as well. It is estimated that the cost of making a single application to USAID for a matching grant can be as high as $20 000. And any NGO, American or Southern, receiving more than $25 000 from USAID must comply with auditing requirements so complex that a 70-page explanatory booklet is needed to understand them.[19] Just as planting seasons do not wait for donor decisions, real life does not unfold according to the dictates of a logical framework analysis. And participation does not come in a jar.

A further problem: NGOs are increasingly *used* as implementing agencies for larger donor initiatives: water projects, credit programmes, immunization efforts. NGOs are hired to conjure up the thing called participation, because current development wisdom says it is important. But if NGOs are treated as clerks and are only expected to get the jar off the shelf, participation will be illusory. Participatory techniques may be helpful in reaching fixed goals determined by outsiders, but in such cases they will be just that, techniques: an 'input' rather than a result; a methodology rather than the institutionalized involvement that contributes to long-term sustainability.

Dichter rewrites his list, asking what it would take to get those of us who talk and write about participation to actually participate in something, like a road or a health clinic, initiated by an outsider. Our answers would be obvious:

o a sense that we are being respected;
o a sense that we will be heard when we have something to say (such as: are the road or the health clinic priorities for us?);
o a sense that we are being treated fairly and that we understand the rules;
o a sense that following the rules will bring about the desired effect;

o a sense that we will get something in return for our participation;
o a feeling of confidence that we are not giving up anything, as an unfair tradeoff in return for what we are getting.

Human rights

Power does not corrupt men; fools, however, if they get into a position of power, corrupt power.

George Bernard Shaw

In 1935, Winston Churchill, then a political outcast, wrote an article about the absence of human rights in Nazi Germany. The Jews, he wrote, were being 'stripped of all power, driven from every position in public and social life, expelled from the professions, silenced in the press, and declared a foul and odious race. The twentieth century has witnessed with surprise, not merely the promulgation of these ferocious doctrines, but their enforcement with brutal vigour by the government and the populace.' Hitler instructed the German ambassador in London to lodge a strong protest against Churchill's 'personal attack on the head of the German State', and when the article was about to be reprinted two years later, the Foreign Office attempted to have it stopped. 'It is hardly to be thought that this article would be at all palatable to the powers that be in Germany,' wrote an official. 'In the present rather delicate state of our relations with that country . . . it might therefore be questioned whether republication just now was advisable.'[20]

The article *was* reprinted, but the same sordid exercise in pre-emptive cowardice, in attempting to stifle independent comment on human rights abuse, is repeated on a daily basis in a hundred ways. Northern NGOs which advocated an end to colonialism in Portuguese Africa and to apartheid in South Africa during the 1960s and 1970s were attacked as agitators, fellow-travellers and sometimes as communists. The phenomenon still exists. A 1989 example is provided by the International Freedom Foundation, whose Executive Director wrote about the 'systematic transformation' of British NGOs, and of the emergence 'under the cloak of famine relief and development aid, of highly politicized "charitable" organizations whose traditional functions have been relegated to a secondary role, behind a narrow political agenda. Organizations such as Christian Aid and Oxfam seem to have been "captured" at their centres by small cliques of ideologically motivated individuals . . . Radical socialist and Marxist campaigns are now a daily occurrence from some of Britain's largest charities.'[21]

Government pressure on an NGO can manifest itself in many ways: a slap on the wrist; public condemnation; cancellation of charitable status; reduced financial support. In 1979, the Government of New Zealand removed CORSO's charitable status for 'left-wing' political activity, dealing a massive and permanent financial blow to what was then the country's largest NGO. In 1991 the Charity Commissioners for England and Wales censured Oxfam for criticizing an aspect of British aid spending. Apparently oblivious to concepts of free speech and human rights, they found that 'it cannot be acceptable for any charity to run public campaigns against the policy of any government (whether at home or abroad)'.[22]

The closer an NGO gets to the centre of a human rights issue, the more it risks. The International University Exchange Fund (IUEF), an international Geneva-based NGO, began supporting South African political refugees in the early 1970s. In addition to publicizing the atrocities of apartheid, it also supported the advocacy and human rights work of activists within South Africa. The Black Consciousness Movement, founded by Steve Biko, was an IUEF beneficiary until 1976 when the Soweto uprising, which resulted in the deaths of hundreds of people, shocked the South African Government to its foundations. Ways were sought to destroy any organization, inside the country or outside, that was involved in awareness-building, human rights and political advocacy. Biko was arrested and killed, but the groundswell continued. The secret police began to bone up on their Fanon, Freire and Marcuse, reading Stokely Carmichael long into the night. They concluded that community development, including cottage industry, literacy courses, clinics and crèches, also posed a major danger to the regime.[23]

Black consciousness organizations were outlawed, their surviving leaders arrested, and outside agencies like IUEF were targeted for destruction. The notorious South African Bureau of State Security (BOSS) managed to place an agent inside the organization, disguised as a left-wing anti-apartheid refugee. Incredibly, this police major rose to the rank of deputy director within two years, gathering invaluable and highly destructive information about the anti-apartheid movement. When the BOSS infiltration was exposed by a defecting South African agent in 1980, donors withdrew their support from IUEF and the organization collapsed — the ultimate BOSS objective once the cupboard had been looted.[24]

Indonesia offers another variation on the NGO-human rights issue. East Timor, a Portuguese colony forcibly annexed by Indonesia in 1976, has been the subject of harsh authoritarian rule — criticized from afar by some Northern NGOs — for two decades. Following the 1991 massacre of dozens of students in an anti-government demonstration, the Netherlands, Canada and Australia suspended their aid programmes. The Indonesian reaction was swift. The official Dutch aid programme was cancelled by Indonesia itself, and all Dutch NGOs were expelled as well. It was a message from Indonesia that it would not tolerate external interference in its own affairs and it served to *encourager les autres.* Canadians and Australians took note. Official aid was quietly resumed, and NGOs with programmes in Indonesia remained mute. Some, in fact, responded to generous offers from bilateral donors to open programmes in East Timor. Although perhaps not a bad thing from a welfare point of view, this had no likelihood of advancing human rights or Timorese civil society: the only NGOs with any possibility of government clearance were those with spotlessly apolitical track records.

To speak or not to speak is one question. Another, when a decision to speak has been taken, is what to say. NGOs rarely, if ever, speak with one voice, and NGOs certainly do not all see human rights in the same way. The human rights activities of NGO workers in Central America, for example, have been very mixed. Many were used, or allowed themselves to be used, as foot soldiers in the cold war. Before 1980, the region was virtually unknown to most NGOs. With the 1979 Sandinista revolution in Nicaragua, however, with a brutal civil war in El Salvador and a cornucopia of murder and abuse in Guatemala, Central America developed pivotal cold war importance. NGOs rushed in. Between 1980 and 1987, aid spending tripled in the region, 15 per cent of it provided by and through NGOs.[25] European governments, opposing US policy but not wishing to confront the US directly, channelled additional money through NGOs. European and Canadian NGOs, working with peasant groups and human rights organizations, spent as much as 30 per cent of their budgets in countries that most had never visited five years earlier. The rush of 'progressive' NGOs, vying for the correct analysis and approach, encouraged other donor agencies, notably USAID, to contract 'apolitical' NGOs like Project Hope and World Vision for the implementation of projects: a kind of NGO counterinsurgency. As one observer put it, 'only two institutions have consistently flourished in the Central American crisis: the military and the NGOs'.[26]

Obviously there are costs associated with speaking out about human rights abuse, and NGOs are often faced with a cruel choice. Many work closely with refugees. Some work intimately with Southern human rights organizations in repressive situations, and their presence can provide political protection. If they speak out against the authorities, therefore, they run the risk of expulsion, putting their beneficiaries and partners at risk. Médecins sans Frontières was thrown out of Ethiopia in 1985 for declaring that the government's forced resettlement programme had cost the lives of 100 000 people. World Vision, the Lutheran World Federation and the Action Committee for Relief of

228

Southern Sudan were expelled from the Sudan in 1986 because of perceived political partiality.[27] All NGOs and international church organizations working in Biafra were expelled by the victorious Nigerian Government at the end of the war, because during the conflict they had urged international political action against what they saw as genocide. Relief agencies working with Hutu refugees in Zaire knew that many in their midst were politicians, militia and soldiers who had authorized and participated in the earlier bloodthirsty reign of terror against innocent Tutsis. By pointing out known war criminals, however, they could have placed their own workers at risk, endangering the larger effort they were mounting on behalf of the innocent.*

Influencing policy

Both Northern and Southern NGOs can and do influence policy: aid policy; specific development policies; the broader policy framework in which development takes place. NGOs in almost every OECD country have at one time or another campaigned vigorously and often successfully to protect and increase official development spending. Singly and in coalitions they have urged their governments to reduce the debt burden of beneficiary countries, to apply more official assistance to basic human needs, to consider the damaging effects of structural adjustment programmes. They have been active and influential at world gatherings, from the 1972 Stockholm Environment Conference to UNCED, Cairo, Beijing and beyond. And because of their direct field experience they have been major informants for parliamentary studies and international inquiries such as the Brandt and Brundtland Commissions. They have challenged their governments at different times on relations with Cambodia, South Africa and Central America. They are, effective or otherwise, both a watchdog for, and the conscience of the development business: roles perfectly in keeping with the historical traditions of the voluntary sector.

Writers cite their achievement in developing a code of conduct for the marketing of baby milk, their contribution to an essential drugs list and their work on reducing trade restrictions against Southern textile

---

*A few did speak out. At the height of the refugee crisis in July 1994, CARE said that it would consider halting its relief effort to 150 000 (Hutu) Rwandans if the UN did not act on a report recommending the arrest and trial of people suspected of genocide against the Tutsi minority. (Mark Hubbard, *The Observer*, as reported in the *Ottawa Citizen*, 20 July 1994.) By early October, seven CARE workers in Katale Camp had been placed on a Hutu death list. CARE withdrew. James Fennel, CARE's Emergency Director, said, 'We are not willing to work with a bunch of killers. These people should have been weeded out months ago.' (*The Economist*, 8 October 1994.)

manufactures.[28] Oxfam was able to modify a World Bank-induced policy in Malawi aimed at dismantling parastatals. It proved that the Agricultural Development Marketing Board provided an important food security role for poor farmers and woman-headed households in some of the most vulnerable parts of the country, and the policy was modified. SCF (UK) worked with the Government of Uganda for five years to produce legislative change that would establish the standards of care required of organizations running children's homes. The legal reform included detailed approval procedures and a regulatory system which would maintain and supervise the new standards.[29]

Gonoshasthaya Kendra, a Bangladeshi NGO, was almost single-handedly responsible in the early 1980s for the creation of a National Drug Policy, making pharmaceuticals less expensive and less dangerous for the poor. Improved standards were established, retail prices dropped between 30 and 85 per cent, transfer pricing in international firms was halted, and the share of drug production by locally owned firms increased from 35 per cent of the market to 75 per cent by 1991.[30]

The difficulty with policy change, however, is that it is expensive and time-consuming. It is expensive in the sense that real NGO workers, who might be doing something else, must devote time and energy to research, writing and to meetings that do not deliver an immediate, identifiable result. This is a serious problem for organizations on tight budgets and limited overheads. Policy development is not an attractive fundraising tool, and so it is rarely if ever mentioned in NGO publicity material. It does not lend itself easily to project support of the type favoured by bilateral donors. And the investment is inherently risky because changing policy does not necessarily mean that reality will change. The SCF efforts in Uganda were only the start of a process: implementation would require a change in attitudes and values; there would be heavy costs involved in training and supporting an inspectorate, costs that would have to be shouldered by a government cutting services back under adjustment programmes.*

Policy work can be costly. Having achieved an important policy goal, Gonoshasthaya Kendra in Bangladesh found itself under direct and regular attack from private pharmaceutical firms. It also came under indirect attack from the medical establishment, and from politicians bowing to private-sector pressure for de-regulation of the industry.[31] It also sacrificed its position in the Bangladeshi NGO community

---

*During the 1980s, Uganda negotiated one World Bank Economic Recovery loan, four IMF standby arrangements and one structural adjustment facility. During this period, Ugandan Government per capita expenditure on education dropped by 11 per cent, and health expenditure fell by 29 per cent (Berg, pp.62 and 65).

because it had worked at high levels on policy change with an unpopular and undemocratic government. Wearing their democratic hearts on their sleeves and conveniently ignoring the fact that many of them had also worked with government departments, the NGO community reacted with inaction and silence when mobs (allegedly hired by pharmaceutical firms) attacked the Gonoshasthaya Kendra offices during the 1991 democracy movement.

NGOs make governments nervous when they become involved in policy work. This is especially true in countries where the democratic process is weak or ineffective. NGOs tend, in such cases, to become something of an unofficial, political opposition. Like an opposition political party, they are quick to criticize, and they can be both doctrinaire and simplistic. They seldom provide comprehensive alternatives to the intricate web of interacting forces that have created the situation they seek to influence. NGO supporters try to be tactful when they discuss this problem. Alan Fowler deals with it by saying politely that 'many NGOs are not informed by deep political insight'.[32] The blanket NGO condemnation of structural adjustment provides a good example. Historically blind, socially myopic, economically flawed, and hurtful in many ways, adjustment programmes have nevertheless become one of the few comprehensive tools for re-calibrating badly skewed national economies. In 1989, for example, Nicaragua's annual rate of inflation was more than 3400 per cent. In Argentina it was 3700 per cent and in Peru it was 3000 per cent. NGOs certainly provided much of the evidence that adjustment programmes were hurting poor people, and helped inform the authors of UNICEF's groundbreaking book, *Adjustment with a Human Face*.[33] But they offered no real alternative, expending most of their energy on ritualistic criticism of the World Bank and the IMF, criticism which has done little to help beleaguered governments or people submerged in poverty.*

Kwesi Botchwey, the Ghanaian Minister of Finance who presided with integrity over a decade of extremely difficult and modestly successful structural adjustment, believes that the NGO perspective is narrow and selective. For example NGOs are quick to attack user fees in the health system, saying they hit the poorest with an unaffordable

---

*Maybe this judgement is too harsh. Without the attacks, adjustment programmes might never have been adjusted as they have been to take social questions into greater concern. Susan George and Fabrizio Sabelli, however, reinforce the image of ritualistic and largely impotent NGO criticism of the Bank: 'Most NGOs are not lobbying to make sure that EDs [Executive Directors] responsive to poverty and environmental concerns are named to the board, or even to make sure that their votes are a matter of public record. With few exceptions, NGOs haven't a clue as to who their representative on the board is anyway, nor any idea of what s/he does all day. (George and Sabelli, (1994), p.221)

tax. But Botchwey believes that the fees, which represent one-thirtieth of the actual cost of health provision, helped make a moribund Ghanaian health system functional. The real problem for the poorest, he believes, is illegal billing by doctors, not user fees. He points to a 15 per cent decrease in infant morbidity, a manageable inflation rate and a stable currency as tangible results of adjustment: as important for the poor as for anyone else.[34] (While Botchwey acknowledges the importance of Bank and IMF loans, he has also said that many government programmes were 'crushed under a labyrinth' of foreign aid conditions. 'This is no way to run a country.'[35])

The World Bank has frequently hit back at NGOs, criticizing their facts and the quality of their research. Attack and counter-attack are not always the norm, however. ASOCODE, an association of Central American NGOs, has met regularly with Central American presidents, making useful and constructive social and economic recommendations. Supported by the Ford Foundation, CECADE (*Centro de Capacitación el Desarollo*) and a number of Costa Rican peasant organizations studied the impact of structural adjustment on the poor and held a roundtable meeting with senior politicians during an election campaign. The result was a commitment to key policy changes by the incoming president.[36]

A reckoning

It is obvious that only certain facets of development can be measured in national statistics. For the poor, development is a process of change that permits them to improve and manage their own lives, and to understand and influence the larger context in which they live. This requires confidence, skills, independent institutions and responsive, responsible government. The official donor commitment to responsible, democratic government had never been more vocal than it was in the early 1990s. Nor was it ever so confused and ambivalent. For example 'democracy' is often used in the same sentence as 'human rights', as though they are synonymous and fully compatible. One of the weaknesses of majority decision-making, however, is that the rights of minorities can be ignored. In finely tuned systems of government with strong, pluralistic civil societies, there are checks and balances against this. Where the checks and balances are weak, however, external agents pushing hard on simple majority rule can well contribute to damaging human rights.

Donor confusion and ambivalence has an impact on NGOs and their effectiveness. Some NGOs have taken terrible risks in the name of democracy and human rights. Workers have died or been jailed, organizations have been crushed, lives ruined. There have been failures, but there have also been celebrated successes. And for every one of these, there have been a hundred more successes observed in silence, in order to protect the innocent. There can be no question that NGOs have strengthened civil society, by educating people, by enhancing the participation of women, minorities, the poor and the marginalized. Northern NGOs have helped create and sustain an entire generation of Southern organizations. And these Southern NGOs have taken civil society a step further, recognizing and strengthening traditional institutions at village level. Together, these organizations constitute an important buffer between people and the state, helping to change the odd but persistent notion that people are responsible to government, rather than the reverse.

This is a by-product of the investment in Northern NGOs, one that was largely unforeseen in the 1960s and 1970s. It may yet prove to be their most important long-term contribution to development.

There are problems, however. NGOs can be politically doctrinaire and many are 'not informed by deep political insight'. NGOs are often seriously compromised in their ability to speak out, for example, on the human rights abuse they see at first hand, because it can put their workers, their programmes and their beneficiaries in real jeopardy. Fear, of course, has always separated the wheat from the chaff where reform and justice are concerned. The cost of speaking out can be very high, as Martin Luther King Jr., Malcolm X, Steve Biko, Chico Mendes, Nelson Mandela, Aung San Suu Kyi in Burma, and many other activists have discovered.

NGOs are slow to share or co-operate with each other. Stockholm and UNCED notwithstanding, development NGOs have for decades been largely oblivious to environmental NGOs, and they have been equally detached from human rights organizations. Amnesty International, Human Rights Watch, the International Commission of Jurists and others are unknown to far too many development NGOs. Competition for money and limelight, as in so much NGO endeavour, works against a co-ordinated voice, co-ordinated research, and co-ordinated programming. Different philosophies, structures, histories and approaches add fuel to the contest for money. When external NGO coalitions have been formed for the protection that anonymity can provide — as happened on the East Timor issue — these tend to be the exception rather than the rule. All this isolation and competition has obvious costs. Because policy research is expensive, and because few donors will support it explicitly, NGOs must squeeze the money out of general revenue — either adding it to overheads or concealing it. Low budgets can mean low quality. Bigger NGOs have a natural advantage, but most big NGOs did not get big by taking political risks with donors or with governments.

Sadly, NGOs can be used as window dressing, as demonstrations of pluralism and of commitment to participatory development in countries where these things are in short supply. Guatemala's 1985 constitution guarantees civil and political rights, but the space for dissent and reform, despite the presence of local and foreign NGOs, has been highly restricted. It can also work the other way. Sri Lanka, ostensibly an open parliamentary democracy, conducted a massive witch hunt against NGOs between 1990 and 1992, allegedly seeking out mismanagement and corruption, but aiming mainly to quell criticism of the government's development failures and human rights abuse. In Indonesia, India and Malaysia, NGOs can be banned or, equally damaging, prevented from receiving foreign contributions, on the whim of a single well-placed civil servant or politician. For NGOs working under such circumstances, circumspection and self censorship can become the guiding light.

Where participation is concerned, the culture of donor agencies, riddled with risk-averse blueprints, targets and jargon, is unfriendly, if not hostile. Many NGOs are tied to inflexible project budgets and time-frames that work against constructive participation. Despite the rhetoric of responsiveness and support, NGOs are seen increasingly as channels and as executing agencies for priorities determined by larger donor agencies: feeding programmes, child immunization, irrigation, water and sanitation projects. In such relationships, NGOs become contractors rather than independent actors, beholden to the agenda of the funder. Participation becomes a way of getting communities — which often means women — to undertake for free what once fell to governments.

For Northern NGOs, dependency on government is a short-cut to self-censorship and a 'reasonable voice'. But for Southern NGOs there is a double problem. Heavily reliant on outside donors, they are often expected to provide the voice of democracy that outsiders cannot or will not articulate themselves. In 1983, the Dutch NGO, NOVIB, temporarily withdrew all support from Sarvodaya because it believed Sarvodaya had not been forthright enough in its condemnation of Tamil massacres. But Southern NGOs cannot simply get on a plane and leave — as the Dutch NGOs were forced to do in Indonesia when their government denounced the massacre in East Timor. They must stay and face the music. For them, fear has a real and human face. At least six Sarvodaya field workers were murdered in the late 1980s. This was not because they were caught in accidental crossfire; they were targeted because their peace message and their relief supplies were viewed by combatants as partisan.

A further problem has to do with the direct funding of Southern NGOs by Northern government agencies, discussed in Chapter X. One area of very serious negative fallout in the diversion of bilateral money to Southern NGOs is that it can place them in direct competition with their governments. By changing funding 'windows' and altering the optics, donors can deal with this to some extent. But the simple fact of an NGO having money and providing services when a government cannot, creates an entirely new dynamic in the traditional politics of patronage. NGOs must be alert to the perils, and aware of the consequences that may result, as must donors and governments.

Those who 'support' NGOs contribute to muffling their voice in another way: by a refusal to contribute to long-term financial independence and sustainability. Endowments, long the most reasonable way to build financial sustainability in Northern hospitals and universities, are still in their infancy among international and Southern NGOs. And an income-earning proposal is one of the most difficult things a Southern NGO can sell to a donor, governmental or otherwise. As long as there is financial dependency, there will be a constraint on the extent to which an NGO is able or willing to speak out on issues that are unpopular with the donor. Ignoring the long-term financial sustainability of any Southern organization only adds to dependence and provokes the question that many Southern NGOs ask: is it deliberate?

What could governments and donor agencies do to change the situation? One option is to encourage the establishment in each country of a legislative, administrative and fiscal structure for regulating non-profit organizations, consistent with international norms.[37] In other words, governments could encourage the development of a formal climate that would give real meaning to the right of association. Expecting NGOs to contribute to civil society and democratization within the chaotic and repressive legal frameworks that are too often the norm is unrealistic. Any new rules should be clear, simple and administrable. They should clarify standards of governance, registration, organization and dissolution, and they should provide for a right of public appeal. They should also specify the means for ensuring NGO accountability: as long as accountability is defined by and for outside donor agencies, NGO legitimacy will be questioned and independence will be compromised. Any regulatory framework should also recognize that non-profit organizations have a useful and legitimate role to play as advocates on public issues.

The problems of donor meddling, risk-aversion and particularism could perhaps be avoided by the creation of arm's-length joint-donor funding mechanisms: foundations that might standardize bureaucratic requirements and leaven political concerns. Poor donor co-ordination and the scramble by each donor, non-governmental or otherwise, for its 'own' projects and project partners are among the most serious financial and political problems facing Southern NGOs today. There are, however, no simple solutions. Two good-looking models are the

Trust for Voluntary Organizations, created in 1990 from a USAID endowment in Pakistan, and the Janasaviya Trust Fund in Sri Lanka, financed by the Government of Sri Lanka, the World Bank, UNDP and the German Bank for Reconstruction (*Kreditanstalt fur Wiederafbau*). The independence of both has been seriously compromised, however, by relentless government meddling and, in the case of the latter, inappropriate World Bank micro-management.

Donors and Northern NGOs should consider broader questions of civil society. The focus on poverty alleviation and development projects has meant that the strongest Northern relationships have been with relatively new development NGOs, often cast in a Northern mould. But there are other types of organization critical to a broad-based civil society. Professional and labour groups, student organizations, religious bodies, welfare agencies, and peasant movements of the sort found in Latin America are all deserving of consideration. Beyond this, donors can expand on other efforts that have been initiated in recent years: support for election observers, electoral commissions, voter registration and training, equipment and technical assistance for representative political institutions, support for the training of independent journalists. Fostering horizontal linkages between these organizations, such as coalitions, partnerships, umbrella groups, would also help to create interactive networks that might be able to influence the North-South, vertical linkages that now predominate.

Shopping lists of what can and should be done sound good: neat conclusions to round out the chapter. But there is a jarring note that spoils the harmony of the apparent potential for democratic collaboration. Many Southern governments find the whole idea threatening. And while Northern governments *say* they believe democracy and the observance of human rights to be precursor of, and a catalyst for good development, their own actions are fraught with situational ethics and ambivalence. A trade embargo may be placed on undemocratic Haiti, but a major trading partner such as China is treated very differently. Despite widespread Western condemnation of the Tianenmen massacres of 1989, official development assistance to China grew by 42 per cent between 1989 and 1992.[38] Aid to Ghana, which complied during the same period in every way with World Bank and IMF adjustment programmes, and which held its first multi-party elections in more than a decade, saw an increase of only 13 per cent. Bangladesh, which also returned to parliamentary democracy during this period, experienced a 4 per cent *decline* in official development assistance. Canada, having boasted to taxpayers about reducing aid to Kenya and Tanzania in order to induce multi-party elections, rewarded the new, democratically elected governments by closing its bilateral aid programmes entirely in 1993. And UNDP, roundly attacked by Southern governments which disliked its bold 1991 'Human Freedom Index', quietly allowed the idea to drop out of sight.

In September 1991, a military junta overthrew the democratically elected Haitian Government of Jean-Bertrand Aristide. Three years later, US troops entered Haiti in order to restore human rights and democracy. This might have been a powerful message for dictators and human rights abusers elsewhere. But in the three-year interim there had been military coups in Sierra Leone and the Gambia, annulled elections in Nigeria, on-going bloody war in Liberia, and Rwanda had rocked out of control. Except for mild expressions of dismay from the world community, the villains largely prospered. In the autumn of 1994, around the time of the invasion of Haiti (and the pullout of US troops from Somalia), US Commerce Secretary Ron Brown went to Beijing with two dozen captains of American industry. The Canadian Prime Minister followed a month later with nine of the country's ten provincial premiers. Eager to trade, all appeared to have forgotten Tianenmen Square. None seemed to have noticed reports during the same period from Human Rights Watch, the Hong Kong *Eastern Express*, *The Economist*, the *Times* of London and the BBC about Chinese forced labour camps, and the execution-to-order (for their kidneys, eyes and other vital organs) of prisoners in Chinese jails.[39] Perhaps in celebration, and no doubt as a demonstration of its respect for the visitors, the Chinese Government set off an under-ground nuclear explosion at its test sight in Lop Nor.[40]

This sort of thing makes sad reading for those who take peace, democracy and human rights seriously. Ultimately, there is a question as to how much the 'civil society' discourse and donor infatuation with NGOs has to do with democracy and human rights, and how much it has to do with finding cheaper and more efficient alternatives to faltering governmental delivery systems. To the extent that NGOs are viewed as part of the private sector, the enthusiasm for them may have less to do with a new-found understanding of civil society's role in making democracy work, and more to do with the new orthodoxy. By squinting hard, NGOs can be seen and treated simply as contractors, just another private sector alternative to government in general, and to bad government in particular.

237

CHAPTER XIII

Future conditional

Many have dreamed up republics and principalities which have never in truth been known to exist; the gulf between how one should live and how one does live is so wide that a man who neglects what is actually done for what should be done paves the way to self-destruction rather than self-preservation.

Nicolò Machiavelli.

FOR NGOs, the journey from the optimistic first 'Development Decade' of the 1960s to the grim reality of the century's last years has been one fraught with painful but important lessons, lessons about poverty, community and change; about failure, growth, and sometimes heroic achievement. Today, poised on the brink of a new century, thousands of Southern NGOs and a small army of their Northern counterparts are at a crossroads. This is not the kind of crossroads which marks all human endeavour. It is not two poetic paths diverging in a wood, or one in a series of intersections that can be navigated easily with yesterday's roadmaps. Today's NGOs are at a major interchange where several twelve-lane superhighways meet in a series of high overpasses, dark tunnels, tight curves and fast-merging traffic.

It is an interchange where the value and importance of the nongovernmental movement is acknowledged, but where it is increasingly challenged by forces and temptations which conspire to undermine the very independence that distinguishes it. This book asks questions about NGOs, but it does not have all the answers. It does not, for example, answer P.J. O'Rourke's question about what to do when an uncontrollable, unstoppable emergency begins to unfold. People respond differently when faced with choices. The book does not seek to condemn people who find themselves a little further down the road to hell because they took the exit marked 'good intentions'. Today, however, there is enough knowledge about how the highway works, and where that particular exit can lead, to make some informed choices about what to do at the junction.

Building civil society. In the South, only Southern organizations can build meaningful solidarity, trust and tolerance between Southern individuals, communities and their governments. Northerners can support the effort, but they cannot do it themselves. Good development, sustainable development, cutting-edge projects are all important. But they are not as important as the creation of strong local institutions that can help people make decisions about what to do for themselves. Co-operation and public-spiritedness, even if it is self-interested, does not flow from logical framework analyses or rules, but from people working together on common problems. It arises from the sinking of deeper institutional roots, and the formation of horizontal relationships with the other associations and groups that comprise a broadly based civil society: co-operatives, professional organizations, policy advocates, small community organizations, development NGOs and those working on human rights and environmental issues. This is not a two- or three-year enterprise, to be abandoned if NGO 'articles of faith' turn out to be a little shaky. If Italy is anything to go by, it could take a century. No matter how long it takes, the building of 'civil society', 'social capital' — whatever the name — is essential to a secure future, to a muffling of the tribal and ideological drums that have sounded the destruction of so many lives in the past century.

North-South partnerships. One of the great future challenges has to do with relationships between the 'old' world of the North, and the 'new' world of the South; between seductive old ideas about an endless cornucopia of economic growth, and newer ideas about how to live within the means, economic and environmental, that are available. If not today, then some time in the near future, questions about Northern consumption patterns will have to be figured into the equation.

Governments and multilateral organizations will help to shape the outcome of these challenges. But it is the relationship between *people* that will illuminate and form the basis for lasting solutions. In this there is tremendous scope for North-South NGO partnerships, between organizations with shared obligations working on common agendas, towards common solutions to shared problems. Here Northern NGOs are faced with their greatest test: how to convert what remains a giving-getting connection — a 'lop-sided friendship' based on vertical bonds of dependence — into one that can transcend money. Many will not be able to do it, and aspects of the old order may well survive. But a much more intelligent sort of relationship is possible, one in which institutions of the North and the South challenge each other and work together on problems. This will undoubtedly require people and organizations to surmount the traditional but often artificial barriers between the profit-making and the non-profit worlds, between practitioners and academics, between 'development', 'environment' and 'human rights'. It means that truly reciprocal obligations will have to be constructed in order to create balanced partnerships.

'Partnership' may find expression in new forms of NGO multilateralism, with international groupings of Northern and Southern NGOs creating foundations and financial mechanisms which can surmount today's bureaucratic maze of one-off unilateral financial arrangements. If the dysfunctional aspects of organizational egos can be suppressed, if people realize that money is not the same thing as knowledge, and that knowledge is not the same thing as wisdom, then perhaps the fledgling efforts that abound today can become part of tomorrow's reality.

Professionalism and working together. Robert Chambers has written extensively about the need for 'reversals' and for learning from poor people, and about the need for new approaches to professionalism. 'Development spreading' and self-improvement, aimed at making life better for poor people, can only come about if organizations are able to learn, remember and share; if they are prepared, when they seek to influence policy, to take well-aimed rifle shots and give up their scatter guns. From this will flow the political strength needed to influence governments and the private sector to do what NGOs alone can never do. Far greater attention to listening, learning and sharing is needed between organizations involved in human rights, the environment, development and emergencies.

There are two visions of the many NGOs extant today. One vision is based on principles of sharing and networking, of a 'thousand points of light' brightening the darkness. The other is an archipelago image, one of islands, remotely connected (or not at all) in a vast and stormy sea. Duplication, unproductive competition, isolation, amateurism: all characterize the second image, weakening what NGOs, singly or together, can do for the health of their societies. There is no easy way to build professionalism, broadly defined. The inability of individual NGO communities — in the US or Chile or Ghana — to take matters of co-ordination, ethics, standards, competence and learning in hand is a demonstration of how much larger the problem is at the international level.

Networks, coalitions and umbrella organizations notwithstanding, one of the greatest practical problems facing NGOs today is the fragmentation of effort, the hundreds of lookalike organizations spawned more by ego than goodwill, and maintained more by charity than by clarity of purpose. Fragmentation is the amateur's friend, a haven for wheel inventors; it is the enemy of learning and of teams that can tackle poverty effectively on a broad front. Like small boys playing football, too many NGOs swarm down the field after the ball, without strategy and without positions. Dismissed by bemused spectators, they are easily relieved of the ball by bigger players.

240

Perhaps the impetus for more and better evaluation, more and better dissemination, more and better co-ordination can come from the South, from organizations that have a degree of international credibility and standing: the Third World Network, El Taller, Civicus, DAWN and others. Perhaps it will have to take place on a country-by-country basis. Whatever the answer, the vigour and importance that are attached to this challenge by NGOs will determine both their role in the coming years, and history's judgement of their contribution.

Size and knowledge. Big organizations may very well be effective. Size may help an organization to become more professional, to have greater impact, to keep its market share of charitable giving. But big is not likely to be the major criterion of success in the future. For Northern NGOs in fact, size — which looks so important today — may become irrelevant, especially among transnational organizations that are unable or unwilling to bring the South into their decision-making processes. That World Vision 'sponsors' a million children is almost irrelevant in a world where half a million women die every year from causes related to pregnancy, abortion and childbirth, where 13 million children die every year before the age of five, where 15 million or more are refugees or 'displaced persons', and where tens of millions face unproductive lives because they have never enrolled in primary school. In the future, lighting a candle will not be half so important as knowing something about how to keep it lit, about how to pay for it, about how to make candles and matches — or perhaps better — electricity. Knowledge, combined with heart and commitment, has always been a key to development, and moving away from *ad hoc* charitable amateurism towards lasting, longer-term solutions, and the policies needed to sustain them, will require politically aware, focused, specialized organizations that can learn, that can remember and share what they learn, and that are prepared to build on what they remember.

Independence. Organizations — North or South — that dance to governmental tunes are unlikely to be more than service providers, weak imitations of what government once was. The almost unconscious, but increasingly swift NGO slide into contracting in many countries, and the resulting homogenization of structures and accountabilities to meet the demands of government bureaucrats, will almost certainly lead to more 'lost decades'. It will also lead to the eventual need for new, more resurgent organizations if the slide is not halted. Stopping it will be the responsibility of both NGOs and the governments that support them.

On the NGO side, the development of better and wider accountabilities — to small donors, to partner organizations, to beneficiary communities — is a matter of urgency. Open and rigorous evaluation,

241

from which all participants can learn, would be a start in the right direction. Governments must somehow find ways to back off; to balance their new contracting enthusiasms with the need for strong, independent social sector organizations, organizations capable of independent thought and action, organizations that are instruments of social reform as well as competent delivery mechanisms.

Co-operation with government. To co-operate is not the same as to obey. Nor are co-optation and co-operation synonymous. But what some NGOs view as co-optation may in fact be victory, laying the groundwork for real co-operation. If governments and NGOs can transcend suspicion and the contracting ethic, there is tremendous scope for genuine co-operation. NGOs could become allies rather than antagonists in the development and appraisal of anti-poverty projects, not least because the often-disparaged NGO 'articles of faith' actually have a strong basis in both experience and fact. NGOs *can* be innovative, efficient, effective. Thousands have shown that they *do* reach the poorest in remote areas in ways that governments never have, and probably never will. They can provide important services in health and education, at community, regional and even national levels.

Despite globalization and the much-heralded decline of the nation state, government is not a thing of the past. In fact governments may be more important today than ever before: not in the sense of doing everything, but in providing a framework in which people can, through a range of organizations, live safe and productive lives. It may be a framework in which some traditional power blocks are weakened in favour of others: women, minorities, the poor. But properly managed, this should serve to enrich, rather than weaken society. NGOs have everything to gain from helping government to establish such frameworks. Governments have everything to lose by assuming they can survive without them.

The criticism of government. Criticism of government — fair or unfair — is the hallmark of a healthy democracy. It is exemplified in Northern NGOs' criticism of official aid: its volume, its lack of attention to poverty, debt reduction and fair trade, its preoccupations with politics, tied aid and the blunt instruments of structural adjustment. In the absence of real democracy, where opposition parties, the press and the judiciary have become muted, NGOs — sometimes domestic, sometimes foreign — behave as an official opposition would elsewhere. This is why NGOs have, at various times in countries like Kenya, Brazil and Bangladesh, seemed so antagonistic towards government. Until people can speak freely within the standard institutions of a functional democracy, governments should not be surprised that NGOs behave like critics.

242

Emergencies. Emergencies are not going to cease. Whether they will grow and deepen is perhaps a matter of one's place within the spectrum between predictions of doom and promises of cornucopia. In the meantime, NGOs have demonstrated that they can move quickly, and that they are as efficient and as effective as government and multilateral organizations, or more so. A handful of NGOs are, correctly, beginning to act as leaders, rather than as supplicants in the business of warning and preparing for disaster. With support from UN agencies and their own governments; and with encouragement for strategic alliances, research and the building of better early warning systems, NGOs can and should become much more powerful allies (and critics where appropriate) of the multilateral system than is currently the case.

Predictions about the future are often based on little more than obvious trends. That is why the futuristic spaceships in the *Buck Rogers* films of the 1940s look so much like old-fashioned V-2 rockets. Although writers like Jules Verne, H.G. Wells and George Orwell got some of it right, they also got some of it wrong, as did Thomas Malthus, the Club of Rome and Paul Ehrlich. Few futurologists predicted the oil crisis, the debt crisis or the collapse of communism. Saying what *should* happen in the developing world, therefore, and more narrowly in the work of NGOs, is much easier than predicting what is likely. Before getting to the possibilities, however, an obscure and rather unlikely prediction is perhaps worth recalling.

'Mandela is given a Hero's Welcome', reads the headline in the Johannesburg *Star*. The dateline is Windhoek, capital of Namibia, and Mandela is arriving to attend an OAU conference. He is greeted at the airport by Head of State Sam Nujoma, and is presented with a bouquet of flowers by a fair-haired little five-year old. It isn't much of a story on a front page dominated by reports of a new government budget which will devote massive sums to housing in the townships and improvements in education for black children. There is also a story about South Africa's ambassador to the United Nations, and news about a West Indies cricket tour of South Africa.

The interesting thing about this edition of the *Star*, is that it was published on 15 August 1980. It was a two-page simulation of what the editors thought the news might look like in 1985 if apartheid were to be abolished. As it happened, in real-life 1985 Nelson Mandela was still in jail, and would stay there for another five years. Sam Nujoma's guerilla liberation war was in its twentieth year, and South Africa's seat at the United Nations remained vacant. The *Star's* exercise in journalistic conjecture was a dream, and with the exception of dreamers, few could have taken it very seriously. In the same issue of the paper, in the real news, Prime Minister P.W. Botha thundered against 'leftists' and 'lightheaded' superpowers, saying that South Africa had a 'minorities problem', not a race problem. The actual front page story was about a speech by a former Rhodesian army general who warned that South Africa was on the path to full-scale guerilla war.

And yet . . . And yet within 12 years of the *Star's* exercise in whimsy, Nelson Mandela was President of South Africa, Sam Nujoma was President of Namibia, and most of what the *Star* had put forward as conjecture had come to pass.

The return of Billy Jack

Where development, NGOs and the future are concerned, there may well be reason for optimism, for dreaming about a new kind of future, a 'global citizenship', one of communities and movements and trans-national social forces, a 'globalization from below' that Richard Falk describes as being 'animated by environmental concerns, human rights, hostility to patriarchy, and a vision of human community based on the unity of diverse cultures seeking an end to poverty, oppression, humiliation and collective violence.'[1] Linked by E-mail, modems and computers, networks both real and virtual will, in the words of another writer, 'develop planetary consciousness via electronic democracy'.[2]

This future is part of a broader effort in which governments and inter-governmental institutions take charge, find the political will and the money, and start doing, at long last, the right thing. Each of the global development commissions — Pearson, Brandt, Palme, Brundtland and the 1995 Commission on Global Governance — concluded with lengthy lists of chores for the world community. Some lists have price tags. Lester Brown and Hal Kane suggest that many of the problems ahead could be reduced or eliminated by putting $14 billion a year into population programmes, by spending $6.5 billion annually to get 130 million school-age children into school, $5.6 billion on reforestation, $8 billion on conservation and $5 billion annually on agricultural research. In all, their budget starts at $24 billion in 1996, rising to $61 billion by 2005. This is well within reach of a world that was still spending $800 billion annually on arms three years after the end of the Cold War, where drug trafficking is estimated at $500 billion annually, and where some $85 billion in drug profits are laundered annually through the world's legitimate financial markets.[3] UNICEF provides similar cost estimates. Halving child malnutrition, reducing child mortality by a third, immunizing 90 per cent of the world's children and getting 80 per cent into primary school by the turn of the century would cost about $40 billion more than what is

244

now being spent on aid, a relatively small investment in genuine poverty eradication when stacked up against the $40 billion spent annually on golf, the $160 billion spent on beer, and the $400 billion on cigarettes.[4]

It seems beguilingly simple. Take for example the way the 1994 UNESCO-funded International Commission on Peace and Food makes its recommendation on technology transfer:

> Accelerate the transfer of technology to and between developing countries. One or more profit-making commercial organizations should be established as a public sector joint venture of developing countries to promote the commercial transfer of technology to, within and between developing countries and to channel the profits from this activity towards research in these countries.[5]

About a hundred recommendations like this basically wrap it up. There is a problem with all these recommendations, however. Many, like this one, lack a subject. *Who* will accelerate, establish, promote and channel? The UN? The World Bank? The faltering nation state? This exhortation, like many of the others, is cast in the future imperative: 'must', 'should', 'have to' — 'must' develop the political will, 'should' allocate the money, 'have to' tap the untapped resources that are there for the asking: knowledge about development, values that foster productivity, organization and social cohesion; skills that improve quality and productivity; social attitudes that foster self-confidence, individual initiative and positive responses to new opportunities . . .

As British novelist John Fowles correctly observes, a thousand violins cloy very rapidly without percussion. How these things are to happen in a world of Somalias and Liberias, in a world where the nation state no longer has a monopoly on armed force, where debt and famine — and Northern apathy towards both — are the order of the day; how these things are to happen is not at all clear. Machiavelli warns that neglecting what is actually done, for what should be done is not always the safest way to get to the future. The answer cannot be more of the same. And the answer is surely more than simply hoping for the best, more than vague ideas about 'strengthening over time the institutional forms and activities associated with global society'. Simplistic exhortations to 'accelerate the transfer of technology', after decades of disastrous technology transfer, are not only counterproductive, they are (and here, the percussion) *stupid*.

For those concerned about voluntary organizations, whether as charities, welfare and service providers or communities of citizens, there is something worse. The distinguished American author James Baldwin was surprised and disheartened by the futuristic 1977 film,

Star Wars. It depicted a universe filled not only with humans, but humans interacting with weird, intelligent intergalactic creatures from a dozen universes. What depressed Baldwin was that among all these fantastic creatures and humans, there were no black people. Hollywood, usually the first in political correctness, saw no place in the future for black humans. The same is true of the International Commission on Peace and Food. It talks about new ways of thinking, about 'new types of public and private organization', but with the exception of five brief references, it has nothing to say about the form of interaction that will be necessary between people, governments and the global forces which influence their lives. Like the Pearson and Brandt Commissions, which basically ignored NGOs, (Brundtland gave them three pages to themselves), this commission sees no place in the future worth mentioning for the associations people might make for themselves.*

Second ending

Fowles refused to end his novel *The French Lieutenant's woman* with the heroine's head on the hero's breast, conflict resolved, a Chopin mazurka filtering through the leaves in the sunlit garden. So he wrote a second ending. Galbraith likewise declined to end his book, *The culture of contentment*, with optimistic signposts beside a sylvan path leading to broad sunlit uplands. 'There is a special occasion here for sadness — for a sad ending,' he wrote. He was writing about governments 'accommodated not to reality or common need but to the beliefs of the contented'. Short-run inaction, he says, 'is always preferred to protective long-run action. The reason is readily evident. The long run may not arrive.'[6] But Irish statesman Conor Cruise O'Brien, writing *On the eve of the millennium*, does believe that the long run could arrive. And he also ends on a sombre note, 'because this is warranted and because I believe alarmism to be far less dangerous to us in the late twentieth century, than the witless complacency which set in at the end of the Cold War.'[7]

So for NGOs, there is another type of ending. Some critics of the NGO movement worry that NGOs may be little more than a convenient justification for a continued dismantling of the welfare state, giving the dregs to a patchwork of community organizations and to NGOs ill-equipped to handle the responsibility. Internationally, the situation is more confused. Some fear that NGOs are 'crowding out' the state,

---

*Happily, for the first time in three decades of 'global commissions', this was not the case with the 1995 Commission on Global Governance, which wove NGOs and a broad understanding of civil society through its arguments and findings.

while others, disillusioned with public sector failure and bad 'governance', *want* the state crowded out, supporting a contraction in government services and using NGOs to pick up the pieces while the market, biotechnology and the information superhighway come to the longer-term rescue. Both factions place a faith in NGOs that is probably unwarranted.

Whenever there is a detailed examination, NGOs tend to wilt under the microscope. One of the more famous examples was a 1982 study done by Judith Tendler for USAID, 'Turning private voluntary organizations into development agencies'. Here, and in a widely circulated article five years later, 'Whatever happened to poverty alleviation?',[8] Tendler not only sharpened the focus on the microscope, she started pulling wings off butterflies to see what made them fly. She debunked, not always unfairly, NGO 'articles of faith'. And looking specifically at 'better performing' NGOs like SEWA, the Working Women's Forum and Grameen Bank, she said that even these were 'riddled with problems, mistakes and false starts'. Qualify this as she may, her writing has become an especially bright mazurka to the ears of those who would bash NGOs, as they have bashed others. UNDP, having criticized donors and Southern governments in its first two *Human Development Reports*, found itself under pressure to take a critical look at NGOs. It dug out Tendler's papers and agreed that there had been failures. 'More success than failures? Nobody really knows. What seems clear is that even people helped by successful projects still remain poor.'[9] It said that 'most NGO interventions probably miss the poorest 5–10 per cent' and that even Grameen Bank, impressive though it may be, provides only 0.1 per cent of all national credit in Bangladesh. 'NGOs are in no position to replace government or commercial markets in the provision of credit.'

Even the most hardened NGO critic should have been stunned by these remarks, especially in a report which a few pages earlier said that only 6.5 per cent of official development assistance was earmarked for human priority concerns. A comparison is therefore in order. The report estimated total NGO expenditure in 1990 at $7.2 billion, most of it going to human priority concerns (if not necessarily the poorest 5–10 per cent). Total official development assistance that year was $40.2 billion, which means, if UNDP was right, that only $2.6 billion in government money was going to human priority concerns. NGOs, therefore, despite their failures, were spending almost three times more than governments on direct attempts to reach the poor. But there is a lot more. As observed in other chapters, NGOs are very often the first off the mark in disaster situations, and they stay behind to clean up the mess after the cameras leave. They have blazed new trails for women, in the environment and in human rights. NGOs are a major player in the health field, providing a quarter of all external assistance in 1990, and almost four times more than all the development banks combined.[10]

Despite all this, however, they have no official voice or standing worth the name in global meetings and institutions. Numbers put this in perspective: the membership of only two NGOs — Amnesty International and the Worldwide Fund for Nature — exceeds the combined populations of Namibia, Cyprus, Luxembourg, Barbados and Guyana.* It is perhaps indecorous but not wrong to ask why NGOs should do anything, and why they should be anything but cynical in the face of the monumental failure of governments and the multilateral system to make significant inroads into injustice and poverty.

To say that Grameen Bank was providing only 0.1 per cent of all national credit in Bangladesh is like saying that beside the sea, a river is nothing. The statistic may not be wrong, but apart from one or two donor-insulated government projects, Grameen Bank, BRAC, Proshika and an army of smaller organizations provide virtually *all* of the credit that reaches the poor in Bangladesh other than that available through moneylenders. Unlike bilateral projects, and unlike the formal commercial sector, repayment rates exceed 90 per cent, and many of the biggest NGO operations are no longer in need of foreign assistance. True, a river is not like the sea. But that is not to say rivers have no value. And the farther a river is from the sea, the more important it can be. It can make the difference between life and death: water for drinking; water for irrigation; fish. It is also a highway, connecting people with other communities and the rest of the world. Getting the numbers wrong is bad enough, but misinterpreting the broader value of human organization — organization for self-improvement and for community development — is worse.

This is not to say there is no failure. For every NGO success story, there are many examples of things that have not worked. This is equally true of government attempts to end poverty. But NGOs have been slow to demonstrate concretely what they *can* do. They are fragmented, competitive, localized and increasingly accountable to governments rather than to their own aims, objectives, partners and beneficiaries. So it is not hard to write a pessimistic or, let us simply say a 'technocratic' ending to the story. This would envision greater government acknowledgement of the NGO role and achievement.

---

*To rectify this, the 1995 Commission on Global Governance suggested the creation of an annual UN Forum of Civil Society that would bring together three to six hundred organizations to debate social and economic issues, and to make recommendations which could be brought forward to the General Assembly, and to other national and international bodies.

It would, no doubt, include more money. But it would also mean greater government co-ordination and control, a gradual hardening of the contracting ethic, with concomitant demands for standardization, co-ordination, evaluation and agenda-setting by government. Larger organizations would fare best in this kind of atmosphere. They would be most attractive to the funder, and they would be most able to retain a semblance of their identity in such a regime. Co-opted by the broader culture of contentment, however, their voices would be muffled, limited perhaps to the occasional Brandt or Brundtland or Peace and Food Commission where they might exhort the deaf to 'accelerate the transfer of technology' or some such thing, and feel they were making a difference.

A third ending

Every limit is a beginning as well as an ending . . . the fragment of a life, however typical, is not the sample of an even web: promises may not be kept, and an ardent outset may be followed by declension; latent powers may find their long-awaited opportunity; a past error may urge a grand retrieval.

George Eliot, *Middlemarch*, 1872.

Heading towards the intersection of several twelve-lane highways, the international NGO movement is in a state of profound transition. It is uncertain about what it is, and it is unsure about where it is going. Increasingly studied by outsiders, it no longer seems master of its own agenda. It is beset by competing forces and demands which make its future difficult to discern. The simplest and most balanced conclusion, however, would take as its point of departure the work of people who see voluntary organizations as the new anchor of meaningful citizenship.

With the globalization of the economy, of knowledge and information, the importance of the nation state is declining. As its abilities to protect and to provide services wane, it finds itself increasingly unable to quench the flames of tribalism and fundamentalism that arise from old embers buried deep in the ashes of the human psyche. The social sector — the 'third sector', the voluntary sector — provides an answer, or at least part of an answer. The social sector, meaning NGOs, can provide services that governments are no longer able or willing to provide. This may be a temporary phenomenon, or it may be of a longer-term nature. It may be charity, it may be welfare or self-help, or it may have other names with vaguely disparaging connotations. In the end, it may be little more than the provision of the services that are necessary for a sound community and a decent life.

Things change. Just as there was nothing immutable about the way such services were organized in Lenin's brave new world, there is nothing particularly sacrosanct about the way Western Europeans or North Americans organized themselves to provide health and welfare services after the Second World War.

In fact it was the notion that the government should and could do everything that led many newly independent countries in the South down a slippery slope, one which encouraged them to organize and to attempt to deliver every facet of health, education and social welfare. Foreigners helped them, providing inappropriate technologies and costly, often wrong-headed, technical assistance. In the process, lending institutions helped them to mortgage their future. Now, because the need is so great, there is hope for a new spirit of community, 'community' which is more than a provider of services, 'community' which is also a way of organizing, of providing the integrating power that many governments now lack, a way of restoring active citizenship and the participation of individuals in their own future. This is important to industrialized countries where, for example, a President Clinton could lament the 'stunning and simultaneous breakdown of community, family and work, the heart and soul of civilized society'. It is more true perhaps, in former communist countries, where associational life and citizenship were systematically nullified over a series of generations. And it is especially true in much of the South, where brief, unhappy experiments with the nation state and modern institutions have caused people to retreat into older concepts of community. These are communities based on blood, language, tribe and religious beliefs. Many of them are ill-equipped for survival in a world where education, health, knowledge and trade are essential to life and living. Increasingly, these 'communities' are being hijacked by thugs and warlords, whose own survival is inexorably linked to machine guns and rocket-launchers.

'Communitarianism' is more than a vague concept, it is a terrible word. But in the United States, it has developed a wide intellectual following among those seeking refuge from a socially splintered world. Amitai Etzioni, professor of sociology at George Washington University, has written extensively about it in *The spirit of community: the reinvention of American society*, saying that both the left and the political right have contributed directly to the current malaise. The right has damaged both community and family through its single-minded emphasis on the invisible hand of free-market capitalism. With more and more of the adult population working to make ends meet, old ideas about 'parenting' have been abandoned, and the family has been fractured. On the left, unsustainable welfare benefits and entitlements, handed over without responsibility, have shifted power into the hands of faceless bureaucrats, discouraging people from involvement in any kind of community action, or in the provision of assistance to any beyond their immediate kin.

Some fear the captivating message of communitarianism,[11] saying that it rejects — at the peril of society — the very foundations of individualism, liberalism and liberal economics which have shaped the Western world. This stark conundrum always seems to rise up: how to rationalize the utopian ideals of More, Rousseau and Marx with the suffocation of freedom (and the terror) that some of their followers instituted? How to benefit from Adam Smith's liberal economics without ignoring, and reaping the consequences of, the tremendous social ills that challenge the new millennium?

Philosophers argue that concepts of community and liberty are inimical. As Robert Putnam has shown in the Italian case, however, vibrant civic community has been the most important precursor of a strong, free-enterprise economy. The opposite, a strong economy as precursor to development — often held by economists as the answer for the developing world — was manifestly not the case. The most obvious and most consistent developmental factor was the presence of associations, clubs, self-help societies and voluntary trade unions, and a history of associational life which had built over the centuries a climate of trust, social capital, reciprocity and networks of civic engagement.

A good example of 'social capital' can be found in the informal savings societies that exist everywhere: in Africa, Asia, Latin America. Small groups save money and each month, in turn, one individual 'gets the pot'. This very old and almost universal form of group savings was the basis for Grameen Bank and a dozen organizations mentioned in other chapters. People stay in the group after they have received their share, because to pull out would damage their standing in the community, and would limit their ability to participate in similar schemes in the future. Comparable forms of social capital can be seen in North American barn-raising and quilting bees. There may be a socializing function in such activities, but many people participate simply because they may need such assistance in the future: it is enlightened self-interest, that most famous of conservative values.

Collective action may be another way of saying that the life you save may be your own. But there is more to it than enlightened self-interest. Charity can be based on moral values as well as the goodness of the heart. There is still value and meaning in the idea of 'service'. It is true that, like 'charity', 'service' is fraught with moral ambiguities, self-congratulation, doubt, egoism and hypocrisy. Somewhere in his writings, Steinbeck had a character say 'Whenever I hear the word 'service', I wonder who is getting screwed'. But there is another side

251

to service, one that is central to the values of most societies and religions, and to people for whom *being* is a consequence of *doing*. That is why so many individuals volunteer their time to work with the poor and elderly, why so many make donations to NGOs, why there are so many NGOs, and why so many people make careers in voluntary organizations. It may be a job, but it is usually more than that. It may fulfil a religious obligation or provide the satisfaction of doing something concrete: to learn, to test one's self, to make a difference, to *help*. It may fulfil a moral purpose, righting a wrong, serving justice in some way. Martin Luther King Jr. once said that 'to live out one's idealism brings with it hazards'. And the hazards can be grave, as they were for King. For others, they are more mundane, but they can be hard on morale: ridicule, defeat, fatigue, depression. These can harden the most ardent idealism into cynicism, self-righteousness and despair.

Robert Coles, psychiatrist, biographer and teacher, describes the challenge of service this way:

> To some extent, all those called to social and political activism struggle with that tension between the obvious desire to change a situation, and the necessary respect for those who have had to endure hardship and have learned to survive as best they can — and who have a hard-earned skepticism of outsiders, whatever their good intentions. The activists who stay the course longest seem to have figured out how far they can go in prodding others, how deep within themselves they must look. They have a mixture of political insistence and introspective tentativeness that allows them to be effective in spite of the ever-present frustrations.[12]

What Putnam concludes about Italy, however, has disheartening overtones for the developing world. In the Italian south, centuries of a different kind of equilibrium — one based on paternalism, exploitation and dependence — has created a society where idealists are in short supply, where vertical relationships, extra-legal 'enforcers', clan, family and church are everything, and where trust between neighbours, businesses and politicians is the exception. The result is poverty, ignorance and bad government. 'Effective and responsive institutions depend, in the language of civic humanism, on republican virtues and practices. Tocqueville was right: Democratic government is strengthened, not weakened, when it faces a vigorous civil society.'[13]

Phoenix, Faust and Narcissus

Does this mean that societies with weak civic traditions and limited social capital are doomed to a future more reminiscent of Sicily and

252

Calabria, than of the vibrant, industrial regions of Emilia-Romagna and Lombardia? Can social capital, associational life, a strong civil society be induced? If so, can it be done quickly?

In her book, *Geography and the human spirit*, Anne Buttimer offers a metaphor for themes running through Western thinking about humanity and its interaction with its political and social environment: Phoenix, Faust and Narcissus. The phoenix is a legendary Arabian bird that is said to set fire to itself every 500 years, rising anew from the ashes. According to German legend, Faust was an alchemist, a magician (popularized by Goethe in the nineteenth century) who sold his soul to the devil in exchange for knowledge and power. In Greek legend, Narcissus, a beautiful youth, trifled with the affections of others until one day he caught sight of his own reflection in a forest pool and fell in love with it. Mesmerized by his own beauty, he pined away and died by the pool. The flowers which grew up where he died carry his name through history.

Buttimer sees in the phoenix a symbol for the emancipatory moments in history when new life emerges from the ashes, with prospects for a fresh beginning. 'In individual careers, as well as the course of nations, cultural groups and disciplines, one can identify at least two kinds of emancipatory cry, one seeking freedom *from* oppression, oblivion or constraining horizons, the other seeking freedom *to* soar towards new heights of understanding, being and becoming.'[14] History is full of these moments: the Renaissance, the Reformation, the anti-colonial independence movement. The Northern NGO movement that evolved in the 1960s represents such a moment, a moment that extended into the 1970s and 1980s with the evolution of Southern NGOs and the idea of North-South partnership.

Having captured an audience, however, the liberator succumbs to new orthodoxies, creating structures which can consolidate and maintain. Enter Faust. Once new ideas appear, energies are devoted to building institutions and the legal protection required to ensure their autonomy and identity.

Phoenix, the pioneer, accepts assistance from the architect to help sustain the original emancipatory ideal. But in the legend of Faust, Mephistopheles waits to steal the architect's soul. Catacomb communities become a Vatican, volunteers become a Peace Corps, help for famine victims turns into an Oxfam. The Sarvodaya work-sharing ideal becomes a movement, and the movement becomes an institution. And waiting in the wings is the Mephistophelian institutional donor, ready to exchange the architect's soul for eternal life. Idealism and passion are traded for the unresponsive, uninspiring wilderness of competence.

As organizations debate the tensions, trade-offs and contradictions between goals and activities, between their dream and the reality, an

253

inward-looking, Narcissistic stage sets in. Idealistic plans and innovative, dynamic movements become cautious, unwieldy, self-perpetuating bureaucracies. Certainly, Narcissistic self-examination has led to the paralysis of many once-dynamic Northern NGOs. They restructure and restructure again, decentralizing, re-centralizing, fine-tuning mission statements and debating endlessly the finer points of development theory. Some in the South, although younger, run the same risk. In time, what remains of the beautiful youth is little more than a name and some flowers beside a forest pond.

Galbraith describes the narcissism that destroyed Robert Owen's early-nineteenth century attempt to create utopia in New Harmony, Indiana:

> Idealists did come to New Harmony, although the population was never more than a few hundred. So did an historic collation of misfits, misanthropes and free-loaders. Once there, they devoted themselves not to service but, more or less exclusively, to argument. While the discussions continued, so it was said, the pigs invaded the gardens. Harmony being lost, New Harmony failed . . . It is my unhappy observation that idealists, including liberal reformers in our own time, are frequently less endangered by their enemies than by their preference for argument. Their righteous feeling, very often, is that everything should be sacrificed to a good row over first principles or a fight to the finish over who, if anyone, is to be in charge.[15]

The Phoenix-Faust-Narcissus metaphor is, of course, a poetic version of the youth-maturity-death cycles common to the literature of organizational evolution.[16] The phoenix is an ideal, however, not a structure. Sometimes it is a movement that can rise anew in different places and in different ways. For those concerned about North-South relationships, there is a Gandhian reminder in the Phoenix analogy. Gandhi, whose teachings and example continue to inspire new generations of NGOs, spent more than twenty years working as a lawyer in South Africa. Once, on an overnight train journey from Johannesburg to Durban, he read Ruskin's *Unto This Last*. John Ruskin, a nineteenth-century British art critic, imparted three important ideas to Gandhi:

- that the good of the individual is contained in the good of all;
- that a lawyer's work has the same value as the barber's, in that each has the right to earn a living from his work;
- 'that a life of labour, i.e., the life of the tiller of the soil and the handicraftsman is the life worth living'.

'The first of these I knew,' Gandhi wrote. 'The second I had dimly realized. The third had never occurred to me.' *Unto This Last* brought about 'an instantaneous and practical transformation' in Gandhi's life.

'I translated it later into Gujarati, entitling it *Sarvodaya* (the welfare of all).' And he decided to move the newspaper that he and a dozen others had been producing, to a farm 14 miles from Durban. It became known as 'The Phoenix Settlement'.[17]

This, then, suggests a third possible ending to the story: one of rebirth, of new associations, of new relationships, of new energy and conviction, a clearer awareness of what is at stake; one of new approaches to money, organization and development.

It comes with a warning, however: NGOs in both the North and the South have exploited and taken public trust for granted. In the North, the public is treated as a friendly but rather ignorant milch cow, available for top-ups to the milk container that is increasingly being filled by governments. Starving babies, pandas, flood and drought, sad-eyed seals, war, elephant chain-saw massacres: aided and abetted by media that seem to have had a blow-out on the information superhighway, almost anything seems acceptable in the effort to separate the Northern public from a few more of its dollars. In the South, easy Northern money has swamped domestic philanthropy, creating new dependencies and alienating NGOs from their own people.

Perhaps the problem should be stated differently: many of the world's best NGOs have moved away from concepts of philanthropy, welfare and social care, towards ideas of sustainable development and community participation. But they have not taken their donors and the broader public with them.

Development education — under-resourced, well-intentioned but often dogmatic and amateurish, outpaced and outclassed by starving-baby fundraising — has had almost no effect in galvanizing public opinion behind the urgent development challenges that NGOs and governments face on a daily basis. Somehow this must change . . . Here, however, that awkward imperative tense creeps into the final paragraphs, 'must'; and the magical word 'somehow', used to rather impotent effect towards the end of all those other last chapters that were criticized at the outset of this book.

It should be acknowledged that changing deeply ingrained attitudes, attitudes fuelled by trash television, political spin doctors and simplistic fundraising, will not be easy. But the 'how' of it is not deeply mysterious. The environment became an issue when environmentalists domesticized it, when they made it a domestic issue in Brazil, in Germany, in Pakistan; when it became a subject on the teacher's syllabus and found its way into textbooks and films and television news. Opportunities to domesticize apparently foreign development stories occur every day. Mexico provides a striking example. A liquidity crisis and the precipitate devaluation of the Mexican peso — completely unpredicted by financial gurus — was a consequence of Mexican poverty and a Chiapas uprising, as much as it was the product of an overvalued currency.

This was as domestic and as dramatic an issue as they come for Europeans, South Americans and North Americans. US investors lost more than $10 billion in a few short weeks. It had a negative impact on US and Canadian national debt, on currencies and stock markets throughout the western hemisphere and on the long-term well-being of the North American Free Trade Agreement. The 1995 international bailout included more than $30 billion in US and European loans, and a package of IMF standby lending that was three times greater than any set of loans given to an IMF member up to then. Lenders forced guarantees from Mexico that clearly infringed on national sovereignty. Punitive domestic interest rates were combined with the promise of a dramatic drop in Mexican standards of living.

In terms of global public understanding, however, little changed. Chiapas, and the poverty behind its uprising, disappeared from the news, although perhaps only temporarily. The fact that half of all Mexicans were already living in poverty — one-fifth of them in extreme poverty — did not seem to strike economists as a reason to do anything but applaud wage reductions and tighter emigration controls. The roots of Mexican political and economic instability were simply ignored, except that Mexican debt was increased, along with the country's inability to repay.

The fundamental issue of Mexican poverty, as in Batista's Cuba, Somoza's Nicaragua and all the Rwandas and Somalias of today, became lost in IMF negotiations, stock market shifts and attempts to rebuild investor confidence; in what Conor Cruise O'Brien calls 'wishful fantasy, unwarranted reassurance and intimations of quick fixes'.

Leaders in both the North and the South seem to have lost their ability to lead on such issues. Aid budgets are cut back to all-time lows in the name of solving problems 'at home' first, as though home is unrelated to, and unaffected by Chiapas, Somalia and Rwanda; as though home has nothing to do with the poverty that creates refugees, unchecked pollution and poppy fields. Aid alone is not the answer; in fact it may be little more than a symbol. But when industrialized countries resist the idea that they should spend 20 instead of 10 cents out of their aid dollars on health and education, when they send less than one-third of their money to the countries where two-thirds of the poor live, this too is a symbol, and a powerful one. Among other things, it demonstrates a terrible paucity of leadership and good sense. The consequence is that bigger problems, like trade, debt, human rights, and the global environment, fall further and further down the political agenda.

Here, perhaps, is where the most effective alliances can and should be forged between NGOs in the North, in the South, and across the great divide: alliances aimed at creating public ownership of both problems *and* solutions, at finding ways to help governments make the commitments that will be necessary for real change, through the mobilization of informed public opinion. Compassion for those in distress is an important human value, but alone, this has proved totally unequal to the task of generating the political will and the economic energy needed to change the overall order of things. Enlightened altruism rather than blind compassion, what de Tocqueville called 'self-interest *properly understood*': this is likely to make the most headway in the years to come.

Writing about a related topic and despairing of change, Galbraith said that writers, on taking pen, assume that from the power of their talented prose must proceed the remedial action. Hence the usefulness of three endings. Hence the debate in the opening chapter about doomsters and cornucopians: those predicting the direst of futures and those who believe that all will somehow be well. This book is not really about the future, however. It is about today. It is about a today that has grown out of one of the most productive and technologically miraculous centuries in human history, one that has also been the cruellest and bloodiest. It is about a today in which a great many organizations, created by a great many concerned and caring people, and supported by many more of the same, are trying to sort out a better future for our children. It is a better future, however, which looks, from the perspective of places like Chiapas, the Balkans, the Brazilian rainforest, from most of Africa and much of Asia, more distant than ever.

257

Notes

These include short references to books or articles that are mentioned elsewhere in the book, and for which the full details appear in the bibliography, as well as full references to articles or books that are only mentioned in this chapter.

Introduction

1. Charities Aid Foundation, (1994), p.64; 'The GOP's blind faith in charity', *Business Week*, 6 March, 1995.
2. O'Neill, Michael, (1989), *The third America: The emergence of the nonprofit sector in the United States*, Jossey Bass, San Francisco, p.7.
3. Charities Aid Foundation (1994), pp.14, 39.
4. Canadian Centre for Philanthropy, (1994), p.ix.
5. The OECD counted 1600 such organizations in 1980, and there were well over 3000 in 1993 (Smillie and Helmich, 1993, p.21); Lester Salamon puts the number at 4600 (1994, p.119).
6. Ignatieff, pp.28 and 138.

Chapter I   Doomsters and cornucopians

1. IFAD (1988): pp.xviii-xix; UNDP (1991), p.23; World Bank (1990), p.139.
2. The Bank's 1980 *World development report* was in fact rather cautious, predicting two scenarios: worse *and* better.
3. Berg *et al.*, (1994).
4. See, for example, UNICEF (1995), and Berg *et al.*, (1994).
5. Berg *et al.*, (1994), p.11.
6. World Bank, (1994b): SSA's GDP was $132.3 billion, not including the Sudan, for which figures were not available, or South Africa, compared with Denmark's $123.5 billion.
7. Meadows *et al.*, (1972) pp.56–8.
8. World Resources Institute (1994), pp.338–9.
9. 1970 figures: Meadows *et al.*, (1972) pp.57–8; 1987 figures: World Resources Institute (1990), p.320; 1990 figures: WRI (1994), p.336.
10. The 1974 figure: Brown (1974), p.9; the 1993 figure: Brown and Kane, p.76.
11. Bailey, (1993) pages 88, 161–2.
12. *The Economist*, (1995) 21 June.
13. Quoted in Kaplan, p.52.

14. World Resources Institute, (1992–3), p.180.
15. Brown and Kane, (1994) p.78.
16. Homer-Dixon, Thomas, (1994).
17. Kaplan, (1994) p.46.
18. Palau had, in fact, been struggling for independence from US management of its UN Trust Territory status for years. Huge efforts by the US to retain its influence through a 'compact of free association' led to years of bribery, intimidation, confusion and violence. NGOs such as the International Commission of Jurists and the American Civil Liberties Union assisted in the management of the plebiscites and referendums that eventually led to independence. In 1983, the entire country was honoured with the Right Livelihood Award, sometimes known as 'the alternative Nobel prize'.
19. Creveld, (1991) p.204.
20. *The Economist*, (1994), 'Apocalypse Soon', 23 July.
21. These arguments and more were used in a lengthy rebuttal to Kaplan's article: 'Apocalypse deferred' by Marcus Gee, a member of the editorial board of the Toronto *Globe and Mail*, 9 April 1994. In three articles about global warming in its 1 April 1995 issue, *The Economist* warned against draconian action to avert global warming. 'On present evidence,' its editorial said, 'any huge catastrophe looks highly improbable. There is still time to bask in the sun.' Coincidentally, this is a view shared by the Western Fuels Association Inc. In full page advertisements in prominent American publications (e.g. *Harper's*, April, 1995), this coal industry lobbying firm called for policymakers to 'Repeal Rio', explaining (like *The Economist*) that global warming is not necessarily caused by carbon dioxide emissions that result from burning, among other things, coal. In any case, the advertisement complains, global warming promotes 'greater crop yields and more robust forests. Carbon dioxide fertilization of the atmosphere helps produce more food for people, and wildlife can flourish in more abundant habitat . . .' Smoke, it seems, is not just OK, it is a positive good.
22. Connelly and Kennedy, 'Must it be the rest against the West?' *Atlantic Monthly*, December, (1994).
23. Barnet and Cavanagh, (1994) p.328.
24. UNDP (1993a), p.68. The 1993 OECD DAC Chairman's Report takes some issue with the calculations (p.98), but does not invalidate their basic premise.
25. UNDP (1994), p.54.
26. Kennedy, (1993) p.334.
27. Drucker (1993), p.178.
28. Rich, (1994) pp.301–3.
29. Homer-Dixon, Thomas, 'Environmental and demographic threats to Canadian security', *Canadian Foreign Policy*, Vol. 2, No.2, Fall, (1994).
30. Barnet and Cavanagh, (1994) p.429.
31. Daly and Cobb, (1994) pp.166–7.
32. Hallin, (1994) p.35.

Chapter II Naming the rose: what is an NGO?

1. Patronage of the arts, a variant on charity, runs through the history of most civilizations. The support of artists and artisans by the rich and powerful has been a feature of virtually every successful society, from the time of Hammurabi and the Ch'in emperors, through Islamic Cordoba, Agra and Delhi to the endowment of museums and art galleries today.
2. Dahlén, Olle, 'A Governmental Response to Pressure Groups — The Case of Sweden', in Willetts (ed.) (1982), p.151.
3. Krieger, (1993), pp.195–8.
4. Discussed at length in Chapters 8 and 10 of Boorstin, Daniel J., *The Americans: The National Experience*, Vintage, New York, 1965.
5. Cited in Brodhead and Herbert-Copley, (1988), p.31.
6. This issue is discussed at length in Johnston and Sampson, (1994).
7. Drucker, (1994), p.76.
8. Cited in Gaylin *et al.*, (1978), p.51.
9. Steinbeck, John, *The Log from the Sea of Cortez*, 1951, quoted in Klitgaard, Robert p.13
10. Korten, (1990), p.106.
11. Reich, (1991), p.279.
12. Kuti, (1993), p.5.
13. Korten, (1990), p.124.
14. *ibid*, p.2.
15. *ibid*, p.98.
16. Janashakthi Bank statistics derived from personal interviews in September 1994, and from JB Progress Report 11, 31 July, 1994.
17. Salamon and Anheier, (1992a).
18. Here a word on the expression, 'third sector', which typically lumps everything falling between government and the private sector under one convenient heading. Norman Uphoff argues, as does Korten, that there is a distinction to be made between membership organizations, oriented towards *self*-help of their members, and service organizations that deal with clients or beneficiaries. For Uphoff the true 'third sector' is made up of self-help membership organizations and co-operatives, while charitable, non-profit NGOs belong more correctly in the private sector, which always deals with third parties. (Uphoff, Norman, 'Why NGOs are not a third sector', paper presented at Manchester University Workshop on 'NGOs and development: performance and accountability in the new world order', June, 1994).
19. Some years ago, in describing the Canadian non-profit scene, Samuel Martin developed an evolutionary classification on which this typology is based. See Martin, Samuel, (1975).
20. Lissner, (1997), p.i.
21. Brown, David, (1990), 'Rhetoric or reality? Assessing the role of NGOs as agencies of grass roots development', Bulletin No. 28, University of Reading Agriculture and Rural Development Department.

Chapter III   Northern NGOs: the age of innocence

1. Curti, Merle, *American philanthropy abroad*, Rutgers University Press, New Brunswick, N.J., p.3, cited in Sommer, (1977), p.17. For information on early 'NGO' activity, I have drawn largely on Sommer, Lissner (1977) and Bremner (1988).
2. Theroux, Paul, 'Reminiscence: Malawi', in *Making a difference: the Peace Corps at twenty five*, Viorst Milton (ed.), (1986), p.85.
3. Perinbam, Lewis, (1959), 'Canadian Volunteer Graduate Program', mimeo, Ottawa.
4. Rice, Gerald T., (1981), *Twenty years of Peace Corps*, Peace Corps, Washington, p.1.
5. Cowan, Paul, (1967), *The making of an unAmerican*, Viking, New York, p.48.
6. This section is adapted from Smillie (1991).
7. Willoughby, Kelvin W., (1990), *Technology choice: a critique of the Appropriate Technology movement*, IT, p.66.
8. Whiticombe, R. and M. Carr, (1982). 'Appropriate Technology institutions: a review', ITDG, London.
9. Willoughby (*op. cit.*) reviews the literature and arguments critical of appropriate and intermediate technology, pp.223–63.
10. Schumacher, (1973), p.40.
11. Best, (1990), p.163; see also Womack, J.P., Jones, D.T., and Roos, D., (1991), *The machine that changed the world: the story of lean production*, pp.146–53.
12. The 'Third Italy' is discussed at length in Best, Michael H., (1990) *The New Competition*, Polity Press, Cambridge, pp.203–226.
13. de Soto, Hernando, 'Structural adjustment and the informal sector', J. Levitsky (1989).
14. China: *World Resources* Institute (1994), p.77; Bangladesh: Hossain, Mahabub, (1984), 'Increasing food availability in Bangladesh: constraints and possibilities,' Dhaka Food Strategy Review Exercise, Ministry of Agriculture. See also World Bank, (1985), *Bangladesh: economic and social development prospects*, Vol. III, which estimated that by 1991 only 16 to 18 per cent of the additional labour force would be employed in direct crop production.
15. Gwitira, Joshua C., (1990) 'Small-scale technology for agro-industrial development', ITDG/Zimbabwe Ministry of Industry and Commerce, Harare, October.
16. See Robert Chambers, (1987 and 1994), and Chambers and Conway, (1992), for a more thorough discussion of sustainable rural livelihoods.
17. McCormick, John, (1989), *Reclaiming paradise: The global environmental movement*, Indiana University Press, Bloomington, p.3.
18. McCormick, (1989), *op cit*, p.19.
19. Quoted in Bonner, Raymond, (1993), *At the hand of man: peril and hope for Africa wildlife*, Knopff, New York, p.40.
20. IUCN (1948), Statutes, 5 October.
21. Quoted in Bonner, (1993), *op cit*, p.57.

22. McCormick, (1989), *op cit*, p.183.
23. Ekins, (1992), pp.145–9.
24. World Commission on Environment and Development, (1987), p.2.
25. World Resources Institute (1994), p.13.
26. Kelly, Petra, 'A very bad way to enter the next century', in Brecher *et al.*, (1993), p.141.
27. Bonner, (1993), *op cit*, p.20.
28. Bonner, (1993), *op cit*, pp.189–90.
29. McCormick, (1989), *op cit*, p.85; for a scathing attack on just about everyone in the environmental movement, see Bailey Ronald, (1993).
30. Middleton, Neil, P. O'Keefe, S. Moyo, (1993), *Tears of the crocodile: from rio to reality in the developing world*, Pluto, London, p.209.

Chapter IV   Southern NGOs

1. Kandil, Amani, (1993), *Defining the non-profit sector: Egypt*, Working Papers of the Johns Hopkins Comparative Nonprofit Sector Project, No. 10, The Johns Hopkins Institute for Policy Studies, Baltimore, p.4.
2. Wanigaratne, Ranjit D., (1994), 'The state-NGO relationship: rights, interests and accountability', paper presented at University of Manchester Workshop on NGOs and Accountability in the New World Order, June, p.5.
3. These numbers, drawn from a wide variety of sources, are only barely trustworthy, as definitions are widely inconsistent. Many of the 'NGOs' in one country may actually be small, village-based organizations that are not included in the survey of another country. The numbers serve largely to demonstrate the global dynamism of the sector.
4. BRAC, (1992), 'BRAC at twenty', Dhaka.
5. Black, (1992), p.133.
6. *ibid.*
7. Nyoni, Sithembiso, (1987), 'Indigenous NGOs: liberation, self-reliance and development', *World Development*, Vol. 15, Supplement.
8. Alinsky, Saul D., (1969), *Reveille for radicals*, Vintage, New York, p.90 (originally published in 1946).
9. Rich, (1994), p.131; Reilly, Charles, (1993), 'The road from Rio', *Grassroots Development* 17/1.
10. Sources for the Chipko story include Dankelman and Davidson, (1988); Ekins, (1992); and 'Standing up for trees: women's role in the Chipko Movement' by Shobita Jain in Sontheimer, (1991).
11. This section is based on an extensive study of Ghanaian NGOs undertaken by the author with Siapha Kamara and Daniel Joly in 1992.
12. Thompson, Judith, (1991), 'Managing NGOs: what are the critical challenges for NGOs today in Africa?' ISODEC, Accra. Thompson also includes the problems of networking, umbrella organizations, and gaining recognition at home and abroad.
13. The main sources for details in this section are as follows: Malee Suwana-adth, (1991), 'The NGO sector in Thailand', SVITA Foundation, Bangkok; PRIA, (1992), November *Newsletter* No. 40, PRIA, New Delhi; Perera, J.,

C. Marasinghe and L. Jayasekere, (1992), *A people's movement under seige*, Sarvodaya, Ratmalana; R. Betts *et al.*, 'A strategic assessment of NGO development in Indonesia', DAI, Washington, 1987; International Center for Not-for-Profit Law, 'Report of a visit to Asia', (1994), Farmington.

14. This silly idea was given more prominence than it deserved by its inclusion in the 1993 UNDP *Human development report* (p.99); it is discussed at length in Chapter IX.
15. Schneider, (1988), p.108.
16. Houston, James, (1994), *Strengthening the NGO sector in Africa — the legal and fiscal framework*, Charities Aid Foundation, London, (draft).
17. This did not, however, stop the Government of Kenya from expelling the Director of a German NGO, nor from de-registering Kenyan NGOs (the Mwangasa Trust and the Centre for Law and Research International in 1994) for what it regarded as activities designed to injure the credibility of the government.
18. Sources: Kenya — Gillies D., and M. Muta, (1993), 'A long road to Uhuru; human rights and political participation in Kenya', International Centre for Human Rights and Democracy, Montreal; and Houston, (1994), *op. cit*, p.14; Pakistan — various news articles and NGO position papers.

Chapter V The pink elephant: empowerment and the status of women

1. Mathai, S., (1990), 'Women and new technologies — an organizing manual', in *The Tribune*, No. 34, New York: International Tribune Centre, cited in Moser, (1993), p.46. Interestingly, in 1994 China banned the use of ultra sound for the detection of the gender of an unborn baby.
2. UNDP, (1991), p.27.
3. UNDP, (1994), p.97.
4. Sen and Grown, (1987), p.49
5. The best early critique was produced in 1987 by UNICEF: edited by Cornia *et al*. More recently, Susan George, a long-time critic of the World Bank, went for the adjustment jugular with Fabrizio Sabelli in *Faith and credit: The World Bank's secular empire* (Penguin, London, 1994). A broad collection of NGO views was produced in 1994 in *50 years is enough: the case against the World Bank and the International Monetary Fund* (Kevin Danaher (ed.), South End Press, Boston).
6. World Bank (1994a), p.163.
7. Moser, (1993), p.61.
8. *ibid*, p.62.
9. *ibid*, p.70
10. World Bank, (1994a), p.21 and p.49.
11. Rose, Kalima, (1992), *Where women are leaders: the SEWA movement in India*, Vistaar, Delhi, p.79.
12. Personal visit by the author to Darsano Charno, June 1988.
13. IT Publications, London.
14. Carr, (1984), p.125.

15. Yudelman, Sally, (1987), 'Integrating women into development projects: observations on the NGO experience in general and Latin America in Particular', *Word Development*, Supplement, Vol. 15, Autumn, p.181.
16. Moser, (1993), p.117.
17. Andam, Aba. A., (1990), 'Remedial strategies to overcome gender stereotyping in science education in Ghana', in *Development*, SID, Rome.
18. See, for example, McKee, Katharine, (1989), 'Microlevel strategies for supporting livelihoods, employment and income generation of poor women in the Third World: the challenge of significance', *World Development*, Vol. 17, No. 7; and Tendler, Judith, (1989), 'Whatever happened to poverty alleviation?' in Levitsky, (1989).
19. The CARE case is based on personal study by the author during a visit to the project in August 1990, and on CARE SRCP Quarterly Report, 1 April 1994 — 31 June 1994.
20. This claim is most clearly identified in McKee, (1989), *op cit*, p.101
21. Statistics are taken from 'Grameen Bank Project Phase III; Project Completion Mission, Final Report', January 1994. The report says that 'Grameen Bank has been unable to develop, refine and promote promising technologies that the borrowers can subsequently adopt to increase the productivity of their loans and to enable them to utilize larger loans' (p.ii).
22. This is borne out in the findings of Ponna Wignaraja, (1990), in *Women, poverty and resources*, Sage, New Delhi.
23. The BRAC poultry example is based on visits by the author to BRAC programmes over the years, most recently in October, 1994.
24. Carr, (1984), pp.13–14.
25. Chen, Marty, (1989), 'A sectoral approach to women's work: lessons from India', *World Development*, Vol. 17, No. 7.
26. I am grateful to Brenda Cupper for this imagery. Commenting on a draft of this chapter in a fax from Croatia, she wrote, 'The academics got carried away on theory: people are afraid to stick their neck out and call something successful because it doesn't incorporate every principle from every theory. Even though the theories have been valuable, they have proven to be very, very intimidating to most practitioners in the real world: notably men'.
27. Longwe, Sara H., (1989), 'Gender awareness: the missing element in the Third World development project', FINNIDA; also a revised version of the same paper in *Changing perceptions: writings on gender and development*, Oxfam, Oxford, (1991).

Chapter VI   Disasters: some came running

1. 'Report of the Secretary General on the Situation in Rwanda', 31 May 1994; quoted in Vassall-Adams, Guy, (1994), *Rwanda: an agenda for international action*, Oxfam, Oxford, p.44.
2. Detailed descriptions of Peruvian housing can be found in De Soto, H., (1989), *The other path*, Harper and Row, New York, and Maskrey, A., (1989), *Disaster mitigation; a community-based approach*, Oxfam, Oxford.
3. Smillie, (1991), p.40.

4. See, for example, Ryder, Graine (ed.), (1990), *Damning the Three Gorges: what the dam-builders don't want you to know*, Probe International, Toronto.

5. 'The Three Gorges Dam in China: forced resettlement, suppression of dissent and labor rights concerns', Human Rights Watch/Asia, New York, Vol.7 No.2, February 1995.

6. Homer-Dixon, (1994), pp.5–40.

7. Cited in O'Rourke, (1994), pp.94–5.

8. Sampson, Cynthia, 'Quaker conciliation during the Nigerian Civil War' in Johnston and Sampson, (1994), pp.88–118.

9. Stremlau, J.J., (1977), *The International politics of the Nigerian Civil War*, Princeton University Press, p.244.

10. 'Last month [August 1968], the Red Cross published a figure of eight to ten thousand deaths . . . But all our figures, I would remind you, are likely to be on the conservative side,' said Clyne Shepherd, World Council of Churches (Source: Jacobs, Dan, (1988), *The brutality of nations*, Paragon, New York, p 109); by September, Herman Middlekoop, WCC Relief Director in Biafra was estimating 12 000 deaths a month, and cabled U Thant to predict 25 000 a day by December if the war did not end (Source: Jacobs, *op cit*, p.3).

11. A. Edgell in David, M. (ed.), (1975), *Civil wars and the politics of international relief*, Praeger, New York, p.67.

12. Akpan, N.U., (1971), *The struggle for secession, 1966–70*, Frank Cass, London, p.160.

13. Quoted in Stremlau, *op. cit.*, p.239.

14. Lloyd, Hugh, *et al.*, (1972), *The Nordchurchaid airlift to Biafra, 1968–70: an operations report*, Folkekirkens Nodhjaelp, Copenhagen, p.240.

15. Stremlau, (1977), *op. cit.*, p.241.

16. Lloyd, (1972), *op. cit.*, Appendix 9.

17. Carl, Beverly, Deputy Chief of Nigeria/Biafra Relief and Rehabilitation program, USAID, quoted in Stremlau, (1977), *op. cit.*, p.242.

18. Susan Cronje (1972), puts the figure for Nigerian arms expenditure at $40 million in her book, *The War and Nigeria*, Sidgewick and Jackson, London.

19. Burley, L.A., (1973), 'Disaster relief administration in the Third World', *International Development Review*, 15:1.

20. Senior managers in UNICEF, Concern, the American Friends Service Committee, CARE and others (of which the author was one) would occasionally organize a Nigerian evening in Dhaka to recall earlier adventures.

21. *1994 UN Revised Consolidated Inter-Agency Appeal for Angola; February — July 1994*, UN Department of Humanitarian Affairs, Geneva.

22. Black, (1992), p.223.

23. The 1992 figure, according to the 1993 and 1994 OECD DAC Reports was 8.6 per cent, and in 1993 it was 11.4 per cent. These figures are open to interpretation.

24. Benson, Charlotte, (1993), *The changing roles of NGOs in the provision of relief and rehabilitation assistance: Cambodia/Thailand*, Overseas Development Institute, London, p.93.

25. Benson, (1993), *op. cit.*, p.36.
26. For horror stories on relief assistance gone wrong, see Hancock; these documented examples and more can be found on pp.12–13, and in Shawcross, W., (1984), *The quality of mercy: Cambodia, holocaust and modern conscience*, Andre Deutsch, London, p.386.
27. *The Economist*, 8 October 1994.
28. See for example Mason, L. and Brown, R. *Rice, Rivalry and Politics: Managing Cambodian Relief*, University of Notre Dame Press, 1983, Shawcross, (1984) *op. cit.* and Benson (1993) *op. cit.*, 29. Smillie, (1985), p.335.
30. These two efforts are described in detail in Anderson and Woodrow (1989).
31. O'Rourke, (1994), p.95.
32. *World Disasters Report 1994*, Red Cross, Geneva, 1994, p.87.
33. Mason and Brown, (1983), *op. cit.*, p.131.
34. Benson, (1993), *op. cit.*, p.93.
35. Campbell, (1990), p.93.
36. Borton, (1994), p.85.
37. Borton, (1994), p.19.
38. Hancock, (1989), p.27.
39. According to 'Chronicles of Change' (CIDA, 1994), Canada spent C$1.3 billion in peacekeeping, food and emergency assistance to Somalia between 1989 and 1992. Total Canadian aid expenditure to all African countries — bilateral, multilateral, food, emergency aid and NGO support — was C$1.07 billion in 1992–3 (CIDA Annual Report, 1992–3, Ottawa, 1994).
40. Quoted in Benthall, (1993), p.133.
41. Match International: *Ottawa Citizen*, 22 July 1994; AJJDC/AAI: *New York Times*, 31 July 1994.
42. Shawcross, (1984), *op. cit.*, p.243.
43. *Humanitarian aid between conflict and development*, (1993), Ministry of Foreign Affairs (DVL/OS), The Hague, p.52.
44. 'AIDAB-NGO Cooperation; Annual Report 1993–4', Canberra; and Smillie and Helmich, (1993), p.33.
45. Quoted in Kent, R.C., (1987), *Anatomy of disaster relief: the international network in action*, Pinter, London, p.81.
46. Anderson and Woodrow, (1989), p.97.
47. Oxfam, Oxford, (1993).
48. Vassall-Adams, (1994), *op. cit.*, p.26.
49. Eguizábal, C., D. Lewis, L. Minear, P. Sollis, and Thomas Weiss, (1993), *Humanitarian challenges in Central America: learning lessons of recent armed conflict*, Thomas J. (1993), Watson Jr. Institute for International Studies, Brown University, Providence.
50. Rakiya Omaar and Alex de Waal (1994), use the guinea-pig analogy in 'Humanitarianism unbound? Current dilemmas facing multi-mandate relief operations in political emergencies', African Rights, London, November. De Waal uses it again in (1994), 'African Encounters', *Index on Censorship 6*. Had the guinea-pig survived, the subsequent Rwandan disaster might have been much less severe.

51. *ibid.*
52. Cited in *Humanitarian Aid . . ., op. cit.*, p.4.
53. USAID Office for Disaster Assistance, (1991), *Annual Report*, Washington.

Chapter VII   Mixed messages: NGOs and the Northern public

1. Reported in *The Ottawa Citizen*, 12 May, 1994.
2. Canadian International Development Agency, (1994), 'Public opinion research input for the foreign policy review', February.
3. Norwegian statistics: Statistics Norway, 1993; Sweden: SIDA correspondence with author; United States: Rockefeller Foundation/Belden and Russonello, (1993), 'Americans and Foreign Aid in the Nineties', February.
4. OECD, (1983), Documentation relating to DAC Meeting on Public Opinion and Development Assistance, September.
5. Canadian International Development Agency, (1993), 'Canadian public opinion on international development; analysis of Focus Canada 1993–1 Survey', Public Environment Research and Analysis Group, July.
6. 'Americans and Foreign Aid: A Study of American Public Attitudes', (1995), University of Maryland, January.
7. European Commission, (1992), 'Eurobarometer 36: the way Europeans perceive the Third World in 1991', INRA European Coordinating Office, Brussels, March.
8. Sources: Isopublic, (1994), 'Entwicklungspolitik Berichtsband' Swissaid, Bern; Kelley, Jonathan, (1989), 'Australians' attitudes to overseas aid', Australian International Development Assistance Bureau, Canberra; Government of Japan, (1994), *Japan's ODA 1993*, Ministry of Foreign Affairs, Tokyo.
9. Cited in Yankelovich, (1991), p.32.
10. These included an NGO Coalition for US Support of Equitable and Sustainable Development, The Development Group for Alternative Policies, the Advocacy Network for Development, and the Overseas Development Council. See Smillie and Helmich, (1993), pp.312–3
11. Decima Corporation, (1993), 'Elite study on development assistance', IDRC, Ottawa.
12. 'Summit debates dilute plan', Toronto *Globe and Mail*, 10 March 1995.
13. Randel and German, (1994), p.19.
14. OECD, (1995).
15. Figures derived from annual reports of the NGOs mentioned.
16. Reported in Charities Aid Foundation, (1992), p.13.
17. Source: 'InterAction Member Profiles', InterAction, Washington, 1993.
18. Smillie and Helmich, (1993), p.21.
19. Charities Aid Foundation, (1992).
20. Yankelovich, (1991), p.5.
21. Harris, Lou and Associates, (1993), *Harris Poll 55*, New York, 1 November.
22. University of Maryland, *op cit.* Michael Kinsley criticizes the public ignorance revealed in this study — and the attachment of any political importance to it — in 'The Intellectual Free Lunch', *New Yorker*, 6 February 1995.

23. Times Mirror Center for the People and the Press, (1994), 'Eight nation people and the press survey', Washington, March.
24. Canadian International Development Agency, (1991), *Report to CIDA: public attitudes toward international development assistance*, Ottawa.
25. Intercultural Communications Inc., (1993), 'A new climate for foreign aid?' Washington, May: the Belden and Russonello poll (Rockefeller Foundation, 'Americans and Foreign Aid in the Nineties', Feb. 1993) found support for the UN slightly lower, at 45 per cent; 61 per cent believed multilateral aid programmes would be more effective than bilateral. A word of caution is needed on the US figures: a 1992 UNICEF poll found that roughly the same number (19 per cent) believed US Government support to be effective, however only 22 per cent favoured UN agencies and UNICEF. Religious organizations came out ahead in this poll (37 per cent), and NGOs received only 11 per cent support (Source: InterAction 1994).
26. CIDA, (1988), 'Report to CIDA: Public Attitudes Towards International Development Assistance', Ottawa.
27. European trust in national governments ranges from a high of 15 per cent in Germany, to a low of 1 per cent, 3 per cent and 5 per cent respectively in Greece, Italy and the Netherlands. The highest support for UN agencies was found in Greece and Spain (65 per cent and 57 per cent), and the lowest in Germany and Britain (30 per cent). The greatest confidence in NGOs was found in Ireland and Britain (33 per cent and 30 per cent), and the lowest in Portugal and Greece (3 per cent and 8 per cent). Confidence in NGOs was relatively weak in the Netherlands, Denmark and Belgium (15 per cent, 16 per cent and 19 per cent). Source: European Commission, (1992), 'Eurobarometer 36: the way europeans perceive the Third World in 1991', INRA European Coordinating Office, Brussels, March.
28. Yankelovich, (1991), pp.84–5.
29. Yankelovich, (1991), p.101.
30. Quoted in Bread for the World, (1993), p.70.
31. 'Patterns in Foreign News Coverage on US Network Television' by Weaver, Porter and Evans; cited in Wallis, Roger and Stanley Baran, (1990), *The known world of broadcast news*, Routledge, London, p.156.
32. Riffe D., and E. Shaw, 'Conflict and consonance: coverage of the Third World in two US Papers', *Journalism Quarterly* 63, (1986), pp.617–26.
33. Highlights from French Study, 'L'image du Tiers Monde dans les médias', BarOsud, Commission Développement/Coopération et Ministère de la Coopération, La Documentation Française, Paris, (1992).
34. Rosenblum, Mort, (1979), *Coups and earthquakes: reporting the world to America*, Harper Colophon, New York, p.214.
35. Rosenblum, Mort, (1993), *Who stole the news*, John Wiley and Sons, New York, p.280.
36. Hallin, (1994), pp 14–15.
37. *ibid*, p.35.

38. Source: Eurobarometer 36, *op. cit.*
39. Harris National Omnibus, September, 1989; RSGB General Omnibus Survey, July, 1993.
40. Nikki van der Gaag and Cathy Nash, (1987), *Images of Africa: the UK report*, Oxfam, Oxford; cited in Benthall (1993).
41. See, for example, *New Internationalist*, May 1982 for several stories on child sponsorship.
42. Sources: *New Internationalist*, May, 1982; Plan International Annual Reports 1992 and 1994; World Vision US Annual Report 1993.
43. ACFOA Code of Ethics, adopted September, 1989.
44. InterAction, (1993), *InterAction PVO Standards*, Washington.
45. Phillips, E. Hereward, (1969), *Fund raising techniques and case histories*, Business Books, London; quoted in Lissner, (1977), p.131.
46. Bread for the World, (1993), p.74.
47. Clark, (1991), p.146.
48. *ibid*, p.50.
49. USAID, (1993), 'Evaluation of the Development Education Program', Intercultural Communication Inc., Washington, October, p.5.
50. Kirby, Bob (ed.), (1994), *Education for Change: Grassroots Development Education in Europe* (draft), NGDO-EC Liaison Committee Development Education Group, Brussels, pp.8–9.
51. Pinney, C. (1994), 'Building support for a new foreign policy' (draft), CCIC, March.
52. CIDA's Communications and Development Information Program had a budget of C$15.7 million in 1992–3; in 1991 World Vision Australia spent more than C$20 million on administration and fund raising. Source: CIDA Main Estimates; World Vision Australia Annual Report, (1992).
53. OECD, (1983), 'Present State of Public Opinion . . .', DAC (83)25.
54. Sources: North-South Centre, (1993), 'Education and training in the fields of environment and development', Lisbon, June; Kirby, (1994), *op. cit.*; SIDA correspondence (1994), Riddell, Roger, *et al.*, (1994), *Strengthening the partnership: evaluation of the Finnish NGO support programme*, FINNIDA, Helsinki.
55. For example, Canadian polls between 1987 and 1991 gave NGOs a credibility rating of about 25 per cent: behind television (about 35 per cent) and churches (about 32 per cent), but ahead of newspapers (20 per cent and government (18 per cent).
56. UNDP, (1994), p.71.
57. Times Mirror Poll, *op. cit.*, March 1994. None of the other seven countries surveyed did so badly on Boutros Boutros-Ghali. Only Mexicans had more trouble than Americans with Boris Yeltsin.
58. Scott and Mpanya, (1994), pp.97–8.
59. Cited in Gowing, Nik, (1994), 'Real time television coverage of armed conflict and diplomatic crises: does it pressure or distort foreign policy decision?', Harvard University, Cambridge.
60. O'Brien, Conor Cruise, (1994), p.49.
61. Galbraith, (1992), p.174.

Chapter VIII   Management, memory and money

1. Accurate statistics on NGOs are elusive. This figure is therefore an estimate. Reasonably accurate US figures, which show a total flow of $5.8 billion for American NGOs in 1991, would suggest that a total of $10 billion is probably not an exaggeration. These figures, however, include in-kind contributions and grants from government, which may represent as much as half the total. The 1994 DAC Chairman's Report uses a figure of $6.3 billion in 'grants by private voluntary agencies', but there are serious problems and a likely under-reporting in this number. For details, see Smillie and Helmich, (1993), pp.40–41.
2. Mintzberg, Henry, (1994), *The rise and fall of strategic planning*, The Free Press, New York, p.110.
3. 'The top US charities', *Money*, December, 1994.
4. I realize that Chapter VI cites a figure of $209 million in private donor support to World Vision US in 1993. That figure, taken from the US journal, *Chronicle of Philanthropy* (1 November 1994), differs from the figure in World Vision's published Annual Report — $173 million. This demonstrates one of the issues raised elsewhere in the chapter — the inconsistency and confusion in reporting formats.
5. USAID, (1993).
6. Williams, Grant, (1994), 'More scrutiny for a relief charity', *Chronicle of Philanthropy*, Washington, 5 April.
7. This story was detailed on the British television programme, *Dispatches*: 'In the Name of Hunger', produced and directed by Roy Ackerman, Channel 4, London, 1990. World Vision went to great lengths to discredit the programme, later claiming that a major retraction and apology had been elicited from Channel 4. Damage control became a global effort. For example, World Vision reportedly told officials of the University of Canterbury Students' Association in Christchurch, New Zealand, that legal action might be taken if the Student Christian Movement showed the film on campus. The Student's Association backed down, but faculty members eventually showed the film on university, rather than student-owned property. In Ireland, the film provided background to a debate about World Vision's child sponsorship activities. Apparently quite litigious, World Vision took legal action against the Irish NGO, Trocaire, over allegedly libelous statements. The matter was eventually settled out of court. I am grateful to several people in Canada, Britain, Ireland and New Zealand for documentation and assistance with this vignette.
8. Fowler, (1992).
9. This internal calculation obviously does not come out in the wash inspected by *Money* magazine.
10. World Vision Australia, (1991), *Annual report*.
11. Source: SCF UK Annual Report and Financial Accounts, 1991–2.
12. 'Warm Mailing', *Professional Fundraising*, October, 1994.
13. Cavanagh, John, (1994), 'Fair trade sets out to challenge free trade', *The WorldPaper*, November.

14. 'Charity shops at end of a high street growth road', *Guardian*, 29 June, 1994; 'Trade and prosper?' *Guardian*, 14 December, 1994; 'A flexible way to keep giving', *Daily Telegraph*, 14 December, 1994.
15. Parts of the section on 'results' are based on the author's work with the Aga Khan Foundation Canada and CIDA in Pakistan in 1994.
16. Brinkerhoff, (1991), p.191.
17. Rondinelli, Dennis, (1993), 'Strategic and results-based management in CIDA', CIDA, Ottawa. For a more complete discussion on adaptive development administration, see also Rondinelli.
18. Rossum, Constance, (1993), 'How to assess your non-profit organization', Jossey-Bass, San Francisco.
19. 'Social Audit 1992/93', Traidcraft plc, Gateshead; 'Traidcraft Exchange: Ideas and Action for Fair Trade,' Traidcraft, Gateshead, 1994; Zadek, Simon and Gatward, Murdoch, 'Transforming the Transnationals,' University of Manchester Workshop on NGO Accountability, June, 1994; Zadek, S., 'Notes on Social Audit,' New Economics Foundation, London 1994.

Chapter IX Dependence and independence in the contracting era

1. For example Ralph Kramer, writing in McCarthy *et al.* (1992), of social services in the UK, Italy and the Netherlands, refers to 'growing interdependence' between NGOs and the state, but says that 'contrary to the conventional wisdom, there seem to be few successful attempts of the state to control, regulate, monitor, evaluate or press for greater accountability' (p.93). Robinson (1994) says, 'NGO contracting in developing countries is not a very widespread phenomenon', although he says that 'further substantive research is required'.
2. These figures, drawn from Smillie and Helmich, (1993), cover the years 1991 and 1992. A great deal of interpretation was required in reaching them, as the figures and definitions supplied for the study and to the OECD are often inconsistent. These are, however, the most accurate assessments available, and are based on information supplied from the governments in question. They refer to cash grants that are not tied to government commodities, programmes or priorities. The grants are provided to NGOs only. Universities, professional institutions and others have been excluded.
3. OECD Aid Review 1992/3, Memorandum of Australia, 29 July, 1992.
4. See, for example, Weir, Margaret, 'Entitlements', in Krieger, p.267.
5. Government of Australia, (1994), 'AIDAB-NGO Cooperation Annual Report 1993–4', Canberra.
6. *ibid*, p.310; the figure refers to cash only.
7. Korten (1990), p.102.
8. Discussions of contracting and the PSC, or something like it, can be found in Brodhead and Herbert-Copley, (1988), Clark, (1991), Farrington and Bebbington, (1993) and Robinson, (1994).
9. USAID, (1993b).

10. Smillie and Helmich, (1993), p.278.
11. The Uganda and Bolivian experiences are outlined in Robinson (1994).
12. The author was involved in an evaluation of the JTF in September, 1994. A description of this 'John Cleese poverty project' can be found in Hodson, Roland, (1995), 'Elephant loose in the jungle: the World Bank and NGOs in Sri Lanka', (mimeo).
13. Bell, Bill, (1994), 'The Relationship between NGO service provision and advocacy: the UK experience', Manchester University Conference, June.
14. Smith and Lipsky, (1993), p.45.
15. Drucker (1993), p.57.
16. Clark, (1991), p.65.
17. World Bank, (1993), p.127 and 143. The Brazilian NGO is the Pastoral da Criança, managed by the Catholic Church.
18. Matthias. A., and A. Green, (1994), 'Government and NGO roles and relationships in policy making: the health sector in Zimbabwe', University of Manchester Workshop, June.
19. Barnet and Cavanagh, (1994), p.113.
20. Tandon, Yash, (1991), 'Foreign NGOs, uses and abuses: an African perspective', *Associations Transnationales*, No.3.
21. Personal conversation with Siapha Kamara and others.
22. See, for example, Bebbington and Riddell, (1994); Edwards and Hulme, (1994) and Pearce, J., (1993), 'NGOs and social change: agents or facilitators', *Development in Practice*, Vol.3, No.3.
23. UNDP, (1993), p.99.
24. Palmer, R., and J. Rossiter, (1990), 'Northern NGOs in Southern Africa: some heretical thoughts', quoted in Edwards (1993a).
25. The study was undertaken by Dr Kamal Siddiqui. See *Report of the task forces on Bangladesh development strategies for the 1990s*, University Press, Dhaka, (1991), Vol.II, p.381.
26. Edwards (1993a and 1993b).
27. Polit-Econ Services for USAID, (1973), 'Problems of voluntary agencies in Africa', Washington, p.18.
28. Brodhead and Herbert-Copley, (1988), p.70.

Chapter X   Partners

1. 'Our Values', (*circa* 1993), War on Want publicity material, London.
2. Author's work with Sarvodaya between 1984 and 1990. See Smillie, (1987), 'Northern *donors* and Southern *partners*: arguments for an NGO consortium approach', Commonwealth Secretariat Roundtable, University of Warwick, July.
3. This story is based on the author's work with AMREF. See Smillie, (1987), 'Strengthening collaboration with NGOs: the strangulation technique', AMREF, Nairobi.
4. Speech given at a UNICEF meeting in Manila in May, 1977, reprinted in Ariyaratne, A.T., (1984), *Collected works* (Vol. I), Sarvodaya, Colombo.
5. Bhasin, Kamla, 'Towards South-North NGO partnership: some thoughts', (1994), Manchester University Conference, June.

6. Ford-Smith, (1989), p.100.
7. Tandon, Y., (1991), 'Foreign NGOs, uses and abuses: an African perspective', *Associations Transnationales*, No.3.
8. Malena, Carmen, (1992), 'Relations between Northern and Southern non-governmental development organizations', IDS, University of Sussex.
9. 'South-North linking for international development', *Conference Proceedings*, November, 1990, quoted in Malena, (1992), *op. cit.*
10. See, for example, Bebbington and Riddell, (1994).
11. Zadek, S., and S. Szabo, (1994), 'Valuing organization: the case of Sarvodaya', New Economics Foundation, London.
12. Perera, Jehan, (1994), 'In unequal dialogue with donors: the future direction of Sarvodaya', Manchester University Conference, June.
13. The numbers had a tendency to jump about, which donors found particularly frustrating. In 1978, Ariyaratne used the number 2000 villages. In 1979 it was 3000 and by 1985 he said that 'the Movement is active in 8000 [villages]' ('Development from below', A.T. Ariyaratne). Perera, (1994) *op. cit.*, talked of 8600 in 1994. A mid-term Review conducted in 1988 referred to only 5000, and donor funds, in fact, were targeted specifically at 2000 villages where concrete and verifiable activity was taking place.
14. Sarvodaya, (1994), 'The future directions of Sarvodaya', Moratuwa, June.
15. Perera, (1994), *op. cit.*
16. Pitt-Rivers, Julian, (1954), *People of the Sierra*, Weidenfeld and Nicholson, London, p.40; cited in Putnam, (1993), p.174.
17. James, Rick, (1994), 'Strengthening the capacity of Southern NGO partners' (Draft), INTRAC, Oxford.

Chapter XI Act globally: the rise of the transnational NGO

1. Black, (1992), p.101.
2. *ibid*, p.170.
3. CARE Canada, (1994), *Annual report.*
4. Charities Aid Foundation, (1992).
5. CARE Australia, (1992), *Annual report, 1991/2*; AIDAB, (1992), *NGO Cooperation program annual report, 1991/92.*
6. World Vision, (1993), *Annual report, 1993.*
7. World Vision Canada, (1993), *Childview*, February/March and (1995).
8. World Vision New Zealand, (1994), 'Simplified Statement of Accounts', Year ending 30 September 1994.
9. In 1994, Irish NGOs raised about $25 million in total. World Vision Ireland raised only a tiny fraction of this.
10. Plan International, (1992 and 1994), 'Worldwide annual reports'.
11. Fowler, (1992).
12. Campbell, (1990), p.193.
13. Sources: World Vision Australia, (1991), *Annual report*; World Vision Canada, (1993), *Childview*, Feb/March; USAID, (1993), *Voluntary foreign aid programs, 1993*; Fowler, (1992); World Vision New Zealand, (1992), *Statement of accounts*, 30 September 1992; Plan International, (1994), *Worldwide Annual Report, 1994.*

14. Fowler, Alan, (1992), 'Decentralization for international NGOs', *Develop-ment in Practice*, Vol. 2, No. 2, pp.121–4, Oxfam, June. Debates about decentralization, of course, date back at least as far as the Roman Em-pire. Norman Uphoff discussed decentralization and deconcentration in *Local institutional development: an analytical sourcebook with cases*, (Kumarian Press, 1986); Julie Fisher uses the same terminology as Fowler in 'Local governments and the independent sector in the Third World' in McCarthy *et al.*, (1992).
15. Campbell, (1990), p.192.
16. Black, (1992), p.295.
17. USAID, (1993).
18. The study was conducted by the author on behalf of CARE Canada.
19. Farrington and Bebbington, (1993).
20. Edwards, (1993b).
21. Falk, Richard, 'The making of global citizenship', in Brecher *et al.*, (1993), pp.39–50.
22. Kelly, Petra, 'A very bad way to enter the next century', in Brecher *et al.*, (1993), p.142.

Chapter XII   Democracy, participation and the rights stuff

1. Quoted in Chomsky, Noam, (1992), *Deterring democracy*, Hill and Wang, New York, p.279.
2. World Bank, (1981), p.11.
3. World Bank, (1989), p.61.
4. UNDP, (1991), p.19.
5. These were developed by Charles Humana, and published first in *The world guide to human rights*, Facts on File, New York, 1986.
6. Schmitz, G.J., and David Gillies, (1992), *The challenge of democratic development*, North-South Institute, Ottawa, p.33.
7. *ibid.*
8. de Tocqueville, (1969), pp.517–518.
9. Will, G.F., 'Yeltsin: looking to Locke, he avoid's Kerensky's path', *Herald Tribune*, 25 March, 1993.
10. UNDP, (1993b).
11. Fowler, (1993).
12. Putnam, Robert, (1993).
13. Ignatieff, Michael, (1995), 'On civil society: why Eastern Europe's revolu-tions could succeed', *Foreign Affairs*, March/April.
14. Jazairy *et al.*, (1992), p.343.
15. Bhatnagar and Williams, (1992), p.3.
16. See Ross, Hughes Shapan Adnan and Barry Dala-Clayton, (1994), *Flood-plains or flood plans? a review of water management in Bangladesh*, IIED/RAS, Nottingham; and Kvaloy, Froydis, (1994), *NGOs and people's participation in relation to the Bangladesh Flood Action Plan*, (self-published?), Oslo.
17. UNDP, (1993), p.1.
18. Dichter, Thomas, 'Demystifying popular participation: institutional

mechanisms for popular participation', in Bhatnagar and Williams, (1992), p.89.

19. Smillie and Helmich, (1993), pp.314–15.

20. Quoted in Gilbert, Martin, (1994), *In search of Churchill*, Harper Collins, London, pp.274–5.

21. Quoted in Dolan, Chris, 'British development NGOs and advocacy in the 1990s', in Edwards and Hulme, (1992), p.207.

22. Letter from Robin Guthrie, Chief Charity Commissioner, the *Times*, 10 May 1991.

23. Series of articles by Arthur McGivern, a South African journalist who had acted as a police spy, beginning 6 January 1980, the *Observer*, London.

24. This story is told in detail in Smillie, (1985), pp.236–43.

25. Biekart, Kees, (1994), 'European NGOs and democratisation in Central America: new policy agendas and assessment of past performance', paper presented at IDPM Workshop, University of Manchester, June, p.3. See also Eguizábal, Lewis *et al.*, (1993), *Humanitarian challenges in Central America: learning the lessons of recent armed conflicts*, Thomas J. Watson Jr. Institute for International Studies, Brown University, Providence.

26. Lewis, David, cited in Biekart, (1994), p.4.

27. Borton, (1990), p.30; Fowler, (1991), p.56.

28. Clark, (1991), p.150.

29. Parry-Williams, John, 'Scaling-up via legal reform in Uganda', in Edwards and Hulme (ed.) (1992), p.89.

30. *The News on Friday*, Islamabad, June 24, 1994.

31. In a rather remarkable letter dated 28 October, 1993 to the Bangladesh Secretary of Health, written on joint letterhead created specifically for the purpose, UNICEF, the World Health Organization and the World Bank urged the Government to maintain the National Drug Policy.

32. Fowler, (1993), p.13.

33. Cornia *et al.*, (1987), p.ix.

34. Canadian Parliamentary Committee on Foreign Policy Review, 3 June 1994, 'Notes of a Meeting . . . with Mr. Kwesi Botchwey, Minister of Finance of Ghana', Ottawa.

35. Toronto *Globe and Mail*, 3 October 1994.

36. Draimin, Tim, (1994), 'Potential for partnership', IDRC, Ottawa.

37. This approach is spelled out in 'Principles of Regulation' by Karla Simon of the International Center for Non Profit Law, Washington, May, 1994. Experimental projects were started by UNDP and the World Bank to study the regulatory framework for NGOs in certain countries in 1993.

38. OECD, (1994), p.204.

39. *The Economist*, 3 September 1994; the London *Times*, 26 October 1994; BBC *Newsnight*, 27 October 1994.

40. Travelling with Ron Brown was the President of Chrysler Motors, which reportedly had ties with the New Face Vehicle Refit Factory, a labour camp. Brown's visit took place in September; the Lop Nor nuclear explosion took place on 6 October. The Canadian mission, which took place in November, signed protocols of intent under which Canada would sell CANDU nuclear reactors to China.

Chapter XIII   Future conditional

1. Falk, R., 'The making of global citizenship', in Brecher, *et al.*, (1993), p.39.
2. Stefanik, Nancy, 'Sustainable dialogue/sustainable development', in Brecher, *et al.*, (1993), p.263.
3. Brown and Kane, (1994), pp.214–219.
4. UNICEF, (1995), p.46.
5. The Report of the International Commission on Peace and Food, *Uncommon Opportunities*, Zed, London, 1994, p.102.
6. Galbraith, (1992), p.20.
7. O'Brien, (1994), p.163.
8. Tendler, Judith, 'Whatever happened to poverty alleviation', in Levitsky, (1989).
9. UNDP, (1993b), p.94.
10. Total external assistance to the health sector was $4794 million; the development banks provided $298 million in concessional loans, while NGO disbursements were $1100 million. Source: World Bank, (1993), p.165.
11. *The Economist*, for example, ran a long essay on the subject in its 24 December, 1994 issue, arguing that 'high communitarians', with their 'neurotic fear of the future' are a threat to the very foundations of western liberalism.
12. Coles, (1993), p.40.
13. Putnam, (1993), p.182.
14. Buttimer, (1993), p.41.
15. Galbraith, J.K., (1977), *The age of uncertainty*, BBC-Deutsch, p.30.
16. See, for example, Vincent, Fernand and Piers Campbell, (1989), *Towards financial autonomy*, IRED, Geneva. Their cycle included birth, adolescent crisis, consolidation, prime, maturity, bureaucracy and death.
17. Recounted in Gandhi, M.K., (1927), *An autobiography, or, The story of my experiments with truth* (translated from the Gujarati by Mahadev Desai), Navajivan Publishing House, Ahmedabad, pp.220–1.

Bibliography

Anderson, Mary B., and Peter J. Woodrow, (1989), *Rising from the ashes: development strategies in times of disaster*, Westview, Boulder.

Bailey, Ronald, (1993), *Eco scam: The false prophets of ecological apocalypse*, St. Martin's Press, New York.

Barnet, R.J., and J. Cavanagh, (1994), *Global dreams: imperial corporations and the new world order*, Simon and Schuster, New York.

Bebbington, A. and R. Riddell, (1994), 'New agendas and old problems: issues, options and challenges in direct funding of Southern NGOs', ODI (mimeo), London.

Benthall, Jonathan, (1993), *Disasters, relief and the media*, I.B. Taurus, London.

Berg, Elliot, G. Hunter, T. Lenaghan and M. Riley, (1994), *Poverty and structural adjustment in the 1980s: trends in welfare indicators in Latin America and Africa*, DAI, Bethesda.

Best, Michael H., (1990), *The new competition*, Polity Press, Cambridge.

Bhatnagar, Bhuvan and Aubrey Williams, (1992), *Participatory development and the World Bank: potential directions for change*, World Bank, Washington.

Black, Maggie, (1992), *A cause for our times: Oxfam, the first 50 Years*, Oxfam, Oxford.

Borst, Diane and Montana, Patrick (ed.), (1977), *Managing nonprofit organizations*, Amacorn, New York.

Borton, John, (1994), *The changing role of NGOs in the provision of relief and rehabilitation assistance: northern Ethiopia and Eritrea*, ODI, London.

Brecher, Jeremy, J.B. Childs and J. Cutler (eds.), (1993), *Global visions: beyond the new world order*, Black Rose, Montreal.

Bremner, Robert H., (1988), *American philanthropy*, University of Chicago Press, Chicago.

Brinkerhoff, D.W., (1991), *Improving development program performance: guidelines for managers*, Lynne Rienner, Boulder.

Brodhead, Tim and Brent Herbert-Copley, with Lambert, Anne-Marie, (1988), *Bridges of hope: Canadian voluntary agencies and the Third World*, North-South Institute, Ottawa.

Brown, Lester, (1974), *By bread alone*, Praeger, New York.

Brown, Lester and Hal Kane, (1994), *Full house*, Norton, New York.

Brown, Michael, and May, John, (1991) *The Greenpeace Story*, Dorling Kindersley, New York.

Burnell, Peter, (1991), *Charity, Politics and the Third World*, St. Martin's Press, New York.

Buttimer, Anne, (1993), *Geography and the human spirit*, Johns Hopkins University Press, Baltimore.

Campbell, Wallace, (1990), *The history of CARE: a personal account*, Praeger, New York.

Canadian Centre for Philanthropy, (1994), *A Portrait of Canada's Charities*, Toronto.

Carr, Marilyn, (1984), *Blacksmith, Baker, Roofing-sheet Maker: employment for rural women in developing countries*, IT Publications, London.

Carroll, T., (1992), *Intermediary NGOs: The Supporting Link in Grassroots Development*, Kumarian Press, West Hartford.

Chambers, Robert, (1987), 'Sustainable Livelihoods, Environment and Development: Putting Poor Rural People First', *Discussion Paper 240*, IDS, Sussex.

Chambers, Robert, (1988), 'Poverty in India: Concepts, Research and Reality' *Discussion Paper 241*, IDS, Sussex.

Chambers, Robert, (1993), *Challenging the Professions: Frontiers for Rural Development*, IT Publications, London.

Chambers, Robert, (1994), 'Poverty and livelihoods: whose reality counts?' UNDP Roundtable, 'Change: social conflict or harmony?' Stockholm, July.

Chambers, Robert and Gordon R. Conway, (1992), 'Sustainable rural livelihoods: practical concepts for the 21st century', *Discussion Paper 296*, IDS, Sussex.

Charities Aid Foundation, (1992), *Charity Trends 1992*, Tonbridge.

Charities Aid Foundation, (1993), *Individual Giving and Volunteering in Britain*, 6th Edition, Tonbridge.

Charities Aid Foundation, (1994), *International Giving and Volunteering*, London.

CIVICUS, (1995), *Citizens: Strengthening Global Civil Society*, CIVICUS, Washington.

Clark, John, (1991), *Democratizing development; the role of voluntary organizations*, Earthscan, London.

Club of Rome, *Limits to Growth*, see Meadows, D.M. *et al.*

Coles, Robert, (1993), *The call of service: A witness to idealism*, Houghton Mifflin, Boston.

Commission on Global Governance, (1995), *Our Global Neighbourhood*, Oxford University Press, New York.

Creveld, Martin yan, (1991), *The transformation of war*, The Free Press, New York.

Cyert, Richard, (1975), *The Management of non-profit organizations*, Heath, Lexington, Massachusetts.

Daly, H.F., and J.B. Cobb, (1994), *For the common good*, Beacon Press, Boston.

Dankelman, Irene and Joan Davidson, (1988), *Women and environment in the Third World*, Earthscan, London.

de Tocqueville, Alexis, (1969), *Democracy in America*, Anchor Books, Garden City, New York.

Drucker, Peter, (1990), *Managing non-profit organizations: Principles and practices*, Harper Collins, New York.

Drucker, Peter, (1993), *Post-capitalist society*, Harper Business, New York.

Drucker, Peter, (1994), 'The age of social transformation', *The Atlantic Monthly*, November.

Edwards, Michael and Hulme, David, (1992), *Making a difference: NGOs and development in a changing world*, Earthscan, London.

Edwards, Michael, (1993a), 'International NGOs and Southern Governments in the "New World Order": Lessons of Experience at the Programme Level', INTRAC Workshop, Amersfoort, June.

Edwards, Michael, (1993b), 'Does the doormat influence the boot? Critical thoughts on UK NGOs and international advocacy', *Development in Practice*, Vol. 3(3).

Edwards, Michael, and David Hulme, (1994), 'NGOs and development: performance and accountability in the "New World Order"', Manchester University Conference, June.

Ehrlich, Paul, *The population bomb*, Sierra Club/Ballantine, New York, 1968.

Ekins, Paul, (1992), *A new world order: grassroots movements for global change*, Routledge, London.

Etzioni, Amitai, (1993), *The spirit of community: the reinvention of American society*, Touchstone, New York.

Farrington, J. and Lewis, D.J., (eds.) (1993), *Non-governmental organizations and the state in Asia*, Routledge, London.

Farrington, J. and Bebbington, A., (eds.) (1993), *Reluctant partners? Non-governmental organizations, the state and sustainable agricultural development*, Routledge, London.

Ford-Smith, Honor, (1989), *Ring ding in a tight corner: a case study in funding and organizational democracy in Sistren, 1977–88*, International Council for Adult Education, Toronto.

Fowler, Alan, (1992), 'Distant obligations: speculations on NGO funding and the global market', *Review of African Political Economy*, No. 55.

Fowler, Alan, (1993), 'Democracy, development and NGOs in Sub-Saharan Africa: where are we?', *Development and Democracy*, No. 3, May, Johannesburg.

Galbraith, John Kenneth, (1992), *The culture of contentment*, Houghton Mifflin, Boston.

Gaylin, Willard, I. Glassner, S. Marcus and D.J. Rothman, (1978), *Doing good: the limits of benevolence*, Pantheon, New York.

George, Susan and Fabrizio Sabelli, (1994), *Faith and credit; The World Bank's secular empire*, Penguin, London.

Homer-Dixon, Thomas F., (1994), 'Environmental scarcities and violent conflict: evidence from cases', *International Security*, Vol. 19, No. 1, Summer.

Hallin, Daniel C., (1994), *We keep America on top of the world; television journalism in the public sphere*, Routledge, London.

Handy, Charles, (1988), *Understanding voluntary organizations*, Penguin, London.

Hancock, Graham, (1989), *Lords of Poverty*, Atlantic Monthly Press, New York.

Ignatieff, Michael, (1984), *The needs of strangers*, Chatto and Windus, London.

International Commission on Peace and Food, (1994), *Uncommon Opportunities: An Agenda for Peace and Equitable Development*, Zed, London.

Jazairy, Idriss, Mohiuddin Alamgir and Theresa Panuccio, (1992), *The state of world rural poverty*, IT Publications for IFAD, London.

Johnston, Douglas and Cynthia Sampson, (1994), *Religion, the missing dimension of statecraft*, Oxford University Press, New York.

Kennedy, Paul, (1993), *Preparing for the twenty-first century*, Harper Collins, Toronto.

Korten, David C., (1990), *Getting to the 21st century: voluntary action and the global agenda*, Kumarian Press, West Hartford.

Kotler, Philip, *Marketing for nonprofit organizations*, Prentice-Hall, Englewood Cliffs, New Jersey, 1975.

Kuti, Éva, (1993), *Defining the nonprofit sector: Hungary*, Working Papers of the Johns Hopkins Comparative Nonprofit Sector Project, No. 13, The Johns Hopkins Institute for Policy Studies, Baltimore.

Krieger, Joel (ed.) (1993), *The Oxford companion to politics of the world*, OUP, New York.

Levitsky, J., (ed.) (1989), *Microenterprises in developing countries*, IT Publications, London.

Lissner, Jørgen, (1977), *The politics of altruism*, Lutheran World Federation, Geneva.

Martin, Samuel, (1975), *Financing humanistic service*, McClelland and Stewart, Toronto.

McCarthy, K.D., V.A. Hodgkinson, R.D. Sumariwalla and Associates, (1992), *The nonprofit sector in the global community*, Jossey-Bass, San Francisco.

Meadows, D.H., D.L. Meadows, J. Randers and W.W. III Behrens, (1972), *The limits to growth*, Potomac Associates, London.

Milton, Viorst, (ed.), (1988), *Making a difference: the Peace Corps at Twenty five.*

Moser, Caroline O.N., (1993), *Gender planning and development: theory, practice and training*, Routledge, London.

OECD, (1994), *DAC Chairman's Report 1993*, OECD, Paris.

OECD, *DAC Chairman's Report 1994*, OECD, Paris.

O'Brien, Conor Cruise, (1994), *On the eve of the millennium*, Anansi, Concord Ontario.

O'Rourke, P.J., (1994), *All the trouble in the world: the lighter side of overpopulation, famine, ecological disaster, ethnic hatred, plague and poverty*, Random House, Toronto.

Pearson, Lester B., (1969), *Partners in development: Report of the commission on international development*, Praeger, New York.

Putnam, Robert D., (1993), *Making democracy work: civic traditions in modern Italy*, Princeton University Press, Princeton.

Randel, Judith and Tony German, (1994), (eds.), *The reality of aid 94*, ICVA et al., London.

Reich, Robert B., (1991), *The work of nations: preparing ourselves for 21st century capitalism*, Knopff, New York.

Rich, Bruce, (1994), *Mortgaging the earth: The World Bank, environmental impoverishment, and the crisis of development*, Beacon Press, Boston.

Robinson, Mark, 'Governance, democracy and conditionality: NGOs and the new policy agenda', discussion paper for INTRAC Workshop, Amersfoort, June, 1993.

Robinson, Mark, (1994), 'NGOs as public service contractors', Manchester University Conference, June.

Rondinelli, Dennis, (1993), *Development projects as policy experiments* (Second Edition), Routledge, London.

Salamon, Lester M., (1994), 'The rise of the non-profit sector', *Foreign Affairs*, Vol. 73 No. 4, July/August.

Salamon, Lester M. and Helmut K. Anheier, (1992a), *In search of the non-profit sector I: the question of definitions*, Working Papers of the Johns Hopkins Comparative Nonprofit Sector Project, No. 2, The Johns Hopkins Institute for Policy Studies, Baltimore.

Salamon, Lester M. and Anheier, Helmut K., (1992b), *In Search of the Non-profit Sector II: The Problem of Classification*, Working Papers of the Johns Hopkins Comparative Nonprofit Sector Project, No. 3, The Johns Hopkins Institute for Policy Studies, Baltimore.

Scott, Michael and Mutombo Mpanya, (1994), *We are the world: an evaluation of Pop Aid for Africa*, InterAction, Washington.

Schneider, Bertrand, (1988), *The barefoot revolution: a report to the Club of Rome*, IT Publications, London.

Schumacher, E.F., (1974), *Small is Beautiful*, Abacus, London.

Sen, Gita and Caren Grown, (1987), *Development crises, an alternative vision: Third World women's perspectives*, Monthly Review Press, New York.

Smillie, Ian, (1985), *The land of lost content: A history of CUSO*, Deneau, Toronto.

Smillie, Ian, (1991), *Mastering the machine: poverty, aid and technology*, IT Publications, London.

Smillie, Ian and Henny Helmich, (ed.) (1993), *Non-governmental organizations and governments: stakeholders for development*, OECD, Paris.

Smith, S.R., and M. Lipsky, (1993), *Nonprofits for hire: The welfare state in the age of contracting*, Harvard University Press, Cambridge.

Sommer, John G., (1977), *Beyond charity: US voluntary aid for a changing Third World*, Overseas Development Council, Washington.

Sontheimer, Sally (ed.), (1991), *Women and the environment, a reader*, Monthly Review Press, New York.

Sullivan, Denis J., (1994), *Private voluntary organizations in Egypt: Islamic development, private initiative and state control*, University Press of Florida, Gainesville.

Tandon, Rajesh, (1991), 'Civil society, the state, and roles of NGOs', *IDR Reports*, Boston, Vol. 8, No. 3, August.

UNDP, (1991), *Human development report 1991*, OUP, New York.

UNDP, (1993a), *Human development report 1993*, OUP, New York.

UNDP, (1993b), 'UNDP and organizations of civil society', UNDP, New York.

UNDP, (1994), *Human development report 1994*, OUP, New York.

UNICEF, (1995), *The state of the world's children 1995*, OUP, New York.

United Nations, (1991), *The World's Women 1970–1990: Trends and Statistics*, New York.

USAID, (1993a), 'Civil society and democratic development: a CDIE design paper' (draft); Harry Blair *et al*, Center for Development Information and Evaluation, Washington, August.

USAID, (1993b), 'Voluntary foreign aid programs 1993', USAID, Washington.

Uphoff, Norman, (1994). 'Why NGOs are not a third sector', Cornell University (mimeo), Ithica NY.

Waller, David, (1993), *Rwanda: Which way now?*, Oxfam, Oxford.

Willets, Peter (ed.), (1982), *Pressure groups in the global system*, Frances Pinter, London.

World Bank, (1980), *World development report 1980*, OUP, New York.

World Bank, (1981), *Accelerated development in Sub-Saharan Africa: an agenda for action*, Washington.

World Bank, (1989), *Sub-Saharan Africa: from crisis to sustainable growth*, Washington.

World Bank, (1990), *World development report 1990*, OUP, New York.

World Bank, (1993), *World development report 1993*, OUP, New York.

World Bank, (1994a), *Adjustment in Africa: reform, results and the road ahead* OUP, New York.

World Bank, (1994b), *World development report 1994*, OUP, New York.

World Commission on Environment and Development, (1987), *Our common future*, OUP, New York.

World Resources Institute, (1990), *World resources 1990–91*, OUP, New York.

World Resources Institute, (1992), *World resources 1992–93*, OUP, New York.

World Resources Institute, (1994), *World Resources 1994–95*, OUP, New York.

Yankelovich, Daniel, (1991), *Coming to public judgement: making democracy work in a complex world*, Syracuse University Press, Syracuse.

Index

284